CONTESTED MODERNITIES IN CHINESE LITERATURE

CONTESTED MODERNITIES IN CHINESE LITERATURE

Edited by

Charles A. Laughlin

CONTESTED MODERNITIES IN CHINESE LITERATURE
© Charles A. Laughlin, 2005.

First published in 2005 by
PALGRAVE MACMILLAN™
175 Fifth Avenue, New York, N.Y. 10010 and
Houndmills, Basingstoke, Hampshire, England RG21 6XS
Companies and representatives throughout the world.

PALGRAVE MACMILLAN is the global academic imprint of the Palgrave Macmillan division of St. Martin's Press, LLC and of Palgrave Macmillan Ltd. Macmillan® is a registered trademark in the United States, United Kingdom and other countries. Palgrave is a registered trademark in the European Union and other countries.

ISBN 1–4039–6782–2

Library of Congress Cataloging-in-Publication Data

Contested modernities in Chinese literature / Charles A. Laughlin, editor.
    p. cm.
Includes bibliographical references and index.
ISBN 1–4039–6782–2
    1. Chinese literature—20th century—History and criticism. 2. Modernism (Literature)—China. I. Laughlin, Charles A., 1964–

PL2303.C62 2005
895.1'09005—dc22   2004061675

A catalogue record for this book is available from the British Library.

Design by Newgen Imaging Systems (P) Ltd., Chennai, India.

First edition: June 2005

10 9 8 7 6 5 4 3 2 1

Printed in the United States of America.

CONTENTS

ACKNOWLEDGMENTS

This book owes its existence, first of all, to Letty Chen, Carlos Rojas, and John Weinstein, the organizers of the conference "Contested Modernities: Perspectives on Twentieth-Century Chinese Literature," held at Columbia University on April 7–9, 2000. The conference was made possible by the generous support of the Chiang Ching-kuo Foundation Center for Chinese Cultural and Institutional History, Columbia University. To them and all the contributors, I owe a debt of gratitude for their patience during the long preparation of this volume. The conference host David Wang's support and encouragement over the ensuing years were crucial to the completion of this manuscript. I would also like to thank the anonymous readers invited by Palgrave Macmillan to evaluate the manuscript, and again the contributors to this volume, for all their invaluable comments regarding my introduction and the organization of the volume. Though I was not able to include every paper that was given at "Contested Modernities" in this work, I sincerely wished to, and I think we would all agree that the echoes of many of these other participants' voices resonate throughout.

Notes on Contributors

YOMI BRAESTER is Associate Professor of Comparative Literature at the University of Washington in Seattle. His publications include *Witness Against History: Literature, Film and Public Discourse in Twentieth-Century China* (2003) and essays on cinema and urban planning in China and Taiwan.

CLAIRE CONCEISON is Assistant Professor of Drama in the Department of Drama and Dance at Tufts University, where she is also affiliated faculty in Asian Studies, Asian American Studies, and International Relations. She is author of *Significant Other: Staging the American in China* (2004). Her current project is a collaborative autobiography of the late Ying Ruocheng. In addition to her scholarship, she is an active translator and director.

AMY D. DOOLING is Associate Professor of Chinese Literature at Connecticut College. She is the coeditor of *Writing Women in Modern China: An Anthology of Women's Literature from the Early Twentieth Century* (1998), editor of the sequel volume *Writing Women in Modern China: The Revolutionary Years, 1936–76* (2005), and author of *Women's Literary Feminism in Twentieth-Century China* (2005).

ALEXANDER DES FORGES is Assistant Professor in the Department of Modern Languages at University of Massachusetts, Boston. He has published several articles on nineteenth- and early twentieth-century fiction, and has recently completed a manuscript on the tropes and figures governing Shanghai cultural production. He is currently researching the aesthetics and politics of the "literary" in the nineteenth century.

MEGAN M. FERRY is the Luce Junior Professor of Asian Studies and Assistant Professor of Chinese at Union College, in Schenectady, New York. She is currently revising a manuscript on women writers in early twentieth-century China.

JEFFREY C. KINKLEY is a Professor of History at St. John's University in New York City, specializing in modernism in early twentieth-century Chinese literature, and literary investigations of law, morality, and corruption in Chinese popular fiction. Continuing *Chinese Justice, the Fiction: Law and Literature in Modern China* (2000), his most recent research is about corruption, realism, and the return of the political novel in late socialist China.

DEIRDRE SABINA KNIGHT teaches Chinese and Comparative Literature at Smith College and writes on questions of ethics and bioethics as addressed in twentieth-century Chinese fiction and film.

CHARLES A. LAUGHLIN is Associate Professor of Chinese Literature at Yale University. He is author of *Chinese Reportage: The Aesthetics of Historical Experience* (2002). He is currently completing a book on the modern Chinese essay entitled *The Literature of Leisure and Chinese Modernity.*

EMMA J. TENG is the Class of 1956 Career Development Associate Professor of China Studies at the Massachusetts Institute of Technology, and the author of *Taiwan's Imagined Geography: Chinese Travel Writing and Pictures, 1683–1895* (2004). Her current research focuses on representations of Eurasians.

ROBIN VISSER is Assistant Professor of Chinese Language and Literature at The University of North Carolina at Chapel Hill. She is currently writing a book on Chinese urban cultural aesthetics titled *Cities Surround the Countryside: Urban Aesthetics in Post-Socialist China.*

LINGZHEN WANG is currently teaching in the Department of East Asian Studies at Brown University. Her special fields include modern Chinese literature, gender, feminist and literary theories, and film. She is the author of *Personal Matters: Women's Autobiographical Practice in Twentieth Century China* (2004).

JOHN B. WEINSTEIN is Assistant Professor of Chinese and Asian Studies at Simon's Rock College of Bard. His articles and reviews appear in *Asian Theatre Journal, China Information, CLEAR*, and other U.S. and Taiwan publications. In addition to his scholarship, he has directed, adapted, and translated dramatic work by Ding Xilin, Chen Baichen, Yang Jiang, Yuan Changying, Wang Qimei, and Bai Xianyong.

XIAOBIN YANG is Associate Professor of Chinese at the University of Mississippi. He is author of *The Chinese Postmodern: Trauma and Irony in Chinese Avant-Garde Fiction* (2002), *History and Rhetoric: On Contemporary Chinese Literature* (1999, in Chinese), *Negative Aesthetics: Literary Theory and Cultural Criticism of the Frankfurt School* (1995 and 1999, in Chinese), and *Across the Sunlight Zone* (1994, a collection of poems in Chinese).

INTRODUCTION

CONTESTED MODERNITIES

The term "modernity" was rarely used or examined in the English language study of twentieth-century Chinese literature before the year 1989. For a field defined by the "modern," this seems ironic, but it also draws attention to the ideological nature of the manner in which Chinese modernity is conceived, particularly in the West, and also, to an extent, in China. That is to say, in part because of the influence of the May Fourth Movement, that the equation of "Westernization" with "modernization" has been taken for granted for far too long; so, virtually every discussion of modern Chinese culture up through the 1980s is circumscribed by the questions of "the introduction of things Western" and "the response to the West." Even if this were the sum and substance of Chinese modernity, it is clearly a far different way of looking at modernity than is common in the West.

By the 1980s, Edward Said's *Orientalism* was being discussed in earnest among scholars of Chinese literature, as well as of many other fields.[1] Whether one agreed with Said's arguments or not, the book drew attention to the historicity of cross-cultural academic scholarship (referring here specifically to First-World studies of the Third World). For those who saw the implications of Said's book on Chinese cultural studies, there was something disheartening about the inescapable complicity of Western academic scholarship in the project of Orientalism, as implied by Said's theory; yet Said's challenge was seminal to a major transformation in modern Chinese literary studies. Insofar as the May Fourth Movement itself was arguably an Orientalist project (assuming Western cultural supremacy, promoting disdain for the backwardness of traditional Chinese culture while, at the same time, appropriating certain aspects of traditional culture, negatively or positively, to define the Chinese modern), and the principles and assumptions of the May Fourth generation have influenced Western scholarship on modern Chinese literature (whether or not the Westerners who helped establish this field were inclined to be Orientalist), modern Chinese literary studies can be said to be *doubly* Orientalist. How is it that we came to be studying modern China? Who are "we," and how have demographic shifts altered the conditions of the field? To what extent has our place in history and on the global landscape determined how we define and understand Chinese literature and modernity? What avenues of research methodology or theoretical positioning might there be to circumvent the equation of modernity in China with Westernization, and the assumption of Western cultural supremacy in the study of modern Chinese culture?

The question of modernity in modern Chinese literary studies may be said to have been first brought into focus in Leo Ou-fan Lee's 1989 surveys of modern Chinese literature in the *Cambridge History of China*.[2] While not explicitly concerned with modernity, Marston Anderson's 1990 book, *The Limits of Realism*, was seminal in that it vividly illustrated how the gaps in history, culture, concept, and literary practice between Europe and China inevitably led to distortions that both made "realism" as understood in Europe virtually untenable in China, and "Chinese realism" a very different mode of literary expression than its Western models.[3] Thus, any literary approach to Chinese "realistic" fiction that does not negotiate these gaps tends to perpetuate the myth of "failed imitation," due to which modern Chinese literature is thought never to be able to "catch up" with modern Western literature.

Rey Chow's *Woman and Chinese Modernity* (1991), was the first sustained, critical inquiry into the way in which Chinese modernity is constituted and understood, using the questions of the literary images of women, the generally marginalized practice of women writers, and the awkward relationship between New Literature and popular literature in the Republican period, as angles of entry.[4] *The Limits of Realism* and *Woman and Chinese Modernity* helped inspire various explorations into the complex origins of modern Chinese literature, which made the 1990s the most productive period in modern Chinese literary studies in the English language. Lydia Liu's *Translingual Practice* (1995), by looking at the migration of concepts and language from Europe to China (largely mediated by Japan), has shown that the process was much more multilateral than had previously been assumed, emphasizing the cultural agency of the Chinese in creating their own modernity from partly Western (and often distorted) materials. Leo Ou-fan Lee's *Shanghai Modern* (1999), though not oriented as a critical inquiry, is clearly more focused on modernity than his earlier work on romantic writers and on Lu Xun by its vivid and extensive unfolding of the life-practice of cultural modernity in Shanghai. More recently, Shu-mei Shih's *Lure of the Modern* (2001) is the first book-length study of modernism in China, expanding it well beyond its erstwhile marginalization as flash-in-the-pan Shanghai "New Sensationism" to aspects of modernism in Lu Xun and other May Fourth period writers, and the influential yet little-studied "Beijing School," and even linking the discussion up to the post-Mao period.[5] What these studies and many others that take modernity head-on have in common is not a desire to import the discussion of modernity in the Western context wholesale into the discussion of modern China, but rather to use the compelling case of modern Chinese culture to highlight the complicity between imperialism and modernism/ modernity both in the West and in China.

Any attempt to address the origin of modern Chinese culture, whether consciously or not, has to face the question "What is modernity?" and this is a question that does not and will not have a clear-cut answer in China any more than in the West. Rather, if pursued diligently (and I hope this book will help stimulate this pursuit), the inquiry into the problem of modernity will generate a more sustained and substantive discussion than the field has ever seen, one that could be its greatest contribution to the general study of culture through literature.

Contestation is not just a theme in current research—modern Chinese literary studies is riddled with controversy, all of which is traceable to questions of modernity but not always obviously so. The debate between Jaroslav Průšek and C.T. Hsia in the 1960s over the politics of reading and the possibility of a socialist literature,[6] Fredric Jameson's controversial reading of Lu Xun as typical of "third world allegory,"[7] Stephen Owen's critique of "world poetry" from China,[8] the debate between Liu Kang and Michael Duke on the critical paradigms that vied for legitimacy in the 1980s,[9] and the like, all show that when people sit up and take note of the activities and agendas of participants in the field of modern Chinese cultural studies, it stirs up deep and highly charged issues of broad significance.

Yet the field has also become less confrontational in the 1990s and beyond, with differences more embedded and implicit in research trends. Most of our current fascinations—lesser-known writers, mass print culture, gender, unusual literary genres, literary modernism, postmodernism and the avant-garde, the literary arena as a field of cultural production, visual and performance arts, regional and dialectic literatures—are motivated by a desire to interrogate, discredit, reconsider, or simply ignore the process of canon-making in modern China, which had, by the 1950s, established the authority of the May Fourth tradition and especially its realistic and revolutionary legacies. This has created a wonderful and stimulating diversity of newly uncovered subject matter (overlooked writers made interesting by new concerns, popular print culture including illustrated magazines, advertisements, cartoons, fashion trends, just to name a few), and, consequently, a variety of new approaches influenced by Western Marxisms, feminism, new historicism and sociology of literature, and cultural studies.

Most of these new phenomena in the 1990s have positioned themselves as adversaries of the received canon and the approaches that had prevailed before (often understood to be limited to biographical criticism, new criticism, and the "old" sociology of literature).[10] Particularly in the study of contemporary Chinese culture, there have begun to be interesting challenges to the conventional geography of modern Chinese literature (e.g., mostly mainland China embellished with a bit of Taiwan), which compel our attention to the culture of Hong Kong as well as the various roles played by the Chinese diaspora in the global production and consumption of Chinese culture—their experience as subject matter for literature and film, their increasingly recognized importance as an audience for contemporary Chinese culture, and even their role as producers of culture. This includes the possibility of discussing Chinese American literature and film within the context of, "Chinese culture" and, specifically, "modern Chinese culture," as well as studying Chinese American literature as one of a diverse collection of American literatures. The fact that Ha Jin, a Chinese immigrant living in the United States, could receive The National Book Award (in 1999) for his original English writing, gives us a glimpse of the shifting cultural demography of the

Chinese American community as producers and consumers of culture and is part of what makes this consideration possible. But once we have broken through the limits of China's national borders, how can we delimit or define Chinese culture as a context for the study of literature, art, and film? In the current state of methodological flux, I think, it is sometimes too easy to slip into the comforts of cultural essentialism, using an ahistorical rubric of "cultural China" to bind together these discrete phenomena.

This volume has its genesis in a conference held at Columbia University in the spring of 2000, entitled "Contested Modernities: Perspectives on Twentieth Century Chinese Literature." The organizers of this conference divided the presentations on the basis of various different kinds of boundaries that have defined the field of modern Chinese literature up to the present—boundaries between tradition and modernity, Chinese nation and diaspora, genders, social classes, among literary genres, and other forms of artistic expression, the city and the countryside, and the grand narratives of history and everyday experience. In the course of the conference, however, synergies and affinities emerged independent of the panel divisions, suggesting the outlines of an emerging landscape of modern Chinese cultural studies—one no longer defined in terms of remedies or supplements, but of conceptual reframing, which challenges or overturns conventional assumptions and frameworks. In short, this became a conference about what kinds of tactics were being used to map and negotiate these boundaries, and, to me, this in itself called for a book to define a new moment in the history of this field.

It is along these defining synergies that I have decided to organize this book, since I am more interested in exploring the *intersections* of, for example, nation, gender and city, diaspora and modernity, feminism, and historiography, than in sorting them out in terms of binary oppositions. The resulting categories are as much a result of my own invention as explicitly suggested by the chapters: in the following I will discuss "Rewriting Literary History," "The Quotidian Apocalypse," and "The Moral Subject under Global Capitalism" as emerging themes in modern Chinese literary studies.

REWRITING LITERARY HISTORY

The title of our first section is borrowed from the Chinese *chongxie wenxue shi*, which has been a catchword in mainland Chinese literary historiography for over a decade. It indicates a common desire to depart from the received periodization of modern Chinese literature, which was the product of the Communist Chinese literary and academic institution. It is also a challenge to the assumption originating from the May Fourth Movement that literature is meant to propagate messages of social redemption and national salvation, particularly in the form of realistic fiction. The slogan "Rewriting literary history" has been used widely among Chinese scholars of modern Chinese literature since the mid-1980s, but finds its most sustained practice in the works of Wang Xiaoming and his students.[11] The relevance of this to contemporary scholarship on modern Chinese literature around the globe is quite direct: the current generation enjoys unprecedented international scholarly interaction, and the trend of rewriting literary history is a project shared across different scholarly communities, united in their critique of the received narrative of modern Chinese literary history.

The interesting question is not *whether*, but *how*, to rewrite literary history, and, I think, contemporary English-language scholarship on modern Chinese literature may distinguish itself from others (including Chinese) precisely in the specific alternative directions chosen.[12] One approach is to return to the archive and let its specificity talk back to the generalities of literary history—many scholars are reexamining (or examining for the first time) literary journals, organizational documents, personal papers, and correspondence in an effort to reconceive the dynamics of the modern Chinese literary field.[13] Performances are a kind of "archive" as well, and Claire Conceison and John Weinstein in chapters 7 and 8, respectively, show how reference to instances of theatrical experience have as much to say as published dramatic scripts about the workings of modern Chinese theater, perhaps even more.

In chapter 5, on the other hand, Xiaobin Yang, locates unwritten literary history in the arguably ideological gap between the theory and the practice of contemporary avant-garde writing. Specifically, Yang reconstructs the debate over postmodernism in China, pitting critics whose enthusiasm for the concept conceals conservative identity politics and teleological convictions against others whose opposition to it fails to acknowledge its rejuvenating critical potential. Yang's own notion of the "post-Mao–Deng" classifies Chinese postmodernity as a dynamic response to Maoist revolutionary discourse as well as a dialogue with global intellectual and cultural trends, and he sees the most promising manifestation of the Chinese postmodern not in the polemics of these critics, but in literary practice: ". . . Chinese literary postmodernism (not postmodern theory) is by no means a conservative trend that conceals the conflicts in historical reality, but rather a radical experiment that examines the psycho-rhetorical basis of the authoritarian culture of modern China." Importantly, he emphasizes that conceiving of the postmodern, postsocialist, or post-Mao–Deng in sequential, chronological terms misses the point by adhering to the very modernist teleology these "post-" cultural gestures constantly deconstruct: "the prefix 'post-' does not refer to a chronological subsequence but shows *a temporal force of deferral and a spatial force of deviation within the not completely forgotten but immemorial desire and repression of the modern*" (emphasis in original).

Indeed, the pursuit of the postmodern in China is all too rarely premised on an interrogation of the *modern*. In a way, it is bolder to more directly examine the foundations of the Republican-period canon and take a more critical view of what now appear to have been the dominant strands in modern Chinese cultural development. Alexander Des Forges, in chapter 1, provides a masterful reassessment of the origins of modern Chinese culture, using contemporary redactions of psychoanalytic theory to delve deeply into the motivations and anxieties of the defining gestures of Chinese cultural modernity. Des Forges shows the complicity between the central concerns of May Fourth—to demonize Chinese tradition, to revolutionize China and establish a democratic and scientific new world, to unite workers and peasants with the intellectual elite who would supposedly liberate them—and the central concerns of the defining works in the field of modern Chinese literary studies since the 1960s. For everyone engaged in the study of modern Chinese culture, Des Forges argues, modernity—especially an inflected, Chinese modernity—functions as a fetishistic object, which covers up a distressing lack on the part of modern Chinese identity. This lack generates shame among scholars of modern Chinese literature when compared with both traditional Chinese culture on the one hand and Western European culture on the other. If one accepts this argument, it could shed new light on the significance and functioning of marginal and heterodox cultural practices in modern China, which have attracted so much scholarly attention recently.

The most productive approach to the problem of rewriting literary history among scholars working in the English language, in my opinion, is from feminist perspectives, perspectives that themselves offers variety of constructive critical avenues. Megan Ferry and Amy Dooling, in chapters 2 and 3, respectively, make use of archival and other methods to get around the strictures of the received canon and narrative of modern Chinese literary history. Feminist theory, in practice, can generally be understood as a radical critique of other approaches and the assumptions that underlie them, deriving or beginning principally from how the received patriarchal ideology as well as other critical approaches (such as Marxist, poststructuralist, or postcolonial) ignore or underestimate the cultural productions, as well as the historical and private experiences, of women. The return to the archive recovers lesser known women writers (or lesser known works of well-known women writers), both to enrich the literary historical record as well as to show, through close reading, the aesthetic and ideological elements that may have contributed to the traditional suppression of such works. This has been Amy Dooling's approach in *Writing Women in Modern China* as well as in chapter 3 of this volume, "Desire and Disease: Bai Wei and the Literary Left of the 1930s."[14] Dooling shows, as do some other scholars, how texts, content, and aesthetics are categorized and evaluated differently depending on the gender of their authors.

Megan Ferry uses another approach—examining approaches to women writers contemporary to the period under investigation. By concentrating on the May Fourth period, already well known for making women in history and literature overdetermined signs of the transition from tradition to modernity, Ferry dramatically demonstrates the complicity between the May Fourth Movement's ostensibly "feminist" ideology and the suppression or marginalization of exactly the kind of women's writing that Dooling's work tries to recover—writing that might be said to resist the very canon that prides itself on its "feminism." In other words, since the May Fourth generation, and the tradition of redemptive/revolutionary discourse issuing from it, are based on a confinement of women to gender-based stereotypes, it becomes clearer why the canon of Republican period literature allowed little room for major women writers.

Another significant challenge to the received canon is the increasingly conspicuous variety of modern literary and cultural traditions that lay claim to the term "Chinese," including Chinese-language productions in Taiwan, Hong Kong, and other modern, Chinese-speaking communities, but also more recently Chinese-speaking diaspora all over the world interacting both in local networks and the nationless space of the internet. To this must also be added the consideration of communities of Chinese descent whose creative work is *not* in the Chinese language. What kind of conceptual framework or context would justify the inclusion of works from mainland China, Taiwan, Hong Kong, indeed even works by writers in the Chinese global diaspora, in a course on "modern Chinese literature"? Those familiar with the material know that there is a wide enough gap between Taiwanese, Hong Kong, and mainland Chinese literature to make their shared cultural heritage seem trivial. The differences involve settings, themes, modes of literary cultivation, even character types and events/phenomena that, until recently, could not be shared across geographic boundaries at all.

One way to address this problem is to talk about literature *written in Chinese* as a way to encompass the "three Chinas," as well as some Singaporean, Malaysian, and expatriate Chinese writers in Europe, the Americas, Australia and New Zealand, and Japan.[15] This, like shared cultural heritage, can superficially gloss over the disparity of these literatures, and is complicated by the diversity of dialects concealed within the category of "Chinese language," but from an institutional standpoint, division of literatures by their language of composition is more common than by authors' country of origin (or place of publication).

But what shall we do with works in English by authors of Chinese descent? Emma Teng, in chapter 4, addresses precisely this problem. As she puts it, ". . . what happens when you cross not only geographic, but also linguistic boundaries? Can literature still be considered 'Chinese literature' if it is not written in Chinese, but in English, for example? Or does it belong to the preserve of 'English literature'? If we do consider English-language Chinese diasporic literature to be 'Chinese literature,' then what exactly is 'Chinese' about it? Is it simply a question of the author's ancestry?" Works of Chinese American literature usually appear in courses on English literature or American studies, but when they appear (as they sometimes do) in courses on Chinese literature, presumably, it is on the basis of shared cultural heritage (teaching Maxine Hong Kingston's *Tripmaster Monkey* (1989), e.g., in a course that also includes the sixteenth century novel *Journey to the West* to which it alludes).[16] Although this may seem reasonable at first, examining the supposed avenues of cultural transmission reveals that the basis of shared culture, when not in the form of a direct allusion or usage of a traditional Chinese work like *Journey to the West*, is often unconsciously reduced to a question of race: the shared cultural heritage is assumed to proceed inevitably from Chinese ancestry. Moreover, the study of Chinese American literature reveals that the use of elements of Chinese culture is often less a mode of establishing communication with a knowledgeable readership than the creative appropriation of cultural material to which the author has some kind of access, but addressing an audience to whom these cultural elements often will come across as *exotic*.

When defining the boundaries (however porous) between literatures, I think it is useful to emphasize above all the relationship between readers and authors, and how, in each case, this relationship can be said to constitute a community by virtue of systematically shared reading practices. "World poetry," as discussed by Stephen Owen, for example, can be defined as a literature easily "translatable" into other languages (usually English), one which appeals to common experience that is also not subject to linguistic or national boundaries. Insofar as it can be said to belong to a literature, a text reveals what kind of knowledge or cultural competence is expected of its readership. In this sense, a work like Qian Zhongshu's *Guan zhui bian* (*Limited Views*, 1979) may belong to a very small discursive community, for which extraordinary linguistic competence in Chinese alone may not be adequate. However, there is a large body of work in Chinese that assumes literacy in modern Chinese *and* the shared experience of certain defining moments in modern Chinese history (especially the May Fourth era, the War against Japan, and/or Chinese socialism after 1949), and this is usually what we loosely define as modern Chinese literature. Its experiential base only partially overlaps with that of the literatures of Taiwan and Hong Kong, and even less with that of Chinese diasporic literatures.

THE QUOTIDIAN APOCALYPSE

The increase in awareness of the size and diversity of cultural China over the past generation has been a decisive factor in recent developments in literature, performance, and film among all Chinese communities. It has led to, among other things, a globalization of literary settings, including both a more comfortable imaginative crossing of national boundaries as well as a new emphasis on the contemporary metropolis as a setting for literature and film. Coupled with the transition into the new millennium, this imaginative transformation led to fin-de-siècle styles and themes in Chinese literatures and the resurgence of apocalyptic literary discourse. The apocalypse is, in some sense, a final rejection of teleology, a complete loss of faith in collective social progress to iron out China's historical predicament. Utopia is exchanged for dystopia, or even entropy, and history is no longer morally legible.

The sense of "quotidian" is of the mundane, the everyday, the particular, the individualized perspective, even on history. In literary practice, it involves telling stories of individuals and families who do not clearly fall into types embodying larger historical or cultural forces. Without necessarily being "ahistorical," these people and stories evince modernity not in their typicality and manifestation of characters' immersion in the *Zeitgeist* of twentieth-century China, but rather precisely in the gaps between personally lived experience and the larger forces of capitalism, imperialism, class conflict, and national self-actualization under which personal experience had been continually subsumed. This was pioneered in twentieth-century China by popular writers such as Zhang Henshui as well as certain works by canonic writers such as Lu Xun's "Regret for the Past," and brought to the fore by wartime writing both in occupied (Eileen Chang) and unoccupied (Ba Jin's *Cold Nights*) urban China.

With the idea of *quotidian* apocalypse, I mean to suggest that the culture of the late 1980s and 1990s shifted in such a way as to generate a complex of mutually dependent quotidian and apocalyptic visions, displacing the romantic/realist axis that had predominated before.[17] Because the now discredited redemptive discourse of socialism involved the reconstruction of subjectivity as collective identity, the emergence of apocalyptic discourse in the late 1980s and early 1990s coincided with an unprecedented exploration of the individual model of subjectivity, such that even cataclysmic historic events would now be presented more often as merely the backdrop to private and personal narratives. These elements are actually quite prominent in Taiwanese film and theater of the 1990s, as John Weinstein and Yomi Braester, in chapters 8 and 9, amply demonstrate. Similarly, Claire Conceison's chapter on "The Great Going Abroad" shows how the encroachment of the global on contemporary mainland Chinese culture has helped dislodge the sweeping historical vision from its May Fourth throne, rendering contemporary experience, instead, through historically and culturally foreshortened perspectives.

Apocalyptic visions are, to my mind, complicit with the quotidian in that individualism suggests the universality of truth, its not being constrained by history, particularly the teleological, materialist vision of history that informs Marxism–Leninism Mao Zedong thought. Absent teleology, history from the individualistic perspective is either cyclical or culminates (collapses?) in an apocalyptic moment. It is a vision that equalizes humans as individuals rather than privileging their class, gender, or nation. Thus apocalyptic visions tend not to pit sociohistorical groupings against one another but rather emphasize a universal, common fate, even if it is only imagined or feared.

Jeffrey Kinkley, in chapter 6, reviews the apocalyptic in general literature and, in a masterful discussion of apocalyptic narratives in contemporary Chinese popular literature, reminds us of how unorthodox this vision is in the context of contemporary China. *Yellow Peril* (1991, attributed to Wang Lixiong), is an astonishing science-fiction dystopia of sweeping scope and with strong political overtones, quite unlike anything that had been published in the PRC before. In fact, in its explosion of history and atomization of the role of individuals, as well as certain elements of its style and organization, it resembles so-called traditional-style science-fiction and political novels of the late Qing period as are discussed, for example, in David Wang's book *Fin-de-siècle Splendor: Repressed Modernities of Late Qing Fiction, 1849–1911*.[18] What it lacks in literary quality, *Yellow Peril* makes up for in influence and agency because it occupied that common role of popular literature in China—the intellectual's guilty pleasure. Zhang Ping's *Jueze* (*Choice*, 1997) and Lu Tianming's *Cangtian zai shang* (*Heaven Above*, 1995) are, by contrast, more realistic novels of profound corruption, with an air of quotidian hopelessness that still marks a significant departure from the quasi-sacred teleology of historical and national redemption that characterized mainstream Chinese fiction up to the 1980s. Kinkley's chapter concludes with a reading of Mo Yan's *Republic of Wine* (*Jiuguo, 1992*), a surrealistic tour de force with an unreliable narrator investigating reports of cannibalism in a certain Chinese community. As a whole, Kinkley's chapter runs the gamut of apocalyptic fictional narrative in 1990s China, from the popular, through the "middlebrow," to the elite, demonstrating the unprecedented possibilities created by the perceived rupture of literature and politics after 1989.

Nothing illustrates the apocalyptic paradigm better than the films depicting the demolition, reconstruction, and alienated exploration of the city of Taipei discussed in chapter 9 by Yomi Braester. Braester examines films by Stan Lai, Edward Yang, and Tsai Ming-liang, which dramatize how a metropolis in the convulsions of historically disruptive change shakes the foundations of subjectivity and interpersonal relations: "Rather than simply lamenting the death of an imaginary metropolitan utopia, the films trace the urban ruin to the collapse of the distinction between the private and public realms and at the same time show the creative potential in embracing semipermeable borderlines." The robust fantasy of the urban youth who masters the martial art of flight in Stan Lai's *The Red Lotus Society* (1994) picks up the apocalyptic irrealism of *Yellow Peril* and *Republic of Wine*, while the empty interpersonal transactions and urban anomie in often transnational spaces like McDonald's and Hard Rock Café, in this film as well as *Vive l'amour* (1994) and *Mahjong* (1996), seem to come out of the same experience and imagination as the "belated" fiction of Zhu Wen and Qiu Huadong, discussed by Robin Visser in chapter 11: "The new urban subjects are antiheroes, living in alienating and torn-up spaces, who must find an existence that transcends the unstable structures they inhabit."

Claire Conceison and John Weinstein's chapters share this urban fin-de-siècle vision, yet also demonstrate the critical potential of modern Chinese theater studies to dislodge (as film studies has been doing) the modern Chinese cult of the text. Weinstein presents us with an in-depth, yet broad, overview of the considerable performance corpus of Li Guoxiu and his associates in Taiwan's Ping-Fong Acting Troupe (closely connected with the Performance Workshop and Stan Lai, the director of *The Red Lotus Society*), documented with the author's own viewings as well as video recordings of performances. Avant-garde in its imagination, yet immediately engaging to its large and enthusiastic audience, Ping-Fong's theater exemplifies the best in contemporary Taiwan culture, expressing beyond postmodern alienation a profound yet often sardonic dismay at the apparent decline of everything that is familiar in the dizzying process of globalization.

This ambivalent tension also drives the theater of Wang Gui and Wang Peigong, the contemporary mainland writer–director team, as presented by Claire Conceison. Focusing in more detail on one play "The Great Going Abroad," Conceison delves into the production and performance processes themselves, and how they condition the reception and larger significance of such unofficial theater in China. With what might be called the "narrative promiscuity" of apocalyptic literature as introduced in Kinkley's chapter, "The Great Going Abroad" presents us with an extravagant, lurid plot of cultural and sexual jealousy and murder in the context of Chinese students and professionals residing in the United States. As common as depictions of the study abroad situation are in contemporary cultural works, by taking this violent and surrealistic approach of presentation, "The Great Going Abroad" demonstrates the vitality of the contemporary performing arts. This is demonstrated as much, or perhaps even more, by the performances expertly witnessed and documented by Conceison than by the script, which as Conceison points out, does not exist in any stable form.

THE MORAL SUBJECT UNDER GLOBAL CAPITALISM

Kinkley's study presents definitively, explicitly apocalyptic visions, and as the subsequent chapters demonstrate, this fin-de-siècle worldview resonates with contemporary theater and film in mainland China and Taiwan. What remains to be demonstrated is the important continuity between such apocalyptic visions and the ostensibly opposite perspective of the quotidian—everyday experience with the individual as the ontological center.

In this section, chapters 10, 11, and 12 by Lingzhen Wang, Robin Visser, and Sabina Knight, respectively, illustrate a fascination with contemporary urban experience, particularly from the point of view of marginal or eccentric individuals (the *typical* character being the stock-in-trade of social realism). This focus on the mundane often calls into play issues of personal morality or amorality not intelligible from the point of view of narratives of collective historical experience.

Under these conditions, the individual becomes the context for morality, and moral choices are no longer conditioned by history, at least not entirely. Personal or family narratives can span eras and national boundaries without altering their moral significance, yet, at the same time, moral questions and even personal identity are fraught with ambiguity. Once teleology (and "ideology") has been suspended from its place of sole arbiter of meaning, the significance of any course of events can be attributed to anything from the age-old beliefs in predestination or karmic retribution to the utter meaninglessness of chaos. Where familiar values (the spirit of socialism and the Party) once had a certainty about them, the new certainties conveyed in art and literature are overwhelmingly *demoralizing*, even when they resonate moral significance. This is not only about the aftermath of socialism, it is also about the subjective and moral effects of market capitalism, of globalization.

Lingzhen Wang, in chapter 10, explores the continuity in women's writing—particularly autobiographical writing—from the early period of reform to the much-changed post-Tiananmen culture since the 1990s. It shows, how the evolution of contemporary mainland Chinese literature has been one from a unitary and pervasive discursive community (social realist fiction) to a variety of discrete niche readerships and authorships: "In the early 1980s, Chinese women writers succeeded in carving out a literary space for different personal voices; in the studies of women writers in the 1990s, I found that the personal is still one of the most important and pertinent concepts, even though the meaning of the personal has been differently signified." Wang's chapter is, in this sense, an exercise in *defining* a discursive community (here, that of contemporary Chinese women writers and their readers) in terms of a psychological assessment of what this generation has in common, in particular because of the ways in which historical circumstances have conditioned these women's relationships with their mothers and the ensuing effects on their subjectivity, desires, and modes of self-expression.

Visser discusses this in spatial terms as a literal "dislodging" of individuals from the social space of the *danwei* to that of autonomously chosen living and work spaces, both within an urban environment. Exploring the quotidian, yet in many ways avant-garde, fiction of Qiu Huadong, Zhu Wen, and He Dun (all well-known writers who have received little attention in English-language scholarship), Visser very originally makes reference to trends in contemporary painting to help shed light on the lifeworld of these authors of the everyday. All the authors strive for a vernacular and mundane imagination that is often associated with the so-called belated generation (*wansheng dai*) of poets and novelists. In the process, Visser shows a remarkable facility with contemporary Chinese criticism and theory.

In chapter 12, Sabina Knight takes an approach analogous to Visser's spatial one: she looks at specific changes in economic conditions (in particular the re-introduction of self-ownership in China) as a way to approach unprecedented moral dilemmas dramatized in Yu Hua's *Chronicle of a Blood Merchant* (1995). Knight's approach is unusual in that she sees potential in *Blood Merchant* for the *restoration* of the same Enlightenment values that the "belated generation" writers ridicule. Crucial to this argument is a clear distinction of capitalist and Enlightenment values, which are often confused and are particularly entangled in postsocialist China and its cultural production. Of course, the Enlightenment bears a close kinship with the May Fourth Movement in terms of values and goals, and what Knight perceives in contemporary literature about the thrust toward capitalism is a sense of reservation, even nostalgia for a morally directed, socially redemptive modern project. In alluding to ambivalence about capitalism, Knight is conscious of stepping into the contemporary Chinese debates between liberals and the new left alluded to in chapter 5 by Xiaobin Yang, and she documents this facet of her interpretive strategy also very well.

Second, Knight's choice of *Blood Merchant* foregrounds Yu Hua's transition from one of the foremost avant-garde writers of the 1980s to a humanist writer of more or less realistic fiction, including his celebrated novel *To Live* (1992). This vernacularization of a writer who used to be beyond the edge is the most obvious way in which *Blood Merchant*, Yu Hua, and ultimately Sabina Knight's chapter resonate with the previous section's quotidian theme. Although many of the kind of "belated" writers lack the moral ambivalence about capitalism that Knight celebrates in Yu Hua, on a stylistic level they share the accessible and vernacular vehicle of expression, making this ostensibly transparent language of everyday life and the streets into the medium of communication that may be said to define yet another discursive community within the postsocialist mainland Chinese literary scene, despite the deep moral and political divisions among the various debating camps.

In the end, again, what is being contested by all is a constellation of beliefs about the nature and purpose of modern literature that traces its origins in China to the May Fourth Movement. Because it was a broad cultural project that involved language reform (from classical Chinese to the vernacular), the establishment of a Western-style educational system, and a new literature that would, in part, become the subject matter of a modern Chinese education, it was able throughout most of the twentieth century to control modern Chinese discourse about literature and assert its own values, aims, and aesthetic standards as the only proper ones in the cultural field and the basis of the received canon.

Without detracting from the immense importance of the May Fourth Movement in modern Chinese culture, it is refreshing that we have arrived at a moment when we can step outside the May Fourth parameters of cultural production, giving due voice to alternative visions of Chinese modernity. Some of these visions coexisted with May Fourth literature; others emerged much later in the aftermath of the Chinese Communist revolution in Taiwan, Hong Kong, amongst the international Chinese diaspora, as well or within contemporary mainland China itself. The modes of contestation represented in this volume approach the issue from the point of view of displacing some of the sacred idols of the May Fourth legacy: the orthodox literary canon and its historiography; the dominance of elite mainland intellectual circles as a discursive community; the primacy of the text; and the teleological view of historical experience. They assert the cultural agency of women writers, the culturally active Chinese diaspora, the performing arts, and the full moral and philosophical significance of private, everyday experience. What results is a panoramic view of the future of Chinese literature in the twenty-first century, in which the formerly dominant May Fourth discourse has been given its due place as only one part of a vast and variegated tapestry of new Chinese culture.

NOTES

1. Edward Said, *Orientalism* (London: Routledge, 1978).
2. Particularly the first one: Leo Ou-fan Lee, "Literary trends I: the quest for modernity, 1895–1927," in *Cambridge History of China*, ed. John K. Fairbank and Albert Feuerwerker (Cambridge: Cambridge University Press, 1989) pp. 452–504.
3. Marston Anderson, *The Limits of Realism: Chinese Fiction in the Revolutionary Period* (Berkeley: University of California Press, 1990).
4. Rey Chow, *Woman and Chinese Modernity: The Politics of Reading between East and West* (*Theory of History and Literature 75*), ed. Wlad Godzich and Jochen Schulte-Sasse (Minneapolis: University of Minnesota Press, 1991).

5. Shu-mei Shih, *The Lure of the Modern: Writing Modernism in Semicolonial China, 1917–1937* (Berkeley: University of California Press, 2001).

6. For Průšek's review, Hsia's response, and Průšek's rebuttal, see Jaroslav Průšek, *The Lyrical and the Epic: Studies of Modern Chinese Literature*, ed. Leo Ou-fan Lee (Bloomington: Indiana University Press, 1980).

7. Fredric Jameson, "Third World literature in the era of multinational capitalism," *Social Text*, no. 15 (fall 1986).

8. Stephen Owen, "The anxiety of influence: what is world poetry?" *The New Republic*, November 1990.

9. Michael Duke, "Thoughts on politics and critical paradigms in modern Chinese literature studies," *Modern China* 19:1 (1993); Liu Kang, "Politics, critical paradigms: reflections on modern Chinese literature studies," *Modern China* 19:1 (1993).

10. Rey Chow, "The politics and pedagogy of Asian literatures in American universities," in *Writing Diaspora: Tactics of Intervention in Contemporary Cultural Studies*, ed. Rey Chow (Bloomington: Indiana University Press, 1993), pp. 120–143.

11. See, e.g., the collection Wang Xiaoming, ed., *Ershi Shiji Zhongguo Wenxue Shilun (Historiography of Twentieth Century Chinese Literature)* (Shanghai: Dongfang chuban zhongxin, 1997).

12. Some recent Chinese approaches can be seen in Pang-yuan Chi and David Der-wei Wang, eds., *Chinese Literature in the Second Half of a Modern Century* (Bloomington: Indiana University Press, 2000).

13. The work of Kirk Denton, Michel Hockx, and Denise Gimpel, to name a few, is exemplary in this respect; see Kirk Denton, *The Problematic of Self in Modern Chinese Literature: Hu Feng and Lu Ling* (Stanford: Stanford University Press, 1998); Denise Gimpel, *Lost Voices of Modernity: A Chinese Popular Fiction Magazine in Context* (Honolulu: University of Hawaii Press, 2001); Michel Hockx, *Questions of Style: Literary Societies and Literary Journals in Modern China, 1911–1937* (Leiden: Brill, 2003).

14. Amy D. Dooling and Kristina M. Torgeson, ed., *Writing Women in Modern China: An Anthology of Women's Literature from the Early Twentieth Century* (New York: Columbia University Press, 1998); Amy D. Dooling, ed., *Writing Women in Modern China, Volume II: An Anthology of Women's Literature about War, Revolution, and Socialist Construction* (New York: Columbia University Press, 2005).

15. This is the approach adopted in David Der-wei Wang and Jeanne Tai, *Running Wild: New Chinese Writers* (New York: Columbia University Press, 1994). See Wang's closing article, "Chinese Fiction for the Nineties," pp. 238–258.

16. Gang Yue discusses this pedagogical problem in, "Blending Chinese in America: Maxine Hong Kingston, Jade Snow Wong and Amy Tan," *The Mouth That Begs: Hunger, Cannibalism, and the Politics of Eating in Modern China* (Durham: Duke University Press, 1999), pp. 331–371.

17. Xiaobing Tang, *Chinese Modern: The Heroic and the Quotidian* (Durham: Duke University Press, 2000). Kojin Karatani has suggested that romanticism and realism were two sides of the same coin in modern Japanese literature; I think the same argument could be made for the modern Chinese case. Kojin Karatani, *Origins of Modern Japanese Literature* (Durham: Duke University Press, 1993).

18. David Der-wei Wang, *Fin-de-siècle Splendor: Repressed Modernities of Late Qing Fiction, 1849–1911* (Stanford: Stanford University Press, 1997).

PART I

REWRITING LITERARY HISTORY

1

The Rhetorics of Modernity and the Logics of the Fetish

Alexander Des Forges

It is striking that the fetish, which appears as a significant concept in the works of theorists as varied as Kant, Voltaire, Marx, and Freud, first took shape as a discursive element at a time when European merchants were attempting to join a vibrant broader network of Atlantic trade relations in the sixteenth century. In this sense, the story of the fetish and its origin has interesting parallels with the conventional narrative of Chinese intellectuals identifying "modernity" as a concept through which they could begin to participate in a broader world order in the twentieth century. While these parallels are thought-provoking and deserve a detailed treatment, this chapter aims at a more circumscribed goal: an inquiry into the functions of modernity as a fetish in the field of modern Chinese literature as it has been constituted in the American academy. Starting from an analysis of three distinct strategies that inform attempts to outline the parameters of the field, this chapter will put "literary modernity" itself into question, trace the ways in which interest in modernity relates to the recent accelerated development of the field in its institutional context, and end with a reflexive consideration of how and why we may want to rethink such a fetishization.

Freud's definition of the fetish—a substitute for the mother's phallus, which the young (male) child has discovered to be missing—proposes a substitution that is simultaneously a recognition and a denial of an absence.[1] I invoke this understanding of the fetish not because I want to put the field of modern Chinese literature on the couch, but rather because I see the formation of the fetish as a powerful allegorical resource through which the contemporary rhetorical construction and reconstruction of our object of study can be understood. Over the past two decades, we have moved beyond the simple acceptance of May Fourth claims at face value; numerous critics have pointed out the intensely rhetorical dimension of May Fourth assertions of modernity. But what is not often noted is the extent to which modern Chinese literature, as a field in the American academy, continues to rely on a few key tropes, the figures that allow us to talk about literary modernity in the Chinese context in the way that we are used to talking about it.[2]

Should one suspect that tropes and figures, the language of literariness, are not the most appropriate analytic tools for this discussion, a second look at the introduction to *Modern Chinese Literature in the May Fourth Era* (1977), the first English-language conference volume on the topic, will make their relevance clear. The definitions advanced and the positions taken in this introduction are quite familiar to any scholar in the field and apparently extremely straightforward, because they have been thoroughly naturalized over the last two-and-a-half decades. What surprises the reader, however, is the power of the rhetoric brought to bear in advancing them. In her emphasis on the "brilliance" of the May Fourth movement, the "weight" of tradition, "embrace" of the West and "rejection" of the thinking that was holding China back, the "courageous" use of literature as a "weapon," Merle Goldman manages to summarize the dry scholarly arguments presented in the pages to follow in a text that we can only consider to be poetic. What this suggests is not only that the construction of modern Chinese literature as a field in the American academy since the 1960s is no less a rhetorical project than the May Fourth polemics of the 1910s, 1920s, and 1930s in China—though the preferred modes of textual production now are the scholarly article, the monograph, and the anthology, the stylistic energy of past manifestos lives on—but also, that the many tropes that appear in Goldman's introduction and in the secondary scholarship published since work together to articulate an approach to modernity that is fundamentally fetishistic on three distinct levels.

THREE MOMENTS OF MODERNITY

From its very inception as a field of study in the United States, "modern Chinese literature" has struggled for disciplinary independence from the older, dominant fields of Sinology: the social sciences on one hand, and the study of Chinese literature and culture from the earliest times to the eighteenth century on the other. Well into the 1970s, graduate students in the United States focusing on Chinese literature of the twentieth century often found themselves working toward their degrees under the auspices of graduate programs in history, as the study of this literature as literature— as an enterprise distinct from other disciplines—was seldom emphasized. C.T. Hsia was the first to challenge this approach in 1961 with the publication of *A History of Modern Chinese Fiction*, making the following claim for the autonomy of literary study and the primacy of pure aesthetic value as the criterion for establishing a canon of modern literature: "The present work is not of course designed as an adjunct to political, sociological, or economic studies. The literary historian's first task is always the discovery and appraisal of excellence."[3] This assertion was not, of course, a neutral characterization, but an explicit move against the existing disciplinary structure.

But if the selection of pure aesthetic value—"the discovery and appraisal of excellence"—as the means to constitute the field of modern literature liberated literary scholars from toiling in the vineyards of the social sciences, it immediately confronted them with another problem. The existing sinological discourse of earlier literature, from Tang poetry to Song prose, from Yuan drama to the eighteenth-century novel *Dream of the Red Chamber*, had already laid claim to literary "excellence" as a standard. Furthermore, this claim to excellence was founded, in part, in a conception of Chinese uniqueness—Chinese literature through the eighteenth century was aesthetically superior precisely because it was *not* like European or American literature. Chinese literature of the twentieth century, which frequently advertised its supposed dependence on European literary theories and techniques, was therefore denied entrance to the classic canon.[4] In order to assure the autonomy and validity of modern Chinese literature as an object of study in the United States, the next generation of scholars found it necessary to supplement aesthetic value with another criterion—modernity.

And it is this criterion that we see in action in scholarship of the 1970s and 1980s. In this first moment of concern with modernity, literary modernity is defined as "westernization" and as a radical break from "tradition." The dominant motifs are addition (of new genres, new vocabulary, and new techniques), supplementation (filling "gaps" in the development of Chinese literature), and replacement (the exchange of old, limited forms for new ones with greater potential). This definition amounts to an uncritical reproduction of the discourse of literary modernity found in the same May Fourth texts these scholars read as modern; even the most limited critique of May Fourth writers' understanding of themselves as a unique generation was isolated and rare.[5] Why was this reproduction uncritical? I would like to suggest that many scholars writing during this period attempted unsuccessfully to distance themselves from questions of aesthetic value; even as they emphasized modernity as a substitute, they could not let go of the original standard completely. For this reason, these scholars frequently felt it necessary to apologize—whether explicitly or implicitly—for the "inferiority" or "inadequacy" of the works that they discussed. Under these circumstances, modernity could not be subject to critique precisely because it functions as a fetish, indispensable because it fills in or covers over a crucial absence that is at times recognized and at times disavowed. Freud suggests that, in many cases, the fetish is constructed metonymically; something that is located in close conjunction with that which turns out to be absent is adopted as the substitute.[6] In this case, the frequent articulation of the adjective "modern" together with the ideal that is supposedly missing in China—"good literature"—in the writings of May Fourth authors themselves nominates "literary modernity" as the most likely substitute for aesthetic value.

This substitution was of crucial importance: adoption of western forms and self-conscious distance from previous texts and styles of writing became the focus of scholarly attention, and the "discovery and appraisal of excellence" assigned only a subsidiary role. Furthermore, this fetishization was not static, but generative; once modernity was articulated as a desirable quality in literary works, it was only a matter of time before scholars interested in broadening the nascent canon of modern literature took it up as a means to insure a more diverse field of scholarly inquiry. Subsequent revisions of the canon included: (i) new attention to texts of the Republican period that had been dismissed by May Fourth writers and critics as insufficiently progressive; (ii) a look back to fiction and poetry of the late Qing; and (iii) a projection of the literary modern into the 1980s. In the process, however, modernity became increasingly reified as a standard and an analytic category; expansion of the canon, in this case, often reiterated and reinforced its governing propositions. Two central strategies drive this canonical revision in the 1980s and 1990s: the first presumes the fundamental social embeddedness of literary texts, and insists on careful attention to the social and ideological dimensions of literary practice, reminding us that cultural production does not take place in a vacuum. The second, by contrast, resists the subordination of the literary field to the socioeconomic infrastructure, and moves away from a rigidly determinist understanding of aesthetic modernity, attempting to call into question Eurocentric conceptions of modernity and modernism in literature. Over the last two decades, these two strategies have played a central role in broadening the scope and deepening the theoretical grounding of the field in the United States. They share one characteristic with the concern with modernity of the 1970s and early 1980s that they seek to critique, however: each is structured with reference to a fetish, a term or concept that simultaneously acknowledges and covers a lack. In fact, none of these three approaches (whether canonical or revisionist) is normally found in a pure state; they appear more often in alloyed or compound form together in works of secondary scholarship.

The understanding of true aesthetic modernization as closely, even inextricably, linked to an appropriate stage of economic and technological development has inspired scholars of modern Chinese literature with a variety of very different approaches, from Jaroslav Průšek to Jing Wang. Unlike earlier scholars who insisted on the timelessness and universal relevance of aesthetic standards of European origin, critics who work from this understanding historicize those very standards in crucial ways, and remind us that textual production is ultimately best understood with reference to the historical circumstances under which it is produced. Other scholars of modern Chinese literature are less explicit in their articulation, but, nonetheless, presume this connection as subtext. Whether the literary text constitutes a "reflection" of reality, an "expression" of a social mood, a "refraction" of a particular historical conjuncture, or a "working out" of problems posed by the contradictions inherent in the modernizing process, it is, in the end, technological progress, changes in the mode of production, or a shift to a new type of social organization that make it possible and appropriate for a certain *literary* modernization to begin and come to fruition.

As Jing Wang puts it, "In the 1990s, it becomes more and more obvious that it is the economic, rather than the ideological, political, or cultural that delimits the Chinese social imaginary."[7] While Wang makes this point explicitly with reference to a single decade, it is representative of the more general conviction of the primacy of "social reality" that underlies this approach as a whole. Modernism that appears at the wrong time is doomed to failure—it can only wither on the vine, unappreciated. It is partial rather than full, "spurious" rather than "genuine."[8] The problem of how to define a field of "modern literature" or "modernist literature"—how to justify its existence as separate from "pre-modern" cultural production—is thus removed from the sphere of specifically literary consideration, and transferred to another, more basic domain: modern literature or "modernism" is the literary production that is appropriately dominant (or, at the very least, most fiercely contested) during a period that is economically and technologically modern or rapidly modernizing.[9] Since that period in China is understood to begin after a similar period in Western Europe, when Chinese literary modernity does appear, it must be marked as belated and somehow secondary to *modernity as such*. By extension, this paradigm finds the concept of "Chinese postmodernism," so heatedly discussed in the late 1980s and early 1990s, to be questionable, or even impossible, for the necessary late capitalist infrastructure is not yet in place.[10]

This emphasis on the determining power of the material base is particularly timely in the mid- to late-1990s, as it can be read not only as a decisive rejoinder to Maoist voluntarism of the 1950s and 1960s, but also as a critique of the class biases of the intellectual elite during the "culture fever" of the 1980s. But such an emphasis can end by shortchanging the very power and relevance of the texts that it sets out to study. In his landmark account of cultural production of the 1980s, *Chinese Modernism in the Era of Reforms*, Xudong Zhang refers us to Marshall Berman's definition of "modernism of underdevelopment."[11] Indeed, Berman's highly influential reading of modernity as a social and aesthetic project, *All that is Solid Melts into Air*, supplies a concise, coherent, and powerful statement of the contingency of cultural modernity on economic and technological modernization. One of the distinguishing features of this book is its focus on Russian modernism in the nineteenth and early twentieth centuries: in a discussion that makes up one-third of the book, Berman asserts that since Russian society was technologically and economically backward, its literary and artistic modernisms have both an intensity and an ephemerality that is not to be found in the cultural production of more "advanced" nations in Western Europe. He identifies a close tie between base and superstructure, suggesting that literary modernism in nineteenth-century Russia is almost a mirage since it lacks a material foundation, and goes on to generalize that such a fantastic and unreal modernism is found in Third World nations around the globe as they begin the modernization process in the twentieth century.[12] There are, however, several problematic aspects to Berman's distinction between the modernism of Western Europe and the "modernism of underdevelopment."

While Berman is generally concerned with identifying an opposition between a hearty "modernism of development" and a sickly and feverish modernism of underdevelopment, his more detailed readings work to undercut this distinction. The book begins with an extended reading of Goethe's Faust, which Berman identifies as central to the European experience of modernity: Faust is first presented as a drama of *development*, not underdevelopment.

Yet only pages later, Berman reminds us that German intellectuals of Goethe's era thought of themselves as backward and less developed than England, France, and America (pp. 38–41, 43). In other words, the "underdevelopment" that Berman will later claim characterizes Russian and Third World modernisms lurks at the very heart of the advanced European modern cultural production. And things only get more complicated when Berman takes a closer look at Pushkin, Gogol, and their favorite avenue, Nevsky Prospect, all of which belong to the supposedly underdeveloped and economically backward Russian Empire of the early nineteenth century. According to Berman, Pushkin's bizarre urban visions predate Baudelaire, Gogol "seems to be inventing the twentieth century out of his own head" in the 1830s, and the cosmopolitan and illusory sweep of Nevsky Prospect anticipates Haussmann's Parisian boulevards by a whole generation (pp. 194, 198). In other words, literary modernity in Russia not only precedes its economic modernization by a century; it also appears decades before the full flowering of literary modernity in Western Europe. The disjunction between Berman's general thesis and his specific readings reminds us that he has failed to foreground the constructive potential in literary texts; it is the very possibility of texts to *produce* a certain social reality that could resolve some of these contradictions and make the link he finds between economic development and aesthetic or cultural progress simultaneously more sophisticated and more convincing. Similarly, in scholarship on twentieth-century Chinese literature that makes use of concepts like belated modernity, Chinese modernity, alternative modernity, and so on, contradictions and tensions arise precisely from such a neglect of the processes and products of textual construction. As Raymond Williams points out in his critique of a similar neglect on the part of certain Marxist theorists of literature, assertions that literary production is essentially determined by social infrastructure reproduce the very dichotomy between culture and society basic to idealist criticism that Marx originally set out to challenge.[13]

Numerous scholars of twentieth-century Chinese literature have made the point that in the perceived absence of economic modernization, literary and cultural modernity are freighted with more significance than they would be otherwise. Freud remarks that subsequent to the perception of absence, "Something else has taken its place, has been appointed its substitute, as it were, and now inherits the interest which was formerly directed to its predecessor. But this interest suffers an extraordinary increase as well . . ."[14]

It is just such a juxtaposition of the *perception* of absence with an increased investment elsewhere, in a substitute, that leads me to read the concepts of "Chinese modernity," "belated modernity," and "deferred modernism" as fetishes in this context. The point here is not to rigidly assert one-to-one equivalences (China as mother figure, and so on), but rather to think about how the fetish as metaphor can bring out aspects of this approach to literature that may not be immediately evident. First, the logic of the fetish can be understood as an operation that can be appropriated and repeated. In the case of this approach to the question of literary modernity, we can identify at least two levels of substitution: it is not only, as noted above, that literary or cultural modernity as such gains importance as a kind of substitution, which makes up for economic underdevelopment, but also that belated or Chinese modernity stands in for this very modernity as such when it in turn is perceived to be missing. Second, as Freud notes, the fetish is not a simple substitution, but rather one that marks a double movement of perception and disavowal. If scholars writing in the 1970s and 1980s continually disavow the aesthetic, yet time and again invoke its lack in the texts they study, critics working in the 1990s frequently invoke the concept of "modernity as such," implicitly or explicitly, without ever coming to grips with the contradictions inherent in such a formulation.

The third moment of concern with literary modernity, an alternative critical response to the Westernization paradigm, emphasizes the relative autonomy of the literary realm. Instead of focusing on the contemporary material base grounding (or failing to ground) literary modernity, this approach defines literary modernity or modernities in nineteenth- and twentieth-century China against the textual tradition of the preceding centuries. In a careful and convincing reading, for example, Rey Chow's classic *Woman and Chinese Modernity* recuperates Mandarin Duck and Butterfly fiction as modern, arguing that it does not reproduce "traditional" Chinese mores and aesthetics unproblematically, but rather subjects them to profound ironization, exaggeration, and fragmentation. But in refuting the May Fourth claim that Mandarin Duck and Butterfly literature is nothing but clichés and remnants of feudal tradition, Chow's own argument refers, at two key moments, to an oppressive system that does not change over time—tradition—that pervades Chinese literature and culture *before* the twentieth century.[15] These references to a reified tradition are not coincidental: if literary modernity is no longer tied exclusively to the specificities of a given material base or infrastructure, as in the paradigm discussed earlier, but rather abstracted away from it, then a textual "Chinese tradition" becomes an essential component of the argument, because literary modernity, in this case, derives its concreteness primarily from its opposition to a specific literary tradition.[16]

How, specifically, does this second critical response construct a reified tradition? There are several important techniques employed in such construction; I focus here on the well-known rhetorical strategy in which a counterargument is anticipated, raised in highly abbreviated form, and dismissed summarily, a strategy variously termed procatalepsis or prolepsis. The structure of this type of argument can be expressed most simply as follows: "of course A, but B," where A is the proposition that a certain phenomenon is to be found in a much earlier era, and B is the flat assertion, without detailed argument, that a similar phenomenon in a later era must be understood as so radically different from the earlier instance as to be incommensurable.[17] The paradigmatic instance of this move in discussions of nineteenth- and early-twentieth-century literature employs the Tang dynasty as a straw figure. Clearly, this is not the place for an extensive comparison of Tang technology, political structure, economic development, linguistic change, and characteristic literary forms and content with those of the twentieth century. The key point that I would like to make is that even though such a thorough comparison has never been made, scholars from Merle Goldman to Lydia Liu—indeed, most critics who address the question of literary modernity in the late-Qing and Republican period—find it useful to write *as though* it has been, as though we know the outcome of such a comparison already.[18]

The specificity of the Tang in writers who deal with the nineteenth and early twentieth century, and conversely, the ease with which A and B slide up in discussions of later writers—so accounts of Taiwanese modernist writing in the 1960s and 1970s can simultaneously raise and dismiss the Shanghai modernists of the 1930s and 1940s, and inquiries into the modernism of the 1980s on the mainland can, in turn, mention Taiwanese modernists as well as their Shanghai predecessors, only to put them both aside—suggests that this proleptic rhetoric is somehow at the center of our very conceptualization of Chinese literary modernity.[19] It is this gesture that makes it possible for us to conceive and speak of modern Chinese literature as difference and innovation, not as a mere continuation, repetition, or imitation of what went before or happened elsewhere; as such, it is a key tool in establishing the field in twentieth-century American academia. Such a rhetorical figure constitutes the linguistic correlate of the logic of simultaneous perception and disavowal through the fetish mentioned previously. The fact that the simultaneous perception and disavowal is of a problematic *presence* (tradition) rather than a problematic *absence* (modernity) merely reverses the valence of the structure without altering its form.

The three approaches that I have identified here run almost completely at cross-purposes: the first reluctantly emphasizes the validity of certain aesthetic standards, which are supposedly objective and universal, even as it offers modernity as a substitute; the second finds social "reality" to be the base to which all literary production is ultimately reduced; and the third acknowledges neither of the first two axioms, reifying instead a tradition that presents the foundation from which the modern springs and against which it can be defined. As noted above, however, these approaches are best seen not as a succession of discrete scholarly takes; they are rather three strategies, which often work in concert *within* a single scholarly account. The insistent claim that modernity does not belong to a previous time period in Chinese history, argued in the proleptic presentations, for example, is probably, in part, symptomatic of the repressed sense that modernity properly belongs somewhere else entirely, and can appear in China only in a belated and compromised form (as the approach that emphasizes the determining function of the economic base suggests). Similarly, the trope of the "weight of tradition" serves an important purpose for critics as diverse as Merle Goldman and Fredric Jameson in their very different imaginations of modern Chinese literature.[20] The striking characteristic of these three fetishizations of literary modernity is not, however, that they are identical in content *or even in form*, but rather that they ultimately work together to reinforce the centrality of modernity in our field even as they disagree radically as to its definition, origins, and implications. It is precisely their sameness on this point, despite difference on others, the fact that all else is allowed to vary while the basic "fact" of literary modernity remains unchallenged, that identifies that fact as the fundamental ground of the field as a whole.

In each of these approaches, modernity is the axis around which arguments are made: since the "as such" after this key word has apparently gone missing, it is necessary always to supplement it, to add a word or two in front of the key word as a substitute. And so we have no modernity as such in Chinese literature, but we do have: belated modernity, repressed modernities, semi-colonial modernity, translated modernity, alternative modernity, Shanghai modernity, and Chinese modernity, not to mention their associated modernisms.[21] Which leads one to wonder: is this scholarly emphasis on a modernity that is subjunctive, spectral, limited, failed, problematic, or once removed—a modernity that can't show itself without a prefix—appropriate only in the study of Chinese literature? Or is it possible that literary modernity as such is fundamentally contradictory and problematic?

Marshall Berman suggests that the modernity of Western Europe is most "at home in its world," less contradictory and overburdened than that of the "Third World." Given Freud's analysis of the way in the *unheimlich* relates inevitably back to the *heimlich*, however, being "at home" can no longer be considered easy or unproblematic.[22] And as we saw in Goethe's Faust, belatedness, failure, and contradiction through and through characterize the modern condition even when it is most at home in its world. Indeed, Faust's project to develop a "decadent" empire's coastline not only anticipates European colonial activity in nineteenth-century China in a striking fashion; it is also uncannily reminiscent of nothing so much as the Great Leap Forward in China of the 1950s. As Paul de Man finds in his genealogy of modernity as a literary value back through Nietzsche to the seventeenth-century conflict between the Ancients and the Moderns, the advocacy of modernity in literature has always been a profoundly paradoxical enterprise. Even in the later writers who are now considered epitomes of European literary modernity, like Baudelaire, de Man shows that "assertions of literary modernity often end by putting the possibility of being modern seriously into question" and concludes that if a conceptual definition of literary modernity is attempted, the result is likely to resemble the following: the modernity of a literary period is "the manner in which it discovers the impossibility of being modern."[23] Modernity, in this reading, is something that all literature strives for with no hope of ever reaching.

Approaching through this issue the fetish can actually bring us to a similar conclusion. It is important to remember that the fetish is the result of an *imagined* loss; it simultaneously recognizes and disavows the absence of something that never could have existed. In this sense, we can read modernity as such not as an origin or a presence elsewhere, but merely as an *effect* of one's own doubts. The ideal literary modernity against which Chinese/belated/alternative/etc. modernities are defined is, in part, a back-formation of these and other qualified modernities rather than an Edenic realm from which they have been exiled, just as the "mother's phallus" is an *interpretation* that Freud develops out of existing fetishistic practices.

Is this a problem? Does it matter if the field of modern Chinese literature rests on logic that reminds us of the formation of a fetish? After all, Freud begins his discussion of fetishism by noting that a fetish is "seldom felt by [its adherents] as the symptom of an ailment . . . Usually they are quite satisfied with it."[24] The invention and extension of "Chinese literary modernity" was a productive strategic move, without which the field could not have come into existence: from the 1970s into the 1990s, it posed an important challenge to the hegemonic status of earlier literature within East Asian departments.[25] This fetish is not just an "error"; it is a constitutive error, founding and vouchsafing the field as we currently understand it. Should this chapter present a new "non-fetishist" theory of "literary modernity," it would (paradoxically) merely further reinforce the fetishization of that term by redefining it from a different perspective. Instead of attempting to negate the fetishization of modernity directly, therefore, I would like to supplement the above analysis with a genealogy of the fetish as a term and a concept.

"MODERNITY" AND "FETISH" AS PIDGIN VOCABULARY

As William Pietz has shown, the word "fetish" derives from a pidgin term, "fetisso," which came into use in an attempt by European traders to become active on the West African coastline in the fifteenth and sixteenth centuries.[26] "Fetisso"—which in its roots refers to the Latin for making or constructing— was the name given by these European traders to a fundamental component of the cross-cultural market that they were attempting to enter. It was their attempt to represent the means that they had to master in order to join this existing "transnational" exchange.

> Fetish was a key word in the pidgin "trade language" used by African and Afro-European middlemen who mediated cross-cultural transactions. Various artifacts and sites, prescribed and proscribed behaviors, and norms for sanctioning new social relations whose meaning and logic were incomprehensible to European merchants were identified as fetish for the pragmatic purpose of furthering peaceful trade.[27]

Should we merely replace "European" with "Chinese," "African" with "Western," "merchants" with "intellectuals," and "fetish" with "modernity," this account has striking similarities with the conventional narratives of early-twentieth-century Chinese elite culture.

In this sense, finally, we can see one more link between the fetish and the modern; both function as *names* of practices through which subjects in a linguistic system attempt to insert themselves in a broader world order understood as radically exterior. The predictable objection that Chinese intellectuals in the nineteenth and twentieth centuries were situated in a set of power relations quite different from Spanish and Portuguese merchants of the sixteenth century is relevant only if one understands "European imperialism" as a monolithic entity, springing forth ex nihilo and immediately dominant, rather than unfolding through a set of complicated and highly variable historical processes. As Pietz has shown, fetisso first appears not as an attempt to assert political control, military supremacy, or economic dominance (colonization), but rather as a means for entry as relative equals into an existing trade system.

By the nineteenth century, of course, the discourse surrounding fetishism in Europe had changed radically in character and become exclusively pejorative. The presence of beliefs in "fetishes" served to mark West Africa off from Europe as "inferior" and "requiring enlightenment"; similarly, beliefs that *resembled* fetishism were used to define backward and superstitious elements *within* European societies. What is striking is that the formal parallelism with the modern in the Chinese context continues: it is merely that the values are inverted. In late nineteenth- and twentieth-century China, the words *modeng, jindai, xiandai*—modern—serve to mark Europe and America off from China as advanced and able to enlighten; similarly, modernized elites within China were understood to be well positioned to encourage their backward compatriots to move forward. It is not only that modernity works as a fetish in the study of modern Chinese literature, but also that the dynamics of self and other that attach to words like "modeng," "wenming," and "xiandai" are inescapably reminiscent of the binary identities connected with the word fetish in earlier centuries and different regions.

As we have seen, the fetish stems from an etymological lineage that finds its roots in the Latin *facticius*—"manufactured" or "artificial"—derived from the past participle of *facere*, to make or construct.[28] I am convinced that at this historical moment, when modern Chinese literature has decisively asserted its intellectual, structural, and economic independence from other sinological fields, our task is now to question the very coherence of the fictional construct that grounds our sphere of inquiry, by asking: how is it made? Who made it? What are the diverse textual characteristics and dynamics that have been forcibly articulated and eventually fused through ceaseless repetition into an object (or objective quality) that we can speak of, and just as significantly, teach to our students?

Extending Gayatri Spivak's suggestion that the postmodern be understood not merely as a rupture, but also as a repetition, I would like to call attention to the ways in which the specific components that are amalgamated into a fetishized literary modernity in the twentieth century can otherwise be understood as echoes of and/or dialectic successors to figures, vocabulary, genres, and problematics first appearing in various previous—and radically mutually incompatible—historical periods. This is not a proposal to search for "sprouts of modernity" in pre-modern literature, but rather a suggestion that looking back can help us to understand the contingency and incompleteness of modernity even at its supposed moments of greatest triumph.

Attention to literary modernity as a perpetually reworked amalgam of materials of different origins and different vintages has the power to call narratives of literary progress and modernization into question; what I propose is not that the fetish of literary modernity be abandoned, but rather unearthed from its fixed and inert position as a boundary marker and grounding concept, and put into play as a subject of more intense and wide-ranging inquiry. Such an inquiry could move empirically to address texts from earlier periods, investigating in detail the extent to which aspects of certain pre-modern texts fit any definition that we propose (explicitly or implicitly) of literary modernity. It could move temporally to ask whether literary criticism must necessarily adopt a model of linear progression or dialectic advance instead of another kind of chronological structure, whether recursive, aperiodic, or aleatory. And finally, it could move analytically to radically rethink the simple rhetoric of identity and difference that determines the form of so many discussions of the modern in opposition to what went before (tradition) or what comes after, whether by taking into consideration Derrida's conception of repetition with a difference (what appears to be the same is not the same), or by making use of the trope of complementary difference as another form of identity suggested in the work of Benjamin and Heidegger (what appears to be different is not necessarily ultimately different).[29]

NOTES

1. "Fetishism" Sigmund Freud, *The Standard Edition of the Complete Psychological Works of Sigmund Freud*, trans. James Strachey, 24 vols., vol. 21 (London: Hogarth Press, 1966–1974), pp. 152–157.
2. Some examples of these figures—not by any means limited to the field of modern Chinese literature, of course—include the growth of plants (sprouts, coming to fruition, maturity), the battle or contest of strength (the weight of tradition, with which one wrestles, by which one is constrained), the race (fell behind, lagged, tried to catch up), evaluation (the question of the Nobel Prize), and translation.
3. C.T. Hsia, "Preface," *A History of Modern Chinese Fiction: Third Edition* (Bloomington: Indiana University Press, 1999) pp. x/vi.
4. See Rey Chow, "The politics and pedagogy of Asian languages and literatures," in *Writing Diaspora: Tactics of Intervention in Contemporary Cultural Studies* (Bloomington: Indiana University Press, 1993), pp. 120–143, for a detailed discussion of this dilemma.
5. The primary exception in modern Chinese literature in the May Fourth era is Milena Dolezalova-Velingerova's essay titled "The origins of modern Chinese literature," in *Modern Chinese Literature in the May Fourth Era*, ed. Merle Goldman (Cambridge: Harvard University Press, 1977), pp. 17–35; the care with which even her partial differences from the overall paradigm are marked off and contained in the introduction reveals the extent to which more radical challenges would be inconceivable. Similarly, Dolezelova's *The Chinese Novel at the Turn of the Century* (Toronto: University of Toronto Press, 1980), which focuses on the two decades preceding the May Fourth Movement, has had relatively little influence on the development of the field of modern literature.
6. Freud, "Fetishism," p. 155.
7. Jing Wang, *High Culture Fever: Politics, Aesthetics, and Ideology in Deng's China* (Berkeley: University of California Press, 1996), p. 97. See also pp. 55, 234–235.
8. Ibid., pp. 192–193; see also Xudong Zhang's discussion of "the changing historical

conditions under which modernism failed to come to its full actualization . . . in the pre-revolutionary decades," "Literature of the new era: historiography and ideology," *Chinese Modernism in the Era of Reforms: Cultural Fever, Avant-Garde Fiction, and the New Chinese Cinema* (Durham: Duke University Press, 1997), pp. 105–107.

9. It is worth noting here that Paul de Man identifies a willingness or even drive to abandon the literary as one of the contradictory components of modernity. "Literary history and literary modernity," *Blindness and Insight: Essays in the Rhetoric of Contemporary Criticism* (Minneapolis: University of Minnesota Press, 1983), pp. 155–156.

10. Wang, *High Culture Fever*, pp. 233–259.

11. Zhang, *Chinese Modernism*, pp. 20–21. Cf. Marshall Berman, "Petersburg: The modernism of underdevelopment," *All That is Solid Melts into Air: The Experience of Modernity* (New York: Penguin Books, 1982), pp. 231–232.

12. "The modernism of underdevelopment is forced to build on fantasies and dreams of modernity, to nourish itself on an intimacy and a struggle with mirages and ghosts. In order to be true to the life from which it springs, it is forced to be shrill, uncouth and inchoate. It turns on itself and tortures itself for its inability to single-handedly make history—or else throws itself into extravagant attempts to take on itself the whole burden of history. . . . But the bizarre reality from which this modernism grows, and the unbearable pressures under which it moves and lives—social and political pressures as well as spiritual ones—infuse it with a desperate incandescence that Western modernism, so much more at home in its world, can rarely hope to match." Berman, *All That is Solid Melts into Air*, p. 232.

13. "Instead of making cultural history material, which was the next radical move, it was made dependent, secondary, 'superstructural': a realm of 'mere' ideas, beliefs, arts, customs, determined by the basic material history. What matters here is not only the element of reduction; it is the reproduction, in an altered form, of the separation of 'culture' from material social life, which had been the dominant tendency in idealist cultural thought. Thus the full possibilities of a concept of culture as a constitutive social process, creating specific and different 'ways of life,' which could have been remarkably deepened by an emphasis on the material social process, were for a long time missed, and were often in practice superseded by a abstracting unilinear universalism." Raymond Williams, "Basic Concepts: Culture," *Marxism and Literature* (Oxford: Oxford University Press, 1977), p. 19.

14. Freud, "Fetishism," p. 154.

15. Rey Chow, *Woman and Chinese Modernity: The Politics of Reading between East and West*, ed. Wlad Godzich and Jochen Schulte-Sasse (Theory of History and Literature 75) (Minneapolis: University of Minnesota Press, 1991), pp. 39, 52, 59–60.

16. See, e.g., David Wang's discussion of late-Qing fiction, in which he challenges the May Fourth narrative of literary modernity; this challenge depends, however, on the definition of nineteenth- and early twentieth-century fiction against an existing "tradition." David Der-wei Wang, *Fin-de-siècle Splendor: Repressed Modernities of Late Qing Fiction, 1849–1911* (Stanford: Stanford University Press, 1997), pp. 6, 14, 20.

17. To a certain extent, such a trope is standard in late-twentieth-century American academic writing: it grows out of the grant-writing tradition in which the conditional acknowledgment of what went before serves as the springboard for a description of one's own potential contributions.

18. "At no other time, even in the period of Buddhist influence, was China so exposed to an alien culture." Goldman, "Introduction," in *Modern Chinese Literature in the May Fourth Era*, p. 11. "Needless to say, lexical borrowing or loan translation is unique neither to China nor to modern times . . . But the massive influx of neologisms in the late nineteenth century and the first quarter of the twentieth century was unprecedented in terms of scale and influence." Lydia Liu, "Introduction: the problem of language in cross-cultural studies," *Translingual Practice: Literature, National Culture, and Translated Modernity, 1900–1937* (Stanford: Stanford University Press, 1995), pp. 18–19. See also David Wang, *Fin-de-siècle Splendor*, pp. 5–6: "The late Qing integration of non-Chinese elements into Chinese literary tradition is admittedly not unique. . . . But late Qing novelties arose in response to Western provocations and Chinese restlessness during a time when Chinese culture was no longer historically isolated and indeed was becoming part of 'modern,' international culture."

19. Sung-cheng Yvonne Chang, "Preface," *Modernism and the Nativist Resistance: Contemporary Fiction from Taiwan* (Durham: Duke University Press, 1993), p. vii; Wang, "Mapping aesthetic modernity" *High Culture Fever*, pp. 192–193; Zhang, "Literature of the new era: historiography and ideology," *Chinese Modernism*, pp. 105–107.

20. Goldman, "Introduction," in *Modern Chinese Literature in the May Fourth Era*; Fredric Jameson, "Foreword" to Liu Kang and Xiaobing Tang, eds., *Politics, Ideology, and Literary Discourse in Modern China: Theoretical Interventions and Cultural Critique* (Durham: Duke University Press, 1993), p. 5.

21. A list of some titles that have appeared in recent years suggests the range of possibilities: David Wang, *Fin-De-Siècle Splendor*; Zhang, *Chinese Modernism*; Chow, *Woman and Chinese Modernity*; Chang, *Modernism and the Nativist Resistance*; Shu-mei Shih, "Gender, Race, and Semicolonialism: Liu Na'ou's Urban Shanghai Landscape," *Journal of Asian Studies* 55:4 (November 1996), pp. 934–956; Liu, *Translingual Practice*; Leo Ou-fan Lee, *Shanghai Modern: The Flowering of a New Urban Culture in China, 1930–1945* (Cambridge, MA: Harvard University Press, 1999), Xiaobing Tang, *Chinese Modern: The Heroic and the Quotidian* (Durham: Duke University Press, 2000).

    In a slightly different context, Rey Chow has noted the problematic dimensions of the insistent insertion of "Chinese" as a qualifier in front of a wide variety of different terms in contemporary scholarly practice. Chow, *Writing Diaspora*, p. 6.

22. See Berman, *All That is Solid Melts into Air*, 232; and Freud, "The Uncanny."

23. de Man, "Literary history and literary modernity," pp. 144, 152.

24. Freud, "Fetishism," p. 152.

25. See, e.g., Rey Chow's 1991 explanation of her project with reference to Nietzsche's concept of "critical history," a judgmental history that enables its author to throw off an oppressive burden. Chow, *Woman and Chinese Modernity*, p. xv.

26. "It was a middleman's term, a pidgin word that expressed an immense, yet highly functional, misunderstanding." William Pietz, "The problem of the fetish, II: The origin of the fetish," *Res*, 13; see also "The problem of the fetish, I," *Res*, 9; "The problem of the fetish, IIIa: Bosman's Guinea and the enlightenment theory of fetishism," *Res*, 16; and "The spirit of civilization: blood sacrifice and monetary debt," *Res*, 25.

27. Pietz, "The Spirit of Civilization," 25; see also "The problem of the fetish, II," 23ff.

28. See Pietz, "The problem of the fetish, I," 5, and "The problem of the fetish, II," pp. 24–25.

29. Jacques Derrida, "Différance," *Margins of Philosophy* (Chicago: University of Chicago Press, 1982), pp. 1–27. Walter Benjamin, "The task of the translator," *Illuminations: Essays and Reflections* (New York: Harcourt, Brace & World, 1968), pp. 69–82; Martin Heidegger, *Identity and Difference* (New York: Harper & Row, 1969).

2

Woman and Her Affinity to Literature

Defining Women Writers' Roles in China's Cultural Modernity

Megan M. Ferry

In 1934, Chinese essayist Huiqun declared "without women there would be no literature."[1] Her pronouncement joined other voices countering the male-dominated literary sphere, which defined Chinese culture until the twentieth century and which sought women's vindication. Her statement reveals Chinese women's contested relationship with literature at the beginning of the twentieth century. Some people argued that women lacked the ability to write anything that contributed to the literary field because they wrote from an emotional and subjective standpoint. Women, they argued, were better suited for biological rather than literary production.[2] Conversely, other people admired women's appreciation of beauty and meticulosity. Although such traits enhanced the quality of women's embroidery, they were better employed in more useful ways, such as in painting, music, and literature. These people required modern women to get an education so that they could enhance their talents and, ultimately, make a living from the arts.[3] In general, despite much press dedicated to defining women's relationship with literature, Chinese women writers' role in creating a modern China was far from certain.

The varied sentiments reflect a common assessment of women's affinity to literature up until the early 1940s, positing women's new social roles in relational terms to underscore the social characteristics of women. Cultural reformers' essays, variously entitled "women and literature," "women and society," "women and culture," "women and education," measured women as objects against the foundational elements that transformed China into a modern culture, and predicated their greater social presence along the lines of accommodation to these institutions. Major proponents of China's and women's liberation, who were themselves writers seeking to change Chinese society, focused their essays on women and culture or women and the arts so as to reevaluate China's literary culture. For reformers of the time, the emerging literature of the modern era served a new social function as a moral conductor of a reconstituted culture, which incorporated women's revised social roles.

Although cultural intellectuals uniformly agreed that women had an inextricable relationship with literature, they differed as to the nature of this relationship in a reformed China. They also differed in their attitudes toward women themselves; some saw them as potential agents; others, as symbolic of China's modern national identity. But all agreed that feminine and emotive qualities characterized Chinese literature and women's "true nature." This view takes up a timeworn notion that literature expresses personal feelings and that women best manifest emotions. It reflects modern intellectuals' preoccupation with literature's autonomy and the self's role in the creative process. Such an autonomy would allow intellectuals to recast a specifically local Chinese heritage and also redefine the self within a global context. Women's social transformation played an important part in this process because they symbolized the status of China's modern condition. Thus many of the essays did not distinguish between women's physical and figurative presence.

Employing the term woman (*nüxing*) to denote actual women and also their representation, Huiqun and other essayists equated female biology with feminine qualities. They imbued *nüxing* with Western-based sexological concepts, which tied femininity to biological womanhood and thus created a new foundational category for womanhood at the turn of the twentieth century.[4] Yet as contemporary Chinese scholar Li Xiaojiang has illustrated, the term denoted social, not natural, characteristics.[5] Although *nüxing* may have divested women's ties to Confucian ideology, it still bound them to a representational femininity. This lack of distinction between actual and symbolic women affected the growing number of modern women writers, whose very presence forced society to rethink women's contribution to China's cultural modernity.

In order to understand women's multivalent affinity to literature, we must examine how early-twentieth-century discourse constructed identities that relegated the sexes to differing forms of gendered cultural production. Moreover, we must examine how woman, according to Rey Chow, reveals "the power-invested processes of hierarchization and marginalization that are involved in readings of culture."[6] Although intellectuals generally discussed women's relationship to literature positively, their understanding of the terms woman (*nüxing*) and literature (*wen*) did not radically alter the historical position of the woman writer.

Diverse intellectuals from leftists to neo-traditionalists shared a sentiment prevalent since the late nineteenth century that women were slaves as a way to identify China's inferiority within the global context and its women as its most abject citizens.[7] Women represented the negative aspects of Chinese culture that hindered China's progress; thus they became the ideal subjects for social and personal change. As part of this process, intellectuals downplayed women's past literary production so as to imagine a new discursive relationship to literature via the figure of the New Woman—an ideal popular then in

European literature and society but yet to be realized in China. The New Woman appeared in the early part of the twentieth century when print media became ever more accessible to a broad reading public, women had more access to education, and key social and cultural institutions began emphasizing "woman" in their agendas. She reflected a modern ideal who was aware of her historical condition and successfully severed ties to traditional values that previously defined her.

In the following pages, I outline how cultural intellectuals' concept of an autonomous literature allowed them to serve as arbiters of reconstituted cultural and moral values, while constraining women's literary authority. These intellectuals believed that China could only advance as a modern nation if it educated its citizens to internalize modern ideologies derived from Enlightenment concepts of a universal humanism and individualism. These concepts valorized the modern individual as belonging to a universal community, yet circumscribed Chinese women's position because society viewed them as yet to become participants in this community. Male and female intellectuals' tutelage stressed teaching women to participate in society as autonomous individuals, rather than remaining as Confucian ideology would have them, subservient wives and mothers that not only denied women individual status but rendered them socially invisible. Although many claimed that educated women might possess the self-awareness to speak to their historical oppression, none of the essays examined here considered contemporary women writers to have achieved such status.

DEFINING A MORAL COMPASS FOR MODERN FEMALE SUBJECTHOOD: THE DISCOURSE OF SELF-AWARENESS

The literary revolution throughout the early twentieth century—its theorization and implementation, as well as reconfiguration of cultural production—reflected largely male intellectuals' preoccupation with their emancipation from social and political authority. Their break from traditional authority gave rise to their status as intellectuals (*zhishi fenzi*), which, like *nüxing*, was a newly created term, and also established them as helmsmen of a new cultural production.[8] Political changes around the beginning of the twentieth century challenged the credibility of Chinese culture and society's foundations. The establishment of a republic in 1911 forced China to reevaluate its history as well as its relations with the rest of the world. In response to China's defenselessness against foreign aggression of the last 50 years,[9] and the dissolution of the imperial system, the New Culture proponents borrowed heavily from Western literary stylistics, language, and philosophy and adopted a Western Enlightenment model that privileged the individual.[10] With literature no longer beholden to its political ties, as in the traditional civil service examinations and government service ranking, intellectuals rearticulated the function of literature as a vehicle for individual self-expression, yet retained its purpose as "a guide for self-understanding, determining proper moral comportment and one's place in society."[11] Chinese intellectuals saw writing as a means to emancipate the Chinese people from what they considered the shackles of a feudal tradition. It was also a means to strengthen a national identity and liberate the oppressed individual through exposing social and cultural ailments, which left China vulnerable to foreign domination.[12] This new literature was liberational in a double sense: it freed China from its traditional moorings and led it toward a universal modernity; yet it also helped China to preserve a unique national identity in light of this universality.

The new literature embraced what Theodore Huters calls "representationalism": the ability to find a new order to understanding "all levels of life."[13] For Chinese intellectuals, Western narrative expressed the subjective view of the individual and an objective presentation of everyday life at once; something that they thought Chinese literature lacked. According to Rey Chow, Chinese intellectuals' "recurrent obsession with 'reality' " meant that intellectuals considered " 'truth' as personal and historical *at once*" (p. 95). Realism expressed both the particularity of the individual and the universality of humanity; a means to realize the self in its own specific social or cultural context, and to create connections between the self and others. Although realism allowed the self to turn inward to explore one's emotions, it also reflected a fundamental difficulty of its adaptation in China. As Huters notes, representationalism appealed to Chinese intellectuals because it doubly recorded the real world and the imaginary world of social and cultural change as "faithful transcriptions of reality" (p. 162). This vision, however, illustrates cultural reformers' constant crisis to produce literature that simultaneously addressed the "dismal actualities of modern Chinese life" alongside an idealized reality. To show too much of the negative aspects of society would destroy the possibility of realizing their "utopian fantasies" (p. 162). Moreover, Huters argues, as both the creative writers and the critics of the new literature, intellectuals did not pay too close attention to literature's development, preferring instead to be directed by ideological pressures external to literature.[14] Much of the literature produced during the New Culture era focused on the subaltern (minorities, peasants, and women), whereby intellectuals could construct subject positions for themselves against a primitive other.[15] Such constructions gave intellectuals agency in the process of social transformation and allowed them to maintain their elite status, despite political changes.

Representationalism allowed intellectuals to reclassify the view of the world and to assign their own set of morals and values. The self in their writings underwent cultivation to the new norms of society. What predominates in their discussion of women's relationship to literature is the way they link the Chinese female self to a native, national self valorized for its essential cultural elements that lacks completeness or maturity. They recognize women's position in the literary field (as author, literary subject, and muse) and, at the same time, deny them cultural agency. Rarely do they consider women as agents of social change.

Shu-mei Shih notes that othering was a recuperative strategy to overcome the crisis of the self/other split and to conceive of Chinese culture as part of a universal reality by recognizing the coexistence of the Chinese and Western, the modern and traditional in a kind of hybridity.[16] This link between the self and the outer world, which found itself in the conception of a "universal moral community" (Kang Youwei)[17] and a "globalist nation" (Liang Qichao)[18] at the turn of the century, echoed in the writings of intellectuals into the 1920s and 1930s; especially in regards to a writer's subjectivity and her/his political or ideological commitment during a time of internal political struggles and foreign aggression.[19]

Foundational to intellectuals' conception of women's relationship to culture was Liang Qichao's *Bianfa tongyi* (*General Discussions of Reform*) (1897), which linked women's education to the fate of the nation.[20] A leading reformer, Liang voiced his concern for China's position vis-á-vis the world by claiming traditional Chinese women were "ignorant, apathetic and sequestered."[21] Discrediting women and their contributions to Chinese culture, he preferred to view their history as superfluous and detached from the realities at hand. Talented women (*cainü*) from past history served as his metonym for a feminized or weak cultural tradition. Changes in their education, he considered, could resolve women's and China's "backwardness" and strengthen the nation. Accordingly, female literacy formed the basis of a new cultural epistemology wherein women's social participation should serve the nation, not just the family. But as Joan Judge illustrates, aside from economic independence, the primary educational goals included teaching mothers to educate the new citizenry.[22] Liang's thinking encouraged reformers to overlook women's historical contributions to education and literature. Instead, modern women had to be taught culture.

New Culture era intellectuals encouraged women's (and thereby the nation's) cultural transformation because they thought traditional views of the self and society caused China's semicolonial crisis. Traditional learning, they argued, failed to recognize women and denied their humanity. Value systems such as "emphasizing the man and overlooking the woman" (*zhong nan qing nü*), "a dutiful wife and loving mother" (*shangi liangmu*), "the three obediences and four virtues" (*sancong side*)[23] enslaved women and hindered their individuality. An emancipation movement encouraged women's self-awareness of their predicament and reformers emphasized newly founded women's schools, as well as new literature as ways to combat women's "enslavement." They urged women to "awaken" to their social condition and liberate themselves from oppressive kinship ties. Once "awakened," reformers thought women would be productive to society.

These female emancipation advocates stressed the difficulty women faced in adapting to the new sociocultural norms that removed them from the traditional family courtyard into more (male-inhabited) public spaces. They stressed that since women lacked access to "public" life for thousands of years, they did not develop a personhood or moral character (*renge*). *Renge* meant something roughly like individual autonomy and social mobility, and women could only have it once they left the boudoir to interact with society. Yet their introduction to society required the maintenance of a strict sexual binary.

In the minds of some thinkers, those few women who had public lives in the past were too masculine (*nanxinghua*).[24] Their writings on women helped to define a feminine personhood.

Male writer and critic Ye Shaojun understood *renge* to mean an individual spirit within the group. One needed to develop one's instinct to become independent.[25] He embraced the then popular discourse that since society traditionally defined women in relation to others, as wives, mothers, and daughters, or used like machines, played with, bought or sold, they lacked independence and, therefore, could not develop their moral character. According to Ye, women lacked a philosophy of life (*rensheng guan*), a crucial part of independent will, because Confucian ideology confined them to the home and made them dependent on others. He equated women's new social role, while supposedly equal to men's, specifically to their biological femaleness and, thus, tied them to the gendered characteristics that many cultural reformers thought inherent to such a biology. Some reformers stressed that women's "true" nature was to reproduce and rear children. Others considered women's reproduction and child rearing as innate creative talent that could be fostered in other areas. These reformers, then, recognized a new kind of social individual in modern China whose charge, by nature of her biology, was to produce and educate future citizens.

In other discussions of *renge*, authors often distinguished between two types of human characteristics: the rational and the emotional (or intuitive), whereby they outlined the central characteristics or nature (*xingzhi*) that distinguished men and women.[26] New Cultural critic Mei Guangdi's analysis of "women and culture" saw women as possessing more intuition than reason.[27] As those who possessed intuition were more apt to be artists or writers, Mei argued there should be more women artists. His lecture outlined women's innate talents (*cai*) and virtues (*de*), but confused women's social behavior (household managers, socially interactive, etc.) with common symbolic perceptions of women as they appeared in literature (beautiful, vain, and emotional). He concluded that women faced difficulty developing a sense of self or developing their artistic talents because they suffered social restraint.

Thus without a sense of self or moral character, one reformer likened women to "a small boat that once it leaves port, loses direction."[28] The new morality of the age, however, would serve as their compass. Another writer claimed "the men in this world do not consider the women who make up half of humankind as the same kind of human. They only recognize them as soulless amusement toys, which is the most inhuman, most inegalitarian behavior; a great stain on evolutionary history."[29] This author cited European and U.S. fiction and nonfiction to demonstrate how their writings on the woman question related to Chinese social concerns. Similar to other writers of the time, Ceng Qi saw problems with Chinese culture and society, which treated women inhumanely. He wrote, "Today, despite some awakening, there are still many women who are oppressed under men's control; Chinese women in the East especially represent these brutal and inhumane [conditions]. This problem cannot be resolved in a day" (p. 3). One author wrote of women's ambiguous social position, remarking "the essence of the women who make up half of humanity has not been analyzed clearly," nor have women's duties in the new society been "standardized." "Therefore, the explanation of women, even if it cannot be certain, needs to satisfy the goal of humanity, to realize the aspiration of humanity, which is not a lost cause."[30] Countless other authors offered advice to both women and men on how to accept women's position in humanity and to help them become new social beings. This social being reflected a local as well as a global outlook.

In his speech to the Student Council at Beijing Women's Normal College in 1920, Zhou Zuoren urged Chinese reformers to recognize the globality of humanism (*rendao zhuyi*) and individualism (*geren zhuyi*). He asserted that women belong to humankind, and, therefore, should not be subservient to anyone. But, he argued, they lack self-awareness in a more global sense. "In recent years, the women's world has a new atmosphere, but from my observation, it is just a self-awareness as citizens (*guomin*) and not as individuals."[31] For Zhou, self-awareness meant recognizing one's individuality within a larger, or extra-national context. It "means the awareness that one is part of humanity and that one sees one's self on equal footing with others. There are no barriers within [humanity] so mutual understanding is easy" (p. 7). Accordingly, Zhou argued, "[i]f one does not know the self, then one cannot know others. Thus, to know the self is to know others" (p. 7). The key to understanding universal humanity for Zhou lay in understanding the "essential nature" of literature, which was a true expression of personal experience. He put the onus on women writers to explain their social conditions, yet was critical of past women writers:

> There are quite a few female poets and fiction writers in the world, but there are few who can freely express their sorrows. John Stuart Mill said that the books that past and present women have written about women were composed to flatter men. They did not write about real women (*zhen de nüxing*). This is not an exaggeration. From today on, women ought to use the freedom of literature and the arts to express their true feelings and thoughts to dispel thousands of years of misunderstanding and uncertainty. But this will be limited to just a few women who have creative talent. (p. 8)

Because he recognized few women writers as self-aware enough to serve as role models, Zhou ultimately put his faith in the new literature written by women and men to give voice to women's experiences. His notion of an individual's reality, however, is problematic. Though he sympathized with women and acknowledged that society misconceives their lives, he implied that they lacked self-awareness and, therefore, their writings were not real or accurate representations of women's lives. Moreover, Zhou did not clarify how to read women's texts or male authors who have written about women. Unwittingly, it seems Zhou invalidated women's writings and revealed the chasm between the intellectual and the subaltern for whom he wished to speak. This leaves Zhou, and other intellectuals, to determine when a woman tells the "truth" of her lived experience and when she is self-aware. In general, despite intellectuals' attempts to allow women to become agents of social change, they perceived women as incomplete social beings. They ignored alternative (non-masculine) representations of women.

WHOSE FEMININE AESTHETIC?

When intellectuals recognized women as historical producers of literature, they assumed women wrote lyrical and emotional literature. This notion is based on the gender stereotypes existent in the Chinese poetic tradition, which emphasized women's emotionality and physical confinement.[32] For example, scholars of the Ming and Qing dynasties praised women who wrote song-lyrics (*ci*), an aesthetically feminine genre in which men and women adopted the feminine voice.[33] Women came to dominate in the genre by the seventeenth century and scholars largely accepted this dominance as a "convergence of biological femaleness and stylistic femaleness."[34] Thus, the successful amalgamation of an aestheticized femininity and biological femaleness was nothing new to early-twentieth-century literary scholars and intellectuals. Yet for modern women writers, intellectuals' underlying assumptions of femininity and literary production, though recognizing their artistic talent, defined women's literature as weak and in need of rescue by their intellectual authority. In addition, if men could write in a feminine style too, then women's literature remained symbolic of otherness.

Throughout the history of Chinese literature, male authors often used the feminine voice to position the male narrator as the oppressed other for both literary and political effect. Dorothy Ko notes how seventeenth-century male scholars and editors of women's literary anthologies equated women and "feminine" literature with a different kind of aesthetic, which was not restrained by traditional learning. Women's "natural" serenity, emotions, and exclusion from the male-dominated world defined poetry's essence.[35] Yet women's literature served a dual purpose for the scholar as a subject of aesthetic refinement and purity, as well as a commercially profitable commodity. Ko and Katherine Carlitz have examined scholars' interest in women's texts along this duality.[36] One could argue for a parallel context in early-twentieth-century China, especially since many of the cultural reformers were editors and publishers of the journals that produced essays on women's relationship with literature and culture. For now, I want to emphasize that sympathetic reformers generally read women's premodern writing tradition as proof of their supposed natural affinity to literature. Contrary to Zhou Zuoren and Mei Guangdi, writer and literary historian Hu Yunyi did not see women's historical social oppression as an obstacle to their literary production.[37] While their social oppression affected other parts of society, such as politics, philosophy, history, and economics, this was not the case for literature. Hu claimed past women's texts as valuable and rare works because the more a woman suffered (socially and emotionally), the greater her writing and thus the greater her literary influence. Cai Yan's abduction at the hands of barbarians, Xue Tao's life as a courtesan, and Yu Xuanji's apparent unfulfilled sex life gave literary expression to their tragic female experiences (p. 57). Few of women's literary works appear in Chinese literary histories, he argued, not because women lack innate talent but because of the patriarchal system's prejudice against women.

Hu's legitimization of past women's literature privileged it as part of the very literary tradition from which modern intellectuals sought their freedom. In claiming women's literature as "the orthodoxy of the orthodox school" of China's lyrical poetic tradition, he did not simply valorize women, but a lyric tradition that expresses specifically female experiences (p. 57). Such an evaluation of women's literature creates an aesthetic of female oppression or victimization, which relates to the early-twentieth-century intellectuals' perception of Chinese literature and culture within a global context.

Why Hu should express such an interest in claiming women writer's literary authority and historical presence can be explained if we consider his literary and political agenda. Literature's feminine qualities indicated China's weakness against the developed Japan and the West; yet, it also valorized a voice of dissent. Early-twentieth-century intellectuals used male imitation of the female voice and emphasized female emotions in order to construct a new order of truth counter to social and literary conventions.[38] Hu elevated women's literature as orthodoxy to repudiate a past literary tradition. In so doing, he recast that tradition to claim authority for the intellectuals of his day, against which they could construct a new (male) subjectivity. Yet despite Hu's support for women's literature, he equated historical women with the feminine symbolic. They are objects against which he solidified his contemporary cultural authority.

Hu insinuated this in his short treatment of five well-known writers. He did not totally negate the Chinese past and its male literary tradition, even as he asserted its femaleness. Yet he referred to past women writers as girls (*nühaizi*) when mentioning how untutored they were in the classics and other forms of education, thus, insinuating a lack of maturity in their historical experience. These women writers needed to be educated in the arts and given creative freedom in order to grow.

> Our purpose [in this essay] is not to raise the status of women's literature intentionally, but to know the kind of . . . environment in which those girls with no artistic training lived. . . . [I]n reality, women have innate artistic talent. If we add to it education, give them the freedom to study the arts, then Chinese women's literary history's brilliance cannot be a dreary prospect. (p. 68)

Hu offered a liberatory gesture, underscoring how "evil Confucian ethics can't possibly have hindered women's freedom." He suggested that women can "now finally obtain remarkable success in the creative world" (p. 52). Yet by considering Chinese women writers in this light, he negated their completeness as intellectuals or creative producers and also assumed Chinese orthodox tradition as possessing talent but inferior to what the new Chinese literature could and would create.

In contrast, Ms. Wenna's collected essays on women's relationship with literature agreed that women possessed innate artistic talent but oppressive social conditions did hinder their production. Arguing that traditional schooling kept women from being larger players in the literary field, she called for men and women to receive the same education.[39] She criticized men for overlooking women's minds and sequestering them behind walls just because of their sex and also questioned the altruism of male sympathizers who largely led the woman's movement. Equally, she was despondent at women's inability to act independently. Reflecting a strong anti-Confucian bias current among activists in the women's movement, Ms. Wenna saw no past examples of women to emulate because she used the discourse of self-awareness to read backward into time. Thus, she considered female poet Zhu Shuzhen noteworthy but, ultimately, limited by her conformity to social morality and restricted access to the male-dominated literary sphere.[40] In this respect, Ms. Wenna was even more pessimistic than Hu about women's literary tradition and no less concerned about women's ability to overcome social prejudices.

Embracing the notion of the autonomous individual, many reformers considered that one must first live a life unrestricted by social and moral conventions to become a writer. Frequently, women who wrote about women's issues looked positively to the courtesan. They viewed morally upright women as constrained by traditional Confucian virtue, while the courtesan had the freedom to enter the male-dominated literary world and develop her talent. This reflects women's emancipation advocates' anti-Confucian bias, which suggested that the further one receded from the center of moral uprightness and propriety, the better one's literary production. A woman less bound to the Confucian ethic, as a wife and mother, possessed the freedom to develop her innate talent. In general, contemporary women were systematically excluded from the possibility of possessing literary talent (*cai*) while still tied to moral behavior of women's virtue (*de*).[41] The mobility that the courtesan and prostitute supposedly had, reflected a modern preoccupation with free marriage (a marriage by choice and not arranged), women's access to education, and their increased mobility in public. This kind of thinking embraced contemporary social changes as having a positive outcome toward liberating women from the domestic realm, ignoring the reality that men treated courtesans as objects of connoisseurship and a commodity. Moreover, freedom from the social confines of Confucian patriarchy could also imply unacceptable licentiousness or unruliness. Thus this perceived social freedom did not necessarily guarantee that women would produce quality literature.

Throughout their analysis of Chinese women's relationship to literature, essayists uncritically assume women's universal, ahistorical oppression. Their pervasive belief situates women's inequality as a transhistorical phenomenon. Women in the Tang dynasty faced the same issues of those in the 1930s. As such, reformers' discussion of women's relationship with literature focuses on their objectification and social oppression. An exception to this may be Chen Hengzhe, a female writer and historian, who argued that the achievements of past women writers were "like an age-old tree" that "has been growing for hundreds of years, but has been confined to a narrow courtyard whose share of sunshine and moisture is limited, and whose soil has been impoverished through lack of care and attention."[42]

WHITHER THE MODERN CHINESE NEW WOMAN?

Magazines, such as Shanghai Commercial Press' *Funü zazhi* (*Ladies' Journal*), *Nü shizhong* (*Women's Times*), *Xin funü* (*New Woman*), *Nü sheng* (*Woman's Voice*), *Funü xunkan* (*Women's Bi-monthly*), and newspaper supplements like *Chenbao's Funü wenti* (*The Woman Question*), and *Minguo ribao's Funü pinglun* (*Women's Critic*) published countless articles about women, which addressed several concerns specific to their changing social status and concurrently addressed China's cultural changes. The journals' contributors included both men and women who advocated women's emancipation, economic independence, and political participation. They focused on the educated career woman, a woman who left her home and entered the public sphere. One journal purports to "awaken women thoroughly so that they can in the future collectively take responsibility for a new society."[43] This journal, and others like it, outlined the modern Chinese New Woman, a figure expected to devote herself to realize social change, to sacrifice herself for women's future emancipation and China's freedom from both its own tradition and foreign imperialist aggression. Yet the New Woman incorporated much of the traditional feminine ideal. As Hu Ying notes, translations of the New Woman from Western literature, such as Madame Bovary, the Lady of the Camellias, and Madame Roland created sinified versions of women who lived public lives but maintained the essence of traditional female roles.[44]

Reformers, who wrote about the New Woman in journals, contradictorily demanded that women reject Chinese feudal tradition but cautiously embrace Western ideologies. Their imagination of the New Woman was one who devoted herself to national salvation (in whatever political order) to eliminate women's social oppression for good. Ways in which women could be emancipated borrowed from foreign treatises on women's emancipation, such as those by Friedrich Engels, August Bebel, John Stuart Mill, Margaret Sanger, Alexandra Kollontai, and Yosano Akiko. In addition, bourgeois consumerism offered ways toward women's economic independence. *Xiandai Funü* (*Modern Woman*) under female editor and activist Hu Xiufeng included gossip on the lives of professional women writers, who served as new women role models, as well as essays on sexuality, the Chinese women's movement, and articles on women's physical beauty, and proper comportment. Regardless of the content, much of the discussion in these journals focused on ways in which women could be modern, ways in which they could realize in themselves the idealized New Woman.

Irrespective of political ideology, the woman's movement received full attention because it offered a means by which to awaken and, hence, liberate China's most "backward" people. Male editors Zhang Xichen and Zhou Jianren of *The Ladies' Journal* and *Xin nüxing* (*The New Woman*) embraced a liberal feminist agenda. Female activist and editor Shen Zijiu's *Funü shenghuo* (*Women's Life*) reflected the Communist Party ideas on the women's movement, and Wang Yiwei started *Nüsheng* (*Women's Voice*) with a conservative female activist to create a journal solely by and for women.[45] Male reformers, however, largely drove the woman's movement as editors, publishers, and critics, leaving woman's emancipation ambiguously defined. Male playwright Tian Han thought that the woman's movement divided along gendered lines, noting that, for men, the movement meant the "respect women" question, whereas, for women, it meant the "women's self-awakening" question.[46] Male author, critic, and editor Mao Dun advocated women's emancipation yet criticized women's own attempts at it.[47]

The way reformers thought to solve the woman question was as diverse as those individuals with opinions on the matter. Mao Dun called for new moral standards for the New Woman by advocating the study of Western literature on feminism, such as Mary Wollstonecraft, Ellen Key, and Susan B. Anthony.[48] One author charged women with the responsibility to educate society on women's issues, in order to ease men's and women's suspicions of what awakened women would be like.[49] Chen Hengzhe argued that China needed to selectively adapt Western thinking.[50] Many authors contextualized the Chinese woman question as part of a global movement. Whether they advocated woman's emancipation to ensure the health of the nation or saw the Chinese woman question as an evolutionary teleological development of Western women's movements, they did not all agree that women could take a leadership role.

In "Wenxue limian de funü wenti" (The woman question in literature), Huiqun despaired that no representative New Woman existed in Chinese literature for women to emulate.[51] For her, Western male writers, such as Henrik Ibsen and Hermann Sudermann, raised relevant questions about women's lives, such as sexual morality, domestic abuse, and disloyal husbands. Their fiction, she argued, awakens female readers to their oppressed conditions. Huiqun bemoaned male Chinese writer's lack of sympathy for society's mistreatment of women. Women play a central role not just in literature, she argued in "Nüxing yu wenxue" (Woman and literature), but also in culture. "The woman question is also an intellectual concern in modern times, [and] has become modern literature's most important subject matter."[52] Similar to Zhou Zuoren, Huiqun wanted her readers to understand that women belong to a universal humanity and that women's current social status needs to change. Once recognized as human, both male and female authors could work to redefine and correct the perceptions and mechanisms that deny women individual freedom. For Huiqun, literature that incorporated the woman question did not ignore the hardships that both lower and upper class women endured. It sought both an internal revolution (recognition of the human individual) and an external revolution (material technological changes like the Western industrial revolution).

Huiqun's inability to find Chinese literature sympathetic to women had a lot to do with the fact that the New Woman in China was a projection, not of a pre-textual reality but of an imagined possibility of a future ideal. This is why, nearly throughout the early twentieth century, reformers compared Chinese women to their European or American counterparts, and lamented that a Chinese New Woman had not yet been realized. While many upheld the New Woman as a model for emulation, most reformers did not find a Chinese New Woman whose personhood or behavior could fulfill such a role.

For the most part, reformers limited their discussion to Chinese traditional and European literature, rarely discussing modern Chinese literature. *Funü zazhi*'s special edition on "woman and literature" (July 1931) included male European stories about female protagonists, stories written by foreign female authors, pictures of foreign female authors, an update on women writers in Russia, France, and England, as well as discussion of past Chinese women writers. Only a short piece by contemporary female author Lu Yin appears at the very end of the issue.

Writing in 1929, over 30 years after Liang Qichao's call for women's education, one critic compared "new" and "old/traditional" women to argue that contemporary women had not reached self-realization.

> Regarding knowledge, new women do not necessarily have the upper hand. Even though they are educated—whether it is common or higher education—they at least know the rudiments of home and society, and to not believe in superstition or things that cannot be explained by science. Their good points lie in the arts, crafts, and social intercourse. Because of this, their philosophy of life (*rensheng guan*) is encouraging. It is different with traditional women. Because they never entered a school, their sights and sounds are superficial, so they are not used to new sounds (like music) and colors (like the arts) entering their ears and eyes. They do not know just how big the world is; a town or rural village passes for the world in their hearts. This is indeed their biggest defect. It is also the reason why Chinese women cannot compare with Japanese and Western women.[53]

In a remarkably reductive analysis of women, this essay privileges women who received a modern education, noting their access to a global sphere because of it, while considering women who had not received such an education ignorant of anything outside their own localities. Yet despite educated women's greater public interactions they could not compare with women outside of China. This sentiment was repeated throughout the early twentieth century, especially because reformers continually debated the content of women's educational reform.

In general, however, intellectuals assumed that women's social conditions would be resolved in the future, when women writers would finally awaken. Male and female reformers often cited Japanese poet and female activist Yosano

Akiko, who optimistically saw women's liberation occurring in the future:

> Even though it is said that our women have lost hope in the past and present, there is no reason for despair in the future. If we depend on our will and realize our efforts, who knows, the essence of our womanliness could develop rapidly! Women! We must rise up and use all our strength to create a mighty future.[54]

For both male and female intellectuals, literature that addressed the woman question and reflected the author's awareness of women's social oppression came closer to realizing the New Woman as an icon of Chinese modernity. Thus, they critiqued past or present Chinese women writers on the basis of their lack of self-awareness, which women could only obtain sometime in a distant future. Because of this paradigm, when intellectuals spoke of women's relationship to literature, they conflated women's representation *within* literature with women writers themselves. Women writers must await realization until a future time after they have received a complete modern education.

Conclusion: The Woman Writer as an Icon of Modernity

In order to understand the context for China's new literature and New Woman and their perceived affinity in essays devoted to establishing a relationship between them in the early twentieth century, one must take into account not only the pressing issues that "literature" and woman faced singularly, but the combined effect the two terms had on imagining women as professional writers in modern China. These essays suggest the salient issues for male and female intellectuals of the time: namely, the expression of the intellectual self and articulation of a Chinese national identity in light of an international context.

It would be unsatisfactory to understand these essays on the relationship between women and literature solely as readings of Chinese women as the metaphorical oppressed Chinese Other. More complicated than assuming a simplified dichotomy between self/other, male/female, East/West, reformers' consideration of women's relationship with literature forced them to address the ways in which women's education and increased social participation challenged Chinese male-centric notions of self and modernity. The essays examined earlier, regardless if written by man or woman, overlook women as producers of a viable literary culture. They concur that women's successful relationship with literature will occur in the future, thus indicating a deferment of women's unequivocal authority over the representation of woman to an indeterminate and as yet inconceivable time and place.

Unfortunately, dominant sociocultural assumptions about women created obstacles, which hindered actual women from transitioning into modern new women because these assumptions refused to recognize female subject positions outside preestablished paradigms. These reformers kept the historical woman invested with symbolic meaning through their assumption of a specifically feminine writing practice, which equated women's biological experiences with their literary representation. Women straddled the impossible position of representing both China's feudalist past as products of patriarchal oppression and as extensions of male intellectuals' alienated selves. This phenomenon is "of little help in theorizing the historically specific locations of women in culture and society," because it perpetuates women not as unequivocal producers of literature but its spectacle.[55]

The essays examined here demonstrate the burgeoning iconic formation of the woman writer as representative of China's quest for modernization. Though female intellectuals did not necessarily accept an identical definition of "woman/women," they tended to be no less optimistic about the possibility for the New Woman in China. Both male and female intellectuals emphasize Western epistemologies of the self and nation, as well as self-awakening or self-realization to argue that women writers lacked self-awareness of their historical oppression under patriarchy. Since they measure China's modernity through women's (historically "backward") social condition, they devalue women's historical literary production and privilege men as cultural producers. Their discussions on women's relationship with literature position women writers as pedagogical subjects of China's burgeoning modernity, not its leading proponents. This sentiment precluded contemporary women writers from being recognized as positive agents of social change, and circumscribed their contribution to realizing a modern China.

NOTES

1. Huiqun, "Nüxing yu wenxue" (Women and literature), in *Nüxing yu wenxue*, ed. Huiqun (Shanghai: Qizhi shuju, 1934), pp. 1–9, 4. I have identified Huiqun's surname as Li. She was friends with female authors Lu Yin [Huang Luyin] and Xie Bingying.

2. Ceng Juezhi argued that women are innately emotional and cannot write from an objective perspective "Funü yu wenxue" (Women and literature), *Funü zazhi* (Ladies' journal) 17:7 (1931), 15–23.

3. See, e.g., Zhu Yin, "Nüzi haomei shi buyong shuode" (It goes without saying that women love beauty), *Funü zazhi* 12:1 (1926), 167–170.

4. Tani E. Barlow, "Theorizing woman: *funü, guojia, jiating* (Chinese woman, Chinese state, Chinese family)," in *Body, Subject and Power in China*, ed. Tani E. Barlow and Angela Zito (Chicago: Chicago University Press, 1994), pp. 253–289.

5. Xiaojiang Li, "With what discourse do we reflect on Chinese women? Thoughts on transnational feminism in China," in *Spaces of their Own: Women's Public Sphere in Transnational China*, ed. Mayfair Mei-hui Yang (Minneapolis: University of Minnesota Press, 1999), pp. 261–277, 262.

6. Rey Chow, "Mandarin ducks and butterflies: an exercise in popular readings," *Woman and Chinese Modernity: The Politics of Reading Between East and West* (Minneapolis: University of Minnesota Press, 1991), p. 52.

7. See Rebecca Karl, " 'Slavery,' citizenship, and gender in late Qing China's global context," in *Rethinking the 1898 Reform Period: Political and Cultural Change in Late Qing China*, ed. Rebecca E. Karl and Peter Zarrow (Cambridge: Harvard University Asia Center, 2002), pp. 212–244.

8. Barlow, "Theorizing woman," p. 262.

 9. Events from 1840–1919 forced intellectuals to rethink self, community, nation, and the world, such as the Opium War (1840–1842), which opened the door for colonial control of China's major coastal ports, the Sino-Japanese War (1894–1895), the Russo-Japanese war (1904–1905), disintegration of imperial rulership, the failure of a republic at the hands of Yuan Shikai, and Japan's Twenty-one Demands (1915) that granted it colonial territories in China.

10. See Lydia Liu, *Translingual Practice. Literature, National Culture, and Translated Modernity—China, 1900–1937* (Stanford: Stanford University Press, 1996); Edward Gunn, *Rewriting Chinese: Style and Innovation in Twentieth-Century Chinese Prose* (Stanford: Stanford University Press, 1991); and Vera Schwarcz, *The Chinese Enlightenment: Intellectuals and the Legacy of the May Fourth Movement of 1919* (Berkeley: University of California Press, 1986).

11. Kirk A. Denton, "General introduction," *Modern Chinese Literary Thought. Writings on Literature 1893–1945* (Stanford: Stanford University Press, 1996), p. 25.

12. See Wendy Larson, *Literary Authority and the Modern Chinese Writer: Ambivalence and Autobiography* (Durham, NC: Duke University Press, 1991).

13. Theodore Huters, "Ideologies of realism in modern China: the hard imperatives of imported theory," in *Politics, Ideology and Literary Discourse in Modern China*, ed. Liu Kang and Xiaobing Tang (Durham, NC: Duke University Press, 1993), pp. 147–173, 160.

14. Theodore Huters, ed., "Introduction," in *Reading the Modern Chinese Short Story* (Armonk, NY: M.E. Sharpe, 1990), pp. 3–21.

15. Ching-kiu Stephen Chan, "The language of despair: ideological representations of the 'New Woman' by May Fourth writers," in *Gender Politics in Modern China. Writing and Feminism*, ed. Tani E. Barlow (Durham: Duke University Press, 1993), pp. 13–32.

16. Shu-mei Shih, *The Lure of the Modern: Writing Modernism in Semicolonial China, 1917–1937* (Berkeley: University of California Press, 2001).

17. Evelyn Rawski, "The social agenda of May Fourth," in *Perspectives on Modern China*, ed. Kenneth Lieberthal (Armonk, NY: M.E. Sharpe, 1991), pp. 139–157.

18. Shih, *Lure*, p. 63.

19. See Christina Kelley Gilmartin, *Engendering The Chinese Revolution. Radical Women, Communist Politics, and Mass Movements in the 1920s* (Berkeley: University of California Press, 1995), for a discussion of the May Thirtieth incident, which sparked a national revolution and deepened conflict between the ruling Guomindang (Nationalist) and Chinese Communist Parties. Japan's encroachment on Chinese territory increased in the mid–late 1920s.

20. See Rebecca E. Karl and Peter Zarrow, ed., *Rethinking the 1898 Reform Period: Political and Cultural Change in Late Qing China*; Xiaobing Tang, *Global Space and the Nationalist Discourse of Modernity: The Historical Thinking of Liang Qichao* (Stanford: Stanford University Press, 1996).

21. Hu Ying, "Introduction: the emerging new woman and her significant others," *Tales of Translation: Composing the New Woman in China, 1899–1918* (Stanford: Stanford University Press, 2000), p. 7.

22. Joan Judge, "Reforming the feminine: female literacy and the legacy of 1898," in *Rethinking the 1898 Reform Period*, ed. Karl and Zarrow, pp. 158–179, 169. See also Rawski, "The Social Agenda of May Fourth," p. 142.

23. A woman was required to obey her father, husband, and son, and maintain the virtues of fidelity, beauty, to speak little, and to be efficient in needlework.

24. Shi Guanying, "Nüxing yanjiu de mudi" (Reasons for studying women), *Funü zazhi* 7:3 (1921), 1–3.

25. Ye Shaojun "Nüzi renge wenti" (The problem of women's personhood/character), in *Zhongguo funü wenti taolun ji* (Discussions of Chinese Women's Issues), ed. Mei Sheng (Shanghai: Xin wenhua shushe, 1923), pp. 149–156, 156.

26. Wang Pingling, "Xin funü de renge wenti" (The personhood/character problem of New Women), in *Zhongguo funü wenti taolun ji*, ed. Mei sheng (Shanghai: Xin wenhua shushe, 1923), pp. 156–165; Li Li and Wu Rubin, "Wenxue yu nüzi" (Literature and women), *Funü zazhi* 14:11 (1928), 27–30.

27. In Chen Dongyuan and Zhang Youwan, "Nüzi yu wenhua" (Women and culture), *Funü zazhi* 8:1 (1922), 8–11.

28. Miao Ran, "Xin funü de xin daode" (The new moral virtue of the new woman), *Xin Funü* (New Woman) 1:1 (1920), 9–12, 9.

29. Ceng Qi, "Funü wenti yu xiandai shehui" (The woman question and modern society), *Funü zazhi* 8:1 (1922), 2–7, 3.

30. Shi Guanying, "Nüxing yanjiu de mudi," p. 1.

31. Zhou Zuoren, "Nüzi yu wenxue" (Women and literature), *Funü zazhi* 8:8 (1922), 6–8, 7.

32. Dorothy Ko, "In the floating world: women and commercial publishing." *Teachers of the Inner Chambers: Women and Culture in Seventeenth-Century China* (Stanford: Stanford University Press, 1994), p. 61.

33. Kang-i Sun Chang and Haun Saussy, eds. "Introduction: genealogy and titles of the female poet," *Women Writers of Traditional China: An Anthology of Poetry and Criticism* (Stanford: Stanford University Press, 1999), pp. 4–5, 13, 810. "Appendix A: A note on song-lyrics with a glossary of tune-titles."

34. Kang-i Sun Chang, "A guide to Ming-Ch'ing anthologies of female poetry and their selection strategies," *Gest Library Journal* 5:2 (1992), 119–160, 141.

35. Dorothy Ko, Teachers of the Inner Chambers, p. 62

36. Katherine Carlitz, "The social uses of female virtue in late Ming editions of *Lienü zhuan*," *Late Imperial China* 12:1 (1991), 117–152.

37. Hu Yunyi, "Zhongguo funü yu wenxue" (Chinese women and literature), in *Nüxing yu wenxue* (*Women and Literature*), ed. Huiqun (Shanghai: Qizhi shuju, 1934), pp. 52–68.

38. See Yue Mingbao's "Gendering the origins of modern Chinese literature," in *Gender and Sexuality in Twentieth-Century Chinese Literature and Society*, ed. Tonglin Lu (Albany, NY: State University of New York Press, 1993), pp. 47–65.

39. Ms. Wenna, *Funü lunji* (*A Collection of Discussions on Women*) (Shanghai: Beixin shuju, 1927).

40. Wenna, "Du 'Duanchangji' " (Reading "duanchangji"), in *Funü lunji*, pp. 66–75, 68, 75.

41. Wendy Larson, *Women and Writing in Modern China* (Stanford: Stanford University Press, 1998).

42. Chen Hengzhe, "The Chinese woman in a modern world," in *The Chinese Woman and Four Other Essays* (Beijing: S.H. Chen, 1934), pp. 1–22, 16.

43. Editor "Xin funü xuanyan" (Manifesto of new woman), *Xin funü* 1:1 (1920), p. 1.

44. Hu Ying, *Tales of Translation*, pp. 104, 107, 196.

45. See Wang Zheng, *Women in the Chinese Enlightenment: Oral and Textual Histories* (Berkeley: University of California Press, 1999).

46. Tian Han, "Disi jieji de furen yundong" (The fourth class of the woman's movement), *Shaonian Zhongguo* (*The Young China*) 1:4 (1919), 218–219.

47. Wang, *Women in the Chinese Enlightenment*, p. 62.
48. Mao Dun, "Women gai zenyang yubeile qu tan funü jiefang wenti" (How we ought to prepare to discuss the woman's liberation question), *Funü zazhi* 6:3 (1920), 1–5.
49. C.K., "Funü wenti yu zhongguo funü yundong" (The woman question and the Chinese woman's movement), *Funü zazhi* 8:11 (1922), 55–56.
50. Sophia Zen Chen, "The Chinese woman in a modern world," *Pacific Affairs* 4:12 (December 1931), 1070–1081.
51. Huiqun, "Wenxue limian de funü wenti" (The woman question in literature), in *Nüxing yu wenxue*, pp. 10–51.
52. Huiqun, "Nüxing yu wenxue," p. 1.
53. Yang Songxian, "Xin jiu funü de bijiao" (a comparison between new and traditional women), *Funü zazhi* 15:9 (1929), 23–24.
54. Huiqun, "Nüxing yu wenxue," p. 8.
55. Rita Felski, "Sexual and textual politics," *Beyond Feminist Aesthetics: Feminist Literature and Social Change* (Cambridge: Harvard University Press, 1989), p. 5.

3

Desire and Disease: Bai Wei and the Literary Left of the 1930s

Amy D. Dooling

The rewriting of dominant literary history (*chongxie wenxueshi*) has encompassed important new scholarship on the modern women's literary tradition. As a result, we are in the process of constructing an ever more nuanced picture of the literary roles of women through the gender relations reshaped by social, ideological, and economic factors in the twentieth century. Yet our understanding of women's participation in the cultural left of the 1930s, in particular, remains incomplete, dominated by a single paradigm of "subordinated gender politics." Ding Ling's (in)famous metamorphosis from New Woman writer to pioneer practitioner of social realism, which ignored the woman question, and Feng Keng's exhortation to female radicals to forget their gender identity altogether may be symptomatic of the growing ambivalence of the Chinese Communist Party (CCP) to feminism at the time, but they are not, as it turns out, quite as representative as many have assumed. The following explores the work of the (now largely forgotten) political writer Bai Wei (1894–1983) and analyzes the problem of the relationship between feminist sexual politics and leftist culture of the 1930s. Specifically, I focus on her autobiographical novel *Beiju shengya* (*Tragic Life*, 1936), a somber narrative that traces the vicissitudes of a female intellectual trapped in an abusive personal relationship, including a protracted battle with syphilis.[1] As I will argue, this work consciously defied the trend toward depoliticizing private domestic life (and the so-called women's issues associated with that realm) evinced in other leftist literature of the 1930s.

Returning to a noncanonical text such as this is not simply an exercise in archival recuperation; rather, it gives occasion to consider the mechanisms that produce narratives of literary history, including, in this case, contemporary feminist critical discourse, which has focused its attention, to date, largely on the absence—rather than agency—of women in the narratives of Chinese modernity. On the one hand, of course, this preoccupation has been informed by the post-Mao project of dismantling the CCP's self-image as the liberator of Chinese women. Critique strategically focused on the gaps and contradictions between the official party line on women and the historical record, and on the incommensurability of the modern rhetoric and realities of gender, undertakes the vital task of repoliticizing gender as an arena of unresolved conflict and struggle. And as we might expect, at the heart of this challenge has been an attempt to rearticulate women's issues from a standpoint of gender, *rather than class*, which is now increasingly regarded as an "overbearing" analytical category that erased women's specific issues and problems.[2] On the other hand, however, to the extent that much of this critique has looked mainly at canonical texts, current accounts not only often give the impression of an omnipotent patriarchy that condemned modern Chinese women to silence, but leave unquestioned the processes that enshrined the modern canon in the first place. One lesson that a writer like Bai Wei provides is that a more fully engendered narrative of the relationship between literature and politics in this period is required.

I begin by affirming the fact that politically oriented women writers of the 1930s found themselves in a literary environment that had changed considerably from the previous decade. Once encouraged to add their voices to the chorus of debate on the "Woman Question," women writers now risked being discredited for continuing to dwell on domestic subjects, as Wendy Larson, among others, has documented.[3] And, though gender equality remained on the revolutionary platform, literary radicalism no longer offered any clear direction on how to address women's concerns as part of the broader social struggle. Under these circumstances, it is hardly surprising that one finds a conspicuous bracketing of gender in works by writers such as Ge Qin and Tsao Ming, among others. Yet this is only part of the story, for there were radical women writers who chose to confront this erasure, often through fiction that narrated the travails of female activists caught up in a movement, seemingly unaware of—if not altogether indifferent to—their dilemmas. Stories tracing the trauma of pregnancy and its impact on political commitments, for instance, collapse the boundaries between private and public experience and problematize the revolutionary narrative in which female desire is mobilized on behalf of national salvation.[4] For these writers, a meaningful transformation of the social order can't be achieved by transcending the problem of gendered subjectivity, but requires the transformation of gender subjectivity itself.

One of a small number of women writers actively involved in leftist literary circles in the early 1930s, Bai Wei offers a particularly revealing case to consider in this regard. Like her friend and colleague Ding Ling, she was hailed by critics as one of the few women writers to have "lived up to" the literary challenges of the new era, by going beyond the alleged sentimentality that had characterized her earlier work and instead assuming the noble responsibilities of the socially engaged writer. In a 1933 account of her writing, for instance, the critic Fang Ying divided Bai Wei's literary work into two distinctly hierarchical stages: her early "ivory tower" writing, epitomized by her romantic tragedy *Linli* (1926), which dealt with themes of love and emotional betrayal, and her subsequent works like *Dachu youlingta* (1928), which confronted issues of class conflict and national revolution.[5]

Tragic Life, however, clearly complicates this neat schema. Published in 1936, it is a highly confessional autobiographical novel that foregrounds neither the author's ideological conversion nor her involvement in Shanghai's left-wing literary circles, but instead focuses, at length and in graphic detail, on her traumatic romantic entanglement with the poet Yang Sao (1900–1957). Predictably, the critical response was less than enthusiastic: at a moment of fierce debate among radical intellectuals over how to mobilize culture as an effective force in China's anti-imperialist revolution, subjective individual experience came to be seen by many as a highly suspect literary subject. Why, thus complained one contemporary reviewer, had this "social activist . . . who long stood on the frontlines of the [revolutionary] struggle" chosen to privilege the intimate details of a failed romance over her public career as an advocate of political and social reform?[6]

There are several ways to answer this question: we know, for instance, that Bai Wei's motives were, in part, financial, for she wrote *Tragic Life* to offset costly medical treatment for an advanced case of venereal disease. She was no doubt aware that while the reading public had shown little taste for the healthy revolutionary fare now supplied by the intellectual vanguard, they did seem to have an insatiable appetite for titillating accounts of their intimate affairs. This commercial consideration reveals itself in some of the more sensational details, not to mention the sheer volume of the work. Bai Wei's physical battle with venereal disease, however, was more than just the material subtext of her autobiography: it permeates the narrative as a trope of problematic gendered subjectivity. Her infected body bears witness to the ways in which hegemonic culture deprives the female subject of control over her own destiny and renders the experience of self as one of profound alienation. As a second response to the above question, therefore, I would suggest that in formulating her physical (as well as emotional and psychological) experience, not as the private history of a unique individual but as the product of an endemic patriarchy plaguing modern Chinese society as a whole, Bai Wei envisioned her text as social critique. Although this fact apparently escaped the notice of critics, who dismissed the work as a naive return to the insular realm of feminine experience, *Tragic Life* can be read as a conscious reclamation of the private as a simultaneously social and political subject. Indeed, in a short essay defending the work, Bai Wei herself lambasted fellow revolutionary writers who decried the plight of the working classes while slighting "the far worse plight" of women and claims, furthermore, that what the text articulates is not merely her personal life story but the collective "voice of the oppressed souls of women."[7]

Bai Wei prefaces *Tragic Life* with an intriguing, yet seemingly paradoxical, disclaimer. She offers the conventional claim of the autobiographer by asserting the "absolute truth" of the content of her lengthy personal narrative. Composed in candid, unadorned prose, this 900-page tome was produced in a frantic effort to inscribe the authentic "record" (*jilu*) of her life before undergoing a risky surgery to treat the venereal disease she contracted from her lover (who himself had become infected at a brothel in Singapore).

As she emphatically states, "I have exerted my utmost to get down to the essence of the repetitious facts of the tragic unfolding of daily life, and to record them in simple, objective, and unembellished form, in order to express the truth [*zhenshi*] of these facts . . . the absolute truth."[8] Yet Bai Wei distances herself from the autobiographical subject at the center of her text who, as she informs the reader, is not identical to her true self. This is not due to any modest aversion to self-revelation, however, but because there is no such self to reveal: "In this decrepit and moribund society, this nefarious society permeated by patriarchy, women lack an authentic nature [*zhenxiang*]. Their true nature has been falsified to such a degree that they have forfeited every single aspect of themselves. Women are completely determined by society, their environment, men, reputation, and rumor" (p. 5). Sharply contrasting the claim of her contemporary Yu Dafu that "the greatest success of the May Fourth period lay . . . in the discovery of the individual" (1935), Bai Wei here proposes an alternative, gendered formulation of the self, by openly decrying the continued presence of a masculinist social order where to be/come a woman is to undergo a form of self-alienation. *Tragic Life* proceeds, accordingly, not so much as a romantic revelation of authentic selfhood or unique individual experience but as a critical exposé of the multiple forces that have defined *and disfigured* her as a feminine subject of patriarchal culture. The text is, therefore, an autobiography as biography, the portrait of a self with whom Bai Wei, as the authorial subject of the text, does not identify.

Bai Wei's critique of identity can be registered on many different levels: in addition to displacing the standard autobiographical "I" with a third-person "Wei," the highly fragmented text, which interweaves different temporal and narrative perspectives, as well as multiple generic modes (including poetry, diary entries, and love letters), undermines any understanding of the autobiographical subject as a unified self and reformulates the project of literary self-disclosure by envisioning feminine subjectivity as a form of impersonation. For if, as she proposes, under contemporary conditions, there does exist an authentic female I, but only various imposed modes of femininity, then how can the female self be represented? Rather than make claims to special knowledge about the "real truth" of feminine nature or seek to uncover an "essential" self buried beneath woman's myriad social guises, what Bai Wei strives to represent is how the female self is constructed in social interactions but also how these constructions can render the self as other to itself.

In particular, Bai Wei's concern lies with the problematic female identity engendered within modern romance, the ideal that had become virtually synonymous with notions of free choice, emotional sincerity, and sexual/emotional liberation in the May Fourth imagination. For Bai Wei, far from releasing the core of subjectivity, this identity is instead shown to be ideological in nature and deeply implicated in women's continued subordination to male authority. As the narrative opens, Wei is shown to be thoroughly romantic in her assumptions that her "modern" relationship with Zhan would enable "the fullest possible realization of the self [Lee]." But the narrator soon makes it clear that such a romantic vision is a dangerous illusion—in reality, "love was a chasm, a trap into which I fell, like an ignorant wild creature with no one to rescue me" (p. 196). More than simply a personal tragedy, however, Wei's disastrous quest for liberation and self-fulfillment in heterosexual romance is shown to be a consequence of the asymmetrical power relations that structure male–female interaction. Unlike the typical May Fourth (self) portraits of the romantic hero, therefore, whose suffering in love registers (and valorizes) the extreme sensitivity of his personality, here, the author's examination of the high physical and psychological cost of love is an attempt to demystify romantic ideology itself.

It is worth noting that Bai Wei's "love life" had achieved a certain public notoriety even before the publication of *Tragic Life*. Not only was the author's lifestyle frequently reported on in the Shanghai tabloid press, but, in 1933, a collection of her and Yang Sao's personal love letters, ostensibly coedited, was published under the title *Last Night*,[9] one of numerous such textual contributions to the "whirlpool of love" that swept through the contemporary literary scene.[10] Given the alignment of love with sincerity and freedom, along with what Leo Ou-fan Lee describes as a "vogue of self-exposé" (p. 263), many prominent literati couples published their personal correspondences in celebration of romantic sentiments thought to be the hallmarks of modern identity.[11]

But Bai Wei disowns *Last Night* in her autobiography, claiming that it represents a distorted record of their relationship, which originated in Yang Sao's desire to conceal the evidence of his less-than-romantic partnership. During her hospitalization in 1933, Yang Sao had apparently seized the opportunity to pry through her private correspondences in order to edit a carefully censored version of their romance for the public eye. Although she agreed to its publication (for financial reasons), later she discovered an appalling "diary" that he had fabricated as a companion volume to *Last Night* to be published after her death. In this diary, Yang Sao went even further in rewriting their romance, reversing, in effect, its dynamics by casting himself in the role of self-sacrificing, considerate, and loyal lover while insinuating that it was Bai Wei's deception and sexual promiscuity that wrecked their relationship. Unlike *Last Night*, this diary never made it into print because Bai Wei burned most of it.[12] Her reference to both of these texts, however, provides a number of important clues to understanding *Tragic Life* and the kind of feminist intervention it makes. For one, it sets up a comparison between Yang Sao's pseudo-diary and love letter collection and Bai Wei's pseudo-autobiography. The former exemplifies the deceit of self—namely, the projection of an idealized romantic male self designed to write out or rewrite his subjective relation to women. The latter seems to be designed to identify precisely the processes that allow these gross projections—to show, as it were, how the self may be falsely "prescribed" or coded in alienating and distorted ways. Above all, however, if *Last Night* exemplifies the collusion between the discourse of romance and modern patriarchy, *Tragic Life* can be seen as an attempt to critically explore and expose that complicity—to debunk the myth of true romance as the locus of women's sexual liberation and individual autonomy.

Central to Bai Wei's own reconstruction of the relationship is the physical ordeal she undergoes after becoming infected with a sexually transmitted disease. The narrative dwells at length, and in often gruesome detail, on how the disease takes over Wei's body and her life. Never truly at home in her body (she constantly worries about whether it conforms to contemporary sensibilities of the feminine, on conspicuous display in urban advertising and visual culture),[13] Wei is now even further alienated from it. Abandoned by her lover (who denies responsibility for her condition) and unable to shoulder the costly medical treatment herself, she suffers as the advancing illness robs her of health and sexual drive, and renders her intellectually and politically incapacitated.

The candid examination of this intimate topic is, one could argue, in and of itself provocative: sexual discourse of the 1920s–1930s had raised public awareness and concern about the spread of sexually transmitted diseases (*hualiu bing*) but, as the term itself implies, it was generally thought of (and publically discussed) as an affliction of prostitutes.[14] The stigma attached to the disease was appropriated by writers at the time who (like Ibsen and other European writers they read) exploited it figuratively to denote modern social malaise, whether in terms of the burden of tradition (Lu Xun), capitalist depravity (Lao She), or the alarming unruliness of liberated New Women (Mao Dun).[15] By disclosing that she, a prominent female intellectual, was infected, Bai Wei no doubt hoped to destigmatize sexual disease and expose the potential health threat to all women, regardless of their walk of life or class status.[16]

Bai Wei's account of illness, however, is no banal tale of female victimization. As ruthless and depraved as he comes across, the narrative is ultimately less interested in Yang Sao's masculinist misconduct than in exploring the conflicts and contradictions of the female sexual body. On the one hand, the text explicitly establishes Wei's identification as a "new woman" by representing her as subject who experiences, and acts upon, erotic desire. She is a woman who imagines physical passion as an essential aspect not only of love, but of a creative and politically active life in general, as the reader is shown through Wei's erotic fantasies. On the other hand, sexuality is actually experienced as a self-estrangement: the sensation of losing control over her own body occurs not just with the devastating deterioration of her health, but, time and again, from the harassment she encounters from male employers and comrades, to the gossip columns that circulate rumors about her affairs, to women who offer unsolicited beauty tips on how to look more "feminine" and, finally, to a modern medical establishment, which seeks to "cure" her through the surgical removal of her reproductive organs.

Nowhere is Bai Wei's critique of sexual desire more powerful than in her self-analysis of her masochistic attachment to Yang Sao—the man she considers her lover and comrade and who repeatedly fails her on both fronts. Echoing May Fourth confessional narratives of female disillusionment with the sphere of "free love," the autobiographical protagonist experiences a contradiction between her desires and a domestic reality that subsumes those desires.

Whereas writers like Lu Yin strive to elicit the reader's sympathy for their heroine's tragedy, Bai Wei grapples with the reasons *why* the protagonist remains entrapped in such an obviously self-destructive relationship.[17] Having already once decisively "liberated" herself from an arranged marriage, why doesn't this would-be Nora seize such an initiative again and simply leave her unworthy lover? And what does her inability to do so reveal about the ideology of romantic love and its complicitous role in the consolidation of modern patriarchies? The text offers several answers to these difficult questions, the first being that the protagonist's internalization of romantic scripts prevents her from apprehending the actual nature of her attachment to Zhan. Yet the disillusionment that eventually comes from lived experience fails to have the effect we might expect. Conspicuously absent is the pivotal moment of "awakening," which enables the tormented heroine to "move beyond" her oppressed private existence and decisively into the realm of autonomous selfhood. Instead, inclusion of journal entries reveal that even though past betrayals warn her against this fatal attraction, she is unable to resist the deep infatuation she feels for him.

The predicament, of course, resonates sharply with contemporary feminist theorization of subjectivity in terms of a struggle to divest the (female) self of imposed identities and cultural imperatives, which inhibit an independent sense of self. In Bai Wei's critical account, Wei's very sense of identity and personal worth as a woman is so anchored in her having a man in her life that her romantic delusions, while totally misguided, serve as an inevitable form of self-validation. Accordingly, she continually allows herself to fall for Zhan's hollow declarations of love and commitment and rationalizes his infidelities and abuse. As often as not, however, the protagonist is shown to be painfully aware of the contradictions of her behavior, yet, nevertheless, is at a loss to change: will (*yizhi*) and reason (*zhi*), to use the terms the narrator provides, are apparently no match for the power of love (or control) that Zhan embodies. But rather than simply assign blame to the heroine for her "weakness" (or to Zhan for his "villainy"), what is at issue here is the inordinate difficulty, even for a self-conscious intellectual like Wei, to overcome structures of desire and internalized emotional dependence, which sustain the imbalance of power in conventional male–female relations. Thus while Wei intellectually rejects the *idea* of feminine subordination and self-sacrifice, her own compliance with such norms is exposed in the way she assumes the burden of guilt for the relationship's failure. The culpable party, from Wei's anguished point of view, is not the chauvinistic Zhan but Wei herself, whose inadequacies make her feel "unworthy" of his love.

In many respects, indeed, Bai Wei represents the role Wei assumes in her relationship as precisely one of conventional feminine self-sacrifice. Not only does she repeatedly subordinate her own emotional needs by forgiving Zhan for his endless acts of cruelty, but she even willingly compromises her intense artistic and revolutionary aspirations. For example, after they begin living together, Wei's romantic enthrallment overwhelms her ability to write, absorbing her entire consciousness. "What's difficult is not all the housework," she writes in her diary, "but the fact that he gets into my head and dissolves my will to create and to exert myself; he fills my entire mind" (p. 261). That Zhan openly objects to her activism (preferring that she conform to a more conventional domestic role) places additional pressure on the heroine, and are important narrative details that the author uses to elaborate themes of the embeddedness of personal and political experience.

Wei's difficulty in extricating herself from the romantic entanglement brings on feelings of guilt and profound psychological stress. Lacking an explanation for why she continues to love someone who causes her such pain, she experiences not only a frustrating loss of self-control and vulnerability, but also a disturbing sense of self-loathing. In the final section of the text, entitled simply "Her laugh," the author chronicles Wei's psychic and physical collapse, a condition that, according to the narrator, is indescribable.

Significantly, the narrative offers no simple resolution to Wei's predicament, either through a final act of separation from Zhan or in the discovery of an alternative outlet for her desires. The text ends with a description of the unsuccessful surgery that Wei undergoes to treat her illness, and an enigmatic final comment by the narrator about Wei's fate. Did she get well or not? Bai Wei, of course, survived her surgery, and, interestingly, the material text itself played no small role in her final recovery. In 1937, shortly after *Tragic Life* was published, the editors of the Shanghai magazine Funü shenghuo (*Women's Life*) were flooded with letters from sympathetic readers and decided, along with a group of prominent female intellectuals (including Chen Bo'er, Wang Ying, and Guan Lu), to issue a public letter soliciting donations for her medical bills. Money poured in from fans of Bai Wei's work in and outside China, thus enabling her to go to Beiping for further treatment.[18] But it may be in the creative—and cathartic—act itself that we can locate a more provocative remedy for the social ills named in this text; for by inscribing the *socialization* of the woman's body, Bai Wei confronts her personal objectification, and this is a lesson that *exceeds* her individual history.

NOTES

Portions of this chapter appear in Amy Dooling's book, *Women's Literary Feminism in Twentieth Century China* (Palgrave Macmillan, 2005), and are included here with the publisher's permission.

1. Bai Wei, *Beiju shengya* (Tragic Life) (Shanghai: Shenghuo shudian, 1936).
2. For an excellent analysis of contemporary feminist discourse in China, see Wang Zheng, "Maoism, feminism, and the UN Conference on women: women's studies research in contemporary China," *Journal of Women's History* 8:4 (winter 1996), 126–152.
3. Wendy Larson, "The end of 'funü wenxue': women's literature from 1925–1935," *Modern Chinese Literature* 4:1–2 (spring–fall 1988), 39–54.
4. Both Yang Gang's "Fragments of a lost diary" (Riji shiyi) and Xie Bingying's "Abandoned," (Paoqi) for instance, foreground the experience of pregnant activists. For a brief but highly illuminating discussion of these stories and others,

see Sally Taylor Lieberman, *The Mother and Narrative Politics in Modern China* (Charlottesville and London: University Press of Virginia, 1998).

5. The collection in which this essay appeared, *Dangdai Zhongguo nüzuojia lun* (On contemporary Chinese women writers, 1933) is a classic example of the growing critical distaste for the "personal" orientation of women's writing (especially writers like Bing Xin and Lu Yin) and the new affirmation of writers like Ding Ling and Xie Bingying, whose works were seen as promising alternatives to the alleged "feminine" limitations of *funü wenxue*. See Huang Renying, ed., *Dangdai Zhongguo nüzuojia lun* (Shanghai: Guanghua shuju; Bai Wei, 1933). Ju qu Linli (Shanghai: Shangwu yinshu guan, 1926).

6. That same year, Yang Sao published a series of nationalist poems, including his "Three Fujian songs" (*Fujian chang*). According to his biographer, these poems contain little trace of his individual suffering, which has now been absorbed into his greater concern for his native land. See Qing He, *Yang Sao zhuan* (Fuzhou: Haixia wenyi chubanshe, 1998), pp. 191–192.

7. Quoted in *Sanshi niandai zai Shanghai de zuolian zuojia* (Shanghai: Shanghai kexueyuan chubanshe, 1988), p. 396. From her essay "My motives for writing it" originally published in *Funü shenghuo* 2 (1935), 2.

8. Bai Wei, *Beiju shengya*, p. 2.

9. *Zuoye* (Last Night) (Shanghai: Shanghai nanqiang shuju, 1933).

10. See Leo Lee, *The Romantic Generation of Modern Chinese Writers* (Cambridge: Harvard University Press, 1973). For quite different historical reasons, there has been a recent revival of interest in these public–private writings of the May Fourth generation. Many of the love letter collections from the 1920s to the 1930s have been reprinted in mainland China in recent years, including *Last Night*, which was reissued in 1994 by the Hebei jiaoyu chubanshe.

11. These include Lu Xun and Xu Guangping, Jiang Guangci and Song Ruoyu, Xu Zhimo and Lu Xiaoman—to name just a few illustrious pairs.

12. No doubt Bai Wei would have been disturbed by the new biography of Yang Sao by Qing He (see note 6), which cites frequently from *Last Night*, and seems to attribute the failure of Yang Sao's relationship to Bai Wei to differences in temperament and personality.

13. Leo Lee discusses cinema, advertising, and the popular print media, which comprised the "modern" urban culture of Shanghai during this period in his recent book *Shanghai Modern* (Cambridge: Harvard University Press, 1999).

14. Margaret Sanger's lectures at Beida in the early 1920s sparked a flurry of discussions and organizations devoted to birth control in Beijing and Shanghai while translations of studies by European sexologist Edward Carpenter (*Love's Coming of Age*: A Series of Papers on the *Relations of the Sexes*, Manchester: Labour Press, 1896) and Havelock Ellis (*Studies in the Psychology of Sex*, Philadelphia: F.A. Davis: vols. 1–6, 1897–1910; vol. 7, 1928) also contributed to republican period sexual discourse. Among new Chinese intellectuals active in such debates was Zhang Jingsheng, a philosophy professor from Beida, who played an instrumental role in promoting modern sex education with his magazine *Xin wenhua* (*New culture*) (Shanghai, 1927) and his best-selling book *Mei de renshengguan* (Beauty, a Philosophy of Life; Beijing: Beixin shuju, 1926). *Xin nüxing* (New Woman; Shanghai: 1926–1929), another magazine in circulation during this period, also tapped into the growing public interest in sexuality, sexual anatomy, and physical hygiene. For a discussion of these and related topics, see Gail Hershatter,

Dangerous Pleasures: Prostitution and Modernity in Twentieth-Century Shanghai (Berkeley: University of California Press, 1997) and Peng Xiaoyan, *Chaoyue xieshi* (Taibei: Lianjing, 1993).

15. For a discussion of Lu Xun's use of syphilitic imagery, see Lung-kee Sun, "The Fin-de-siècle Lu Xun," *Republican China* 18:2 (April 1993), 64–92. Two of the most interesting, albeit highly problematic, texts that link sexual disease and figure of the female revolutionary are Mao Dun's *Shi* (*Eclipse*) (Shanghai: Kaiming Shudian, 1930) (Zhang Qiuliu) and Jiang Guangci's *Chong chu yunwei de yueliang* (*Moon Emerging From the Clouds*) (Wang Manying). The latter, Jiang's most popular novel, features a female activist who drifts into a life of prostitution and later takes to sleeping with the enemy in order to infect them with venereal disease (the novel's ironic twist being that she eventually discovers she doesn't have the disease after all).

16. Bai Wei offers a similar vision in a short piece of reportage, almost certainly drawn from her own experience, entitled "Sandeng bingfang" (The third-class hospital ward). In it, the author describes a ward of patients suffering from venereal disease—women of all social classes, ages, and physical types—to show that no woman is immune to the social ills of patriarchy.

17. It is interesting to note that despite critical attacks on May Fourth women's writing in the 1930s, there was obviously still a market for this literature. In 1935, for instance, the Women's Bookstore (*Nüzi shudian*) reissued Lu Yin's fiction from the early 1920s.

18. Tragically, Bai Wei had no sooner arrived in Beiping than the Japanese army occupied the city. Despite the urging of friends, she decided not to flee south but instead remained there until March of 1938 to continue her treatment. During this time, she wrote a patriotic five-act play, which, according to her biographers Bai Shurong and He You, was destroyed.

4

What's "Chinese" in Chinese Diasporic Literature?

Emma J. Teng

In response to the call to reexamine the boundaries that circumscribe and define "modern Chinese literature," this chapter considers the geographic and linguistic parameters of this field.[1] Traditional distinctions between "Chinese literature" and "Asian American literature" rely on geographic, linguistic, and disciplinary divisions: the former being literature produced in China, written in the Chinese language, and studied by China specialists; the latter being literature produced in America, written in English, and studied by Asian Americanists. Recent trends within academia, however, have led to a blurring of these boundaries and a questioning of their continued relevance. This phenomenon, celebrated by some and decried by others, will have major implications for how we define the two fields of Chinese literature and Asian American literature in the new millennium.[2]

With this in mind, I examine how Anglophone Chinese diasporic literature contests the geographic and linguistic boundaries that have delimited the notion of Chinese literature. I argue that this literature poses questions that are relevant to China studies, particularly concerning the formation of "Chineseness," which has been a vital subject of discussion in the past decade. I conclude by asking whether the paradigm of diaspora literatures can serve as a viable alternative to the paradigm of national literatures, on which fields such as Chinese literature and Asian American literature were founded.

Contesting Geographic and Linguistic Boundaries

The geographic boundaries of Chinese literature have, in fact, already been contested by movements within the field and simultaneous developments within related fields such as Asian American studies. Since the establishment of Asian American studies in the late 1960s, this field has existed in tension with the older Asian studies, due to differences in disciplinary imperatives, histories of formation, and institutional locations.[3] In the 1990s, however, there was a notable "transnational turn" in both fields, largely in response to the tremendous growth of Asian migration and the global restructuring of the 1980s.[4] This transnational turn has inspired Asian studies scholars to make overtures toward forging links with Asian American studies, and simultaneously prompted Asian American studies scholars to find new connections with Asian studies.[5] The paradigm of "diaspora" has thus emerged as an important meeting point for the two fields. The canon of Asian American literature is already expanding to include Asian-language writing, but how is the canon of Chinese literature within the American academy responding to these challenges?

The anthology *Running Wild: New Chinese Writers* (1994) is a wonderful example of publications that are actively redefining the field of Chinese literature.[6] As David Wang stated, in editing this anthology of translations, he aimed to broaden the definition of Chinese literature by breaking down the traditional political divisions between the literatures of the People's Republic of China (PRC), Taiwan, and Hong Kong, and also by including "overseas sources" among his "Chinese writers." In his afterword, Wang wrote: "By grouping these stories together under the category of contemporary Chinese fiction, the anthology intends to posit a new image of China, a China defined not by geopolitical boundaries and ideological closure, but by overlapping cultures and shared imaginative resources."[7]

The category of Chinese literature, here, is not defined by its production from within the geopolitical boundaries of China, but as a kind of border-crossing practice constitutive of "overlapping" Chinese cultures. In works such as this, it is evident how the emergent notion of diaspora (a multifarious concept that has been used by scholars as diverse as Rey Chow and Tu Wei-ming) has had a decentering effect on the field of Chinese literature, challenging the privileged position of the PRC as the authoritative producer of "real" Chinese literature.[8] In her call to "reimagine the field," Chow writes that new work on the issues of Chinese diaspora has helped to interrogate and critique "the notion of Chineseness as a monolithic given bound ultimately to mainland China," and has been a driving force reshaping the field in recent years.[9]

One of the most influential (and controversial) paradigms that has emerged from the contestation of geographic boundaries in the past decade is that of "Cultural China," described by Tu Wei-ming, Leo Lee, and others in *The Living Tree: The Changing Meaning of Being Chinese Today* (1994). Tu defines Cultural China as an "emergent cultural space" that extends beyond the boundaries of the Chinese nation-state. He models this cultural space as produced through the interaction among "three symbolic universes." The first symbolic universe includes mainland China, Taiwan, Hong Kong, and Singapore—societies populated by ethnic Chinese majorities. The second includes "overseas" Chinese. The third is comprised of non-Chinese individuals who try to understand China.[10] This paradigm of cultural space has provided an alternative to the dominant paradigm of national literatures in the teaching of Chinese literature and culture by professors such as Leo Lee and others. If "China" is no longer a fixed geographic entity, then Chinese literature has become a moving target.

Yet despite their geographic dispersal, the authors collected in *Running Wild* share one fundamental thing in common—their stories were all originally written in Chinese, a fact that serves to unify the collection. In other words, if we want to identify a "core" element that defines this material as Chinese literature regardless of the authors' diverse geographic locations, it is perhaps language.

But what happens when we cross not only geographic, but also linguistic boundaries? Can literature still be considered Chinese literature if it is not written in Chinese, but in English, for instance? Or does it belong to the preserve of "English literature"? If we do consider Anglophone literature from the Chinese diaspora[s] to be Chinese literature, then what exactly is "Chinese" about it? Is it simply a question of the author's ancestry? Does this matter of ancestry impart some essential Chineseness to an author's writings? These have become imperative questions at a time when texts like Maxine Hong Kingston's *The Woman Warrior: Memoirs of a Girlhood among Ghosts* (1975) are taught with increasing frequency in Chinese literature courses.

I certainly do not wish to suggest that there is anything essentially Chinese about literature written by authors of Chinese ancestry, any more than I wish to suggest that "English literature" belongs exclusively to those of English ancestry. Rather, I ask these questions about language and diasporic identity in order to examine how various authors grapple with what it means to be Chinese outside of China, and to probe the limits of Chineseness. These questions are inspired, in no small part, by Tu Wei-ming's assertion that Cultural China is a "cultural space that both encompasses and transcends the ethnic, territorial, linguistic and religious boundaries that normally define Chineseness" (p. v). This is an intriguing suggestion. However, we might ask if Cultural China truly transcends linguistic boundaries. Or will Chinese language remain the ultimate litmus test for what we consider Chinese literature in the age of transnationalism, displacing geographic borders as the fence that circumscribes the field?

It is this issue of language and linguistic borders, then, on which I focus my discussion of the question of what it means to be Chinese outside of China. How is language related to Chineseness? What does Chineseness mean for those who choose to write in English (or other languages)? Language is a central issue for many reasons: perhaps most obviously, language is a key component of ethnicity and culture. It often serves as a means of distinguishing the in-group from the out-group. Linguists and writers have argued that intangible aspects of culture are often embedded in language, for language patterns and unique phrases embody habits of thought or expression. Language, especially when conceived of as the "mother tongue," is deeply infused with primordial sentiment and emotion. Language can also be a very political issue: it is tied in with issues of nationalism, colonialism and decolonization, assimilation, and cultural purity or authenticity. For writers, certainly, language is crucial because it is the medium of their craft, and they are highly conscious of the complex issues surrounding it.

In describing Cultural China, Tu Wei-ming makes two very provocative statements about language. First, he identifies language as a site for a primordial ethnic Chinese identification. As he writes, "the potential for language, especially . . . as the mother tongue, to evoke sympathetic responses or great indignation is even stronger [than territoriality]" (p. vi). Second, he posits the written Chinese language as a kind of glue that binds (literate) Chinese together, as a building block of the Chinese imagined community. He argues: "written Chinese (*hanzi, kanji* in Japanese), as a distinct cultural symbol significantly different from an alphabet, gives literate Chinese a strong sense of membership in a unique discourse community" (p. vi). Tu references here the notion that Chinese separated by regional dialects can all read Chinese characters, and are, therefore, able to communicate with one another, and unified despite their linguistic diversity and regional identities. Thus even as he defines Cultural China as a space that *transcends* the linguistic boundaries that "normally" define Chineseness, Tu nonetheless suggests that the Chinese language lies very close to the heart of Chineseness.

Indeed, if we shift our attention away from the privileging of culture in Cultural China to consider Chineseness in relation to a notional "Chinese race," we might note that the idea of a genetic propensity for speaking Chinese is fairly widespread, indicating a continued tendency to perceive culture as somehow inscribed in our genes: we find it in the presumption that Chinese in the diaspora ought to speak Chinese, and in the reverse presumption that "foreigners" (especially Westerners) cannot possibly ever fully learn to speak Chinese. Ien Ang has challenged this notion in her provocative *On Not Speaking Chinese: Living between Asia and the West* (2001),[11] which interrogates the cultural and political implications of a person of Chinese descent "not speaking Chinese." By contesting the linguistic boundaries of Chinese literature, this essay challenges both the concept of a racial mother tongue, and the notion of Chinese characters as a unifier of Chinese in the diaspora(s).

I approach the issue of language through a comparison of Anglophone literature produced by authors of Chinese ancestry from America, Malaysia, and Singapore.[12] There are many points of similarity as well as differences among the Chinese diasporas in these three locations, which lend themselves to productive comparison. Not only do writers from these places produce both Sinophone and Anglophone literature, but they also deal with similar language issues, cultural themes, and politics. These examples also provide the opportunity to compare the situation of Chinese American authors, as racial minorities within the U.S. nation-state, with the situation of Chinese diasporic writers living within Asian nations—as ethnic minorities in the case of Malaysia, and as members of the majority in the case of Singapore. Without any doubt, what it means to be Chinese in America, Singapore, and Malaysia is drastically different, but there are also points on which writers from these diverse locations speak to one another. Indeed, writers from Singapore and Malaysia often make references to Chinese American literature and draw parallels between their situations. Much of what I say here will be specific to these particular, and quite different, locations of the Chinese diaspora(s), but there will also be many points of dialogue for those from other regions as well. This simply points to the fact that the meaning of Chineseness is at once a global and a local problematic.

In any case, my remarks here are necessarily very general, as it is not my intent to offer exhaustive readings of the "fields" of Chinese American, Chinese Malaysian, and Chinese Singaporean literature. Rather, I examine specific issues raised by selected authors as a starting point for critically rethinking the linguistic boundaries of Chinese literature. Despite the title, this chapter actually does not ask the question of "in what ways is this Anglophone literature Chinese." Instead, I ask, "in what ways is it *not* Chinese?" Ultimately, I suggest that the Chineseness of the particular authors examined here lies not so much in their Chinese ancestry, as in their active engagement with the question of what it means to be Chinese outside of China.

CRAFTING A CHINESE AMERICAN VERNACULAR

In Asian American literary studies, which emerged in the late 1960s and early 1970s, language has always been a key issue. The first MLA bibliography of Asian American literature defined it as literature written in English by authors of Asian descent living in America.[13] The English-language basis of the field has been important to an area of study that explicitly defined itself as panethnic, encompassing writers of diverse Asian ancestry. Although recent scholarship has done much to bring Asian-language writing into the fold, this is predominantly how the canon has been defined until this time.[14]

Despite the fact that Anglophone writing has been the mainstream of Asian American literature, or Chinese American literature more specifically, bilingualism, translation, and the problematics of language have been central issues in the field. Most Chinese American literature makes use of some form of bilingualism, whether through code switching, pidgin, translations of Chinese phrases, or imaginary Chinese dialogue rendered in English. In addition, bilingualism early on emerged as a central trope of Chinese American literature. In one early model, bilingualism was conceptualized as a split between the mother tongue and the language of the dominant society. Writers thus employed bilingualism as a trope to talk about cultural and generational conflicts. Bilingualism was used to express the notion of Chinese American as a hyphenated, or dual identity—the person torn between English and American culture, on one hand, and Chinese and Chinese culture, on the other. The public self, the American self, was the English speaker; the private self at home, the Chinese self, was the Chinese speaker.

This model of bilingualism represents a very static notion of biculturalism as a kind of cultural schizophrenia, and has been discredited by much more nuanced work on the complexities of "living in translation."[15]

In the late 1960s, with the emergence of the Asian American movement, activists began to challenge this model of the dual identity and the either/or model of bilingualism. For those writers who explicitly identified themselves as "Chinese American" (or panethnically as "Asian American"), the question arose—what language should they use? This question was loaded with emotional and political tension, and the difficult relation of the Chinese American writer to language became a central issue in the literature. To begin with, most second-generation (or third- or fourth-generation) Chinese Americans were not necessarily fluent in Chinese, and almost certainly not literate. They thus faced accusations from the older generation or the Chinese-born that they were "*jook sing*," inauthentic "hollow bamboo," inferior for their inability to write Chinese. From the other side, writers faced pressure from publishers who demanded that authors write in standard English, and often rejected Asian American works on the grounds of language. Given these linguistic limitations, it seemed that there was no other choice for writers but to write in standard English. Yet many Chinese American writers regarded the use of standard English as a sellout, a rejection of the community. Frank Chin was one of the most outspoken on this issue. He wrote: "That college white in your mouth was the sound of shame on us, the sound of teachers calling us stupid, and you talking like a teacher grading papers meant you were too good for Chinatown and Chinamen. It meant if you weren't thinking of graduating the town for whiteness, you'd better."[16]

Thus the question of language was related to both ethnic and class issues. Caught between these two sides, radicals began to resist. Why choose between Chinese and standard English? Why not have a language of our own, an Asian American or Chinese American vernacular that would reflect the "authentic" experiences of the community? This desire for a new language went hand-in-hand with a rejection of the hyphenated, either/or identity. Writers experimented with using hybrid languages like Chinatown English, Hawaiian creole, pidgin, and Asian American street slang. Unfortunately, many of these experiments with language failed. And Chin felt this keenly. As he wrote, "the development of Chinese American English has been prevented, much less recognized. The denial of language is the denial of culture," and "language is the medium of culture and the people's sensibility."[17] Chin and his associates argued that the powerlessness of Chinese Americans as minorities in the United States was directly related to the lack of a language of their own.

Of course, issues of language raise issues of audience. For whom is this literature written? Early Chinese American writers such as Wong Chin Foo, Jade Snow Wong, and Pardee Lowe were writing to explain Chinese Americans and Chinese culture to a mainstream audience, and hence the choice of standard English seemed natural. But what about the writer who uses Chinatown English? Is s/he writing literature for the "community," or writing for a wider audience? And who has the power to determine the appropriate audience for Chinese American literature? These highly fraught cultural politics of representation, which are beyond the scope of this chapter, were at the center of the authenticity debates in Asian American literature, epitomized by the decades-long pen war between Frank Chin and Maxine Hong Kingston beginning in the 1970s.[18] This debate culminated in Chin's drawing a line in the sand between the "real" and the "fake" authors.[19]

If Chin had early on attacked writers who used standard English as sell-outs, he also accused writers like Maxine Hong Kingston, and later Amy Tan, of distorting language to pander to the mainstream audience's taste for Orientalism.[20] There are a number of linguistic practices that come into play here. One literary technique developed by Chinese American writers is based on code-switching, which is usually signified through the use of translated or transliterated Chinese phrases. In Kingston's *The Woman Warrior*, for example, she renders "eclipse" as "frog-swallowing-the-moon," giving a literal translation of the Chinese phrase. This use of language drew fire from Frank Chin and others, who accused her of using such "quaint" translated Chinese phrases for exotic effect. Other reviewers also accused Kingston of mistranslating Chinese phrases in her work. For example, Maxine refers to mainland China as the "Big Six," a mistaken translation based on the Chinese homophones for "mainland China" and "big six." Critics declared that this demonstrated Kingston's inauthenticity, and her distortion of the culture.[21]

Amy Tan employs a different form of code switching in her work, based on transliterated Chinese phrases. In some cases, Tan uses code switching to convey the notion of a linguistic gap between generations. As she writes in *The Joy Luck Club* (1989): "mother said the two soups were almost the same, *chabudwo*. Or maybe she said *butong*, not the same thing at all . . . I can never remember things I didn't understand in the first place."[22] In this scene, the Chinese American protagonist's inability to understand her mother is symbolized by her incomplete comprehension of the Chinese language. At other times, Tan employs code switching to convey the foreignness of the speaking character. As first-generation Auntie Lin says, "I was *chiszle*," "mad to death" (p. 24). Tan's use of this literary technique here is not intended to represent direct speech in the same manner as Frank Chin's Chinatown English. Rather, the reader is meant to hear Auntie Lin say "*chisele*," and understand that this means "mad to death" in translation. Unlike the earlier attempts to write Chinatown English, which were intended to be "faithful" renderings of how people actually speak, the main function of this type of code switching is to signify difference, Chineseness. This practice is controversial, and, like Kingston, Tan has been criticized for exoticizing her work.[23]

LOST IN TRANSLATION

Aside from the issue of finding an appropriate language for Chinese American literature, Chinese American writers have also treated the problematics of language as a theme, and addressed the existential challenges of "living in translation." The protagonist of Maxine Hong Kingston's *The Woman Warrior* grows up in a bilingual and bicultural world where she shifts between Chinese and English, thereby inhabiting two cultural domains. But Kingston does not conceptualize these domains as a simple split between the English-speaking public world and the Chinese-speaking world of home. Rather, these two domains are complexly intertwined, with Chinese serving in the external world as a language of secrets, of paper sons, of cursing *lofan* to their faces, of tactics of survival in a hostile environment. The Chinese language thus connects Maxine not so much to the "homeland" of China, but to a racialized experience as an ethnic minority in America.

Kingston also demonstrates how, for the bicultural subject forced to negotiate between two linguistic realms, issues of translation loom large. Her work addresses fundamental questions such as: what gets lost in translation? How can you translate ideas across cultures? How can you translate the nuances of culture? Throughout *The Woman Warrior*, Kingston shows the subtle ways in which culture is embedded in language. As Maxine recalls, "I remember telling the Hawaiian teacher, 'we Chinese can't sing "land where our fathers died." ' She argued with me about politics, while I meant because of curses."[24] This instance of miscommunication demonstrates how the phrase "land where our fathers died" has very different meanings in the American and Chinese contexts, meanings that do not translate across cultures even if the words themselves can be rendered translingually. To put it another way, the *same* English words signify differently in the Chinese and American cultural contexts. Chinese American Maxine hears both meanings. Without reference to the Chinese language, then, Kingston conveys Maxine's Chineseness to the reader through her interpretation of this American anthem, her refusal to sing "fathers died," and her utterance of the phrase "we Chinese."

Amy Tan also writes about the difficulties in translating across cultures in *The Joy Luck Club*:

> Back home, I thought about what she said. And it was true. Lately I had been feeling *hulihudu*. And everything around me seemed to be *heimongmong*. These were words I had never thought about in English terms. I suppose the closest in meaning would be "confused" and "dark fog."
>
> But really, the words mean much more than that. Maybe they can't be easily translated because they refer to a sensation that only Chinese people have, as if you were falling headfirst through Old Mr. Chou's door, then trying to find your way back. (p. 210)

In this passage, Tan proposes that certain concepts are specific to Chinese culture (or as she puts it, "Chinese people"), and therefore can only partially be translated. As a result, cultural misunderstandings inevitably arise between Chinese and non-Chinese. This split between the Chinese and English languages is consistent with the way that Tan sets up Chinese/American binary oppositions throughout her novel. As she writes elsewhere: "Chinese people had Chinese opinions. American people had American opinions" (p. 214).

If this is the case, then can Chinese Americans be authentically Chinese without access to the Chinese language, and through it, "Chinese thoughts," "Chinese sensations," and "Chinese opinions"? Or are they doomed to be "hollow bamboo"?

Kingston and Tan refer not only to the impossibility of translating across cultures, but also across generations. In *The Woman Warrior*, Maxine's limited knowledge of Chinese, and her mother's limited fluency in English means that much is "lost in translation" between mother and daughter. *The Joy Luck Club*, with its four mother–daughter pairs, follows the same essential formula, identifying the linguistic gap as the source of the generational conflict. Both Kingston and Tan are primarily concerned with the second generation's limited understanding of Chinese, which not only creates difficulties in understanding their mothers, but ultimately Chinese culture. The linguistic gap thereby serves simultaneously as a metaphor for the generation gap and for cultural loss.

FROM BILINGUALISM TO MULTILINGUALISM

These issues of language become infinitely more complex when we turn to writers from multilingual societies, where the paradigm of the mother tongue versus the language of the dominant society tells only part of the story. Chinese–Malaysian–American writer, Shirley Geok-lin Lim, takes up the difficulties of "swimming among languages"[25] in a number of her works, including her memoir *Among the White Moon Faces: An Asian–American Memoir of Homelands* (1996), the first half of which is set in Malaysia and Singapore, and the second half in America. If, as Lim shows, the issue of bilingualism is supplanted by multilingualism for those in the Chinese diasporas in Malaysia and Singapore, writers in these places share the Chinese American concern with the issue of their relation to the mother tongue, and the challenges of crafting a vernacular for their work. One important point on which they differ from Chinese American authors, however, is that their relationship to the English language is mediated by the legacy of British colonialism.[26] In addition, whereas Chinese American writers frequently refer to the struggle between English and a monolithic Chinese (by which some writers mean Mandarin, and others Cantonese, or other regional "dialects"), Southeast Asian writers often highlight the multiplicity of "Chineses," and the power dynamics of Mandarin versus nonstandard Chinese languages. As the writers I examine in this section demonstrate, the politics of Chinese language(s) in the local contexts of Malaysia and Singapore are highly contentious, and serve as informative comparisons for Chinese American literature. This comparison demonstrates at once the "shared imaginative resources" of the Chinese diaspora(s), and the profound differences arising from the local contexts of particular national locations, not simply in relation to the Chinese language, but the English language as well.

THE MOTHER TONGUE AND THE COLONIAL TEAT

In *Among the White Moon Faces*, Shirley Geok-lin Lim outlines her complex relationship with language. Lim describes a kind of triangulation between languages for a "Chinese girl" growing up as a minority in a Malay-speaking society under the legacy of British colonialism. She writes:

> I heard Hokkien as an infant and resisted it, because my mother did not speak it to me. This language of the South Chinese people will always be an ambivalent language for me, calling into question the notion of a mother tongue tied to a racial origin. As a child of a Hokkien community, I should have felt that propulsive abrasive dialect in my genes. Instead, when I speak Hokkien, it is at the level of a five-year-old . . . it remains at a more powerful level a language of exclusion, the speech act which disowns me in my very place of birth.
>
> Chinese-speaking Malayans called me a "Kelangkia-kwei,"—or a Malay devil—because I could not or would not speak Hokkien. Instead I spoke Malay, my mother's language. My peranakan mother had nursed me in Malay, the language of assimilated Chinese who had lived in the peninsula, jutting southeast of Asia, since the first Chinese contact with the Malacca Sultanate in the fifteenth century. And once I was six and in a British school, I would speak chiefly English, in which I became "fluent," like a drop of rain returning to a river, or a fish thrown back into a sea.[27]

In this passage, Lim problematizes the notion of a racial mother tongue, for although she is Chinese by descent and Hokkienese by patrilineal inheritance, Hokkien does not mark her inclusion, her membership, in an ethnic in-group. Lim draws a distinction here between the mother tongue and the "mother's tongue," which for her is Malay—the language in which her peranakan mother nursed her.[28] Milk, and not blood, thus becomes the source through which language is transmitted: language is not genetically inherited, but imbibed, drawn from the teat (an image Lim will later use in reference to English).

Being "at home" with language is not associated with Chinese, but instead is conjured up in this passage by the image of the fish thrown back into the sea, through which Lim figures her "fluency" in English. By contrasting her discomfort in Chinese with her comfort in English, Lim further deconstructs the notion of a racial mother tongue. And yet, this image of fluency, bracketed by quotation marks, highlights the problem of colonial language relations. That is, as a Chinese–Malaysian, Lim can never claim English as her "native tongue" no matter how fluent she becomes: the English language is something over which she gains mastery; it is not something she inherited or was weaned on. Which language, then, can she claim as "her own"?

In a chapter of her memoir, "Pomegranates and English Education," Lim describes how language becomes a carrier for ideology (much as Kingston and Tan described language as a carrier for the intangibles of Chinese culture). Lessons in Western culture and colonial ideology are learned through children's songs in English. Nonetheless, Lim's relation to English language was not a simple one of colonial domination. As a child, she falls in love with the English language, and her mastery of English becomes crucial to her identity, especially her formation as an individual outside of the family. Her desire to become a writer is directly connected to her love of English. Lim never learned to write Chinese, nor even Malay, which remained a language of familiarity, affection, and home. It is English, then, that draws her into creativity and transports her into other worlds beyond the strictures for a Chinese girl in a Malayan convent school.

One might be tempted to attribute Lim's embrace of the English language to her internalization of colonial domination. However, Lim herself resists such readings. As she argues: "I have seen myself not so much sucking at the teat of British colonial culture as actively appropriating those aspects of it that I needed to escape that other familial/gender/native culture that violently hammered out only one shape for self. I actively sought corruption to break out of the pomegranate shell of being Chinese and girl."[29] Lim thus highlights individual agency in relation to language choice.[30]

Yet despite Lim's active choice to speak and write in English, and her mastery of this language demonstrated by her numerous literary prizes, she cannot escape the colonial dynamics of being a Malaysian English speaker. As she writes: "We had grown up in a compulsory language system, but, as if to strip us of all language, we were constantly reminded that this language did not belong to us. Depriving us of Chinese or Malay or Hindi, British teachers reminded us nonetheless that English was only on loan, a borrowed tongue which we could only garble."[31] I will return to the trope of the "borrowed tongue" below.

First, let me note that the issue of colonial language relations also points to the problematics of a postcolonial language in Malaysia. The complex politics of decolonization and language are beyond the scope of this chapter, but I want to briefly outline a general problem for ethnic Chinese in a postcolonial nation like Malaysia: if Malay was constructed as the "native tongue" of postcolonial Malaysia in nationalistic reaction to Western imperialism, how did ethnic Chinese stand in relation to this language?[32] As citizens of the new nation, would they adopt this national language or should decolonization enable them to reclaim "their own" language? And what about a "Malay-speaking devil" like Lim? In fact, as Lim reminds us, the idea that decolonization can lead to a return to an original, uncorrupted, native tongue is only a myth, for all language is always already corrupted, inherently hybridized by numerous cultural encounters, past and present.

The impossibility of returning to pure, uncontaminated roots, both cultural and linguistic, is also highlighted in a novel by Singaporean writer Tan Mei Ching, *Crossing Distance* (1995).[33] In this story, an old grandmother goes back to her village in China, a self-conscious act of "going home." The old woman thinks that she is speaking Hokkien to the villagers, but she unconsciously infuses her language with Malay and English words, much to the puzzlement of her relatives. Again, as in Amy Tan's work, language is used to symbolize estrangement from one's cultural roots. The grandmother's inability to communicate with the villagers "back home" in their "shared" native tongue reveals to her how diaspora has reshaped her Chinese heritage. But *Crossing Distance* also reveals how the linguistic content of a language monolithically identified as "Hokkien" changes from one local context to another. Tan Mei Ching's work reminds us that language is a living medium that changes as loan words enter over time, and old words pass out of usage. Sometimes, the version of the language that immigrants speak in diaspora is the "old-fashioned" language, a fossil that has remained static while new words and slang have entered the language that is used in "the homeland." Since language is dynamic and constantly evolving, it becomes impossible to definitively identify a racial mother tongue.

A LANGUAGE OF ONE'S OWN

To return to the notion of the borrowed tongue, Singaporean writer Suchen Christine Lim also talks about the dilemma of not having a language of one's own in a slightly different context—that of postcolonial Singapore. Like Malaysia, Singapore was a British colony, and is now a multiethnic society inhabited by ethnic Chinese, Malays, and Indians. An important point of difference, however, is that ethnic Chinese form the majority in Singapore. As Beng-Huat Chua has argued, the multicultural (or "multiracial") policies of the Singaporean state are complex and contradictory, seeking, on one hand, to create a unified Singaporean national identity, and, on the other hand, to reinforce the distinctions between its official racial/cultural groups—the Chinese, Malaysians, Indians, and "Others"—as a tactic of diversity management.[34]

Multilingualism in Singapore operates within the delicate balancing act of celebrating pluralism and suppressing ethnic tension. Because there is a threat of ethnic conflict if any language group seems favored over the others, there is a need for a neutral lingua franca to tie together the "imagined community" of Singapore. In the educational system, English has served as this language, and the primary medium of instruction. In addition, students must enroll in classes in their so-called mother tongue, defined "racially" as Mandarin for Chinese, Malay for Malays, and Tamil for Indians. The educational system thus at once promotes the integration of Singaporeans as "global citizens" into the (English-dominated) world of modern transnational capital, and seeks to maintain its citizens' diasporic, or ancestral, identifications and "traditional values."

Suchen Christine Lim's novel *Fistful of Colours* (1993) talks at length about the intricacies of language politics in Singapore, the richness of the multilingual heritage, on one hand, and the tensions of multiculturalism, on the other. Lim also addresses the problematics of Singapore's postcolonial relationship to English. Describing a campus event at a British university, the central protagonist, Suwen, laments on the difficulties of singing in a borrowed tongue:

> You see, we were supposed to take part in a concert. International Night or something. All of us, the participants, had to contribute an item. Most people

sang or recited something in their national language. But the three of us from Singapore didn't know what to do. I mean our national language is Malay but we didn't know Malay. And the two girls from Malaysia had already recited a Malay pantun. And two guys from China recited some poems in Mandarin. The girl from Hong Kong even sang an aria from a Cantonese opera. . . . So, in the end, we sang "Sing Your Way Home." The applause, well, was lukewarm. Some of the Caucasians wondered why we sang in English. . . . like I had no tongue of my own, and that I had to use a borrowed tongue. . . .[35]

Plagued by this notion that English is a borrowed tongue, Suwen tries to establish the right for Singaporean Chinese to speak and write in English. But she is also attacked in the press by Chinese nationalists for not writing in Chinese. As her fictional attacker, who styles himself "Son of China," writes:

Our nation is swamped with numerous geh angmos [fake foreigners]. They dress outrageously and insist on speaking English or Singlish. They do not want to speak Chinese. They cannot even read the Chinese signs in the public places. Some even claim to dream in English! Such people have forgotten their Chinese ancestors and their five-thousand-year-old history and civilization! (p. 9)

The faction represented by Son of China considers those who cannot speak and read Chinese to be "*geh angmo*," or fake foreigners: in other words, inauthentic, just like the "*jook sing*" of Chinese America. The tension between two camps of Chinese, the Chinese-educated and the English-educated, is a major theme of the novel. Suwen challenges the idea that language defines the wo/man. She argues, "I was born ethnically Chinese. I grew up speaking English. Am I not Chinese still? Or am I just half-Chinese? Not because of a physical change but because of a language change" (p. 83). She further challenges the "Chinese should speak Chinese" idea by asking, what is Chinese? For Singapore, this means: Cantonese, Teochew (Chaozhou), Hokkien, Hakka, and Hainanese. But the government attempts to impose Mandarin as a lingua franca for all Chinese through the yearly "speak Mandarin" campaign.[36] As she writes: "We're living in an age of cultural lobotomy. Forget about your Cantonese, Teochew and Hokkien. Think Mandarin. Drop the dialects. That's what the authorities want. . . . they want to sculpt a new kind of Singapore Chink. The Mandarin-speaking sort" (p. 83).

For Suwen, Mandarin is not only *not* her mother tongue, as the government would insist, it is more foreign to her than English, the language in which she was educated, or than pasar-Malay, the market language that she learned on the streets. Suwen challenges not only the denigration of Chinese dialects, but also the notion of literacy in Chinese as a marker of authentic Chineseness. She declares: "I am as Chinese as my Cantonese-speaking grandparents have brought me up to be. And they were illiterate non-Mandarin speakers. And it wouldn't have occurred to anybody at that time in the fifties to label them as less Chinese or what!" (p. 218). Mandarinization is presented here as distinctly a class issue. Suwen reads the imposition of

Mandarin and the so-called 5000-year heritage as an attempt to deny the true roots of Singapore's Chinese immigrants as coolies, rickshaw pullers, bondmaids, and prostitutes. Mandarin is not their native tongue, she declares, but the language of the educated class.

Suwen sees her struggles with language as directly related to those of other writers, including Maxine Hong Kingston. In making the case for English as an authentic language for Chinese in the diaspora(s), she explicitly links Singapore with the situation of Chinese Americans, declaring, "thousands of Chinese Americans spoke to one another in English, and it's no shame" (p. 217). She further asserts the individual's right to choose a "language of one's own": "Our language is our choice. And sometimes it's the result of a quirk of history" (p. 218).

Like Frank Chin, Suchen Christine Lim resists the false choice between (Mandarin) Chinese and English. Instead, she shows Singaporeans, like the early Asian American activists, striving to create their own language. In this case, it is the vernacular of Singlish. Singlish is a form of Creole, a hybridized language in which English words are arranged according to Chinese grammar and interspersed with Chinese, Malay, and Tamil phrases. It is a unique and local language, which reflects the colonial history of Singapore and its multicultural heritage. Singlish at once draws on Singapore's linguistic diversity and attempts to transcend it. For many Singaporean writers, the use of Singlish directly connects to efforts to form a new Singaporean identity, the New Asian who is not specifically Chinese, Indian, or Malay, but simply Singaporean. The use of Singlish can also be an act of resistance: it is a hybrid language, which represents the efforts of the colonized to take the language of the colonizers into their own hands.

Hwee Hwee Tan provides a vivid description of Singlish in her novel *Foreign Bodies* (1999):

> Singlish sounds like "broken" English—to foreign ears it can sound unintelligible, uneducated, even crude. However, we didn't speak "broken" English because we lacked the ability to speak the Queen's English; we spoke Singlish, because with all its contortions of grammar and pronunciation, its new and localized vocabulary, Singlish expressed our thoughts in a way that the formal, perfectly enunciated, anal BBC World Service English never could. Besides, who wants to talk like some O level textbook, instead of using our own language, our home language, the language of our souls?
>
> I don't speak either standard English or Singlish consistently. When I'm with friends like Eugene, I enjoy switching between the Queen's English and the *Ah Ma's* English, randomly, arbitrarily and often in mid-sentence. It's just the Singaporean way, this totally jumbled, multi-lingual lingo—just part of our melting pot, *rojak* way of speech, thought and life.[37]

Tan not only emphasizes the local character of Singlish, but also brings out some of its class associations as street language. The educated slip in and out of this language as they choose: for many less educated, however, Singlish is the only form of English they speak. The case of Singlish, therefore, touches on many of the same class issues as Chinatown English, a similarly hybrid "street language" produced in a different context.

AN IMAGINED COMMUNITY OF DIFFERENCES

Ironically, perhaps (or perhaps not), one common strand that links many Chinese American, Chinese Singaporean, and Chinese Malaysian authors together is *not* their uniform assertion of their essential Chineseness in the diaspora, but rather a shared desire to carve out particular, local, and often highly individual, spaces of their own. Their "shared imaginative resources" are often devoted to contesting hegemonic notions of Chineseness, including the demand to write in Chinese. Difference and hybridity are their common denominators, not the homogeneity of "we are all Chinese." All the writers examined here problematize the notion of Cultural China as a community bound by language, particularly Tu Wei-ming's notion that written Chinese plays a key role in providing a sense of membership in this imagined community.

The authors discussed here show that literacy in Chinese cannot be taken for granted in the Chinese diaspora(s). There are a number of reasons for this: first, many Chinese overseas are descended from illiterate classes of immigrants; second, even for those from the educated classes, it is harder to transmit literacy in Chinese than the ability to speak Chinese; and third, certain locales have laws against written Chinese, such as Indonesia under the Suharto regime. Rather than seeing the Chinese language, especially the written language or Mandarin, as a marker of a global Chinese identity, then, these authors seek to find the meaning of being Chinese outside of language.

Southeast Asian writers already have the example of the peranakans, for whom the meaning of being Chinese is separate from the question of speaking Chinese. In turning away from Mandarin as a global Chinese language, writers turn instead to local languages that reflect particular local histories—the pidgins and Creoles, such as Chinatown English, Hawaiian Creole, Singlish, pasar Malay, and Asian American slang. These are hybrid languages that grew out of contact between linguistic groups, from the conditions of immigration, segregation, assimilation, colonization, and decolonization. Language is, therefore, not only inherited, but also invented. Furthermore, in insisting that language cannot belong to any one group, these writers attempt to sever language from nationalism at the same time that they assert their identity as part of the Chinese diaspora(s), no less real in their own way than the "Chinese from China."

DIASPORA AS A MERGING POINT FOR ASIAN AND ASIAN AMERICAN STUDIES?

If diaspora currently serves as a meeting point for Asian and Asian American studies, we might well ask whether diaspora studies will eventually become a merging point for the two fields. This may be an attractive model for some universities in a time of cost cutting, but it would have major implications for those of us who study and teach literature. I must admit I am skeptical in this regard. The paradigm of diaspora has great liberating potential, as the critical work of Rey Chow has powerfully demonstrated, helping us to move beyond monolithic notions of Chineseness, beyond nationalism, and beyond the disciplinary divisions of national literatures.[38] Moreover, as Chow argues in *Writing Diaspora: Tactics of Intervention in Contemporary Cultural Studies* (1993), the critical spirit of diaspora can help us "to *unlearn* [the] submission to one's ethnicity such as 'Chineseness' as the ultimate signified even as one continues to support movements for democracy and human rights in China, Hong Kong, and elsewhere."[39]

However, as Ien Ang has cautioned, diaspora can be a double-edged sword. As Ang writes: "it can be the site of both support and oppression, emancipation and confinement."[40] Therefore, although I have argued here that the paradigm of diaspora enables us to contest the geographic and linguistic boundaries of Chineseness, it also poses certain dangers. Sau-ling Wong, for example, has suggested that the denationalizing effect of diaspora may deflect attention away from issues of racial inequality for Asian Americans as minorities within the United States.[41] The same might hold true for those of Chinese ancestry within other nation-states. For some, the idea of a Chinese diaspora also implies a certain kind of transnational homogeneity, essentializing the Chinese as Chinese, no matter where they are located globally or for how many generations.

How can we harness the emancipating effects of diaspora without giving in to the hegemonic ideology of "Global Chineseness," which the authors I examine here so actively contest? How can Asian and Asian American studies productively incorporate diasporic perspectives, while also maintaining national and local perspectives? What we need to seek is a type of practice that neither homogenizes those in the various Chinese diasporas as essentially and eternally Chinese, erasing the differences between local contexts, nor patrols the fences of Chineseness so vigorously that the nation-state of China becomes the sole standard for what is authoritatively Chinese. What I advocate here is a kind of crossover practice, in which Asian-language texts are admitted to the canon of Asian American literature, and Anglophone texts can be read as Chinese literature rather than dismissed out of hand as "un-Chinese" or "inauthentic." While I am suggesting, then, that there is nothing *essentially* Chinese about Chinese diasporic literature, I am also suggesting that there is nothing essentially *un-Chinese* about not writing in Chinese.

NOTES

1. This material was originally presented at the "Contested Modernities: Perspectives on Twentieth-Century Chinese Literature" conference at Columbia University in April 2000. Subsequent versions have been presented at other venues; I do not have the space here to acknowledge all those who have provided feedback, but

special thanks to the following: Arundhati Tuli Banerjee, Isabelle de Courtivron, Alison Groppe, Evelyn Hu-DeHart, Tseen Khoo, Charles Laughlin, Leo Lee, Shirley Geok-lin Lim, Daisy Ng, James St. Andre, Min Song, David Wang, Jing Wang, Wong Sin Kiong, and Wong Yuan Wah.

2. See King-Kok Cheung, "Re-viewing Asian American literary studies," in *An Interethnic Companion to Asian American Literature*, ed. King-Kok Cheung (New York: Cambridge University Press, 1997), pp. 1–38; Arif Dirlik, "Locating Asian American studies today: origins, identities, and crises," *Amerasia Journal* 29:2 (2003), 167–169; Shirley Hune et al., *Asian Americans: Comparative and Global Perspectives* (Pullman: Washington State University Press, 1991); Shirley Geok-lin Lim, "Immigration and diaspora," in *An Interethnic Companion to Asian American Literature*, pp. 289–311; Lisa Lowe, "Heterogeneity, hybridity, multiplicity: marking Asian American difference," *Diaspora* 1:1 (1991), 24–44; Jonathan Y. Okamura, "Asian American studies in the age of transnationalism: diaspora, race, community," *Amerasia Journal* 29:2 (2003), 171–193; Sau-ling Wong, "Chinese American literature," in *An Interethnic Companion to Asian American Literature*, pp. 39–61; and "Denationalization reconsidered: Asian American cultural criticism at a theoretical crossroads," *Amerasia Journal* 21:1 and 2 (1995), 1–28.

3. On Asian and Asian American studies, see Shirley Hune, "Area studies and Asian American studies: comparing origins, missons, and frameworks," in *Asian Americans*, pp. 1–4; Sucheta Mazumdar, "Asian American studies and Asian studies: rethinking roots," in *Asian Americans*, pp. 29–44.

4. On the "transnational turn," see Okamura, "Asian American studies in the age of transnationalism."

5. See, e.g., the articles collected in Kandice Chuh and Karen Shimakawa, *Orientations: Mapping Studies in the Asian Diaspora* (Durham: Duke University Press, 2001); Evelyn Hu-DeHart, *Across the Pacific: Asian Americans and Globalization* (Philadelphia: Temple University Press and the Asia Society, 1999); Elaine H. Kim and Lisa Lowe, ed., "New formations, new questions: asian american studies," *positions: east asia cultures critique* 5 (special edition) (1997); and the section edited by Arif Dirlik in the special issue on "Pedagogy, social justice, and the state of Asian American studies," in *Amerasia Journal* 29:2 (2003), 167–228, especially David Palumbo-Liu, "Re-imagining Asian American studies," pp. 211–219.

6. David Der-wei Wang and Jeanne Tai, *Running Wild: New Chinese Writers* (New York: Columbia University Press, 1994). On redefining the field, see also Rey Chow, *Modern Chinese Literary and Cultural Studies in the Age of Theory: Reimagining a Field* (Durham: Duke University Press, 2000).

7. Wang and Tai, *Running Wild*, p. 238.

8. See, e.g., Rey Chow, *Writing Diaspora: Tactics of Intervention in Contemporary Cultural Studies* (Bloomington: Indiana University Press, 1993); Leo Ou-fan Lee, "On the margins of the Chinese discourse: some personal thoughts on the cultural meaning of the periphery," in *The Living Tree: The Changing Meaning of Being Chinese Today*, ed. Tu Wei-ming (Stanford: Stanford University Press, 1994), pp. 221–244.

9. Rey Chow, "Introduction: on Chineseness as a theoretical problem," in *Modern Chinese Literary and Cultural Studies*, p. 6.

10. Tu Wei-ming, *The Living Tree: The Changing Meaning of being Chinese Today* (Stanford: Stanford University Press, 1994).

11. Ien Ang, *On Not Speaking Chinese: Living between Asia and the West* (London: Routledge, 2001).

12. One could well extend this discussion to other parts of the Chinese diaspora. In addition, much of what I have to say here relates to language issues in Hong Kong and Taiwan as well, where the politics of Mandarin versus "nonstandard" forms of Chinese, or "dialects," are highly fraught. For a discussion of this last issue, see Chow, "Introduction: on chineseness as a theoretical problem," p. 6.

13. King-Kok Cheung and Stan Yogi, *Asian American Literature: An Annotated Bibliography* (New York: Modern Language Association of America, 1988).

14. On Chinese-language Chinese American literature, see Wong, "Chinese American literature."

15. See Isabelle de Courtivron, *Lives in Translation: Bilingual Writers on Identity and Creativity* (New York: Palgrave Macmillan, 2003). On the complex issues of cultural translation, see Homi K. Bhabha, "How newness enters the world: Postmodern space, postcolonial times and the trials of cultural translation" *The Location of Culture* (London: Routledge, 1994), pp. 212–235.

16. Frank Chin, "Confessions of the Chinatown cowboy," *Bulletin of Concerned Asian Scholars* 4:3 (1972), 59.

17. Frank Chin and Jeffrey Paul Chan, "Racist love," in *Seeing Through Shuck*, ed. Richard Kostelanetz (New York: Ballantine Books, 1972), pp. 76–77.

18. See Sau-ling Wong, "Autobiography as guided chinatown tour? Maxine Hong Kingston's *The Woman Warrior* and the Chinese–American autobiographical controversy," in *Multicultural Autobiography: American Lives*, ed. James Robert Payne (Knoxville: University of Tennessee Press, 1992), pp. 249–279.

19. See Frank Chin, "Come all ye Asian American writers of the real and fake," in *The Big Aiiieeeee!: An Anthology of Chinese American and Japanese American Literature*, ed. Jeffrey Paul Chan et al. (New York: Meridan, 1991), pp. 1–92. On the gender politics of the authenticity debate, see King-Kok Cheung, "The woman warrior versus the Chinaman Pacific: must a Chinese American critic choose between feminism and heroism?," in *Conflicts in Feminism*, ed. Marianne Hirsch and Evelyn Fox Keller (New York: Routledge, 1990), pp. 234–251.

20. Chin, "Come all ye Asian American writers of the real and fake."

21. See Deborah Woo, "Maxine Hong Kingston: the ethnic writer and the burden of dual authenticity," *Amerasia Journal* 16:1 (1990), 173–200.

22. Amy Tan, *The Joy Luck Club* (New York: Putnam, 1989), p. 6.

23. Chin, "Come all ye Asian American writers of the real and the fake." For the cultural politics of Amy Tan's use of Chinese phrases, including mistranslations, see Sau-ling Wong, " 'Sugar Sisterhood': situating the Amy Tan phenomenon," in *The Ethnic Canon: Histories, Institutions, and Interventions*, ed. David Palumbo-Liu (Minneapolis: University of Minnesota Press, 1995), pp. 174–212.

24. Maxine Hong Kingston, "At the Western Palace," *The Woman Warrior: Memoirs of a Girlhood among Ghosts* (New York: Vintage Books, 1989), p. 167.

25. I take the phrase "swimming among languages" from Shirley Geok-lin Lim, "The im/possibility of life-writing in two languages," in *Lives in Translation: Bilingual Writers on Identity and Creativity*, ed. Isabelle de Courtivron (New York: Palgrave Macmillan, 2003), pp. 39–48.

26. The complex issues of colonialism and language are beyond the scope of this chapter.

27. Shirley Geok-lin Lim, "Splendor and squalor," *Among the White Moon Faces: An Asian–American Memoir of Homelands* (New York: Feminist Press, 1996), p. 11.

28. The peranakans are descendents of Chinese immigrants who settled in Southeast Asia generations ago, often intermarrying with the locals and becoming highly assimilated.

29. Lim, "Pomegranates and English Education," Among the White Moon Faces, p. 65.

30. See also Lim, "The im/possibility of life-writing in two languages."

31. Lim, "Outside the Empire," Among the White Moon Faces, p. 121.

32. For more on Malaysian language politics, see Carolyn Cartier, "Diaspora and social restructuring in postcolonial Malaysia," in The Chinese Diaspora: Space, Place, Mobility, and Identity, ed. Laurence J.C. Ma and Carolyn Cartier (New York: Rowman and Littlefield, 2003), pp. 69–96; Donald Macon Nonini, "Shifting identities, positioned imaginaries: transnational traversals and reversals by Malaysian Chinese," in Ungrounded Empires: The Cultural Politics of Modern Chinese Transnationalism, ed. Aihwa Ong and Donald Macon Nonini (New York: Routledge, 1997), pp. 203–227.

33. Tan Mei Ching, Crossing Distance (Singapore: EPB Publishers, 1995).

34. Beng-Huat Chua, "Culture, multiracialism, and national identity in Singapore," in Trajectories: Inter-Asia Cultural Studies, ed. Kuan-Hsing Chen (London, New York: Routledge, 1998), pp. 186–205.

35. Suchen Christine Lim, Fistful of Colours (Singapore: EPB Publishers, 1993), p. 81.

36. See Chua, "Culture, multiracialism, and national identity in Singapore."

37. Hwee Hwee Tan, Foreign Bodies: A Novel (New York: Persea Books, 1999). Rojak is a Singaporean dish composed of a diverse mix of local foodstuffs.

38. See Chow, Modern Chinese Literary and Cultural Studies in the Age of Theory.

39. Chow, Writing Diaspora.

40. Ang, On Not Speaking Chinese.

41. Wong, "Denationalization reconsidered."

5

Toward a Theory of Postmodern/Post-Mao–Deng Literature

Xiaobin Yang

If Adorno's aphorism "To write poetry after Auschwitz is barbaric"[1] epitomizes the crisis of modernity that Europe faces in the post–World War II era, the Cultural Revolution marks both the culmination and the abyss of modernity in China. The Holocaust ends the belief in a rational, progressive world history that the Hegelian–Marxist theory envisions. The Cultural Revolution, too, both consummates and undermines the project of Chinese modernity,[2] which has exposed itself not only as an utmost pursuit for historical progress and social perfection, but also as a striking presentation of the ruin of the grand History. The Cultural Revolution, like the Holocaust, defies any rational interpretation, for it blends grandiose discourses and atrocious realities that have gone far beyond reason. The simultaneously attractive and hideous experience of the Cultural Revolution has produced the emotional ambivalence that ultimately traumatizes one's rational faculty. The Cultural Revolution, again like the Holocaust, has shattered subjective integrity in every way, for the Maoist omnipotence of human power, which promises a prosperous future, is met with a disastrous outcome that invalidates its original imagination. The most profound destruction lies not only in physical victimization, but also in psychic traumatization, which deprives the nation of its faith in the historical truth and the ethical good.

If, as David Hirsch suggests, the concept of "postmodern" can be replaced by the "historically rooted term, 'post-Auschwitz' "[3] in the Western context, it can also be understood as "post–Cultural Revolution," as far as contemporary China is concerned. Nevertheless, post–Cultural Revolution as a "historically rooted term" in China does not, and cannot, exclude the traumatic experience of other historical events, insofar as the Cultural Revolution was not the only spiritually devastating event in the recent history of China. In the second half of the twentieth century, besides the Cultural Revolution, China has undergone Anti-Rightist Campaign (1957–1958), Great Leap Forward (1958–1960), Anti-Spiritual Pollution

Campaign (1983–1984), Anti-Bourgeois Liberalization Campaign (1987), and June Fourth Incident (1989), as either preludes or postludes to the Cultural Revolution. The post–Cultural Revolution, therefore, is to be conceived not so much as a specific periodization as a term to sum up the general psychohistorical condition of the post-catastrophic China. The imagination of the modern (infinite social progress and subjective capacity) eventually gives way to its own negation or deconstruction.

In his article "Answering the question: what is postmodernism?," Jean-François Lyotard proposes that "*Post modern* would have to be understood according to the paradox of the future (*post*) anterior (*modo*)."[4] Lyotard has repeatedly emphasized the link between the prefix "post-" in the term postmodern and the Greek prefix "ana-," as in analysis, anamnesis, anagogy, and anamorphosis, that is, as an evocation of the immemorial. What is immemorial, in the case of postmodernism, seems to be the overpowering, violent modernity. The prefix post-, therefore, can well be associated with the German prefix "Nach-" as in the Freudian concept *Nachträglichkeit*, a deferred action that reactivates the traumatic experience of historical violence.[5] The postmodern, in this sense, is to be understood as the modern (the splendid idea fraught with bloody disasters) reactivated as a traumatic memory-trace, as a massive psychic burden, which has been carried over (the meaning of *tragen* in the term *Nachträglichkeit*) to the present. The ambivalent attitude of attachment and resistance of the concept of *Nachträglichkeit* also implies that Chinese postmodernism does not launch an antagonistic literary movement. Without confronting political oppression from a self-assumed superior position, Chinese postmodernism is an implosion within the modern cultural paradigm, which serves as the basis of political authoritarianism. Chinese postmodernism can thus be characterized as post-catastrophic, post-traumatic, post–Cultural Revolution, and post-Mao–Deng.

The dissolution of a rational, omniscient subject in contemporary Chinese fiction attests to the psychohistorical phenomenon of postmodernity that is, as I have shown, comparable to the post-Auschwitz cultural scene in the West. Therefore my concept of Chinese postmodernism is radically different from, though not irrelevant to, that which has been either welcomed or repudiated over the past few years by Chinese scholars and critics. Chinese postmodernism has more to do with the historical reality of modern politico-cultural paradigm (sociopolitical totality, grand national imagination, and the discourse of rigid historical teleology are among the most distinctive manifestations) than with the global postmodern civilization. The latter, ironically, has been increasingly utilized by the central authority and successfully integrated into the project of Chinese modernity.

DEBATES ON "POST-ISMS"

Postmodernism was introduced into contemporary Chinese literary criticism in the late 1980s through Fredric Jameson's Beijing University lecture and other translations.[6] But it was not until the early 1990s that postmodernism became a heated topic for debate among Chinese theorists and critics such as Chen Xiaoming, Wang Ning, Xu Ben, Zhang Yiwu, and Zhao Yiheng. Jameson's definition of postmodernism as the cultural logic of late capitalism seems to exhilarate the Chinese critics who find a new concept corresponding to the market economy-oriented nation-state into which China is transforming itself.[7] The historical scenario from modernity to postmodernity or from modernism to postmodernism has replaced the one from capitalism to socialism as the newest variation of Hegelian–Marxian teleology. Jing Wang, despite her perhaps too hasty conclusion that postmodernism is entirely a "pseudo-proposition," keenly observes that the postmodern fever is "part of the syndrome of the Great Leap Forward myth" (p. 235).[8] But postmodernity viewed as a sociohistorical, as well as cultural, stage (a higher phase of civilization) that succeeds modernity entails more questions than answers.

Ever since they were first imported into China, such terms as postmodernity and postmodernism have been befuddling and disconcerting. To many who believe that China has already embarked onto the global market, postmodernity sounds a more than adequate concept to define China's current cultural status. Accordingly, those who do not embrace the term postmodernism whole-heartedly, base their opinion on the judgment that China does not yet have sufficient sociocultural conditions of postindustrialism or transnational capitalism. From these standpoints, postmodernism has been declared either impossible or unquestionable, depending on different assessments of the nature of Chinese society measured by the degree of development of civilization or the production–distribution mode.

Wang Ning, for example, believes that literary postmodernism in China cannot be considered a major genre, since the socioeconomically underdeveloped China is still a Third World country.[9] Following the official discourse of "four modernizations," he claims that Chinese postmodernism can only be an auxiliary style rather than a dominant trend, because "our country is still situated at the primary stage of socialism and the realization of the four modernizations is still a goal that needs much endeavor."[10] Since the chain of evolution requires the development *from modernism to* postmodernism, those cultures that have not fully developed modernist literature are believed to be impossible to grow postmodernism. Therefore Wang Ning expanded this theory beyond China and alleged that "postmodernism could only appear in the West simply because of specific Western literary tradition and because specific mechanisms of literary evolution. . . . On the other hand, in Oriental and Third World countries, there is no such background of a gradually evolving cultural tradition and an innovation oriented literary convention. . . . [B]ecause of its relations and partial continuity with modernism, the emergence of postmodernism is a 'natural' development in Western culture."[11] The agenda of literary evolution in Wang Ning's theory prevents him from seeing that cultural transformation has its own dialectic that goes beyond the rigid and often hypothetical rule of societal and civilizational progress. Having said all this, nevertheless, Wang Ning does carefully admit that Western postmodernism has a great impact on Chinese writers, though he predicts that it is impossible that postmodernism can become a predominant cultural trend in China.[12] This, I believe, is a dilemma for Wang Ning: while still insisting on the previous theoretical assumption, he sees the swift, undeniable cultural transmutations at the end of the millennium. But the cultural transmutations, in fact, had started long before the advent of globalized civilization.

Based on the same logic, but different premise, Zhang Yiwu, a critic who deserves credit for provoking enormous discussions concerning postmodernism, reaches almost the opposite conclusion: "the postmodern is a global cultural phenomenon, a condition culturally correspondent to postindustrialization and commercialization that the development of modern society is facing. It not only functions in the First and Second Worlds, but also enters the Third World culture because of the globalized communication and information."[13] The emphasis on the "culturally correspondent condition" seems to have neglected the Marxist subtext in Jameson, to whom late capitalism, which many Chinese intellectuals have embraced, is certainly *not* the peak of civilization. In any case, even though Wang Ning and Zhang Yiwu have different perspectives, their theoretical presumptions are close: the Marxist theorem that "the economic base determines the superstructure" remains the potential ideology in the discussion of postmodernism. We have seen that it is from this same perspective that Wang Ning slightly shifts his standpoint in the late 1990s, when, it seems, economic globalization has arrived in China in a rapid and unexpected way.

The question thus lies in whether material civilization or economic level is the determinant factor of the sociocultural formation in contemporary China. It must be noted that, in modern China, political powers and events have been holding sway over the entire sociocultural superstructure far more significantly than the development of material civilization, even in the 1990s and beyond. Since the economic policies in China today depend ultimately on the political policies, economic development is not controlled by an "invisible hand," but rather largely by the visibly manipulative hand of the party, and of the politico-cultural condition created by both the central authority and the citizens.

In the present lexicon of the master discourse, the old concepts such as revolution, emancipation, socialism, and international communism are not replaced by, but find their new variations in, the new keywords of Chinese modernity such as commercialization, globalization, and transnational capitalism. I would like to argue that the latter set of terms, far from having dissociated from the revolutionary idea, retains the logic of revolutionary modernity—that is, the radical change and progress of society—so as to justify its legitimacy. As Arif Dirlik and Xudong Zhang have forcefully remarked, "If Chinese society experienced modernity as revolution and socialism, Chinese postmodernity is to be grasped not only in its relationship to modernity in general but also in the relationship to a socialist and revolutionary modernity."[14] The origin of postmodernity in Chinese avant-garde literature—the deconstruction of totality and unity, the emphasis on indeterminacy and randomness, or the problematization of grand, absolute history—cannot be sought simply against the background of the globalization of the consumption society, the commercial society, the mass media society, or the information society.[15] Commercialism and cultural massification have prevailed in China under the sway of, or even in complicity with, its overshadowing political authoritarianism. The concept of the modern in China has depended heavily upon the entity of the modern nation-state defined by Lenin, which subsumes the concern for economic and technological advancement. If Jameson's Western postmodernism is a corollary of (what he calls) late capitalist civilization, then Chinese postmodernism has to do with the cultural psychology provoked by the particular political condition as the very basis of sociocultural superstructure. Accordingly, it is inevitable for us to focus the study of Chinese postmodernism on politico-cultural mentality rather than material civilization. It is precisely from the politico-historical perspective that I adopt the notion "the post-Mao–Deng," as correlated with the concurrent and correspondent cultural paradigm, "the postmodern," which is intrinsically linked to its political environment.

By taking the "distribution of global power" into consideration, however, Zhang Yiwu, among others, has later shifted toward a native "Third World" stance to confront "First World" oppression. Chinese postmodernism, as Zhang Yiwu conceives, counteracts to the so-called hegemony of Western discourses, from which contemporary Chinese culture is said to be suffering. Here, the national Subject recurs to support a discourse of national emancipation, whereas, however, the real "native" problem and "endemic" malady are dodged, consciously or unconsciously. The 1996 *Yaomohua Zhongguo de beihou* (*Behind the Demonization of China*), a book compiled by a number of domestic and overseas Chinese academics (Li Xiguang, Liu Kang et al.) to wage a sweeping attack on American representations of China, only reveals the danger of allying anti-Occidentalism with official nationalism. To oppose the Western cultural colonization, unfortunately, leads to the concealment of the native totalitarianism. The grand Subject that speaks for the nation, in effect, stands for the native/national political power, the most hegemonic power to "demonize," or at least dehumanize, the autonomous individuals within the nation. Insofar as the fact that modernity or modernization belongs exactly to the central national discourse is disregarded, the notion of the postmodern or the multicultural claim in the global scene, conjoined with that of the modern nation-state of China, serves only to reinforce the hegemony of the native political authority. Here, Homi Bhabha's warning is more than pertinent: "The marginal or 'minority' is not the space of a celebratory, or utopian, self-marginization. It is a much more substantial intervention into those justifications of modernity—progress, homogeneity, cultural organicism, the deep nation, the long past—that rationalize the authoritarian, 'normalizing' tendencies within cultures in the name of the national interest or the ethnic prerogative."[16]

I would like to argue that, ironically, the anti-Occidental sentiment packaged in Chinese postcolonial theory is truly subject to the "hegemony of Western discourses" for its unconditioned acceptance of a theory from the West.

To draw the Chinese political culture into the context of the postmodern is exactly an attempt to avoid the "invasion" of the hegemony of Western discourses, for the danger of being trapped into another system of discourse would occur only when the concept of the postmodern is imported without contextualization. Such a danger perhaps lies not in the loss of "native discourse," but in the fact that a misleading discourse obstructs the insight into the discursive condition genuinely relevant to the specific culture. In other words, a simplistic appropriation or a simplistic rejection of appropriation of the concept of the postmodern relies only on the Western discourse of postmodernity, whereas postmodernity in China, set against a different cultural background, is sacrificed due to theoretical innocence.

Entering the 1990s, postmodernism, along with other new Western theories such as postcolonialism and poststructuralism, ascended to a superior intellectual status where it enjoys great popularity, if not dominance. The discussion of postmodernism, in the mid-1990s, developed into heated debates between the postmodernists on the one side, and anti-postmodernists on the other. Zhao Yiheng, in a series of articles he published in 1995 and 1996 in the influential, Hong Kong-based intellectual magazine *Ershiyi shiji* (*The Twenty-First Century*), attacked the native Chinese "postmodernists" for deteriorating radical Western theories such as postmodernism, postcolonialism, and poststructuralism into conservative theories, which help endorse the status quo in current China.[17] Zhao's main targets, labeled "post-ism" as a whole, included not only such advocates of postmodernism as Zhang Yiwu and Chen Xiaoming, who were believed to embrace mass culture uncritically, but also such veterans writers as Zheng Min, who attempted to incorporate Derridean theory into her otherwise unfashionable literary ideas. In accordance with Zhao Yiheng's critique of Chinese "New Conservatism," Xu Ben, another overseas Chinese critic, wrote extensively to question the native critics' post-1989 acquiescence to the indigenous political oppression by redirecting the critical focus toward "Western hegemony."

Zhao's self-admitted elitist stance and Xu's politically righteous stance offended more than one group of people and triggered immediate counterattacks from Zhang Yiwu and Liu Kang. Zhang accused Zhao and Xu of accepting the "Western discourse of modernity" by "deliberately 'forgetting' and 'erasing' " its "cultural hegemony,"[18] and denied the label of conservatism or "nativist" position, which Zhao and Xu have assigned to him. He insists that his exploration of postmodernism emphasizes "the context of hybridity in present China" (p. 134). What this "context of hybridity," is, however, was not elucidated; on the contrary, he complains about the invalidation of the dichotomy between the East and the West and between the native and the foreign (p. 130). By establishing the binary opposition between the Third World and the First World, Zhang Yiwu not only conforms to the prevalent nationalistic fervor (which is, to a great extent, supported by the political authority), but also simplifies the "hybrid" situation of reality. The hybridity exists, indeed, in the fact that it is exactly by way of the official policy of China today that this Third World country is placed under the First World economic and cultural domination. On the other hand, it is the discourse of modernity, imported from the West that has become the ideological basis of this Eastern nation and supported the power and stability of the regime.

In this sense, Zhang Yiwu, who advocates a sensitivity to "nativeness," is responsible for the evasion of the hybrid hegemony of modernity from both the Eastern political and Western economic authorities. His theoretical premise misconceives the "First World discourse" as the sole threat and ignores the fact that such a First World discourse in China has been exploited by the producer of the "Third World discourse" to support its own power. In China, as a matter of fact, the supreme hegemony of discourse comes from the eastern totalitarianism, which has the power to manipulate, within a certain scope, the First World discourse or any other discourse.[19] If postmodernity in the West is, at least in part, a reaction to the late capitalist society, what it faces in China is not only a globalized commercial totality, but primarily a political totality. Commercial civilization has not yet possessed as strong a cultural power as the political authority, and has even become one of the effective modes of political manipulation (despite the fact that commercialism, to a certain extent, does engender potential hazards to the political control). Commercial society has been itself part of the teleological discourse of economic modernization to sustain the political legitimacy. The attempt to gauge Chinese postmodernity simply with postindustrial or commercial civilization is a result of misconception of the characteristics of Chinese culture under the hegemony of the Mao–Deng discourse.[20]

Of all the Chinese postmodernists, Chen Xiaoming and Dai Jinhua (who, unlike her Beijing cohorts, never advocates postmodernism explicitly) are the central figures of, but not the most ardent participants in, the debate, perhaps because their positions are more ambiguous than easily definable.[21] Chen Xiaoming differs radically from Zhang Yiwu in that he, while fully aware of the power structure in the global arena, attends more to the politically conditioned native experience (of the past and the present). In direct contrast to Zhang Yiwu and Liu Kang, Chen Xiaoming expresses an idea actually not so different from Zhao Yiheng's: "Having been living under the native cultural space, all Chinese intellectuals who seek freedom of thinking would know clearly that the Western culture is not the spiritual pressure and cultural hegemony that they are actually confronting."[22] Without denying overdetermination in contemporary China's cultural scene, Chen acutely perceives the predominance of "revolutionary discourse," a specific form of modernity, over China: "Chinese postmodernism displays all the complexities and contradictions, and is caught between the odd correlations of cultural production and the revolutionary discourse."[23] In a necessarily sophisticated tone, Chen Xiaoming warns against the naive desire to attain the native self-identity, for the paradox is that the "pure" native characteristic is exactly the cultural imaginary of the global capitalism (*Fangzhen* 207).

Keen and insightful as it is, Zhao Yiheng's criticism of the Chinese "postists" throws the baby out with the bath water. Although he claims that the Chinese postmodernists apply the radical theories from the West to their conservative objectives, he never intends to probe the possibility of recovering the radical potential of postmodernism in the Chinese context. By concluding that "[p]ostmodernism has actually turned itself into a conformist theory in China which serves to justify the institutionalized mainstream culture,"[24] Zhao refuses to see the possibility of turning it back into a nonconformist theory, which as in the West, serves not to subvert the "institutionalized mainstream culture" in a confrontational way, but to penetrate its politico-historical memory and deconstruct its repressive power. In this sense, Chinese literary postmodernism (not postmodern theory) is by no means a conservative trend that conceals the conflicts in historical reality, but rather a radical experiment that examines the psycho-rhetorical basis of the authoritarian culture of modern China.

Zhao's rejection of Chinese postmodernism is echoed, though from different perspectives, by other overseas scholars, such as Jing Wang, who acutely discerns a teleological undertone in some theorists' espousal of Chinese postmodernism, but, at the same time, misses the opportunity to explore its intimate relevance to historical reality. Jing Wang is certainly correct to find in avant-garde fiction "a belated rebellion against textual repression, a radicalism that by itself is an ideological act."[25] Is it, however, "relevant only to the Chinese context" (p. 258)? To be sure, the deconstructive "textual politics of the experimental fiction" (p. 258) is not exclusively "Chinese"; rather, like those postmodern literary trends in the post-Auschwitz Europe, Chinese avant-garde literature expresses a discrediting of the grand narratives of modernity, of which the Mao–Deng discourse is but a regional, though typical, case. The urgency to conceptualize Chinese postmodernism is a result not necessarily from a teleological impetus to emulate a certain kind of literary development in the West, but from the discovery that the politico-cultural totality that Chinese avant-gardism faces up to belongs to the same discourse of modernity that Western literary postmodernism attempts to cope with. To emphasize the particularity of Chinese literary experimentalism and to avoid linear, teleological literary history should not lead to a denial of the connection between the Chinese experience of post-Mao–Deng culture and a universal experience of postmodernity. As long as we see that modernity has been serving as the basis for the grand historical narrative significant to all nations in the twentieth century, postmodernity is a *problem* not unique to the Western, industrialized world, but pertinent to all cultures, including Third World cultures, under the impact of modernity (even though most cultures cannot be defined as postmodern as a whole). To understand Chinese postmodernism against the global background may help us see the connections among various manifestations of modernity and postmodernity.

To me, then, it is not only possible, but inevitable, to theorize contemporary Chinese culture in light of postmodernism, not because China has entered an economically and technologically advanced, postmodern age, but because the "modern" spirit has still been haunting China, whose literary postmodernity, however, reveals the repressed, self-deconstructive elements from within Chinese modernity.

DEFINING THE POSTMODERN/POST-MAO–DENG

One of the remaining questions is, then: what is the connection between the political condition and cultural production? Are we returning to the orthodox literary theory in communist China, which subjugates the cultural to the political? Here, the crucial point is how we read the political paradigm in terms of culture. If the political paradigm is understood as a cultural paradigm rather than an entity of the state apparatus or specific policies and activities, the political system of an age, particularly that of contemporary China, can be regarded as based on the production of discourses. Since the (post-)revolutionary discourse and the (post-)Enlightenment discourse are inseparable in the historical context of modern China, my concepts of modernity and postmodernity are not purely political or cultural ones, for their cultural significance is destined to derive from their political implication, and vice versa. Chinese modernity and postmodernity always demonstrate their *politico-cultural* power, which defines sociohistorical orientations.

From this hypothesis, the puzzling notion post-Mao–Deng can be approached in a more profound way. In terms of cultural production rather than material production or chronological history, Mao's and Deng's ages do not belong to different political paradigms, even though they adopt different political schemes. Deng's polity follows Mao's insofar as it has only "reformed" the instrument of discourse production. The consequence of such a reform is that the utopian discourse centered on material economy replaces the utopian discourse centered on spiritual community. Because of the collapse of Mao's spiritual community, Deng's polity resorts to the more vulgar and more pragmatic picture of elysium, through which the depressed citizens can be awakened to reconstruct a new utopia on the ruins of the previous utopia—or rather, dystopia.

The same teleological pattern of grand history remains, since the economic development is envisioned as the ultimate emancipation today—an emancipation that aims at worldly pleasure, without spiritual transcendence. The distinction between Mao's "spiritualistic" age and Deng's "sensualistic" age is merely a superficial one. Mao's ideal of egalitarian commune, as Jiwei Ci insightfully observes, appeals to lower-class people especially for its promise of ameliorating their material life, in addition to improving their social status. Ci points out that, insofar as the great temptation of Maoist utopianism lies in its acceptance as "a quick way out of poverty,"[26] Chinese communism is a "movement from utopianism to hedonism, with hedonism both as an essential, though sublimated, component of utopianism and, in an overt form, sequel to nihilism" (pp. 2–3). Without assuring economic prosperity in the collective sense, the political discourse of Maoism could not have prevailed beyond the intellectual circles. In other words, despite its depreciation of individual pleasure, Maoist discourse contains within itself a pleasure-oriented teleology as a basis of its utopian imagination. If in Mao's era, economic interest had to be expressed in political terms, post-Mao China has invented an economic vocabulary, which, indeed, renovates and bolsters the political agenda, rather than weaken it.

In Deng's era, as Ban Wang argues, "under the leadership of the party, the people are striding forward to a better future in a long march toward 'modernization' (the present substitute for the now-discredited 'Communism')."[27] But communism, stripped of pseudo-altruism to serve a new arena of combat (no longer against the "class enemies" but among the "economic animals"), is still the officially sanctioned desire to realize the brave new world in which materials are so abundant that the principle of distribution is, as Marx anticipates, "to each according to his needs."[28] At stake is the fact that it is the same grand narrative that, with its idealistic and teleological code, serves the political authoritarianism and bars all the discourses in conflict with it. A commercialized, transnationalized civilization in today's China is created primarily as the social base of political power to consolidate the one-party dictatorship.[29]

Yet, in any case, socialism is still the officially defined sociopolitical and economic system of China. If Chinese socialism best renders the cultural formation of modernity in a non-Western context, Arif Dirlik's notion of "postsocialism" is indeed pertinent to the concept of Chinese postmodernity, which challenges that cultural formation. Dirlik tells us that his "use of 'postsocialism' is inspired by an analogous term that has acquired currency in recent years in cultural studies: postmodernism," whose prominent feature "Lyotard has described as [. . .] an 'incredulity toward metanarratives.' "[30] Just as the fact that Mao is "every bit as 'postsocialist' as Deng" (p. 376), so is Mao's era subject to postmodern examination along with Deng's era. Postsocialism, if I push Dirlik's idea further, can thus be understood as a self-questioned and self-disseminated potential of the Mao–Deng socialist idea/ideal. As a special form of social modernity, the Mao–Deng version of socialism (or postsocialism, to better phrase it) is accurately illustrated in literary postmodernism, for Chinese postmodernism forcefully unmasks the problems in the Mao–Deng metanarratives.[31]

Thus understood, the notion of "the post-Mao–Deng" refers to the politico-cultural paradigm, rather than historical chronology. Chinese avant-garde literature, avant-garde fiction in particular, emerged during the heyday of Deng's era, an era that would even continue after his death. In what sense can we use the prefix "post-"? The post-Mao–Deng politico-cultural paradigm, I would like to argue, does not necessarily manifest itself chronologically after Mao's and/or Deng's reigns, just as the postmodern cultural paradigm does not come out after the modern age but indicates a deconstruction of the modern paradigm from within. If Lyotard's claim that the postmodern exists in the modern is valid,[32] we can also declare that the post-Mao–Deng must be located within the Mao–Deng paradigm. It is not far-fetched, therefore, that the post-Mao–Deng can be placed on a par with "the postmodern," for the post-Mao–Deng tendency in culture and literature to challenge the totality of political discourse is correspondent to the postmodern subversion against the grand narratives of modernity. The postmodern is to be understood as a cultural paradigm generating *within* and rebellious *against* the cultural paradigm of "the modern" without being confined in the material or economic structure of contemporary civilization.

Postmodernism in Chinese avant-garde literature can be defined as both a psychic reaction to the politico-cultural modernity imbedded in the Mao–Deng master discourse and a rhetorical reaction to the literary modernity exemplified by the representational paradigm of twentieth-century Chinese literature.[33] The politico-cultural discourse of modernity and the literary paradigm of modernity share the totalistic mode of conceptualization. The grand history, which presupposes an absolute coherence between practice and telos and a transparent correspondence between representation and meaning, is certainly the most powerful concept propelling both political modernity and literary modernity.

What is inseparable from the literary idea of the modern is, therefore, not only the emancipatory politico-cultural agenda—the Mao–Deng regimes being its particular expressions—but also the formalistic literary paradigm as such, that is the mode of absolutizing and totalizing discourse. In this respect, the complicity between literary modernity and politico-cultural totalization in the Mao–Deng regimes can be traced back to their common origin. As a literary paradigm, then, the Mao–Deng discourse that prescribes unified historical imperatives corresponds to the representational subjectivism in modern Chinese fiction to a great extent. It is *the same subjectively centered totality and rationality that construct modernity* in both sociopolitical arbitrariness and literary/aesthetic absoluteness.

Maoism, in particular, relies on this literary/aesthetic absoluteness. The function of Maoist discourse lies in its aesthetic magic, which absolutizes the grand narrative by enforcing signifying relationships. The most violent expression of modernity exists in *Quotations from Chairman Mao* and *Mao Zedong xuanji* (*Selected Works of Mao Zedong*), the most widely read books in the Cultural Revolution. (Apparently, *Deng Xiaoping xuanji* [*The Collected Works of Deng Xiaoping*] has never been able to emulate its model.) Maoist discourse becomes a rhetorical paradigm that coerces the affinity between the signifier and the signified. Apart from such indubitable political statements as "the force at the core leading our cause forward is the Chinese Communist Party,"[34] the diegetic mode in Mao's writings is another example of the power of representational subjectivity in modern Chinese literature in establishing the Historical Subject. In his "Jinian Baiqiuen" (In memory of Norman Bethune), one of his so-called three prime articles (*lao san pian*), Mao, despite the fact that "Comrade Bethune and [he] met only once," confidently characterizes Bethune's personality in highly subjective, approving terms: "his utter devotion to others without any thought of self," "his great sense of responsibility in his work and his great warm-heartedness towards all comrades and the people," "true communist spirit," "the spirit of absolute selflessness," etc.[35] Before the reader is able to decide whether one can be "without any thought of self," whether there is such thing as "absolute selflessness," or what the "true communist spirit" really is, the signified of representation has been unmistakably prescribed without any latitude for hesitation or suspicion, even though the link of signification may well be fictitious and illusory.

In those literary passages, Mao's narrative mode evidently corresponds to the canonical paradigm of representation in modern Chinese literature. In "Yugong yishan" (The foolish old man who removed the mountain), another of his "three prime articles," Mao rephrases a parable from *Lie Zi* and ends with this conclusion: "Having refuted the Wise Old Man's wrong view, he went on digging every day, unshaken in his conviction" (p. 272). In the original text of *Lie Zi*, the authorial tendency in the description of this event is reduced to a minimum: "Mister Simple of North Mountain [i.e., the Foolish Old Man] breathed a long sigh, and said [. . .]. Old Wiseacre of River Bend [i.e., the Wise Old Man] was at a loss for an answer."[36] In Mao, however, the objective narration is intruded by such words as "refute," "wrong," "unshaken," each strongly imposing subjective judgment upon what is being represented. Apparently, the master discourse exists in the way of narration in which the modern narrative subject is endowed with an omniscient and omnipotent character.

To Mao, the Foolish Old Man, whom he has imbued with a heroically "unshaken" image as opposed to the wrong, "refuted" Wise Old Man, symbolizes the historical power that Mao assumes himself to represent. Only by dichotomizing and absolutizing the characterization of the good/positive and the evil/negative can the representational subject of Maoist discourse outline an indisputable totality of history. Historical modernity must rely upon the accordingly totalizing and rationalizing mode of discourse, which can be seen as literary modernity. Since the political Mao–Deng is precisely the cultural and historical modern applied in the practical domain, it must ground itself on the literary modernity essentialized by the representational subject.

It is on this basis that, as Xiaobing Tang observes, "the function of [Chinese] postmodernism is to dismantle various master-narratives about modernity and create a new field of uncompromising demystification."[37] In any case, then, as the cultural modern lies in literary rationalization and absolutization—the master discourse of the political Mao–Deng—the prefix "post-" does not refer to a chronological subsequence but shows *a temporal force of deferral and a spatial force of deviation within the not completely forgotten but immemorial desire and repression of the modern*. The postmodern "style," as we have seen from the avant-garde texts, does not exist as a distanced critique of the modern but rather suggests a self-involvement in historical destiny. It thus implies, simultaneously, a preoccupation with and a deviation from the original/primal. The reemergence of the cultural/literary modern in avant-garde narratives, that is, the recurrence of the antecedent affects in the unconscious, or the concurrence of the past and the present, signals the denial of the conception of linear historical progress. In other words, the postmodern is not a diachronic transcendence of the modern but a synchronic evocation and expulsion of its repression.

The subjective self-suspicion becomes the most perceptible feature of the postmodern Chinese avant-gardism. As a deconstruction of the modern representation within the subjective narrative, which conforms to a political totality, literary postmodernity is, formalistically, a confession of the traumatizing violence of modernity within its deep formation. In this sense, the Chinese avant-garde is not only an affront to the externally imposing master discourse, but a conjuring up of the internalized discourse of modernity with which the subject has been culturally possessed. The impetus of the subjective self-critique stems from the awareness that historical catastrophes in China cannot be simply imputed to external, historical evil forces (such as the Communist Party, as might be considered), but has to be examined within the collective/individual cultural subject, which adheres to the same paradigm of the dominant political discourse. The fact that it was always the intellectuals themselves who not only collaborated in, but elaborated, the persecutions of other intellectuals in the numerous political movements in the history of communist China is certainly a practical consequence of the supreme cultural paradigm of the discourse of modernity shared by the intellectuals and the political apparatus.

As an implosive disruption of the transparent and absolute genre that constructs the master discourse, postmodernity necessarily involves self-reference to such a genre in modern Chinese literature. Postmodernity is thus a parody of modernity: the topoi of the modern are still lurking, while at the same time whirled into the involute labyrinth of multiplied signifiers, the signifiers that fail to capture the signifieds in a transparent way. Then, a literary encounter with reality in the post-Mao era becomes, in the first place, an encounter with a language that is already culturally and historically intertextualized, overdetermined, contaminated, and, in particular, associated or entangled with the master discourse as something etiologically modern but pathologically/symptomatically postmodern.

The disintegration of the modern subjectivity in Chinese avant-garde literature is a disintegration of a subjectivity that lacks self-reflection on its own limitations and nonidentities. The Chinese avant-garde does not applaud the death of subjectivity, but launches a self-deconstruction of the totalistic, repressive subjectivity. The irrational narrative subject in avant-garde literature persists in the paradox of self-consciousness: it displays its own quandary to repeal ignorance, while this quandary is precisely the boundary of the subject that rejects the totalized utopia. In other words, the transcendentality of self-consciousness can only be achieved in the self-conscious recognition of its own impossibility of transcendence. Such a postmodernity is not even the eruption of the Deleuzean, productive desire: the irrational subject is to be considered as being activated by the pressure of the politico-historical discourse rather than spontaneously self-generating. Thus a postmodern subjectivity is a self-questioning and deconstructive one, which breaches the absolute, rational, and totalistic oppression of both the politico-historical Mao–Deng and the culturo-literary modern.

NOTES

1. Theodor W. Adorno, "Cultural criticism and society," *Prisms*, trans. Samuel and Shierry Weber (Cambridge: MIT Press, 1981), p. 34.

2. Many scholars now admit that Maoism, or Chinese communism, is a distinctive formation of modernity. As Arif Dirlik and Xudong Zhang conclude, "Chinese communism was arguably the most forceful, and ultimately most successful, expression of an ideological commitment to modernity" ("Introduction: postmodernism and China," *boundary 2* 24:3 [1997], 9).

3. David H. Hirsch, "Three: Martin Heidegger and pagan gods," *The Deconstruction of Literature: Criticism after Auschwitz* (Providence: Brown University Press, 1991), p. 85

4. Jean-François Lyotard, "Answering the question: what is postmodernism."

5. See also Lyotard's exposition of *Nachträglichkeit* in Jean-François Lyotard, "the jews," *Heidegger and "The Jews*," trans. Andreas Michel and Mark S. Roberts (Minneapolis: University of Minnesota Press, 1990), pp. 15–17.

6. According to a comprehensive bibliography of Chinese postmodernism (see Zhang Guoyi, 323), my 1987 essay "Yiyi shang, pintieshu yu xushu zhi wu: Ma Yuan xiaoshuo zhong de houxiandaizhuyi" (Entropy of meaning, collage and the dance of narration: postmodernism in Ma Yuan's fiction), *Wenyi zhengming* 1:6 (1987), 6, was the first to apply postmodern theory to Chinese literary criticism.

7. Such a partial understanding of postmodernism comes mainly from the Chinese translations of Fredric Jameson's works, especially his *Houxiandaizhuyi yu wenhualilun* (*Postmodernism and Cultural Theories*), trans. Tang Xiaobing, (Xi'an: Shaanxi shifandaxue chubanshe, 1986). Of course, it is not these translations, but the lack of more comprehensive studies and translations of other works on postmodernism, that is responsible for the partiality.

8. Jing Wang, "The pseudoproposition of 'Chinese postmodernism': Ge Fei and the experimentalist showcase," in Jing Wang, *High Culture Fever: Politics, Aesthetics, and Ideology in Deng's China* (Berkeley, CA: University of California Press, 1996), pp. 233–260.

9. Wang Ning "The mapping of Chinese postmodernity," *boundary 2* 24:3 (1997), p. 38.

10. Wang Ning, "Jieshou yu bianxing: Zhongguo dangdai xianfeng xiaoshuo zhong de houxiandaixing" (Reception and transformation: postmodernity in contemporary Chinese avant-garde fiction), in *Shengcun youxi de shuiquan* (*The Rings of Ripples of the Game of Existence*) ed. Zhang Guoyi (Beijing: Beijing daxue chubanshe, 1994), p. 136. The same theme recurs in Wang's postscript to the 1991 book *Zouxiang houxiandaizhuyi* (a Chinese translation of *Toward Postmodernism*, ed. Douwe Fokkema), in which he offers again a materialistic and social Darwinian perspective toward literature: "Postmodernism is a specific cultural and literary phenomenon of the Western post-industrial and postmodern society, so it can only appear in the area where the material civilization of capitalism is highly advanced, with rich soil of modernist culture. But in China, where only a few writers and works of modernist tendency have existed and such cultural soil and social condition are fundamentally lacking, it is impossible to have a postmodernist literary movement. The experiment of a small number of avant-garde writers with postmodern tendency can perhaps bring limited 'bombastic effect' in the circle of writers and critics, but ultimately cannot become the major current of contemporary Chinese literature." "Yihouji" (postscript to the translation), in *Zouxiang houxiandaizhuyi* (*Toward Postmodernism*), ed. Wang Ning (Beijing: Beijingdaxue chubanshe, 1991), p. 324. It is especially baffling that, even if he ignores the postmodernist tendency in Latin American literature,

Wang Ning neglects the essay on postmodern Soviet Russian theater in the book to which his postscript is written.

11. Wang Ning, "Constructing postmodernism: the Chinese case and its different versions," *Canadian Review of Comparative Literature* 20:1/2 (March–June 1993), 58–59.

12. See, especially, his "The mapping of Chinese postmodernity," in which he acknowledges that "postmodernism undoubtedly has a marked presence in China" (p. 36), though he still maintains that it "will remain secondary" (p. 40).

13. "Lixiangzhuyi de zhongjie: Shiyan xiaoshuo de wenhua tiaozhan" (The end of idealism: cultural challenge of experimental fiction), in *Shengcun youxi de shuiquan* (*The Rings of Ripples of the Game of Existence*), ed. Zhang Guoyi (Beijing: Beijing daxue chubanshe, 1994), p. 119.

14. Arif Dirlik and Xudong Zhang, "Introduction: postmodernism and China," *boundary 2* 24:3 (1997), 8.

15. Zhang Yiwu is indeed far-fetched to imply that "discontinuities, fragmentations and instabilities" in contemporary Chinese narratives are "feasible practical modes" "resisting *the repression of the First World culture*" in *Zai bianyuanchu zhuixun: Disanshijie wenhua yu Zhongguo dangdai wenxue* (*Pursuing at the Margin: Third World Culture and Contemporary Chinese Literature*) (Changchun: Shidai wenyi chubanshe, 1993), p. 90, emphasis added. Having said this, nonetheless, I must add that the most recent development of urban fiction in China (especially the works by Wei Hui and Mian Mian) has developed interpretations of the post-utopian subjectivity with fluxional, diffused desire. But even Wei Hui's and Mian Mian's writings are not devoid of reactions to mainstream political modernity and its cultural ramifications.

16. Homi K. Bhabha, ed., "Introduction: narrating the nation" *Nation and Narration* (London, New York: Routledge, 1990), p. 4.

17. " 'Houxue' yu Zhongguo xinbaoshouzhuyi" (Post-isms and Chinese new conservatism) is the first and the most frequently discussed of this series of articles. Most of the arguments are later presented in his 1997 article in English, "Post-isms and Chinese new conservatism" (see "Post-isms").

18. Zhang Yiwu, "Chanshi Zhongguo de jiaolü" (The anxiety of interpreting China), *Ershiyi shiji* (*The Twenty-First Century*) 28 (April 1995), p. 130.

19. Zhang Yiwu's emphasis on nativeness is more obscure than illuminating. He once acknowledges that "commercialization is a prerequisite for 'postmodernity,' and it is internationalized"; but then, when claiming that "our Third World condition has imbued commercialization an indigenous color," he cannot proceed to specify anything related to this "indigenized commercialization." *Zai bianyuanchu zhuixun*, p. 97).

20. I am not claiming, of course, that transnational capitalism has no impact on contemporary Chinese cultural scene. Especially in the film industry, to some extent, "Chinese filmmakers are obliged to operate in accordance with logic of global commodification" (Sheldon Lu, "National cinema, cultural critique, transnational capital: the films of Zhang Yimou," in *Transnational Chinese Cinema: Identity, Nationhood, Gender*, ed. Sheldon Lu [Honolulu: University of Hawaii Press, 1997], p. 132). But, as Chen Xiaoming has accurately pointed out, the complexities that characterize postmodernism as regards Chinese cinema include not only "the subordinate/resistant relationship between the native and the global cultural imaginary" but also "the parasitical/disobedient relationship

between the domestic cultural production and the revolutionary discourse" ("The mysterious other: postpolitics in the narrative of Chinese film," *boundary 2* 24:3 (1997), 140).

21. As a major target of Zhao Yiheng's harsh critique, Chen Xiaoming never responded directly to Zhao except in a footnote, where he briefly denies Zhao's accusation of a unified conservative school of "post-isms" (*Fangzhen de niandai [The Age of Simulation]* [Taiyuan: Shanxi jiaoyu chubanshe, 1999], p. 213). Dai Jinhua, on the other hand, never advocates postmodernism. Rather, she, like Jing Wang and many others, finds the naiveté of conceptualizing the postmodern "on the legitimate basis of the need to conjoin and parallel to the Western world" (*You zai jing zhong* [*As If Still in the Mirror*] [Beijing: Zhishi chubanshe, 1999], p. 251).

22. Chen Xiaoming, *Fangzhen de niandai*, p. 213.

23. Chen, "The Mysterious Other," p. 140.

24. Zhao Yiheng, "Post-isms and Chinese new conservatism," *New Literary History* 28:1 (1997), 42.

25. Jing Wang, "The pseudoproposition of 'Chinese postmodernism'," *High Culture Fever: Politics, Aesthetics, and Ideology in Deng's China* (Berkeley, Calif.: University of California Press, 1996), p. 258.

26. Jiwei Ci, "Introduction," *Dialectic of the Chinese Revolution: From Utopianism to Hedonism* (Stanford, Calif.: Stanford University Press, 1994), p. 3.

27. Ban Wang, "The angels of history: The fantastic, schizophrenic, and grotesque," *The Sublime Figure of History: Aesthetics and Politics in Twentieth-Century China* (Stanford, Calif.: Stanford University Press, 1997), p. 241.

28. Karl Marx, "Critique of the Gotha programme," in *The Marx–Engels Reader*, ed. Robert C. Tucker (New York: Norton, 1978), p. 531.

29. Having said this, however, I am not denying that commercialization in reality has complex effects. In today's China, commercialization is not so much a decentering of communist ideology as a reorientation of Chinese modernity—a modernity that now justifies the hedonistic social trend. At the same time, commercialization has a critical impact on the development of Chinese avant-garde literature. Especially in the 1990s, avant-garde literature faces pressure not only from the old, orthodox, official cultural apparatus, but also from the new, commercial, popular cultural environment. It is the latter, i.e., the overshadowing market, that diminishes experimentalism in avant-garde fiction in the 1990s. In other words, Chinese avant-garde fiction as a movement, having fought against the official, orthodox cultural apparatus, can hardly resist the allure, or pressure, of cultural commodification and consumerism. Yu Hua's sacrifice of narrative revolution to more or less complete and dramatized plot lines after 1989 is a typical example.

30. Arif Dirlik, "Postsocialism? Reflections on 'socialism with Chinese characteristics,'" in *Marxism and the Chinese Experience*, ed. Arif Dirlik and Maurice Meisner (Armonk, NY: M.E. Sharpe, 1989), p. 374.

31. Herein lies a more negative understanding of "postsocialism" that Paul G. Pickowicz's offers in his study of new Chinese cinema, especially Huang Jianxin's films: "Postsocialist [. . .] refers in large part to a negative, dystopian cultural condition that prevails in late socialist societies" ("Huang Jianxin and postsocialism," in *New Chinese Cinemas: Forms, Identities, Politics*, ed. Nick Browne et al. [Cambridge: Cambridge University Press, 1994], p. 62). Part of the reason that Pickowicz chooses the term postsocialism, as he explains, is to see the "cultural

identity" that "links China to such societies as Poland, the former Soviet Union, Hungary, eastern Germany, and the former Czechoslovakia, all of which underwent long periods of difficult Marxist–Leninist rule" (p. 61). Dirlik, to avoid confining the concept postsocialism as a narrowly defined one, argues that "postsocialism is of necessity also postcapitalism" ("Postsocialism?," in *Marxism and the Chinese Experience*, p. 364). My preference to the concept of postmodernity, then, further reflects the endeavor to understand socialism, communism, and capitalism under the category of modernity, which can help theorize various historical phenomena such as the May Fourth Movement, the Cultural Revolution, the Holocaust, industrialization, globalization, etc., as long as attention to specifics and particularities is duly paid.

32. Lyotard declares that "modernity is constitutionally and ceaselessly pregnant with its postmodernity" because of modernity's own "impulsion to exceed itself into a state other than itself" (*The Inhuman: Reflections on Time*, trans. Geoferrey Bennington and Rachel Bowley [Cambridge: Polity Press, 1991], p. 25).

33. Examples can be found in almost all the canonical works in twentieth-century Chinese literature before mid-1980s. See my article, "Whence and whither the postmodern/post-Mao-Deng: historical subjectivity and literary subjectivity in modern China," in *Postmodernism and China*, ed. Arif Dirlik and Xudong Zhang (Durham: Duke University Press, 2000), pp. 379–398.

34. Mao Tse-tung, *Quotations from Chairman Mao Tse-tung* (Peking: Foreign Language Press, 1966), p. 1.

35. Mao Tse-tung, *Selected Works of Mao Tse-tung* (Peking: Foreign Language Press, 1965), vol. 2, pp. 337–338.

36. Lieh-tzu, *The Book of Lieh-tzu*, trans. A.C. Graham (London: John Murray, 1960), p. 100.

37. Xiaobing Tang, "The function of new theory: what does it mean to talk about postmodernism in China?," in *Politics, Ideology, and Literary Discourse in Modern China*, ed. Liu Kang and Xiaobing Tang (Durham: Duke University Press, 1993), p. 296.

Part II

The Quotidian Apocalypse

6

MODERNITY AND APOCALYPSE IN CHINESE NOVELS FROM THE END OF THE TWENTIETH CENTURY

Jeffrey C. Kinkley

Most Chinese writers and intellectuals in the first five and final two decades of the twentieth century yearned for Chinese modernity, but saw a China that was "feudal" in an era of accelerating world progress. There were also traditionalists, early on, who rejected mainstream versions of modernity that embraced Westernization and nation building.[1] Their contestations of "modernity" found echoes in the 1990s talk of "alternative modernities" and "modernity with Chinese characteristics."

Apocalyptic views contest the discourse of modernity more radically. If time has no forward motion, or is not linear to begin with, great endings and cycles may be discovered in the human record. China has its own prophetic visions of universal corruption and doomsday, possibly portending a great, new, social–moral dispensation arising from the ashes, even a new spiritual or civilizational "revelation" (Greek: *apokalypsis*). Personal salvation by a healing savior, and not just for the oppressed, may be a concomitant. Such ideas have generally been nurtured collectively, in secret societies and millenarian sects,[2] although Kang Youwei thought he saw great cycles in the classics. Orthodox twentieth-century modernizers considered such sectarian worldviews superstitious, even primitive, and Kang Youwei, a charlatan. The modernizers believed in linear time.

Yet apocalyptic creeds thrive in the most technologically advanced societies, as became evident when Christian millennialist true believers aroused worldwide anxiety in the run-up to the year 2000.[3] Millenarian ideas can be accommodated even in the learned and eclectic skepticisms of modernism and postmodernism. Giambattista Vico's and Joachim of Fiore's circular notions of time have recently been, in a word, recycled. Apocalypticism contests and also coexists with mainstream thought, feeding modern angst— seeds of destruction in modernity itself.

Millenarian sects sprang up again in rural China in the late twentieth century.[4] Chinese Christian sects that arguably fit the category and the

Falun Gong also grew strong. This chapter, however, analyzes individualistic visions of Chinese apocalypse communicated by the printed word. Like their fellow-countrymen wrapped up in quotidian consumerism and the pursuit of private pleasures, apocalyptic writers of the 1990s and their readers were not engaged in communitarian endeavors, or any kind of violence, though the government feared some of them enough to censor their writings. They did contest the teleological and sociological (collectivist, class-based) visions of Marxism–Leninism, which had prevailed in the fiction, propaganda, and morality of Maoist China. Yet their new apocalypticism had roots not only in old millenarianism, patriarchalism, and anti-Westernism, but also Marxism— a utopian philosophy with millenarian roots in which "modernity is seen as a monster,"[5] and great world forces clash, bringing an end to (class) history. Even in practice, as Mao went to extremes constructing new socialist citizens during the Cultural Revolution, many questioned whether the rapid technological advancement of China was foremost on his mind.[6]

In the following, I analyze four apocalyptic Chinese novels of the 1990s. In the plot of *Yellow Peril* (1991), the first and most epic work, a limited nuclear exchange in a near-future Chinese civil war leads to a full nuclear exchange between Russia and the United States, hence nuclear winter and a global demise of civilization.[7] Reflecting the pessimism of Chinese intellectuals after the June 4, 1989 Beijing massacre, this novel was published in Taiwan under a pseudonym. Western media lent the work international fame. Though banned in China, *Yellow Peril* circulated widely there as *samizdat* on computer disks and printouts.[8] In 1998, Wang Lixiong, 45 and at liberty, claimed credit for the work. His is the only work discussed here to describe a Golden Age *after* the collapse of the world as we know it.

The three other novels do not prefigure the end of civilization, but they portray a corruption so vast as to require a great fall, morally and politically— the fall of Chinese communism. Like the collapse of world capitalism predicted by earlier moderns, this other fall has long been prophesied. It portends chaos, at least during a transitional period, and seems to be the product of "inevitable forces" of global modernity—the "end of history," in the words of another prophet of the 1990s, Francis Fukuyama.[9] Lu Tianming's *Heaven Above* (1995) and Zhang Ping's *Choice* (1997) delve into the details and the sociology of corruption in the manner of nineteenth-century realistic novels.[10] Mo Yan's *Jiu guo* deploys images of corruption, drunkenness, and cannibalism more fantastically and symbolically. His novel appeared in Taiwan in 1992, then in China, and was released in English in 2000 as *The Republic of Wine*; the Chinese characters making up the book title are rendered in the English text sometimes as "Liquorland"; other translations might be "Besotted Nation" or "National Liquorification."[11]

Mo Yan is a celebrated writer. His work combines the difficulty of modernism with accessible mixed-genre postmodern and premade-for-cinema effects, including sensationalistic themes like the eating of baby boys. His novel was probably the most "popular" of the four, if that means most widely read in book form. The subject matter, vocabulary, and suspense-generating devices of the other three suggest that they were deliberately written for a mass audience.[12] Even so, they were accompanied variously by prizes, prefaces, and postfaces as if they were classics. In China, "realistic" subject matter (social problems), technical "information" (*Yellow Peril* is something of a techno thriller), and being banned are three imprimaturs of seriousness. Yet the novels of the 1990s discussed here were, like other works described in this volume, products of an individualistic age, distributed as mass *consumer* goods.

RECONCILING THE IRRECONCILABLE THROUGH SYNCRETISM AND SYNCHRONY

China's apocalyptic novels of the 1990s are filled with incongruity. System collapse is conceived both in ancient terms (as corruption, if not doomsday) and in patently modern terms (as environmental decay, if not cosmic entropy). Characterization still reflects Maoist social categories (workers, cadres, intellectuals), even as the social values and literary techniques are post-Marxist, perhaps postmodern. Collective damnation is the theme, yet it is "consumed" as private entertainment—with all the further guilt that that may entail. Time is both linear and cyclical.

How did any of China's ancient apocalyptic heritage get into modern literary works? Notions of apocalypse lie dormant in China's heritage, much as intimations of Millennium survive in societies of Judeo-Christian background. Chinese state orthodoxy and established "Western" churches have long suppressed populist millenarian sects, fearing them to be antiestablishment and anticlerical.[13] But attempts to brand apocalyptic creeds as heretical have never been completely successful in China or in the West.

David Ownby argues that, in medieval China, some apocalyptic creeds were mainstream, and "by the sixth century, Daoism and Buddhism had largely fused in the popular mentality, providing a potent mix of symbols and discourses that was to nourish Chinese millenarian thought down to the present day."[14] The vocabulary of sectarian thinking remains broadly diffused among the public in modern times, reinforced by the mildly apocalyptic and prophetic Mandate of Heaven theory in orthodox Confucian thought, traditional moralism bewailing corruption and fall from a Golden Age, popular novels and histories about millenarian rebels, and remnants of cult knowledge in everyday life. One need not belong to a cult to be able to read the "signs." Underground fears of sorcery and occult arts can break out as mass hysteria in the best-ordered societies.[15]

Fostering these survivals are persistent tendencies, in both mainstream and dissident thought, of syncretism (the blending of different philosophies) and expectations of synchrony (the simultaneity or recurrence of what otherwise might be thought unique moments in time). Syncretism has popped up in ancient and modern millenarian creeds of "the West," notably in "new religious movements," but Chinese cosmologists have anciently and consistently sought a unified field theory that would, "in Joseph Needham's words, 'reconcile the irreconcilable' through discovering the supposed regular interrelations of the sexagenary cycle, the lunar cycle, tropical years, eclipse periods, the 'year-star' Jupiter's synodic revolutions, and conjunctions of the five naked-eye planets—all in accord with the celestial and terrestrial movements of the Five Phases."[16] Still more cycles were thought to exist in "two microcosms that in their normal functioning were in perfect correspondence" to the cosmos: "the liturgical order of both government and religion" and "the life-maintaining order of the human body." Their movements were "a remarkably articulated nest of cycles, with the life trajectory of the mayfly or the diurnal rhythm of the human body representing the smallest wheel, and, as the largest, the practically infinite great cycle—from the beginning to the end of time—integrating all the astronomical periods, all the smaller cycles turning within it like a superbly complicated train of gears."[17]

If, then, Confucianism, Daoism, and Buddhism were syncretistically combined, as in millenarian cults (the twentieth-century Yiguandao or Way of Pervading Unity added Islam and Christianity), then a Heavenly mandated end of dynasty, shift of Daoist phase, and end of a Buddhist kalpa might all occur at once. The odds of that would be dismissed by modern probability theory, if the mixing of creeds did not already offend modernity's "jealous god" of rational consistency, but millenarians, like gamblers, expect a full reversal of fortune *imminently*.

Cosmic syncretism and synchrony, and stories of cultist rebellion, are old not just in Chinese folk belief,[18] but also in the Chinese novel. Works such as the *Romance of the Three Kingdoms* and *Water Margin* keep alive olden images of corruption and the signs of a future fall. They also preserve and embody principles of syncretism and synchrony in their structure. Given the many kinds of time in traditional Chinese thinking, it seems strange that Benedict Anderson has inferred that only the modern novel has any "device for the presentation of simultaneity in 'homogenous, empty time.' "[19]

Modernity's own anxieties about the future can be deflected when doomsday is merely literary, or when it leads to a restoration or a new Golden Age. Moreover, the mixing of apparently irreconcilable elements can produce the cafeteria-style pleasures of postmodernism, keeping the plot fresh and unpredictable—not nearly so boring as cyclicalism might suggest. Add apocalyptic violence or a looming holocaust, and you have a thriller.[20]

FORMULAS OF CHINESE APOCALYPTIC NOVELS IN THE 1990S

Popular apocalyptic novels in the 1990s have formulas. The setting is a time of declining morality, in the present or near future. The looming collapse will be moral; the fall of institutions, total. Not just a nation, but a great "system," is set to expire. Corruption starts at the top, in the performance of official duties, continues downward through ordinary citizen greed and "consumerism," and ends in bestiality. Even exemplars, unlike most Chinese heroes, may fall into the abyss for a time. Adversaries are demonized.

Portents of future collapse heighten anticipation without giving away the game. Catastrophes and prophesies throw out "astronomically" large numbers (to use a favorite neologism in *Yellow Peril*), though not the exact dates of calamity, which obsess Chinese and Western millenarians in life.

A great leader—a male—restores the old system on the brink of its fall, or ushers in a new one. There may be competitors and false prophets. Women tempt the true prince and may corrupt him for a time. They are not evil in essence; it is their nature to tempt men.[21] After many tests, the hero attracts a mass following. He triumphs by his message, not by charisma. He may have apostles who will not fully understand him until the time has come, as in *Heaven Above*. *The Republic of Wine* is the exception. Its antihero is not up to the task.

Coming down through the great vernacular novels, such as *Romance of the Three Kingdoms*, is a concept of "the times." Good times allow good men to prevail; the times produce them. Bad times reveal *jianxiong*, talented opportunists who serve well in a good age, but cause great harm in bad times, when they can seize power. The concept has been called fatalistic, yet it also has a cosmic sense like the ancient Greek concept of *kairos* (time), with the connotation "of the right season, the right time for action, the critical moment."[22] *Yellow Peril* has three major *jianxiong*, all of whom, by doctrine and character, contest mainstream modernity.

The domain of the action is a microcosm. In *Yellow Peril*, China by its sheer size and centrality determines the world's fate. In the middlebrow novels, the battleground where the hero fights is a city—a microcosm of China—or really something bigger: communism, "China's system," whose fate has global implications. And yet, world, system and nation remain territorial rather than abstractly cultural. In *Yellow Peril*, the Chinese people mostly spread their humanity-saving new culture by emigrating, not through new communications media.

The manifold instances of human struggle are signs, and most of them will have transpired in uncannily similar form in a previous era. History repeats itself in nested microcycles, some of which may be visible in a lifetime. At the end, historic macrocycles and microcycles fall due simultaneously—which is not to say, in the modern novel, that the next fall may not also be "final" in the new, linear time of ecological doomsday-sayers.

These are lengthy suspense novels. The last three, which are not quite so cataclysmic, begin as crime thrillers with the hero in the usual role of detective. In the course of the novel, the mystery shifts from whether he can solve the crime(s), to whether he is the chosen one (succeeding others who have failed) who can understand the pattern of corruption, rise above it, and delay the fall of the old system or form a new one. The possibility that he is not elect, but will be drawn into the abyss like his predecessors, looms ever larger, until he extricates himself and restores the old order (in *Choice*, the most "popular" and establishment novel), falters but retains enough dignity to point the way to salvation (in *Heaven Above*), or succumbs (in *The Republic of Wine*, the highbrow novel). *Yellow Peril* has several competing saviors, each with his own doctrine. The mystery is whose doctrine will prove correct at each successive, deepening stage of the apocalypse, and then, which message will suit the post-holocaust era.

YELLOW PERIL

Multiple beginnings—opening with one subplot, beginning all over again with another, and beginning from scratch yet again—is an old technique, as in *The Story of the Stone*. The multiple beginnings may represent simultaneity, and each may be informed by a different cosmic worldview, so that the beginnings are syncretistic as well as synchronic. Suppose also that each small beginning recapitulates a microrevolution from a different period of history, as a small cog, while presaging the future turn of the great cog, when all history-repeating microrevolutions will make a final turn together. These are the ramifications of *Yellow Peril*. As in the traditional novel, the number of narrative units is premonitory—not 100 or 108 lucky chapters, but 13 unlucky superchapters.

Yellow Peril's Yuan-Ming-style prologue or "wedge" (*xiezi*) depicts the earth at an indeterminate future time as if seen from space. Every known phenomenon pointing to global collapse is about to climax. The Nile is desertified. A snowstorm quells civil insurrection in San Diego arising from American decadence and AIDS. Brazilian gold miners destroy the last rain forest. A vastly "overdetermined" end is near. Who could imagine that Armageddon would still be caused by China?

The novel's "first beginning" in chapter one presages the division of China, *Three Kingdoms*-style. Regime power is so weakened by demographic pressure and social–political decay that a moderate new Chinese Communist Party secretary general (a Hu Yaobang figure) has reopened Tiananmen Square to dissidents. This recapitulates May/June 1989, but now the democracy movement itself—China's hope—is fractured. Democrats the secretary general has released from prison battle exiled activists returned from abroad. Violence in the contest for the sacred space of Tiananmen suggests not just 1989, but also the Cultural Revolution, 1966–1967. Heroes are introduced. Shi Ge, head of a mysterious government organ that copes with national emergencies (easily imagined as a dirty-tricks agency), is caught by the ex-prisoner faction. Their charismatic leader is Ouyang Zhonghua (Zhonghua meaning "China"), head of a Green Movement, who wants to found a utopian postindustrial and postconsumerist society of new spiritual beings. Only in the fullness of time will Ouyang be revealed as a *jianxiong* who speaks of peace (and might be an asset in good times), but serves the devil in bad times. The unassuming Shi Ge, a quiet, secret prophet of another new order, is the true savior, disguised as an agent of Caesar. Other factions will in time see through their respective doctrines of naturalism-cum-spirituality ("Eastern") and the West's god (or goddess) of "democracy." Those doctrines' truths are incomplete.

Such events, imagined by an author writing in 1990–1991, bespeak a nearer future than that in the preface. Wang Lixiong foresaw not only a nuclearization of India and Pakistan, as well as of Israel, Iraq, and the Koreas,[23] but also the passing of the Taiwan presidency from the old Kuomintang to the Democratic Progressive Party. Deng Xiaoping has died. Wang knew of communism's fall in Eastern Europe, but not in Russia; it is the USSR that launches the strike on the United States. Historical change almost outpaced his imagination.

A second beginning, in chapter two, recalls China's modern subservience to Japan. At a live sex-show bar, hidden in a maze of tunnels deep below the Ginza, where the sex is literally bestial—animal on woman—a plot is hatched to assassinate the new secretary general. He is seen on TV ceding Heilongjiang to Japan for 50 years, in return for investment and debt forgiveness. Japan's ultranationalist Black Dragon Society of the 1930s is alive and well again, spearheading a new Japanese conquest of debilitated China.

The third opening chapter has a portent directly evoking the Mandate of Heaven. Yellow River dikes break for the first time since 1949, creating 20 million refugees. Without people's communes to organize collective labor, China can only ask the PLA (army) to save the ancient cradle of its civilization. Hens do not turn into cocks, but newspapers divide into two editorial lines—the PLA's and the secretary general's.

It is the setting of the fifth chapter, in the Western Hills, that recalls the eponymous right–KMT faction, hence the Chiang Kai-shek era. Here lies the gravely ill old paramount leader, "the Chairman," with his protégé, a careerist young general named Wang Feng—the antichrist. He has the secretary general assassinated as he cuts the ribbon for the Three Gorges Dam (a touch belonging to the linear discourse of environmental doomsday). Wang uses the power of the PLA at the Yellow River to launch a coup and set up a "fascist state" (Wang Lixiong's term), while a hired *qigong* master literally manipulates the comatose chairman. The general also has a private submarine with 40 nuclear warheads. Eventually, he launches its deadly payload at the United States, in long-delayed retribution for a (UN sanctioned!) joint U.S.–USSR strike with low-yield nukes that, in mid-novel, surgically destroys all Chinese land-based missiles to prevent a Chinese nuclear civil war from starting a world conflagration. The United States launches a thousand warheads at the USSR, the USSR responds in kind, and the armies of both sides, after occupying and devastating the southern hemisphere and Europe early in the nuclear winter, mutiny to go home, with predictably awful consequences.

And so on. Particularly moving in the first volume is a scene of mass labor building a new bed for the Yellow River, broad enough for a 1000-year flood. The parade of astronomical numbers recalls Mao's Great Leap Forward. After Wang Feng and his stooge the premier (a Li-Peng-like figure) set up the military dictatorship, the length of the construction site, with its hundred millions on a starvation-rations dole, is turned into one giant, elongated prison camp that now recalls the building of the Great Wall.

As China reenters the "Fourth World," hyperinflation recalls the last days of the Kuomintang in 1949.

These "small" cogs of history-repeating crises are set to climax simultaneously with a secular demographic one (linear, or cyclical on a vaster time scale): the whole earth may now be insufficient to feed China. It is time for new dispensations, embodied in *Yellow Peril*'s heroes, who otherwise are stock heroes competing for the throne with marvelously interlaced pasts.[24]

Ouyang Zhonghua, prophet of Green spirituality, is a mass movement leader and literally a god to peasant survivors of the North China Plain. They build a tall, green idol to *his* god, "Beauty" (a dig at the Goddess of Democracy of Tiananmen, 1989), until the PLA corrals them behind barbed wire after Wang Feng's coup. Ouyang's movement is millenarian, for he predicts, ecstatically, a cataclysmic destruction of consumer–industrial society from its own excesses. His Green solution is to establish utopian collectivist rural societies in China's last remaining wilds. Like Mao Zedong, he will encircle the cities with the countryside. Shi Ge, the emergency coordinator, grants the Greens six wilderness bases disguised as nature preserves, where they can make not Red, but Green Revolution.

Shi Ge condones the bases under a different system only to gain time, until Ouyang is revealed as a false prophet. In good times, he is an idealist and a check on rampant consumerism; in bad times, he becomes a hegemon. China descends into anarchy, not from radiation after the U.S.–USSR joint strike, but from loss of faith in the government. Wang Feng falls, organized life disintegrates, and the Chinese people start emigrating. Ouyang expands his bases, like Mao, using the gun and a Green *Party* to conquer China's new Mad-Max society. But the Green Movement splits. Ouyang descends into feeding a private army of attack dogs with human corpses, in an episode uncomfortably like the Lord of the Canines scene in Mo Yan's *Red Sorghum*.[25]

The *qigong* master, with the People's Armed Police as his puppets, also gets to rule the superstitious masses of North China as emperor (literally). But ancient ways cannot unite China, much less establish a Great Peace to pacify the world.

The South has its candidate: Huang Shike, venal Party boss of Fujian, supported by a smuggling empire and wealthy local entrepreneurs who detest the North's antediluvian despotism and Yellow River obscurantism.[26] Inspired and assisted by Taiwan, the South secedes, Wang Feng nukes Taibei, and the Southern retaliation brings chaos, until the joint U.S.–USSR strike triggers a total meltdown of China. Huang Shike, America's favorite, reincarnates Chiang Kai-shek. He rules from Nanjing.

Shi Ge is revealed as the true savior, but only in the fullness of time. He protects the autonomous bases and promotes their new hybrid "potato–melons," which grow rapidly in portable pipes from a feeding liquid made of virtually any kind of waste. They need neither soil nor, portentously, sunlight.

Shi Ge is not a revolutionary cult leader, but a Kang-Youwei-style sage with a Hundred Word Constitution in three articles: "1. With a two-thirds majority, each social unit of n individuals (with $3 < n < 9$) elects its leader. These leaders, in a group of n individuals, then elect their leader, level by level on up. Terms are not fixed. Units may choose a new leader whenever they please. 2. Those who belong to multiple social organizations have the franchise in each. 3. Assisting in carrying out public duties shall be those with power delegated by the leader" (1:88). This system might seem utopian, a recipe for endless meetings, or a revisiting of the ancient *baojia* mutual surveillance system. But to Shi Ge, bottom-up rule by voters having face-to-face knowledge of their elected is a perfect middle path between top-down dictatorship and "mechanical" representative democracy, where voters elect strangers and are powerless between elections. This is Wang Lixiong's revelation (*apokalypsis*) for humankind.

Whence the "yellow peril"? Shi Ge has planned all along for the last judgment. As UN-named premier of China after the U.S.–USSR surgical nuclear strike, Shi Ge preplans dissemination of the miracle potato–melon technology worldwide (as advance payment for what China is about to do), while buying up all the world's big ships. The portable potato–melon-growing apparatus will feed the conquerors and the conquered.

A miracle occurs as the refugees stand poised to occupy their first European target area, now in nuclear winter. The great Chinese host, in divisions and squads named after provinces and counties of the mother country, transforms itself into a bottom-up Hundred Word Constitution command system. A Chinese commander is captured, but Shi Ge's system works. A newly elected officer inherits the position in minutes.

The morality and logic of Chinese neocolonialism is never questioned, nor is the effect of nuclear radiation given its due. The inference is that the world was on the road to destruction even before the war, and it was an evil consumerist place anyway. Having found the key to utopia in the Hundred Word Constitution, China will plant its salvational cultural-political "seeds" (which is the Chinese millenarian word for "the saved") worldwide through its emigrants, and they will convert the natives. Shi Ge has saved the world not from Armageddon, but for a millennium that will come once the sky lights up again. Wang Lixiong takes his Constitution seriously; *Yellow Peril* is ultimately a "scholar's novel"—a platform for his political theories.

MIDDLEBROW ANTICORRUPTION NOVELS

Lu Tianming's *Heaven Above* and Zhang Ping's *Choice*, with their socially besieged reformer heroes, resemble the full-length *Bildungsroman* of a young or middle-aged party loyalist fighting the system, pioneered by Ke Yunlu in *New Star*,[27] and Jiang Zilong in his 1979–1980 stories about factory managers. Those episodic works, in turn, recall the *Romance of the Three Kingdoms*. A new man born to lead (like Jiang's "Manager Qiao") builds coalitions against a rival faction for power, aided by a master strategist and personal confidant who alone understands him (a *zhiji*, playing Zhuge Liang to his Liu Bei). Edward Said finds similar male pairings, likewise undistracted by any "domestic or amorous connection between the sexes," in adventure, frontier, and picaresque tales of the West, from Don Quixote and Sancho Panza to Batman and Robin.[28] Zhuge Liang, however, serves not just Liu Bei, but all his Han ancestors. The heroes of *Choice* and *Heaven*

Above do not seem loyal to Mao any more, although they may still owe some allegiance to Marx.

In both *Heaven Above* and *Choice*, the hero heads a large city, which gives him oversight of a giant state enterprise—respectively, a new joint-enterprise car factory and a huge sunset-industry textile plant employing 20,000. The reader is expected to get a *frisson* just to see a mayoral-level official leave his car and walk freely among the people. In both cases, corruption has reached an end-of-dynasty level. In *Heaven Above*, 42-year-old (young!) technician Huang Jiangbei returns in an emergency to be the acting mayor of his home city after the suicide of the previous mayor, who had taken bribes. He will answer the question: so if you complaining intellectuals were put in charge, what would you do about corruption? Li Gaocheng, who in 1996 is the mayor of a city of three million in the more conservative novel *Choice* (printed by the publishing arm of the Ministry of Public Security), was promoted to the municipal level some years before, from the position of factory manager of the textile plant. It is now bankrupt and unable to repay its loans. The workers, who have not been paid in a year, go hungry and without utilities in slum-like dormitories on the factory grounds. The managers want to declare the plant bankrupt—after stripping it of its assets. The car plant in the other novel, a sinkhole for money, has not produced a single vehicle after years of preparation. When a testing facility goes bad from substandard construction, the American coinvestors prepare to pull out. These are mystery novels. The puzzles are: where did the money go, who got it, why, and can the corrupted be replaced, or does their backing go too high? There is also a more "serious" interest in character. Will the hero reformer survive, or will he join the corrupted?

It appears that the corruption does go just too high. The end is surely near. When Li Gaocheng investigates the factory he once ran, he discovers that every person he put in power to carry on after he joined the municipal government—his handpicked plant manager, plant party secretary, purchasing officer—have all gone bad. The provincial party committee secretary, who promoted Li to mayor, heads the whole racket. Li's wife and her relatives are also on the take, which requires him to prove his own innocence. *Choice* is establishmentarian because Li extricates himself through superhuman incorruptibility (he must reject his wife and lose his children, who side with her), with help in the end from Party Central.

By creating polar clashes of interest, as in Mao-era fiction, *Choice* proceeds through four quasi-dialectical stages. In the first, "discovery" stage, workers-say chapters alternate with managers-say ones. Either side could be telling the truth. The second stage moves on to action and investigation, with attacks, counterattacks, and counter-counterattacks by the good and the bad. Mayor Li visits a portion of the factory that has been privatized and turned into a successful sweatshop. Security guards beat him up. The third stage alternates between fast and slow movements, as Li discovers his own unknowing complicity in the crimes. The final dialectic, the denouement, is one of high and low, as Li is rescued by the very highest party levels, but partly because demonstrating factory workers demand it. He is a prophet of less corrupt days to come, but not from charisma like Ouyang Zhonghua's; more like

Shi Ge, he delivers technical facts (in world-ending numbers), which he has uncovered as an unassuming detective. He displays integrity with inner strengths and motivations as fully masked as those of the incorruptible Judge Bao on the Peking opera stage.

Heaven Above, by contrast, is the rare mystery thriller that lets its savior fall, though the plot and characters remain stereotyped. The head conspirator is at the provincial level again: Vice Governor Tian, who leads a sybaritic life and has put an extraordinary number of Tians on the car factory payroll. His sons are his agents. One has built an airplane factory in Russia with a slush fund provided by the car factory. Huang's temptress is a Tian, too. The mayor is surrounded; his own secretary is a spy for the vice governor.

What is to be done when the stolen money is found? Should it be kept, as evidence, or should it immediately be plowed back into the system to fill people's unmet needs? The first choice establishes rule of law; the second keeps the reforms going and food on the table for the masses. There is also a struggle between the powerful, themselves divided into inner and outer palace factions, and the disempowered, who are likewise divided against themselves, into geographically outer, poor mountain farmers who need classrooms for their children, and factory workers, who need employment and bread on the table. Regardless of Huang's war on corruption, the Americans must see the factory produce cars or they will pull out and the municipality will be held back for a generation. Acting Mayor Huang—who fears rocking the boat before he is formally appointed mayor—chooses to hire teachers and preserve jobs. That means cutting corners; he has, unfortunately, declined to shut down a corrupt brake-manufacturing subsidiary of the plant, in order to maintain employment and start production. On the day of Mayor Huang's triumph, the first car off the assembly line, overloaded with teachers and students from the mountain village (a former revolutionary base, symbolic of the communist party), comes down the slopes toward town. Its brakes fail; the price of Huang's compromise falls due. His plans for village, factory, and administrative reform crash simultaneously.

Yet it is *Choice*, the more establishment novel, that directly broaches the fall of communism. Why do China's leaders risk their careers by stealing so much cash *money*, when they already live in such luxury through the party free supply system? Because, having lost faith in the party's future, they are preparing for life abroad after the regime falls. Unlike Wang Lixiong in 1991, these officials *have* seen the end of the USSR.

Still, Lu Tianming and Zhang Ping exalt stoic figures working toward a restoration of old values and preservation of the regime a few years longer. This is "elite messianism" like that of China's medieval Daoists. Danger evidently lies in *self-appointed* messiahs from the masses.

THE REPUBLIC OF WINE

Before *The Republic of Wine*, Mo Yan had written of corruption in his 1987–1988 work, *The Garlic Ballads*. It, too, has apocalyptic overtones.

Early chapters tell of age-old rural conflicts, in nonlinear fashion, until, finally, local officials aggravate the peasants to riot. The layered flashbacks and uncertainty about which narrative voice is speaking are Faulknerian in difficulty, and each chapter is headed by a piece of a blind minstrel's folk ballad. His premonitions of antigovernment sentiment are mystifying until the climax, at which point they are revealed as prophetic, like the little boys' ditties in a Ming novel.[29]

Mo Yan, like Su Tong, Li Rui, Han Shaogong, and A Cheng, lets his rural characters speak in a timelessly apolitical idiom like their forebears', which seems perforce anachronistically "pre-Mao." Peasants refer to local leaders not as cadres, but as "officials" (*guan*). This contests the very existence of communist social change, if not the modernity of the twentieth century. It takes *The Republic of Wine* to contest the modern logic that characters cannot exchange identity, and that if A precedes B, B cannot be the cause of A.

The Republic of Wine originated amid post-Tiananmen hopelessness, like *Yellow Peril*. Mo Yan began his novel in 1989, three months after the massacre. The final 1992 version is a novel of outrageously tall tales far more comic and ribald than *The Garlic Ballads*, and with widescreen technicolor images like *Red Sorghum*'s, not all of which occur in nature.[30] In *The Republic of Wine*, a detective from the procuratorate goes out to verify a report that corrupt urban officials in Liquorland regularly feast on cooked baby boys. Evidence of the crime is everywhere and yet never definitive, for the perpetrators claim that they serve *mock* baby. At the end of the novel, the befuddled hero is a wanted murderer and the only verified criminal in the book—by his lights, which, certainly, can at every stage be contested.

The theme of cannibalism recalls Lu Xun, whose 1918 story "A Madman's Diary" imagined China as a society in which every citizen hungered to eat every other.[31] A Borgesian variation on the whodunit formula seems obvious when Ding Gouer, the investigator, calls Liquorland a labyrinth.[32] There are surrealistic and hallucinatory metaphors and much magical realism; García Márquez was all the rage in China when Mo Yan wrote. A run-on unpunctuated soliloquy in Mo Yan's own voice at the end (which he deleted from the PRC edition) is like Molly Bloom's, though, to some readers, it may evoke classical Chinese, which seems acronymic when read today and is unpunctuated.[33] Because, in life, official banqueting is at the taxpayer's expense and grossly elaborate, it has been an emblem of official corruption throughout the post-Mao era. The fastidiousness of Chinese gastronomy has been satirized and critiqued as decadent long before socialism; Mo Yan pushes the satire to new extremes.[34]

Consumerism is the root of evil, as in *Yellow Peril*. There are portents, bestiality, and numerology. But *The Republic of Wine* is a postmodern, metafictional work, "about writing": the relationship of texts to other texts, of appearances to reality, and of writing to celebrity. Yet, in the plot, writing decays, in modern Chinese practice, generally, and in "Mo Yan's" art in particular. The metafictional subject is thus enfolded within a framing narrative of corruption. The novel ends when all its narrative threads, with all their micro-, macro-, and meta-cogs, make one final turn together, toward a moral and historical abyss. That feels apocalyptic.

The narrative threads are four in number, and are separate. Each thread is narrated serially, one installment per chapter. The installments link up if one skips the intervening installments from the other three threads, yet, in any given chapter, the four threads also relate to each other, reflexively. The first thread is the story of Li Gouer, a detective. Its plot is conventionally narrated, but the characters are fantastic and clues lead only to bewilderment. The second thread is letters from an imaginary and sycophantic would-be disciple of Mo Yan, the celebrity writer, one Li Yidou (One-Pint Li), a doctoral candidate of liquor studies at the Liquorland Brewers University. He wants to change his line to literature and hopes Mo Yan can help. The third thread is letters in response from "Mo Yan," self-dramatized. The fourth thread is nine short stories by Li Yidou, sent to "Mo Yan" for them to be published.

We know Mo Yan to be the meta-author of all four threads of writing, but "Mo Yan" is also a character. The first thread, ostensibly a draft of "a novel by Mo Yan" called *The Road to Liquorland* (according to the third thread), borrows characters that Li Yidou describes in his letters and puts into his short stories, since Li is a Liquorland native. "Mo Yan's" letters in the third thread have many irreverent things to say about current Chinese literature, and Li's letters make some witty observations about Mo Yan and his colleagues. Thus go the nine main chapters (nine is *jiu*, yet another homophone of "liquor"). Chapter ten is a metafictional epilogue.

In the primary narrative, Procurator Ding Gouer travels to a mine in Liquorland to prosecute crimes of cannibalism, which epitomize the arrogance and corruption of the mine director, the party secretary, and their abettor, the deputy head of municipal propaganda, Diamond Jin. The officials are unremarkable; the party boss and mine director are so indistinguishable (at least to Ding, who is in his cups by the time he meets them) that even the narrative voice, evidently dependent on the inadequate Ding, resorts to citing them, with crescendoing comic effect, as "the mine director or party secretary, whichever." The local custom is for all citizens to drink dozens, yea scores of glasses of liquor at every meal, to drink toasts in multiples of three or nine to commemorate every change of venue, and to cure drunkenness with more infusions of alcohol. At one decadent banquet, the director or party secretary, whoever, sets a braised boy before the detective. Though ready to make his arrest, Ding is soon convinced, perhaps by the liquor, that it is mock baby; he samples a little arm that may just be an oddly shaped lotus root. He is assailed by doubts again, but passes out. So it goes; evidence accumulates on both sides of the case that decadence has reached the point of cannibalism, and then again that it might be a misunderstanding. Ding Gouer also meets an amorous but foul-mouthed female truck driver whose fickleness will be his ruination, and a wine shop proprietor who is a dwarf. There are few characters; it is magical how they are all related to each other. The truck driver seduces Ding, and she is also Diamond Jin's wife and the dwarf's ninth mistress. Ding murders both the woman and the dwarf out of jealousy. At the very end, he slips into an open public toilet and drowns.

Li Yidou's creations have plots that connect up in serial fashion, too, though the individual installments stand alone as stories and are written in different styles. All are dreadfully solipsistic, focusing on Liquorland, the author Li Yidou and friends, Li's father-in-law, a professor of brewery who lived with the apes and discovered how they invented liquor millennia ago ("ape wine" is a homophone of "original wine"), Li's mother-in-law, born into a family that gathered swallows' nests (a decadent gourmet food) and whom he loves more than his wife, and, finally, the dwarf. Besides being bad, sophomoric writings that overuse plot management techniques of the traditional Chinese novel for self-promotion ("dear reader, I'll bet you were wondering how I learned to make Red-maned Stallion Wine. Well, now I'm going to tell you"), Li Yidou's stories appear to be parodies and pastiches of modern Chinese literary styles and authors. They resonate horizontally with the other, parallel, threads, but considered individually and vertically, they seem to be: (i) a platitudinous lecture by Diamond Jin (possibly a representation of Chinese reportage); (ii) a story of "grim realism" about ignorant peasants taking their baby boy to the slaughterhouse (a pastiche of Lu Xun stories like "Medicine"); (iii) a tale in which a horrific scaly dwarf disguised as a "meat child" (a baby bred specifically for the market and not, therefore, seen as human) leads a rebellion of "meat boys" to escape from the slaughterhouse (this is described by "Mo Yan," acting as critic in the third thread, as "demonic realism"—it may be a take-off on Wang Shuo, the "hoodlum writer"); (iv) a description of Liquorland's Donkey Avenue, where, for centuries, donkeys have been slaughtered for banquets, with the genitals as the *pièce de résistance* (an appearance by the scaly demon as a knight-errant transforms this into a martial-arts novel of the sort popular in China since 1985); (v) a hagiography of the hero dwarf, his sexual conquests, and his heroic entrepreneurship, backed up by historical chronicles (a send-up of titillating novels and literary promotions of entrepreneurs—almost prophetic of Jia Pingwa's 1993 sensation, *The Ruined City* [*Feidu*], and mid-1990s "enterprise fiction," respectively); (vi) "Cooking Lesson," in which Li Yidou's mother-in-law teaches a class on how to braise babies (touted by "Mo Yan" as neo-realism); (vii) "Swallows' Nests," about the mother-in-law's childhood (a seeming parody of Mo Yan's own *Red Sorghum*, which amazed Chinese readers because it has a grandson tell the story who imagines himself as his grandmother); (viii) "Ape Liquor," in which the father-in-law quarrels with his wife and takes off to find the primal liquor of the primates (this is "literature in quest of roots," the 1986 style of Han Shaogong, Li Hangyu, and Mo Yan); and (ix) "Liquorville," one long advertisement for Liquorland dressed up as literature, like the crassly commercial literature that, according to many writers, dominates China today.[35]

Rabelaisian humor, punning, and plot magic accompany the characters as they undergo transformations, perform miraculous feats, and turn up in plots of the wrong thread. Sometimes a character or trope will appear in

"Mo Yan's novel" before it appears in Li Yidou's stories, a paradox. Oxymorons like those in *Red Sorghum* are everywhere.[36] A sense of uncanny coincidence comes from the preoccurence, in unremarkable expository sentences, of particular words ("scaly," "loach," "40 thieves," "sharp teeth," "ape," and "donkey") that a chapter later turn out to be referents for emerging subplots. The oxymorons and linguistic precognition, like the novel's self-referentiality, beget a dreamlike sense of free association. They also function as foreshadowing, if not prophecy, like the blind minstrel's songs in *The Garlic Ballads*. The final, tenth, chapter, with the "Molly Bloom" finale representing "Mo Yan's" musings as he detoxifies in the Liquorland hospital, is explicitly metafictional. "Mo Yan" has finally come to Liquorland as a character, for a visit; his actions are related by a Super Ego who speaks of him in the third person, as the hermit crab's shell he must inhabit.

Yet there are even more allegorical themes that let the end of *society* frame the abstract metafictional themes. Drunkenness is a recurring motif that climaxes at the end, when the four separate cogs of drunken decadence come together. After his Lu Xun pastiche, Li Yidou's writing descends progressively into absurdity and solipsism, until finally he merely writes advertisements for his land and his people (like so many Chinese nationalists). "Mo Yan" as critic (the voice of the third stream) tries persistently to nudge One-Pint Li onto a more literary path, only to embrace his crassest work in the end.

This serves as a foil to a parallel problem in the first thread, the artificiality of "Mo Yan's" "own" novel, about Ding Gouer's inept investigations. As Ding acts more and more outrageously, "Mo Yan's" own writing becomes ever more desultory. Ding shoots off his pistol and takes off his pants at the wrong times because he has become a drunkard. So has "Mo Yan," author of the first thread of narrative, who takes his materials from the nine stories of the potted Li Yidou. At the end, the self-dramatized "Mo Yan" fully succumbs to temptation and joins Li Yidou in Liquorland—to help write copy for its self-promotion, and even an authorized heroic biography of the dwarf, since he is the richest entrepreneur around. "Mo Yan," thus, embodies the decadence of literature as fully as One-Pint Li. In the end, "Mo Yan" passes out.

One may call this ending, of the first thread and of the novel as a whole, anticlimactic and absurd, rather than apocalyptic.[37] But literature is in decline; witness Li Yidou's stories. The decadence that "Mo Yan" claims for his characters is a genuine historical tragedy. "Mo Yan's" decadence, too, is tragic, and it makes sense because four cogs turn together. There looms an end to Li Yidou's authorial ambition, to whatever was promising in the new Chinese literature his stories mimic, to "Mo Yan's" detective novel, *his* creativity, and Liquorland.

Further, the characters' mindless drunken antics, even when they congeal as a trope of the high cultural artifact called literature, point back to social causes *behind* literature's decadence. The real Mo Yan was a teenager during the Cultural Revolution; he has seen the stark transition from utopian socialism to a dog-eat-dog market economy. Not only Diamond Jin, the woman trucker, and the dwarf, but the whole syndrome of liquor production, the liquorification of society, and the production of new culinary delicacies—human babies if need be—appear to signify the new market economy. A final confirmation is the prominence of Maoist slogans in the five-page single-sentence unpunctuated stream-of-consciousness passage that ends the novel. The problem of social coherence and unity has been transposed, as in socialist fiction, into a conventional problem of system.

Ding Gouer, thus, signifies the remnants of Chinese government, no longer committed to socialism, but hoping to discover some kind of integrity beyond commercialism—some higher mission for himself (itself). The Liquorland mine director and Communist Party secretary, whichever, no longer belong to Ding's calling (the stewardship of governance), having been wholly captured by the market; they glory in their locality's notoriety for producing great new liquors and culinary inventions for export. Flanking Ding Gouer, on the other side, is an old revolutionary who guards the martyrs' cemetery. Rats have already gnawed away his face when Ding Gouer reencounters him after having murdered the trucker and the dwarf in a mad rage; as a representative of the Chinese government as it now is, Ding shoots in the direction of the revolutionary to preserve his corpse from the rats, but, in so doing, inadvertently hits the face and makes a bigger hole. Those who come later will naturally charge him (the government) with the murder— with killing the revolution(ary). Yet none of the deaths—of the revolution, the government as it is now, or the most outrageous entrepreneurs—will stop the final turn of the cycle, which will bring down the whole corrupt society with all its little cogs turning within their respective Maoist, capitalist, or market socialist cycles. Gazing at "a rotten head of cabbage, half a clove of garlic, and a hairless donkey tail, silently clumped together," "the investigator mused agonizingly that these three lifeless objects should be taken together as symbols for the flag of a kingdom in decay; even better, they could be carved on his own tombstone" (p. 243/203).

CONCLUSION

Apocalypticism is not the norm in China today, although it infuses the burgeoning evangelical Christian and *qigong* sects. "Crisis consciousness" and interest in Samuel P. Huntington's ideas of civilizational clashes have also come and gone.[38] It is unfashionable, in this era of Chinese economic prowess, to contest Cold War discourses of modernization and modernity, even if their justifying morality creates malaise and guilt. No novel discussed herein opposes "progress" or advocates "traditional values."

Expectations of a cataclysmic destruction of the current system are, nevertheless, common. The triumph of Chinese apocalyptic thinking may be that communism, which aimed at its own end-time utopia, has been absorbed into Chinese history as just another impermanent dynastic regime. Cyclical ideas of history are, at least, more comforting than the idea of a future dissolving of Chinese culture and power in a Western-defined globalization.

Certainly Marxism's narrative has lost most of its force. Great political–economic systems are to regimes as kalpas are to dynasties. It is hard to imagine kalpas rising and falling within the span of a mere dynasty, or rival economic systems rising and falling during a single regime. The novels fear reversion to Maoism, whose permanent revolution was actually cyclical, reactionary, restorationist, or, as Wang Lixiong hints, "fascist." Communism's real linear meaning was permanent deferment of gratification.

The Chinese have waited over a century for a revelation of a new purpose for humankind on earth. The nation's writers and intellectuals will surely remain in the forefront of the search for it. They need not forget the ancestral knowledge, that many cycles in succession can add up to a vast, forward-moving line, and that lines, at the micro level, may be composed of endless cycles end-on-end.

NOTES

I thank the Rutgers University Center for the Critical Analysis of Contemporary Culture, John Gillis, Eviatar Zerubavel, and Carolyn Williams for critiquing an earlier version of this chapter, and also Columbia University's April 2000 "Contested Modernities" conference and its conveners, Charles Laughlin and David Der-wei Wang, for their friendship and advice.

1. Susan Daruvala, *Zhou Zuoren and an Alternative Chinese Response to Modernity* (Cambridge: Harvard University Press, 2000).

2. Li Shiyu, *Xiandai Huabei mimi zongjiao* (Chengdu: Academia Sinica, 1948); Susan Naquin, *Millenarian Rebellion in China: The Eight Trigrams Uprising of 1813* (New Haven: Yale University Press, 1976); Daniel L. Overmeyer, *Folk Buddhist Religion: Dissenting Sects in Late Traditional China* (Cambridge: Harvard University Press, 1976); Zhou Yumin and Shao Yong, *Zhongguo banghui shi* (Shanghai: Shanghai renmin chubanshe, 1993); David Ownby, "Chinese millenarian traditions: the formative age," *American Historical Review* 104:5 (December 1999), 1513–1530.

3. Paul A. Cohen, "Time, culture, and Christian eschatology: the year 2000 in the West and the world," *American Historical Review* 104:5 (December 1999), 1615–1628.

4. Deng Zhaoming, "Recent millennial movements in mainland China: three cases," *Japanese Religions* 23:1–2 (January 1998), 99–109. Ownby, "Chinese millenarian traditions," p. 1513.

5. Anthony Giddens, "A phenomenology of modernity," *The Consequences of Modernity* (Stanford: Stanford University Press, 1990), p. 138.

6. Revulsion at the Cultural Revolution gives an apocalyptic edge to dystopian post-Mao novels such as Bai Hua's *Yuanfang youge nüer guo* (Beijing: Renmin wenxue chubanshe, 1988).

7. Bao Mi (pseud. of Wang Lixiong), *Huang huo* (Taibei: Fengyun shidai, June 1991), 3 vols.

8. Geremie Barmé, "To screw foreigners is patriotic," *In the Red: On Contemporary Chinese Culture* (New York: Columbia University Press, 1999), p. 261.

9. Francis Fukuyama, *The End of History and the Last Man* (New York: Free Press, 1992).

10. Lu Tianming, *Cangtian zai shang* (Shanghai: Shanghai wenyi, 1995). Zhang Ping, *Jueze* (Beijing: Qunzhong chubanshe, 1997).

11. Mo Yan, *Jiu guo* (Taibei: Hongfan shudian, 1992). *The Republic of Wine*, trans. Howard Goldblatt (New York: Arcade, 2000). *Jiu³ guo²* (lit., "liquor nation" or "liquoring up the nation") puns on "national salvation," *jiu⁴ guo²*.

12. Most post-Mao Chinese fiction was "popular" in style; Jeffrey C. Kinkley, "Introduction: the revival of law and literature in China," *Chinese Justice, the Fiction: Law and Literature in Modern China* (Stanford: Stanford University Press, 2000), p. 9, "Politics," 242, 244, 260–269. Yet Chinese literature's self-appointed "mission," from 1917 through the 1980s, was averse to commercial success, much as theorized by Pierre Bourdieu, *The Field of Cultural Production: Essays on Art and Literature*, ed. and intro. by Randal Johnson (New York: Columbia University Press, 1993). That time has passed.

13. Raymond F. Bulman, "Millennial religious response," *The Lure of the Millennium: The Year 2000 and Beyond* (Maryknoll, NY: Orbis, 1999), pp. 62–66. Eugen Weber, "Conclusion," *Apocalypses: Prophecies, Cults, and Millennial Beliefs Through the Ages* (Cambridge: Harvard University Press, 1999), p. 234.

14. Ownby, "Chinese millenarian traditions," p. 1528.

15. Philip A. Kuhn, *Soulstealers: The Chinese Sorcery Scare of 1768* (Cambridge: Harvard University Press, 1990).

16. Stephen R. Bokenkamp, "Time after time: Taoist apocalyptic history and the founding of the T'ang dynasty," *Asia Major* 3rd ser. 7:1 (1994), 64.

17. N[athan] Sivin, "On the limits of empirical knowledge in the traditional Chinese sciences," *Time, Science, and Society in China and the West*, ed. J.T. Fraser, N. Lawrence, and F.C. Haber (Amherst, MA: University of Massachusetts Press, 1986), p. 152. Cf. Wall Street's "triple witching hour"; or the simultaneous ending of a business cycle, a Kondratieff long wave (20 years), and a post-dependency-theory 300-year really long wave; André Gunder Frank, *ReORIENT: Global Economy in the Asian Age* (Berkeley: University of California Press, 1998).

18. Anna K. Seidel, "The image of the perfect ruler in early Taoist messianism: Lao-tzu and Li Hung," *History of Religions* 9:2/3 (November 1969 and February 1970), 216–247. B.J. ter Haar, *Ritual and Mythology of the Chinese Triads: Creating an Identity* (Leiden: E.J. Brill, 1998), and *The White Lotus Teachings in Chinese Religious History* (Leiden: E.J. Brill, 1992). See also Li Shiyu, *Xiandai Huabei mimi zongjiao*; Overmeyer, *Folk Buddhist Religion*.

19. Benedict Anderson, "Cultural roots," *Imagined Communities: Reflections on the Origin and Spread of Nationalism*, rev. ed. (1983; London: Verso, 1998), pp. 24–26. The interior phrase is from Walter Benjamin, "Theses on the philosophy of history," "Editor's Note," *Illuminations*, trans. Harry Zohn (1955; New York: Harcourt, Brace, & World, 1968), pp. 263, 265. Cf. Sivin, "On the limits of empirical knowledge," p. 152.

20. As known not just by Michael Crichton and Tom Clancy, but also Tim LaHaye and Jerry B. Jenkins. Their *Left Behind: A Novel of Earth's Last Days* (Wheaton, IL: Tyndale House, 1995), about "the Rapture," and 11 subsequent books (over 40 million copies sold) and films end with Christ's Second Coming in *Glorious Appearing: The End of Days* (Wheaton, IL: Tyndale House, 2004).

21. Lu Tonglin, *Misogyny, Cultural Nihilism, and Oppositional Politics: Contemporary Chinese Experimental Fiction* (Stanford: Stanford University Press, 1995), argues that avant-garde novelists, including Mo Yan, are misogynist, perhaps from opposition to the larger system of communism, which upheld feminist discourse. Some millenarian sects of North China, such as those called "White

Lotus," had a female savior—the Eternal Unborn Mother (see Li Shiyu, *Xiandai Huabei mimi zongjiaro*, Overmeyer, *Folk Buddhist Religion*).

22. Bulman *The Lure of the Millennium*, p. 229.

23. These dyads launch their A-bombs at each other after the U.S.–USSR full nuclear exchange. The power that prevails in the aftermath is Japan. Wang did not surmise that both Koreas' missiles might be aimed at Japan.

24. For example, in the weaker "apocalypse" of the GPCR, Shi Ge saved Ouyang Zhonghua from the extreme left.

25. Mo Yan, *Red Sorghum*, trans. Howard Goldblatt (New York: Viking, 1993), pp. 207–220.

26 Like the banned 1987 TV series that pitted an ingrown "Yellow" civilization of the North China Plain against a littoral and ocean-going "Blue" civilization of modernity. Su Xiaokang and Wang Luxiang, *Deathsong of the River: A Reader's Guide to the Chinese TV Series HESHANG* (Ithaca: Cornell University East Asia Program, 1991).

27. Ke Yunlu, *Xin xing* (*New star*), *Dangdai* suppl. 3 (August 1984).

28. Edward W. Said, "The pleasures of imperialism" *Culture and Imperialism* (1993; New York: Random House, 1994), p. 138.

29. Mo Yan, *Tiantang suan tai zhi ge* (Taibei: Hongfan, 1989); *The Garlic Ballads*, trans. Howard Goldblatt (New York: Penguin, 1995). This novel seems prophetic of the 1992–1993 tax protest by 15,000 peasants who burned down the county offices in Renshou, Sichuan, but Mo Yan says the plot is based on a real 1987 revolt of garlic farmers in his native Shandong. Personal interview, March 26, 2000.

30. Small-screen, but uniquely Chinese, is Mo Yan's description of rats who, in their hurry to flee, "cursed their parents for not giving them four more legs" (p. 379/326). (Chinese edition pagination first, followed by the English translation.)

31. Mo Yan has not read Swift. Personal interview, March 23, 2000. A Qing dynasty book of literati stories that Mo Yan read before penning *The Republic of Wine* is Ji Xiaolan (Ji Yun, 1724–1805), *Yuewei caotang biji* (*Jottings from the Cottage of Intensive Scrutiny*), (Beijing: Sheng Shiyan, 1800), which speaks of *cairen* (dinner-course people). Personal interview, March 26, 2000.

32. For the record, Mo Yan says he dislikes Borges, who is too difficult; it is other Chinese writers of his generation who idolize Borges. Jeffrey C. Kinkley, "A talk with Chinese novelist Mo Yan," *Persimmon* 1:2 (summer 2000), 64.

33. Wang Meng, "Introduction," *The Stubborn Porridge and Other Stories*, trans. Zhu Hong (New York: George Braziller, 1994), esp. pp. 159–167, parodies China's imitation-Joyce writing.

34. Drinking "Overlapping Green ants," a wine distilled from mung beans, "is akin to listening to a classical beauty play a zither, a magically conceived rendition that has you pondering things from the remote past," *Republic of Wine* (p. 394/339).

35. These inferences about contemporary styles are my speculations only. Mo Yan, in personal interviews, March 23 and 26, 2000, said that story one represented Maoist rhetoric; denied that story seven satirizes *Red Sorghum* ("No, I would never satirize myself!"); denied the (to me, obvious) connection of story eight to root-seeking literature; and said he felt that Li Yidou's stories were "not too bad, though not of the very highest caliber." He does admit to the pastiche of Lu Xun in story two, and at a March 23 talk at Columbia, he hinted that one

of his stories had to do with Wang Shuo—although, in the interview, he said that story three was in the style of Ming and Qing *chuanqi* (supernatural) tales.

36. "Northeast Gaomi Township is easily the most beautiful and most repulsive, most unusual and most common, most sacred and most corrupt, most heroic and most bastardly, hardest-drinking and hardest-loving place in the world." Mo Yan, *Red Sorghum*, p. 4.

37. Xiaobin Yang, "*The Republic of Wine*: An extravaganza of decline," *positions: east asia cultures critique* 6:1 (spring 1998), 12.

38. Jing Wang, *High Culture Fever: Politics, Aesthetics, and Ideology in Deng's China* (Berkeley: University of California Press, 1996), p. 38.

7

A Cruel World: Boundary-Crossing and Exile in *The Great Going Abroad*

Claire Conceison

Both the storyline of the 1991 play *Da liuyang* (*The Great Going Abroad*) and the story of its production are narratives of the dangers and exhilaration of border crossing.[1] In the play, as in its production process, boundaries are contested through adventures of great risk, yielding both tragedy and triumph. In keeping with Una Chaudhuri's definition of geopathology as "the characterization of place as problem"[2] and her identification of protagonists of contemporary drama as displaced subjects inclusive of exiles, immigrants, and refugees, *The Great Going Abroad* presents the geopathic trauma of exile through its protagonist—and he, in turn, embodies the internal exile of his bold and daring creators, Wang Gui and Wang Peigong.

Going Abroad depicts the experience of Gao Yuan, a young Chinese entrepreneur who "strikes it rich" and ventures overseas to the United States, following in the footsteps of his identical twin Gao Shan, a research assistant to a university anthropology professor. After sharing his excitement with the audience in song and animated conversation, Gao Yuan soon "lands" in a land full of linguistic confusion, physical danger, and mistaken identity. He is immediately accosted by lewd women and thieves, and later is intended as the next victim of the butchers who have already viciously murdered his brother. In the process of trying to make sense of the alien environment into which he has been thrust, he is embroiled in a love triangle involving Gao Shan (for whom he is mistaken), the professor's daughter (Susan), and an unwitting villain (Wen Jun), who vies for the affection of both the professor and his daughter and is used as a pawn by the professor's housekeeper (Sisi) to accomplish her evil ends.

Director Wang Gui and the writers of *Going Abroad* used humor and innovative staging techniques to bring to life the contrasts and tensions of Sino-American cross-cultural experience and personal self-discovery. The geopathic figure of Gao Yuan inhabits a physical stage space representing America that is fluid, undefined, and ever-changing: America is even veiled behind the ambiguous pseudonym of "*waiguo*" (foreign country), although it is referenced specifically by cultural markers such as English language use, local colloquialisms, and contemporary American pop songs (and Wang Gui himself referred to the professor and Susan as "American" when discussing the play).[3]

The dark, bizarre fantasy world of *Going Abroad* is characterized by constant motion: bodies, props, and set pieces are always moving. The exiled subject is continually dislocated, disoriented, and even disembodied and dismembered. Time is sometimes displaced along with subject: past and present intersect, overlap, then separate, mirroring the doubling and splitting of the twin protagonists; time is distilled and dizzy, passing rapidly through the series of events (which also are mirrored in contrasting slow-motion dance sequences, which frame the action of the play). One critic compared the performance to "a winged horse galloping freely on stage."[4] The play's treatment of the crisis of self in a frivolous framework, and its mingling of horror and humor, form an uneasy contrast, which threatens to render the narrative ridiculous.

Critical assessment of the play depends on whether its playful "corniness" was intentional or whether it hoped to be taken seriously. If the writers and director consciously adopted such an uncanny and unconventional style, then the play was brilliant: it was so "bad" it was good. On the other hand, if the production was intended as an honest attempt at a morality play dressed up for the 1990s with the added glamour of a star cast, it was indeed ridiculous. This dialectic was later hinted at in one reviewer's commentary: "Some artistic works seem very coarse on the surface, but actually that surface roughness goes through a process of careful composition, craftfully woven into something entirely different than crude and sloppy."[5]

Seen in this light, the project was a triumph of Brechtian *Verfremdungseffekt*, with its variety of distancing stage elements and its invitation to the spectator to reflect in a dialectically critical mode on a multiplicity of available meanings while, at the same time, being thoroughly entertained.

Colleagues who attended the two November 1991 Shanghai performances, as well as artists who participated, were puzzled that a foreign scholar had taken such an interest in this frivolous "plaything," and could not quite grasp the aesthetic paradox described above. It would not be until five years later that director Wang Gui would specifically address the unique and easily misunderstood style of the piece, and also reflect upon the deeper resonances of the play's subversive message. Not only was experimentation in the production evidenced by its innovative stage aesthetic and dangerous subtext, but the play crossed untested boundaries, from the moment of its inception, in other ways as well.

RISK, RUIN, REWARD: CROSSING POLITICAL, ARTISTIC, AND GEOGRAPHICAL BOUNDARIES

Significantly, *Going Abroad* was not produced in the usual fashion by a premier professional theater in a major city for a local audience; on the contrary, it was conceived and sponsored by an independent business entrepreneur from Hebei and was performed on tour in remote provinces from June 1991 into 1992. When the production eventually reached Shanghai, it did so as an unpublicized pair of performances in the relatively private setting of the Shanghai Theatre Academy, primarily because its star, popular screen actor Zhang Qiuge, is a 1984 graduate. The only published reviews (cited earlier) appeared two months later in *Shanghai Theatre* magazine, a local subscription periodical. These articles describe the play as "fashionable [and] stylish"[6] and "a super-amusing variety play"[7]; audiences, likewise, reacted to the play as playful entertainment, enjoying the pertinent theme, diverse performance modes, and Zhang's comic portrayal of the protagonist(s).

From the preceding description, one might infer that the play was unimportant: it did not reach large urban audiences, did not attract the attention of the press and theater critics, and was not a focus of public discussion. One would be grossly mistaken, however, because *The Great Going Abroad* was a small miracle pulled off by one of China's most famous and controversial directors, a dissident playwright, and a crooked and naive businessman.

The play was a unique interpretation of the (by then) popular and well-worn theme of going abroad: on the surface, it was a parody of the motif and the experience itself, but underneath the glossy, hilarious surface was a searing criticism of the Chinese ethos and national character. *Going Abroad* was also the most ambitious experiment in *form* to date; its elements of dialogue, song, dance, and "action sequences" combined realism and absurdism, comedy and tragedy, parody and farce, the beautiful and the grotesque, frustrating those who attempted to classify it. Its portrayal of America and Americans is multifaceted, paradoxical, and open to incongruous readings. Ultimately, the play's setting in America and absurdist presentation masked its utterly serious assessment of China's current predicament. It is a risk Wang Gui had taken before, but 1991 was a particularly precarious time to test such waters again.

The period between *Liu si* ("June Fourth," the massacre in Tiananmen Square on June 4, 1989) and Deng Xiaoping's tour of southern China in early 1992 was an especially tense time for Chinese intellectuals and cultural workers: not since the Cultural Revolution had there been such fear of imprisonment and other repercussions for suggesting opinions counter to the communist/socialist establishment. Wang's play is situated squarely in this context. Its final performances came just before the reform and opening launched by Deng's economic campaign, which loosened the tight ideological grip of the government as it promoted free-market capitalism. Later that year, Politburo propaganda chief Li Ruihuan announced a relaxation of political control for the first time since June Fourth, deemphasizing the use of art for "political education" in an official speech, which invited increased production of "politically harmless, artistically superior, crowd-pleasing works."[8] Wang's project came too early to enjoy the protection of such a policy.

Although it emerged after the 1989 crackdown, *Going Abroad* aspired to the principles of the cultural discourse of the late 1980s that June Fourth had interrupted. In the words of Zhang Longxi, the 1980s was "a period of

cultural critique and the attempt at liberation of the mind . . . in which
Chinese intellectuals played an important role . . . in opening up windows
toward the outside world and introducing new ideas and values into the cultural arena of post-Mao China."[9] Despite intermittent periods of repression
signaled by campaigns against "spiritual pollution" and "bourgeois liberalization" throughout the 1980s, literature and art that contested the status
quo (party corruption, official versions of the Cultural Revolution, the government's approach to modernization) *was* publicly produced and debated
during the decade preceding June Fourth.

In fact, it was during this time that Wang Gui became the controversial figure he remains today. He was centerstage as a director, playwright, and critic
during the mid-1980s when a string of "controversial" plays was publicly produced in theaters, then printed and discussed in published journals. Among
these plays was a play called *W.M.*, penned by Wang Peigong and later revised
for performance by Wang Gui, who directed its premiere in Beijing in 1985.
W.M. boldly addresses the emotional turmoil and ideological disillusionment
triggered by the political upheavals its characters (returned "sent down"
youth from the rural reeducation campaigns of the Cultural Revolution) have
endured, including the reform period that was then underway.

Wang Gui, head of the Air Force Drama Troupe at the time, faced severe
criticism from authorities, but opened dress rehearsal to an influential public,
which included artists and the press. The production was subsequently dis-
mantled and internally "sealed off" and both Wangs were dismissed from
their posts in the Air Force. Though stigmatized by the establishment, Wang
Gui ironically felt more freedom after his dismissal and was able to pursue
projects independently throughout the country.[10] After *W.M.* was banned by
the Air Force, Wang was invited to Shanghai to oversee a production of the
play[11]; at great personal risk, he also restaged it "unofficially" in Beijing when
theater colleagues helped him gather artists from various troupes to form the
cast, a model that would be adopted again for producing *Going Abroad*.

Considering the fate of the two Wangs in the mid-1980s, it is not surprising that Wang Gui forbade their next collaboration, *The Great Going
Abroad*, from being staged in the capital:

> They intended to go to Beijing, but I didn't let them. One reason was because
> there would be problems—there are lots of people looking for problems. The
> other was because the Beijing theatre community would see the play as
> garbage, as something base; and also because in Beijing there are too many
> people trying to find fault, in terms of thinking and politics—there are so many
> "experts." Shanghai was their own idea, they wanted to go. I told them to go
> to cities in central China to perform. I told them not to go to Beijing and
> Shanghai.[12]

By playing remote locales like Xingtai, Shijiazhuang, and Handan (the
producer's hometown), as well as Shandong, Xiancheng, and Nanjing, the play
was able to reach large, enthusiastic audiences without reaching hard-nosed
party officials and cultural bureaucrats.

Wang took considerable risks artistically as well as politically. In addition to the expressionistic modern dance sequences, he devised karaoke-style songs: actors sang into microphones to prerecorded music (or lip-synched to prerecorded vocals) of pop songs written specifically for the play by celebrity artists. He also incorporated slide projections throughout, and commissioned scenic designer Xu Xiang to create the playful, distorted set pieces. One of the most effective innovations was the absurdist approach to physical scale in the play, particularly in the form of under- and over-sized props, which served to elicit both humor (as in the use of hand-held toy cars with realistic sound effects for car chases) and grotesque horror (the exaggerated knives with which victims are butchered for their internal organs). The world of the play is at once playful and eerie, colorful and morose, energetically charged and weighted with doom. These aesthetic paradoxes are very much in keeping with Wang Gui's overall artistic style and outlook; he categorizes his plays as "relatively course and unrefined [with] a folky flavor (*minjian secai*) to them, and more fun in terms of language, etc."[13]

The hybridity of *Going Abroad* is one of its salient features—not only in terms of its amalgamation of aesthetic elements, its cross-cultural content, and its expansive touring itinerary, but also in its collaborative realization by a diverse group of participants ranging from the remote entrepreneur producer to actors from various provinces and several artists from Beijing. Although the play itself was not staged in the capital, many of its key contributors dwell there and, thus, it can still be classified somewhat as a "*jingpai*" (Beijing-style) play.[14]

Had I not spoken with production participants in 1991 and 1996, I would never have known that Wang Peigong actually wrote the play, since his name does not appear on the script, in the few published reviews, or even in the unpublished list of main contributors to the production. With six other collaborators listed in such sources—including three playwrights given credit for various drafts, Wang Gui for production revision, and two lyricists for the original pop songs in the play—Wang Peigong's omission is undoubtedly intentional, and with good reason. Not only was *Going Abroad* produced in the immediate aftermath of June Fourth, but also acknowledgment of Wang Peigong's participation would have linked the play directly to the 1989 democracy movement's most extreme subversive element, Wu'er Kaixi.[15] After the massacre, playwright Wang was accused of helping Wu'er flee the country because the latter had visited his home on June 2 and borrowed 3000 *yuan* (about US$800) from his wife. Wang was not even home at the time, but was arrested anyway and was imprisoned for 14 months. Shortly after his release, Wang Gui met with him in their compound (though dismissed from the Air Force, the two had remained in the housing provided by their work unit) and told him about Hebei entrepreneur Ni Xiancai's invitation to create a new play, upon which he immediately agreed to write the script. According to Wang Gui:

> We talked about it for several days, and then he [Wang Peigong] wrote the draft in a week. Why? Because we had been collaborators for a long time. And when

he came out of prison, he had no money and no creative activity: *Qingyi* [the China Youth Art Theatre, his work unit since leaving the Air Force] would not take him back, so he had no job. In a week, he could get 5,000–6,000 *yuan* from this script: he has a wife and child, so that way he could get by. As soon as I mentioned it, he was thrilled. "How should I write it? How should I write it?" [he said].[16]

At that point, all that existed was a rough storyline, apparently conceived by Ni. In writing the script, the names of the main characters were retained, but Wang Peigong was depended on to shape those characters and create the plot.

Like *W.M.* before it, *Going Abroad* became a collaboration between the two Wangs, with the participation of several other writers as well. The original draft was written by Wang Peigong in Beijing and was rehearsed in Xingtai (in Hebei province), where it was periodically revised. It was Wang Gui who assembled the actors: first Zhang Qiuge (whose work unit was playwright Wang Peigong's former employer, the China Youth Art Theatre), and then Sha Jingchang of the Central Experimental Theatre, and Wang Deshun, an expert mime actor. The female villain was originally played by an actress from Tianjin, later replaced by Mao Lixin of Hebei.[17] Ni Xiancai paid the actors 2000 yuan per month, about 10 times the monthly base salary at a state-owned theatre at the time.

Ni's total investment in the project was considerable, several hundred thousand yuan in Wang Gui's estimation, including 60,000 yuan for the set design, and the cost of the ad hoc troupe's travel and lodging expenses throughout China. When the show docked in Shanghai for its visit to the Theatre Academy, Ni jumped ship; it was at this point that actor Chen Ziqiu stepped in as temporary manager of the ensemble. According to Wang Gui, Ni had borrowed up to 500,000 yuan from the Hebei cultural bureau and other sources (obtaining small amounts of 10,000–20,000 yuan from each lender), thinking that he would make a profit on the production and be able to repay his debts. His business dealings in the past had included opening a factory and a bar, but he was unprepared for an artistic gamble. Even star actors, popular singers, modern dance, and trendy costumes could not draw large affluent audiences to remote locations. Had he known more about the circumstances of theater in China at the time, Ni would have risked his fortune elsewhere: theater in China had been concerned over loss of audiences since the mid-1980s, and its most successful efforts came in the form of highly publicized, long-running plays in Shanghai and Beijing—the two cities in which this project could not be staged. While Ni's financial fiasco ended in his arrest, Wang's creative efforts resulted in a unique production, which sheds light on the shifting position of the newly exiled Chinese individual in a sea of confusing identifications.

Although *Going Abroad*'s protagonist Gao Yuan is not overtly intended as an autobiographical metaphor for his creators, he shares many similarities with them. Like Ni Xiancai and Wang Gui, Gao embarks on a risky venture. With the naiveté and laissez-faire optimism of Ni, Gao finds himself trapped in alien circumstances for which he is utterly unprepared; but with Wang's cunning and wit, he devises an ingenious scheme to overcome his adversity and establish his superiority. Unlike Ni, Gao adapts to his circumstances and prevails, but not completely unscathed; like Wang, his experiences bring him from the brink of his own ruin to confidence in his survival, but with a somber education in the darkest capabilities of humanity along the way.

Wang Gui and Gao Yuan are both survivors. A party member, soldier, and government cultural worker since age 13, Wang endured several humiliating campaigns in his adult life, including three years of hard labor in frigid Heilongjiang with his wife and children, a year of planting rice during re-education in Hubei, and his aforementioned dismissal from the Air Force after staging *W.M.* In this light, critic Lin Xi's classification of Gao Yuan as a *"yang chadui"*[18] has an ironic resonance (*chadui* is the term for urban school graduates who were sent down to rural areas for reeducation during the Cultural Revolution; the prefix *yang* makes Gao Yuan an "overseas *chadui*" and carries a humorous political tone).

Gao Yuan's traumatic encounters overseas can serve as a metaphor for the internal domestic suffering reflected in Wang's own life experiences; Gao's alienation in the dark and confusing environment on an-Other shore is a reflection of the Chinese intellectual exiled in his own homeland. The barbaric foreign Other that murders Gao's brother and then threatens to rip out Gao's heart for personal profit is actually the cannibalistic Chinese Self that Wang Gui recognizes in his fellow countrymen:

> The central point the play expresses is that Chinese people are shooting themselves. The surgeon Wen Jun and Gao Shan are both Chinese; but [Wen] kills Gao Shan and sells his heart to someone else: this is Chinese beating themselves, fighting themselves, and it is very intentional . . . this is a characteristic of our culture [*minzu de liegenxing*], especially during the Cultural Revolution.[19]

Placing the action of the play in an overseas country automatically provides leeway for depictions of unsavory characters and unsettling events; it takes some pressure off of the artists in terms of possible repercussions for investigating darker complexities in Chinese society. This strategy can also be seen as a clever riff of the Brechtian gesture of invoking estrangement by setting action in distant distorted lands. In this case, situating the play in a foreign country can actually encourage negative portrayals of humanity and society, since the gloomier "*waiguo*" appears to be, the brighter China seems in comparison.

Taking Wang Gui's cue, the play is open to interpretation as symbolizing the self-destructive cultural ethos forced onto well-meaning Chinese citizens by the Maoist hysteria of the Cultural Revolution (an allegory that casts Sisi in the role of Mao manipulating the Chinese masses, represented by Wen, in their mutual debilitation). As candidly as Wang Gui summarized the meaning of the play as exposing the murderous tendencies of his own people, he could just as easily (and at far less risk) say that the play condemns idolatry of the overseas Other and the eager embrace of all things Western without consideration of the potentially hazardous consequences. At least one critic interpreted the play's content in this more superficial manner:

> The first thing I felt when seeing *The Great Going Abroad* is that the play did not describe overseas as golden, didn't make it seem like everything over there is wonderful and that everything here is horrible. On the contrary, over there it's dripping with blood, cannibalistic.[20]

The action of the play consistently works on both levels: it materializes the contrasting essentialized images Chinese hold of the United States as both paradise and hell. Americans in the play can be interpreted as catalysts for the destructive sequence of events—but they can also be seen as caught up in the vortex of China's own self-mutilation. Capitalism is imagined as both liberating and deceptive. It is Gao Yuan's financial luck as a *getihu*[21] in China that affords him the resources to leave its confines and venture overseas. Upon arrival in the United States, he exclaims:

> Hey! Pals! What can I say? In this world today, if you have money, you can perform all kinds of miracles! Look: passport, plane tickets, visa, genuine goods at a fair price, everything one would expect. It's just like a fucking dream![22]

But soon after crossing the border, he is stripped of his fortune by street thugs, triggering his geopathic trauma. Double signifiers continually surface: Gao Yuan is impressed with the professor's fast fancy car, but, later in the play, these same "toys" become the instruments of a deadly car chase. While American songs by artists like Michael Jackson and the Talking Heads are incorporated for lighthearted sequences, they also set moods of fear and catastrophe.

America is a place for birthday parties and dancing, the land where Gao Shan and Susan once frolicked on the beach in their young love; but it is also the location of the clinic in which innocent people are led like lambs to the slaughter by evil butchers who sell their organs for profit. In a scene reminiscent of *Hamlet*, Gao Yuan is approached by the ghost of his beheaded twin brother and warned:

> I'm suffering, little brother. They took my heart out and sold it . . . my life was destroyed by them. They will hurt you, too. This place is a cruel world. It's not the place we lived. Get away from here fast—the farther the better.[23]

Although the first Americans encountered by Gao Yuan upon his arrival are unintelligible passersby who confuse him, seductive women who maul him, and violent thugs who rob him, subsequent local citizens attempt to befriend him, and positive images of Americans are also embodied by the kind professor and his innocent daughter, Susan.

In a significant gender reversal of stereotypical Sino-American sexual relations, Susan clearly has a preference for Chinese men. The following exchange occurs during a memory sequence at the beach when she recalls Gao Shan promising to put an engagement ring on her finger at her upcoming birthday party (the actor playing Gao Yuan doubles in the flashback as Gao Shan, who, at this point in the play, is mysteriously missing):

SUSAN:	Gao [Shan], will you stay?
GAO SHAN:	I don't know.
SUSAN:	Mr. "I-don't-know," then what do you know, you pitiful Chinese child?
GAO:	I know that I love you.
SUSAN:	Gao, I need you! Wherever you go I will follow, whether it's to China or West Africa, or even to the moon! . . . [The dreamland disappears. WEN JUN still stands in front of her, clenching her hand.]
WEN JUN [in English]:	I love you [In Chinese]: I love you. Sue! I am also a Chinese man! Why have you never noticed me?
SUSAN:	I can't be without him!
WEN JUN:	He has already disappeared. I am better than Gao Shan in every way . . .[24]

Later, when her father brings Gao Yuan to the party and she believes it is Gao Shan returned after his long absence, Susan concedes to Wen Jun, "If Gao Shan had not come back, maybe I really could have loved you." The presence of several other men at her birthday party (all American men, played by the ensemble of actors) is barely acknowledged by Susan, whose romantic attractions are limited to the Chinese male characters in the play. And yet she never recognizes in any of her scenes with Gao Yuan that he is not her lover, even when he does not know her name, knows nothing about the promised engagement ring, recoils when she tries to kiss him, and cannot play the cello at her request. Characters less involved with Gao Shan notice that Gao Yuan differs from him in physique, intellect, and personality, leading one to speculate whether Susan is deeply connected to the man she wants to marry or is attracted to him as an exotic Other of her imagination.

BLURRING THE BOUNDARY BETWEEN SELF AND OTHER

The racial contrast of Chinese and American characters was handled differently in various staged versions of the play. In the Shanghai production, the actress playing Susan had dyed reddish-blonde hair, clearly designating her as Caucasian. Even more strongly marked was her father, whose western suit, cane, and white wig and beard made him a dead ringer for the Colonel from Kentucky Fried Chicken, by then a common figure in urban Chinese advertising (though the likeness was officially unintentional). In other productions of *Going Abroad* (those in which Susan and the professor were played by different actors), the American father and daughter had no special costume or makeup to indicate they were not Chinese; physical codes of American Otherness such as skin tone, hair color, facial hair, and differences in speech, mannerisms, and style of dress were discarded in favor of signifiers within the text and plot.

Significantly, the ethnicities of the characters encountered by Gao Yuan in the play are determined primarily by his reactions to them. It is in terms of Gao's cultural crisis of self-identity that their Otherness, ethnically and otherwise, takes on meaning. Gao's identity crisis, in turn, is bound to his geopathic trauma as a voluntary exile in a strange land—a land that he expects to welcome him, but that instead confuses, alters, and threatens him. With Gao Yuan as the thematic and physical reference point (the entire play literally revolves around him, both in terms of plot development and actual spatial physicality), other characters take on degrees of Otherness as determined by Gao's interactions with and reactions to them.

The audience must independently register nonvisual cues provided by Gao Yuan in order to continually reconstruct the combinations of ethnicity on stage at any given moment. Because all of the characters, both Chinese and American, wear contemporary Western-style clothing and speak standard Chinese (the language of the play in real time and space, though not in the imaginary world of the play[25]), there are no conventional theatrical semiotics to establish their ethnicities. Awareness that the professor, his daughter, and the various groups played by the ensemble are all American is maintained purely through the cognitive skills of each audience member in association with the linguistic and plot-based indicators that initially establish each character's identity.

One of the effects of this type of representation is that it downplays foreign Otherness and privileges a kind of universality by erasing conventional markers of difference. This approach is in keeping with another of director Wang Gui's objectives:

> My perspective in writing this play was that all humankind is friends, everyone on earth is equal . . . We were not thinking, "down with Americans" (*dadao laomei*) or about Americans putting us down. Everyone at that time [late 1980s–early 1990s] was beset with crises: local wars persisted, famine, AIDS, natural disasters, environmental pollution . . . no one felt like examining these issues . . . everyone should work to comfort the world, comfort the existence of mankind . . . everyone must help carry the load; people must live in community, not keep warring and killing each other . . .[26]

Wang's reflections situate the creation and staging of the play (from 1989 to 1991) in the moment preceding the convergence of the government, intelligentsia, and public in the fervent expression of anti-Americanism that was prevalent by the mid-1990s, the time when I discussed the production with him. The characters' physical representation also foregrounds Wang's intention that the play be considered on a domestic as well as intercultural level: even if the audience is cognizant of the fact that characters engaged in street brawls, car chases, holding each other at gunpoint, and butchering one another for organs are of differing ethnicities, they remain *embodied* by Chinese actors with no striking physical dissimilarities to distinguish their mutual Otherness or distract from their apparent Selfness. The mind may conceive that a street thug is American and Gao Yuan is Chinese, but the eye sees two Chinese men beating one another—wearing the same clothing and speaking the same language. Thus the dual level discussed earlier (of the play seeming to espouse the inherent dangers of naive intercultural contact while simultaneously identifying a ruthless intracultural violence) continues to gain strength as the plot thickens and the play reaches its climactic—and surprising—conclusion.

With its characteristic juxtaposition of comic absurdism and grotesque horror, *Going Abroad* culminates in multiple scenes of violence, which, though tempered by humor, are nonetheless ultimately disturbing. The most shocking and sobering moments come when Gao Yuan unintentionally kills the professor, intentionally murders Wen Jun, and takes a dying Susan into his arms.

Gao's showdowns with the professor and Wen Jun are initially approached with great comic effect. After Gao Yuan is tricked into believing it is the professor who murdered his brother Gao Shan, he holds the professor at gunpoint. When his gun fails to fire, the professor helps him repair it and then turns the gun on him, but soon places it down, laughing, and offers him coffee. During this exchange, Gao Yuan's patriotic holler, "Go ahead and kill me, but the Chinese people can not be exterminated!" elicited applause from the audience. When the professor realizes that Wen Jun has murdered his beloved student Gao Shan, he vows to kill Wen and then allow Gao Yuan to kill him. Gao refuses, reaching for the gun and saying: " 'Repayment for a life taken is the same as for a debt drawn' (*sharen de changming; qianzhai de huanqian*) . . . Now who is the real 'class enemy' after all? Give me the gun!"[27] At this point, the humor is abruptly mixed with melodrama: the professor is accidentally shot in the struggle for the gun and bleeds profusely into a bucket Gao Yuan provides. Gao turns to the audience and quips, "All that blood is fucking capitalist blood!" and offers to donate his own blood, which is *genhong miaozhuang* (red-rooted and strong-seeded) O-type blood. The professor responds by saying that whichever Gao he is (Gao Shan or Gao Yuan), he is a wonderful person and must promise to love his daughter and have a wonderful child. His dying words are, "expose Wen Jun, save Susan!" Gao Yuan is overcome with guilt at the professor's death:

> GAO YUAN: I am so deeply grieved. In this foreign country that was his native place, I grieve this old man whose name I did not know. Forgive me! I was willing to think you were a class enemy, an "old stinking ninth."[28] It never occurred to me that *laowai* (old outsiders) also had good people![29]

This entire exchange between the professor and Gao Yuan first counter-poses, then integrates, Chinese nationalism and intercultural understanding, beginning with an initial conflict in which Gao is blinded by his anti-Americanism, but through which he tragically comes to a resolution of his irrational xenophobia.

Gao's confrontation with Wen Jun is markedly different in that the object of his hatred shifts from the foreign Other to the enemy at home—a fellow Chinese. This final duel is the most dramatic, the most gut-wrenching, but also the most comic. It begins with Gao Yuan disguising himself as a priest to officiate at Wen Jun and Susan's wedding ceremony. Asking Wen Jun to place his hand on the Bible and repeat his vow three times, the "priest" reveals a tape recorder and plays a previous recording of Wen's reluctant agreement with the professor's housekeeper to murder Susan on her wedding day:

WEN JUN'S VOICE: You wanted me to earn the trust of the professor, and secretly collude in the selling of human organs, and I did. You wanted me to get rid of Gao Shan, and I did. You made me blame the professor's death on Gao Yuan, propose marriage to Susan and get the inheritance rights to the clinic, and I did. What else do you want from me?

SISI'S VOICE: I want you to have Susan meet the Lord on her wedding night—that is the only way to guarantee the clinic stays in our hands from the start![30]

Fighting among all the major characters erupts, including combat choreography borrowed from kung-fu films, a shoot-out during which the participants hide behind movable set pieces, and a car chase (using toy cars), which culminates in a crash. In the final confrontation between Gao Yuan and Wen Jun, the latter substitutes playing the trumpet for all his lines of dialogue, up until Gao shoots him and he drops to the floor, speaking his only words: "Brother—thank you."

The juxtaposition of comic performative elements with the suffering and death of the play's main characters forms an unexpected and highly effective contrast. Use of the trumpet throughout his dying moments would seem to risk making Wen Jun's death laughable; yet the discordance between this comic mode (as he drags himself across the floor playing notes that include the melancholy American song *Feelings*) and his subsequent utterance serves to imbue his parting words with the kind of weight that Wang Gui anticipated when he identified his interpretation of the play as "Chinese people are shooting themselves." The fact that Gao Yuan and Wen Jun remind each other (and other characters) repeatedly throughout the play that they are "brothers" and compatriots makes the hero's murder of Wen, though justified, difficult to absorb.

Nor is there any relief to follow. Wen Jun's death is the final plot element before the powerful closing dance sequence that frames the entire play. The ensemble of actors opens the performance with interpretive modern dance reflecting the trauma of life from birth to death, and they close the show by slowly filling the apron of the stage with their writhing bodies, symbolically echoing the suffering just enacted in the play. During this movement sequence set to eerie music, Susan crawls toward Gao Yuan, calling out only his last name (signifying her conflation of the twin brothers into a single desired Other). Having been shot by Sisi during the final chaos at the wedding, Susan dies in Gao's arms. He raises her above his head in a crucifixion pose and carries her slowly downstage center, as a huge banner with flags from every country is rolled like a wave over the heads of the dancers. The play's theme song "Ocean Tale" (*haisu*) begins, and the dancers continue to interpret its lyrics with their movements as they pass the banner over them. Eventually, they all end up intertwined, signifying the international universalism alluded to by Wang; they then break free, and each time the theme song's recurring words "great ocean" (*dahai*) are repeated, the dancers strike and hold a new dramatic pose before continuing their interpretive dance. The music, movement, and performance cease when Gao Yuan places Susan down on the stage and kneels beside her.

This entire closing sequence ends the tragicomic play on a dramatic and serious, if also somewhat hopeful, note. Since Susan is not an active participant in—but merely a victim of—the conflicts in the story, her death is unexpected, as is Gao Yuan's emotional reaction. The added symbolism of international unity and understanding conveys the hope that such tragic consequences of cross-cultural contact can be avoided in the future.

EXPANDING THE BORDERS OF EXILE

The contrast between Gao Yuan's initial euphoria in anticipation of his adventure overseas at the play's beginning and the nearly complete destruction of everything his twin brother had established in America (amidst the ruins of which he now kneels) by its end invites further analysis of the overall trauma of the typical Chinese *chuguo* experience.[31] The fact that many works of literature, drama, and film during the 1990s reflected similar crises of identity in conjunction with foreign travel indicates that Gao Yuan's experience is symptomatic of a collective cross-cultural phenomenon.

Examinations of motifs of exile in literature have conventionally focused on Western and Eastern European writers and novels rather than dramatic literature, with works by Asian, Islamic and other minority peoples in the United States only recently gaining more attention. Alongside studies of second and third-generation Asian American writings, a distinct genre of "Overseas Chinese Literature" has emerged, consisting of writers originally from mainland China who continue to write in the Chinese language for a Chinese readership while living abroad: some of these writers reside in Taiwan or Hong Kong, and some live in Europe, America, or elsewhere.

Scholarly studies of Overseas Chinese Literature reflect a pattern in exiled Chinese writing that neatly echoes the trajectory of Gao Yuan's experience in *The Great Going Abroad* and also intersects with Una Chaudhuri's theorization of dramatized geopathology and its central concerns with issues of displacement and the identity crisis that results from the disorientations of immigration, refugeehood, and exile.[32] The first characteristic phase of such exile is "rootlessness" or "drifting," which prompts feelings of "cultural vulnerability."[33] These terms aptly describe Gao Yuan's disorientation when he first lands on American soil: the absence of his twin brother immediately instills feelings of panic and unbelonging, heightened by his inability to communicate linguistically and his bodily vulnerability in the face of physical danger. He is quite literally, to borrow one of Chaudhuri's definitions of the geopathic figure, "out of place."[34]

His displacement is materialized physically on stage through the genius of the set design concept as set pieces move about swiftly and erratically of their own agency, completely overwhelming and alienating the uninitiated visitor and greatly enhancing the intensity of his geopathology.

Gao's sense of being adrift is accentuated by the fact that this new land makes him painfully aware of his Otherness while simultaneously seeking to subsume him in a culture of homogeneity, something Chaudhuri identifies as a hallmark of American multiculturalism. America's claim to privilege tolerance and diversity becomes paradoxical in relation to its resistance to heterogeneity: the United States connotes dispersal, dissolution, progress, and conformity—an articulation of Otherness, which is captured "within a web of sameness disguised as difference" (pp. 3–5). This view of American society is supported by Gao's inability to differentiate between good citizens (such as the professor and the young men who attempt to help Gao) and bad (Wen Jun and the gang that mugs Gao), and even helps to explain the professor's and Susan's inability to distinguish Gao Shan from Gao Yuan. As the ensemble of actors becomes group after group of minor characters with little in the way of costume change, we begin to imagine the sea of sameness on which Gao Yuan is afloat and made keenly aware of his own difference, in spite of the fact that he learns quickly from the alien culture how to disguise it. The dialectic of his ability to adapt to, but his inability to accept, this strange brand of American interculturalism releases his internalized nationalism as a logical response—a survival tactic that becomes necessary because, in the process of negotiating the mores of this new place, Gao's very identity comes into crisis. The glossing over of difference in the American version of diversity (enhanced by the aforementioned refusal to mark cultural difference through costume and makeup) threatens to eradicate Gao's sense of self altogether.

This phase of "cultural confrontation," which culminates in "identity confusion,"[35] is another phase of exile and is identified by Chaudhuri as a contemporary reiteration of the classic interrogation of identity:

Who one is and who one can be are . . . a function of *where* one is and how one experiences that place . . . [T]he new version of "who am I?" is firmly anchored in a new form of "where am I?"[36]

In *Going Abroad*, the trope of the twin protagonists is utilized to enhance this identity crisis, which for Gao Yuan reaches its height when he is continually cast in the role of his brother by utter strangers who seem to know him intimately;

it is best expressed when he and Susan are dancing at her birthday party:

SUSAN: You've forgotten? You've forgotten everything?
GAO YUAN: Please forgive me. I've . . . I've even forgotten myself.
SUSAN: Are you joking?
GAO YUAN: It's true. For example . . . what is my name?
SUSAN: Silly child, Gao Shan. You are my dearest Gao Shan!
                          [Kisses him, then releases him.]
GAO YUAN [confused]:   . . . I am Gao Shan? Then, where did I go? I am
                          here, then where did Gao Shan go? *Aiya*, what a
                          mess. No, I must leave! No. If I do that, the professor
                          and young lady will be hurt. My brother is really a
                          disappointment—he's got it so good here, why would
                          he want to leave? If he's gonna leave, he should at
                          least say hi first! It's not right. First I need to find out
                          where my brother is! But how can I ask?: "Excuse me,
                          where did I go?" Can I say that? *Ai!* This play is really
                          hard to act, there's just no way . . .![37]

Again, a Brechtian *Verfremdung* aesthetic is exercised and heightened, in that the actor self-reflexively indicates both his and his character's performative embodiment of the Self that is Other: Gao's image of himself as an actor in a play enacts a doubled doubling, since he actually *is* an actor in a play, thus tripling the Self contained in one body. It continues while he is at the beach with Susan later:

SUSAN: Gao! Gao! Where are you? (Searching.)
[GAO YUAN swims. He climbs the bank and lies on the sand.]
GAO YUAN: They say that living is just like playing a role, but it is really hard
            to play another person. These past few days, even though I've had
            food and drink, love and pain, I still feel uncomfortable; always
            pretending I am my brother. If this continues, there will be two
            Gao Shans and Gao Yuan won't even exist anymore.[38]

This simultaneous doubling and splitting of the self results in a kind of schizophrenia that ultimately threatens to erase his original identity completely. Chaudhuri isolates this schizophrenia as one of the by-products of immigrant geopathology, providing, in her description, an uncanny summary of Gao Yuan's entire experience:

[I]ll-placement . . . affects every part of immigrant experience, coloring everything seen and felt, producing a sort of split self, even a schizophrenia . . . The schizophrenia of immigrant experience begins, as does exile, with a violent and painful rupture . . . After the break comes a lesson in loneliness, in the numerous forms and qualities of loneliness, and of course the slow, dawning sense of loss.[39]

According to Chaudhuri's vocabulary of geopathology, phases of rootlessness and identity confusion are equivalent to a "victimage of location," the principle that identifies place as the central dilemma of the protagonist; its resolution comes through another principle, which Chaudhuri calls a "heroism of departure" (p. xii), which emphasizes integration and inclusiveness.[40] At this stage, the geopathic figure at least recognizes the need for an eventual departure or homecoming, even if it is not enacted. This is precisely the awareness Gao Yuan has arrived at by the end of *The Great Going Abroad*. As one reviewer of the play summarized:

> At first, he looks at the Western world through the traditional perspective and consciousness of a Chinese person; but in this capitalist society of mutual deception, he runs up against stone walls everywhere . . . In the end . . . at a loss under the intermingling feelings of love and hate, he steps upon the path of return to his native land.[41]

His brother murdered and the murderers avenged, there is nothing left for him in this strange, unwelcoming land. He has reached the depths of loneliness, has seen both the Other and the Self in a revelatory light, and is exhausted from the effort. Dispossessed of his wealth and security, he has little choice but to gather up his overwhelming loss and hard-won wisdom and return home.

If integration is an antidote to exile, then it bears repeating that the creative process of *Going Abroad* can be considered as Wang Gui's reenactment of Gao Yuan's traumatic journey, which, in turn, is a reflection of the director's own experience of exile. Though never having lived outside of mainland China, Wang has led a life of "internal exile" throughout his artistic career, particularly since 1985 and the *W.M.* controversy.

Consideration of internal or metaphorical exile in relation to more traditional geographical separation from one's homeland is a recent topic of Western literary debate, and the definition of exile has expanded with the appreciation of the intellectual isolation of repressive politics and the legitimacy of overseas cultural ties. Current scholarship offers a "looser definition" of exile that includes "the attitudes of writers who [feel] no longer at home in their native country either because of official disapproval or because of their own convictions."[42] The recent reconfiguration of the concept emphasizes that "twentieth century totalitarian regimes have produced a different type of exile often called internal exile . . . exile can occur without one's being driven from a home"[43]

Of the many projects in which Wang Gui has collaborated as writer and/or director, *Going Abroad* is most emblematic of exile itself, not only because it isolates the experience of one man's traumatic venture overseas alongside the exile experiences of fellow dislocated Chinese citizens, but also because of the "exiling" of the very production itself. As detailed earlier, the collaborative process that produced the play is a complicated map of literal and aesthetic migrations, both on behalf of the financial investor, the key designers and other creators, the actors, and the performances themselves. Wang Gui and Wang Peigong are political outcasts who risk their freedom with each new project; as internal exiles in the intellectual community, the product of this collaboration became a literal object of exile on the artistic landscape, traveling continuously to remote provinces (and quietly to a limited and barely public engagement in a major city) in order to avoid political censorship. The exiled performances echo the exiled character of Gao Yuan, who echoes the internal exile of his creators.

The play, as a whole, offers a paradoxical view of exile, and of the Occidental land and its inhabitants, which contain and embody exile. Although the United States is a dangerous and destabilizing place, Americans, for the most part, are positive figures, as represented by the professor and his daughter. Wen Jun as a site of cultural transgression is a hybrid space: he is racially Chinese, and as a foreign transplant is susceptible to absorption of negative aspects of American society due to his long-term residence in the United States, although his ethnic and national kinship to Gao Yuan are distinctly foregrounded.

This availability of contrasting readings in interpreting the action and meaning of the play allows *Going Abroad* to fulfill cross purposes: to adhere, on one hand, to the superficial message regarding the potential social ills of excessive foreign influence, and, on the other, to address Wang Peigong and Wang Gui's deeper intention of exploring the mutually self-destructive tendency of Chinese citizens, which has troubled them since the Cultural Revolution. In addition to carrying these two rather serious messages, the play also cleverly parodies the Chinese *chuguo* tidal wave and overall craze for domestic appropriation of things American, which prevailed at the time and continued afterward.

In a 1987 essay entitled "Theater: Look Forward" (*xiju: xiang qian kan*), Wang identified the primary purpose of theater as entertainment.[44] Wang's plays are indeed noted for their entertainment value, and sometimes, accordingly, misjudged as frivolous (as I believe was the case with several colleagues at the Shanghai performances). Critic Lin Xi, in extolling the praises of this particular play, goes on to defend it against its detractors in this regard:

> Some say that *Going Abroad* tries too hard to entertain and doesn't resemble a spoken drama, an opera, a dance piece, and they conclude that it isn't standard or normal. This kind of hypercriticism is unnecessary . . . *Going Abroad* does not adhere to one artistic style, and that is probably its strong point. From the point of view of the law of artistic development, isn't innovation the life and soul of the theatre?[45]

Wang Gui himself would heartily agree with Lin Xi. In fact, in his essay, Wang bravely asserted: "A theorist once said, 'innovation is breaking rules.' These words have powerful logic. If we don't break through outmoded conventions, how can we set new standards?" He warned that if theater continued to adhere blindly to the "superficial propaganda and education model," it would lose touch with the times and its contemporary audience, concluding, "once theatre's function of serving real society weakens, it will become a destitute phenomenon."[46] These are bold words from a man who had just suffered such humiliation in the wake of *W.M.*, but, as stated before, the mid-1980s were bold times, and artists spoke out more freely than they have ever since. As Wang reflects, "before and after 1985 many directors, after just one play, were looking through new eyes" (p. 453).

Wang Gui's advice to directors of the mid-1980s serves as an apt summary of his mission as an artist, and his objective in creating and staging *The Great Going Abroad*: "Directors must fully trust their own existence and, with distinct creative personalities, break through the sealed up burdens in their hearts in order to face this open world" (p. 453).

Wang Gui is a director who has heeded his own advice for more than a decade, and his unique theater of internal exile challenges like-minded artists to take the risk of joining him in crossing boundaries into unstable territory. Like Gao Yuan, Wang emerges from such projects sobered by their disappointments, but unshaken in his belief in both the collective universality of human experience and the potential of a single individual to make an enormous difference.

NOTES

Thanks go to University of Hawaii Press for permission to publish this chapter, which is a revised portion of a chapter of Claire Conceison's book *Significant Other: Staging the American in China* (University of Hawaii Press, 2004).

1. A longer version of this chapter appears in *Significant Other: Staging the American in China* (Honolulu: University of Hawaii Press, 2004).
2. Una Chaudhuri, *Staging Place: The Geography of Modern Drama* (Ann Arbor: University of Michigan Press, 1995).
3. Interview with Wang Gui, Beijing, February 8, 1996. Since only the twin Gao brothers and Wen Jun are specifically defined as ethnically Chinese in the *dramatis personae*, it is implied that all other characters are native to "*waiguo*," though Sisi's ethnicity is somewhat ambiguous. Gao Yuan and Gao Shan are both visitors from China (Gao Shan is an overseas Chinese student and potential emigré), and Wen Jun is specified as a "foreign citizen of Chinese origin," implying a long-term residency (perhaps upbringing) outside of China. Most likely, Wen has acquired U.S. citizenship after holding a green card, but he was definitely born in China.
4. Lin Xi, "*Da Liuyang* daigeile women shenme?" (What has *The Great Going Abroad* brought us?), *Shanghai xiju* (January 1992), 25. All translations are mine unless otherwise noted.
5. Wei Ming, "Kan *Da Liuyang* you gan" (My feelings on seeing *The Great Going Abroad*), *Shanghai xiju* (January 1992), 24.
6. Ibid., 24.
7. Lin, "*Da Liuyang* daigeile women shenme," 25.
8. Kaye, Lincoln, "Exit emperor, stage left: 'theatre of the absurd' may describe today's reality," *Far Eastern Economic Review* (October 1, 1992), 32–33.
9. Zhang Longxi, "Postmodernism and the return of the native," *Mighty Opposites: From Dichotomies to Difference in the Comparative Study of China* (Stanford, CA: Stanford University Press, 1998), p. 184.
10. Wang, February 8, 1996.
11. Wang Gui supervised as executive director the Shanghai People's Art Theatre production of *W.M.* directed by Hu Xuehua. For more on *W.M.* and the controversy it generated, see Tom Moran, *Down from the Mountains, Back from the Villages: Wang Peigong's WM* (M.A. thesis: Cornell University, 1988) or Yan

Haiping's critical introduction to the anthology *Theater and Society* (Armonk, NY: M.E. Sharpe, 1998), which also includes Moran's translation of the play. For the script published in Chinese along with reprinted concurrent critical commentary, see Li Haiquan, ed., *You zhengyi de huaju juben xuanji (Selected Controversial playscripts)* (Beijing: Zhongguo xiju chubanshe, 1988).

12. Wang, February 8, 1996.

13. Wang, February 8, 1996.

14. This term translates loosely as "Beijing School," in contrast to "*haipai*" (Shanghai School). The phrases "*jingpai*" and "*haipai*" are still often invoked to describe the approach of a certain director or playwright, or the style of a specific play. One critic, in discussing *The Great Going Abroad*, called it "*jingban haipai*" indicating that it is a fusion of the two styles, exhibiting characteristics of both trends. He notes its origins in Beijing, but maintains that it has a strong "Shanghai School flavor," listing Shanghai School characteristics as "disregarding tradition; rather strong innovative consciousness; ability to assimilate artistic benefits of the ancient and modern Chinese as well as the foreign for their own use; and . . . any artistic method can be used as long as the play is good to watch and fascinates the audience." (Lin, "*Da Liuyang* daigeile women shenme," 25). For more on *jingpai/haipai*, see Claire Conceison, "International casting in Chinese plays: a tale of two cities," *Theatre Journal* 53 (spring 2001), 277–290.

15. Wu'er Kaixi was the most prominent and outspoken student leader of the protests and hunger strike in Tiananmen Square in the spring of 1989. He fled China after the massacre and was exiled in the United States, where he was frequently interviewed on television news programs; he later became a radio talk show host in Taiwan.

16. Wang, February 8, 1996.

17. Other cast changes during the play's lengthy tour included Sha Jingchang taking over the lead when Zhang Qiuge left the show for another project (at which point Chen Ziqiu stepped into Sha's role), and Wang Zhiquan replacing Wang Deshun. In the Shanghai production I attended, Zhang Qiuge played the twin protagonists, Chen Ziqiu served as production manager and played Wen Jun, Mao Lixin played Sisi, Jiang Lili played Susan, and Wang Zhiquan played the professor.

18. Lin, "*Da Liuyang* daigeile women shenme," p. 25.

19. Wang, February 8, 1996.

20. Wei, "Kan *Da Liuyang* you gan," p. 24.

21. A self-employed worker or establishment; these emerged and flourished in China during the economic reform period of the early 1990s.

22. *Da Liuyang (The Great Going Abroad)*. Text by Yu Xin, Xian Cai, Yi Gong, and Wang Gui. Song lyrics by Gu Ding and Wang Jian. June–July, 1991 (unpublished script): scene 1, 1.

23. Ibid., Scene 5, 11. In analyses of postcolonial theater, the derogated body is a locus infused with rich political and cultural meaning, often as a site of contestation to imperialism. Helen Gilbert and Joanne Tompkins describe its semiotic power this way: "The body which has been violated, degraded, maimed . . . invariably functions within some kind of allegorical framework." In *Going Abroad*, the decapitated body of the elder twin Gao Shan can connote the evils of foreign capitalism or the extremes of violent dismemberment within Chinese communities during times of political upheaval. In either case, the scene in which Gao Shan's ghost, holding its own head, approaches Gao Yuan serves as a significant moment of simultaneously splitting and doubling of the subject,

enhancing the centrality of Gao Yuan's identity crisis as an exiled Other. For more on the mutilated body in postcolonial drama, see Gilbert and Tompkins, "Body politics" in their *Post-colonial Drama: Theory, Practice, Politics* (London: Routledge, 1996), pp. 203–255.

24. *Da Liuyang*, scene 2, 5.
25. The language of the play in imagined reality is English—or perhaps a hybrid of Chinese and English. Since Gao Yuan immediately reveals a language barrier upon his arrival, we can assume that his interactions with Wen Jun would be in their shared native tongue; furthermore, his direct addresses to the audience throughout the play would also presumably be in Chinese.
26. Wang, February 8, 1996.
27. *Da Liuyang*, scene 6, 13.
28. "Old stinking ninth" (*cao lao jiu*) was an epithet used during the Cultural Revolution, labeling intellectuals as the ninth category of class enemy after the eight officially designated types (such as landowners).
29. *Da Liuyang*, scene 6, 14.
30. Ibid., Scene 8, 19.
31. The tremendous increase in Chinese citizens going overseas during the 1980s and 1990s is commonly referred to as "*chuguo re*" ("going abroad fever"); by one estimate, the number of Chinese students going abroad to pursue advanced degrees between 1984 and 1998 rose from 4000 to 120,000. See Zhang Minjie, "Liumei xueren de 'bianji xintai' " in *Qingnian yanjiu* (January 1997), 45. Translated in *Chinese Education and Society* 31:2 (March/April 1998), 93–101.
32. See Hsin-sheng C. Kao, "Yu Lihua's blueprint for the development of a new poetics: Chinese literature overseas," in *Nativism Overseas: Contemporary Chinese Women Writers*, ed. (Albany: SUNY Press, 1993) pp. 81–107. For discussions of exile in contemporary literature, see María-Inés Lagos-Pope, ed., *Exile in Literature* (Lewisburg, PA: Bucknell University Press, 1988); Angelika Bammer, ed., *Displacements* (Bloomington: Indiana University Press, 1994); Michael Seidel, *Exile and the Narrative Imagination* (New Haven: Yale University Press, 1986); and Andrew Gurr, *Writers in Exile: The Identity of Home in Modern Literature* (Sussex: The Harvester Press, 1981).
33. Kao, "Yu Lihua's blueprint for the development of a new poetics," pp. 103, 84.
34. Chaudhuri, *Staging Place*, p. 75.
35. Kao, "Yu Lihua's blueprint for the development of a new poetics," pp. 83, 103–104.
36. Chaudhuri, *Staging Place*, pp. xii, 4.
37. *Da Liuyang*, Scene 2, 6.
38. Ibid., Scene 3, 7.
39. Chaudhuri, *Staging Place*, pp. 173–174.
40. Kao, "Yu Lihua's blueprint for the development of a new poetics," pp. 83, 104.
41. Lin, "*Da Liuyang daigeile women shenme*," p. 25.
42. Rosmarie T. Morewedge, "Exile in Heinrich Boell's novel: *Billiards at Half Past Nine*" in *Exile in Literature*, p. 106.
43. Lagos-Pope in Lagos-Pope, ed., pp. 9–10.
44. The essay was published in *Theatre News* (*xiju bao*) in 1987 and reprinted in *Xijuguan zhengmingji* (*Anthology on controversial theater*) (Beijing: Zhongguo xiju chubanshe, 1988).
45. Lin, "Da Liuyang daigeile women shenme," p. 25.
46. Wang (1998), 449.

8

STAY OR GO: LI GUOXIU'S
AMBIGUOUS ANSWER TO THE
TAIWAN QUESTION

John B. Weinstein

Within a decade of the 1987 lifting of Martial Law, Taiwan has rapidly transformed into a multiparty democracy with freedoms forbidden on the other side of the Taiwan Straits. The presence of such a society causes the government of the People's Republic of China (PRC) to wrestle with the "Taiwan Question," but the people of Taiwan must wrestle with their own Taiwan Question—"Stay or go?" In 1997, at the end of the first post–Martial Law decade, a poll by the TVBS cable station reported that 25 percent of Taiwan's population wished to emigrate to foreign countries; a Democratic Progressive Party poll reported more than 30 percent.[1] The constant threat of the PRC is one reason for so many wanting to leave, but it is far from being the sole cause. Plenty of dangers abound on the island itself. Ironically, and perhaps irrationally, many of these very dangers make life in Taiwan so exciting. It is in this contradiction between danger and enjoyment that playwright/director Li Guoxiu (Lee Kuo-shiu[2]) finds humor.

Of his many productions with his company, the Ping-Fong Acting Troupe (*Pingfeng biaoyanban*), this phenomenon is most explicitly presented in Li's signature series, *Can Three Make It?* (*Sanren xing buxing?*). *Can Three Make It?* is an ongoing series of plays derived from an overarching experiment of creating relevant, humorous theater with only three actors. In the largely unconnected scenes of *Can Three Make It? Part I* (*Sanren xingbuxing I*, 1987), the actors play more than twenty roles, from office workers in contemporary Taipei to characters in a radio play story set during the Japanese occupation.[3] *Can Three Make It? Part II—City Panic* (*Sanren xingbuxing II—Chengshi zhi huang*, 1988), connects its prologue and six scenes with a narrative thread—three people's increasing frustration as they wander through the urban jungle of Taipei. The actors do not only play the three wanderers; when the wanderers attend a dance performance, the actors play the dancers; when they watch movies, the actors play the characters in the films as well as the various people watching them.[4] *Can Three Make It? Part*

III—Oh! Diverged Paths (*Sanren xingbuxing III—OH! Sanchakou*, 1993) is the first in the series to use a continuous narrative plot. This story of the people of the three Chinas—mainland China, Taiwan, and Hong Kong—is told across the plot of a native Taiwanese man, Mr. Guo, who takes his family to Beijing to meet his long-lost brother. The three actors play five roles each, for a total of fifteen characters, five from each of the three Chinas.[5] Rounding out the first post–Martial Law decade, *Can Three Make It? Part IV—Play Hard* (*Sanren xingbuxing IV—Changqi wanming*, 1997) continues the story of Mr. Guo, his wife, his daughter, and his son-in-law, adding fourteen new characters for a total of eighteen. To accommodate all of these roles, Li Guoxiu redefines the concept of three actors, increasing the cast to six—three men and three women.[6] Besides some shared characters, the plays also share some scenes; in a technique Li calls the "button," the epilogue of each play becomes the prologue of the next installment.[7]

Li's motivation for founding Ping-Fong and creating productions like *Can Three Make It?* arose from two shortcomings he identified in the new experimental theater now known as the Little Theater Movement (*xiao juchang yundong*).[8] First, there were no scripts related to the people of Taipei, and second, theater was too solemn—there was no lighter material.[9] Both of these reduced audience accessibility, for the Little Theater Movement tended to draw aesthetically from an unfamiliar avant-garde and textually from equally unfamiliar foreign plays. Li's goals for a lighter, more local theater may seem modest, but in the world of post–Martial Law Taiwan, combining relevance with laughter is no easy task. From traffic fatalities to the demolition of historic landmarks to the potential destruction of Taiwan in a war with the PRC, Li's topics initially seem not to lend themselves to comedy. Li Guoxiu's Taiwan is filled with destruction yet his theaters are filled with laughter. By repeatedly presenting scenes of destruction and eliciting tremendous laughter in doing so, Li captures the contradictions at the heart of urban life in post–Martial Law Taiwan. People live life to the fullest even though, and in fact precisely because, it could all end in a moment of war. On a daily basis, they flock to KTVs despite great potential for violence or fire, buy new homes despite uneven construction and frequent earthquakes, and cross the streets knowing that a speeding motorcycle could be just around the corner. In such a world, there can be no comedy without tragedy, no optimism without pessimism, and no laughter without tears. Li's plays arise from the dialogue between such opposing elements. The series' ultimate question—"Stay or go?"—is not a question to be answered. The contradiction within it is the answer.

Faces in the Mirror: Creating Relevant Theater

In founding Ping-Fong and realizing his personal vision for Taiwan theater, a major goal of Li Guoxiu's was relevance. Gu Mengren, in one of the earliest reviews of *Can Three Make It?*, hypothesizes the key role relevance must play if theater is to succeed. At that time, notes Gu, theater lagged behind both newer kinds of entertainment like television and film, and more traditional forms of culture like literature, fine arts, music, and dance. The source of the problem, according to Gu, relates to the particular nature of theater: "The reason is clear. Theater needs performance, performance needs an audience, and the audience needs material relevant to their daily lives. Unfortunately, these three requirements have never had any way to break out of this vicious cycle, causing the distance between stage and audience to grow farther and farther."[10] Though Gu does not specifically explain this concept of relevance, Li's plays themselves reveal much about it.

One aspect of relevance is topical, localized subject matter. The first two parts of *Can Three Make it?* bring up a range of issues faced every day by people living in Taiwan in the late 1980s: dangerous traffic, poor public safety, lethal fires, Dengue fever outbreaks, volatile stock trading, political rallies, police crackdowns, and censorship. The button that concludes *City Panic* and begins *Oh! Three Diverged Paths* introduces what becomes the major issue of the third and fourth installments—the topic of emigration. *City Panic* ends with the three wanderers leaving the city and viewing it from afar; Li reveals that one of them is getting ready to emigrate to the United States. *Oh! Three Diverged Paths*, inspired by changes in cross-straits policies, continues the emigration theme through characters from both sides of the straits. The 18 roles in *Oh! Three Diverged Paths* include Peter, a Taiwanese with American citizenship whose parents emigrated to the West Coast 10 years earlier; Osaka, a half-Japanese Hongkonger whose wife emigrated to Canada 5 years prior; and Paul, a mainland resident thinking of emigrating.[11] Initially inspired by Li's 1996 trip to Canada, *Play Hard* revisits Peter and his family 5 years later, after his parents have moved to Vancouver.[12] When Peter brings his native Taiwanese in-laws, Mr. and Mrs. Guo, to visit Canada, the conflict between in-laws comes to represent two potential answers to the play's fundamental question of "Stay or go?"

To maintain such close links with the most current events, scripts are altered up to, and even beyond, opening night. At the first press conference for *Play Hard*, Li said, "The whole of society constantly fluctuates, so the script cannot be absolutely decided until the final moment," a quote headlining newspaper articles about the play as early as August 21, 1997.[13] At least one moment of dialogue had to have been added after that date:

MR. GUO:	(*Taiwanese*) Who told you to sell the Benz I gave you?
OLDER BROTHER:	(*Taiwanese*) Think about it. I'm a farmer. Driving a Benz doesn't fit my identity!
MR. GUO:	(*Taiwanese*) When you're sitting in the car, who knows you're a farmer? It's not about suitable identity, is it?! It's a question of safety!
OLDER BROTHER:	(*Taiwanese*) Right! I saw the news that day. The Benz the American princess drove was the same model as mine. I sold it right away.
MR. GUO:	(*Taiwanese*) It was that pack of dogs that killed her! Besides, you're not Princess Diana![14]

Even taking care to have the provincial Older Brother incorrectly call Princess Diana an American, Li Guoxiu incorporates her death—an event that occurred on August 31—into *Play Hard*. Sometimes revisions are more about place than time. When *Part I* played in Taichung in April of 1988, Li revised some of the dialogue "to bring it closer to the temperament of the central region."[15]

Such fine-tuning, whether for temporal or geographic relevance, helps the audience identify with the plays. Chen Sufeng writes that Li's inserting current events from all parts of Taiwan "puts the people themselves into the play."[16] Wu Wenzhi concurs: "In the play, the audience can see many familiar reflections that surround them, including themselves. This kind of feeling of recognition is the reason why it succeeds."[17] This self-identification is a key element in the accessibility of Li's work, accessibility that lessens the gap between audience and content, a gap so often apparent in the early years of the Little Theater Movement. In an extended piece of theater criticism, Zhang Jinghan goes on at length about the notion that "life is like theater, theater is like life."[18] Looking around at people laughing and crying during a performance of *Oh! Three Diverged Paths*, Zhang comes to feel that they constitute an even more beautiful reality of human life than that being portrayed on stage. Zhang writes, "Li Guoxiu once said: 'We live on Taiwan and make theater.' He was talking about workers in little theater, but laying eyes on the reality of human life offstage, one cannot help but think that these words of his refer to all of us" (p. 28). Zhang goes on: "looking at it from this angle, we, on and off stage, all have the capability to 'live on Taiwan and make theater.' The difference is, in the midst of our making theater off stage, largely unconsciously, Li Guoxiu's *Oh! Three Diverged Paths* makes us unexpectedly see ourselves in the mirror" (p. 28).

Relevance is not simply a matter of presenting familiar faces or familiar events, however. Li Guoxiu's theater is relevant because it strikes at the core aspect of identity in Taiwan: multiplicity. When people in Taiwan look in Zhang Jinghan's hypothetical mirror, they do not see just one face. Life in Taiwan is a magic mirror that produces a multiplicity of related, yet distinct, reflections for each viewer. Ping-Fong's convention of one actor playing many roles is a perfect vehicle for visualizing this phenomenon. Yang Liyin, who performed in the original cast of Parts II and III, and in a revival of Parts I and II, explains the origin of this technique: in his early years as a playwright, since Li Guoxiu had only a few actors available to him, he thought of the idea of one actor playing many roles. Later it became part of the Ping-Fong style.[19] The technique is pioneered in the *Can Three Make It? Part I* scene "Eyewitness"—an experiment in creating a scene in which three actors each play three roles differentiated only by physicality, language, and small props.[20] The "City Lights" scene in *City Panic* further develops the technique; the three actors play characters both on-screen and in the audience during the raid on an illegal screening of a pornographic film. Even the most inexperienced theater viewer can appreciate the difficulty of the rapid changes in characterization and, for *Oh! Three Diverged Paths* and *Play Hard*, complex costuming. On *Oh! Three Diverged Paths*, reporter Li Peiyun writes: "As the plot unfolds, the three people must change clothes and change their mold on stage within a time as fast as eight seconds. This abundant demonstration of their skill at quick role changes is bound to surprise and amaze the audience."[21] When the time comes for *Play Hard*, headlines declare that "Six actors play eighteen roles" and "change clothes in eight seconds."[22] The publicity value of this facet of the Ping-Fong style is undeniable.

The technique's efficacy is not limited to audience appeal. Li Guoxiu's comedy emphasizes a multiplicity of possibilities in dialogue with one another, not just between two people, but within a single person simultaneously holding a range of contradictory views and identities. A single actor in several roles aptly demonstrates such a state of being. When each actor portrays characters of different ages and backgrounds, however drastically the costumes, mannerisms, accents, and even languages may change, the person beneath it all remains the same. Li gives himself two alter-egos in *Play Hard*, both of which he himself plays in performance. The first is Mr. Guo. As the playwright, Li slants the script in Mr. Guo's favor, giving him the last laugh in his battles with his in-law, the elite mainlander Sven. As an actor, Li puts his own shtick into the role, using signature facial expressions and body movements to draw applause. As a director, he allows himself to break the frame of the play for such antics. In all of his duties, he makes it clear that Mr. Guo is his voice in the play. However, that role is not his only voice. Another obvious alter-ego is Little Deng, a would-be film director who, we discover in the course of *Play Hard*, is trying to raise money to make a film: "It's the story about eighteen ordinary people gathering and scattering in this city. When the story begins, a Taiwanese father takes his wife and eldest daughter and son-in-law to Canada to visit relatives. Then, that Taiwanese father and his son-in-law's father because of problems of understanding, have a big argument. . . ."[23] In other words, it is exactly the play the audience is watching. Little Zheng's background, the son of a mainlander, also matches Li Guoxiu's, for this leading nativist playwright is, in fact, of mainland descent. By giving himself multiple identities, Li helps his audience see their own multiplicities.

Such multiplicities can even cross boundaries of age, a seemingly insurmountable boundary in the Little Theater Movement. From the outset, little theater was a strongly youth-identified movement. As early as 1980, Yao Yiwei, a playwright whose organizational work jump-started the Little Theater Movement, was already declaring "Experimental theatre is young people's theatre."[24] The audiences were indeed young; one poll by the Lan-ling Theatre Workshop (*Lanling jufang*), one of the first little theater troupes, found that 94.5 percent of its audience was under 30.[25] Ping-Fong's more recent statistics, based on the 60,000 members of the "Friends of Ping-Fong," show its audience base to be 65 percent under 30, and 90 percent under 40.[26] From the beginning, Li's plays presented young people facing various difficulties. "The Betrayal of Desire," one of the scenes in *Can Three Make It? Part I*, shows Paul and Mary attempting a covert office romance while their older boss Peter tries to seduce Mary and fire Paul. In the end, Paul outsmarts his boss, causing the latter to end the scene with the line, "Young people . . . well, they sure have prospects."[27]

Despite the series' emphasis on youth, there are older characters in significant roles, particularly in *Play Hard*. Of the 18 roles in *Play Hard*, 11 are younger characters, mostly in their twenties or thirties, but there are 7 characters who are older, some of them much older. Furthermore, *Play Hard* relegates many of the younger characters to supporting roles, while their elders become the major players, as well as the heart and soul of the play. The emotional core of *Play Hard* is the scene "Searching," which involves only older characters: Mr. and Mrs. Guo, the Older Brother, and his companion A-man. This scene develops the complex relationship between the two Guo brothers, which Professor Chen Zhengxi, in his review of the play, cites as a comparatively successful example of the play's character development; he also calls the Older Brother the role which "gives people the deepest impression."[28] Compared to these older characters' accounts of suffering during the war, the new condominiums and covert love affairs of the younger characters seem frivolous and unimportant. The Guo brothers form a bond unmatched in its complexity elsewhere in all of *Can Three Make It?* Though complex and moving, the relationship seems to move far away from the notion of appealing directly to young audiences.

Nevertheless, Li does make it relevant for them, by invoking the multiplicity of identity in a visually direct manner. In *Play Hard*, student-aged viewers could literally see themselves on stage, since the crowds in the airport scenes were played by several dozen local students. The artistic benefits of this use of students on stage are rather minimal; the increased realism of actual crowds at the airport detracts from the effect of having six actors play all of the roles. There is, however, one interesting use of the student extras. When the curtain rises for the bows, eighteen of them are lined up in the back wearing the costumes of all eighteen major roles.[29] Not only does the audience finally get to view all of the characters at once; they do so across the bodies of Taiwan's youth. The student–actor dressed as the Older Brother for the curtain call is an apt visualization of transgenerational identification. Even the oldest character in the play has a young person at the core.

Throughout the *Can Three Make It?* series, and particularly in *Play Hard*, having a number of roles drawn from a wide range of identities played by one actor underscores the notion that each individual in Taiwan is a conglomeration of different voices. Such multiplicity informs the lives of everyone in Taiwan in the Post–Martial Law decade; everyone must play a variety of roles at once, just like the actors in Li Guoxiu's plays. It is difficult for any one person to provide a single, unchanging answer to the fundamental question of the series, "Stay or go?" At times, one might feel like Mr. Guo, who chooses to stay no matter what. At other times, one might be more like Sven, abandoning Taiwan with no regrets whatsoever. At still other times, one might be like Peter, who claims to love Taiwan yet enjoys the backup security of American citizenship; he declares, in English, that if anything happens he would "Go! Of course! Who cares about here?"[30] In *Can Three Make It?*, Li Guoxiu asks a question to which every person in Taiwan has not just one answer, but many. And there could be no question more relevant to life in Post–Martial Law Taiwan.

INAPPROPRIATE LAUGHTER: UNLEASHING THE COMICS OF DESTRUCTION

Subject matter drawn from local life was only one way Li Guoxiu bridged the gap between the Little Theater Movement and its audiences. His choice of the comedy genre was equally important. At a time when the Little Theater Movement was taking itself very seriously, perhaps too seriously, Li began to present comedies. His inspiration came on a visit to Japan in 1985, during a half-year-long period he spent observing theater in Japan and New York after deciding to focus his work on theater. In Tokyo, in a tiny theater, he watched three young actors perform while the audience laughed heartily. At that point, he realized that theater did not require such a high-pressure atmosphere.[31] He quickly incorporated a lighter atmosphere into his fledgling theater company's works. Gu Mengren's 1987 review of *Can Three Make It? Part I* recounts, "The entire theater roared with thunder-like laughter. The spirits of actors and audience were extremely elated. This was a spectacular event difficult to experience in theater in general."[32] The laughter continued throughout the series. Mainland theater artist Ying Ruocheng, upon viewing *Oh! Three Diverged Paths* in Taiwan in 1993, commented on the young audience's "unceasing sounds of laughter."[33] This unceasing laughter certainly played a key role in Li's success in connecting with his audiences.

The *Can Three Make It?* series is not pure comedy, however. One preview in the press promises comedy, tragedy, and farce—all in the headline.[34] In a more subtle review, Zhang Jinghan writes, "I still stubbornly believe *Oh! Three Diverged Paths* is not a comedy, but a realistic tragedy."[35] Li himself negates the view that there is any such thing as either pure comedy or tragedy. He frustrates such notions with his oft-used facetious description of Ping-Fong's corpus: "Pin[g]-Fong resists simple-minded labels. But if necessary, this is how I would categorize Pin[g]-Fong's style. In the works of our troupe, 13% of them are avant-gardist, 8% experimental, 26% . . . comical, 10% tragical, 25% tragicomical, 18% comic-tragical."[36] What Li is really saying with this pseudo-analytical breakdown is that such categories do not exist individually. There is comedy in the tragic and tragedy in the comic. In Li's form of comedy, tears and laughter go hand-in-hand. Zhang explains this in both directions. On the one hand, laughing always makes one cry; on the other, one laughs because laughing is the only way to face the tragedy that is reality.[37] Li Guoxiu's plays have comedy despite tragedy—or perhaps it is the other way around.

Throughout *Can Three Make It?*, Li blurs absolute notions of comedy and tragedy by presenting laughter at the seemingly most inappropriate moments. In the prologue to *Can Three Make It? Part I*, someone talks on the telephone while watching a comedy program on television. Simultaneously reacting to both the funny program on TV and the terrible news heard over the phone results in a moment of inappropriate laughter: "Ha ha ha . . . no, I'm not laughing at you, ha ha ha . . . What? A-ming died in a car crash? Ha ha ha . . . Hello? Hello? . . ."[38] In "The Death of a Southern Girl," office worker Paul repeatedly tells his coworker Mary and his boss Peter "jokes" that are not in the least bit funny. First he says, "I'll tell you two a joke. Lately, Iran and Iraq have been fighting something fierce! America is getting in the middle of it . . . (*he laughs loudly*) ha ha ha. . . ." Peter cuts him off with, "Paul! This joke isn't funny!" (p. 35). His second "joke," about a recent outbreak of Dengue fever in Kaohsiung, is no better: "I have a friend named Big Head Su. After he got bit by a mosquito, he went to work and turned this way . . . (*acts frothy at the mouth, shakes his head, waves his rear*)" (pp. 35–36). Peter scolds him again:

PETER: Paul! Dengue Fever isn't a joke.
PAUL: It isn't a joke? What is it?
PETER: It's reality.
PAUL: Oh, reality! Ha ha . . . (*realizes it is not funny, awkwardly stops*) (p. 36)

Peter's differentiation of jokes from "reality" is certainly problematic for a comedy about everyday life. "The Death of a Southern Girl" is, after all, a comic scene climaxing in an all-too-realistic traffic fatality. Though far more effective than Paul's jokes, Li Guoxiu's play also depends on inappropriate laughter. Li rejects the notion, put forth by his own character Peter, that joke and reality are mutually exclusive categories.

In *City Panic*, the disturbing nature of everyday life often triumphs over the need to laugh. The three people who journey through the urban jungle of Taipei keep looking for laughter but cannot find it. Even a movie theater fails to offer escape. After a debate about Taipei's violence, crowdedness, and general mania, the three are in low spirits. A projected slide says, "One person suggests watching a comedy movie."[39] However, the Charlie Chaplin film is soon replaced by a Danish pornographic film, which is subsequently shut down by the authorities. Going to the movies, in the end, shows only the pornographic tastes of local audiences and the intrusive censorship of local authorities. Only the joke-cracking policeman who comes to shut down the screening finds laughter. The sequence of slides leading into the next and final scene say, "At that movie theater, they / Watched that sort of a movie / They felt extremely dejected / Three people together got on a motorcycle . . . / Went far from the city" (pp. 6–1). Again, they find only so much solace. Looking through a telescope, they see a building on fire. A-qiang, one of the male characters, easily lists four all-too-common reasons why the fire might have started: an electrical cable, a gas explosion, a child's firecrackers, or an arsonist's intentional act.

This time, they finally cope with Taipei's troubles by laughing. The woman, A-ying, jokingly tells A-qiang that the fire is right near his home.

When he jumps up to rush home, the other man, Er-mao, laughs, saying "If you return home you'll also burn up!" (pp. 6–2). A-ying then also laughs, pointing out that the fire is clearly not even in the same part of the city where A-qiang lives. This laughter in the face of tragedy is a prelude to the final moment of the play. In the course of the scene, Er-mao, who is about to emigrate to the United States, has revealed that he keeps having visions in which he leaves the city only to find it bombed and destroyed upon his return. Nevertheless, when they are all finally ready to return to the city after a day of gloomy discoveries, Er-mao, out of nowhere, expresses a desire to laugh:

A-QIANG: Let's go! (*About to go, A-ying moves with him*)
ER-MAO: I want to laugh.
A-QIANG: Your spirits are that good, huh?
ER-MAO: It's just that I want to laugh. (*Lightly laughs*)
(*A-qiang, A-ying also laugh lightly with him*) (pp. 6–12).

Loud and increasingly joyful sounds of laughter emanate from the three people, even as the lights dim, while a series of six text slides project the final lines of the play. Only after that does the laughter gradually cease. *City Panic* is often not a happy play, but it culminates in laughter.

In *Oh! Three Diverged Paths*, the members of the audience are confronted with images of destruction, yet find themselves laughing, nevertheless. Destruction occurs on many levels—physical, historical, and moral. Scene 1, "The Wasted City," begins with giant projected photographs of the rubble left after the demolition of Taipei's Zhonghua Market. The scrim onto which the images are projected rises to reveal Peter and his in-laws sifting through the rubble. Though the scene is one of destruction, the audience still laughs. When Mr. Guo goes on and on questioning Peter on how he will explain the demolished market to his daughter, Peter responds to the tirade with a pithy, yet humorous, response: "I'll show her a photo."[40] Their exchange reveals how physical destruction becomes historical destruction as well. The historic marketplace no longer exists; more significantly, the younger generation considers its memory unimportant. As cities develop, buildings and even whole streets must be razed, but they could possibly be preserved through memory. However, with people like Peter scoffing at his future role in passing down the past to the next generation, such preservation is unlikely to occur. Given his attitude toward his father-in-law's question, he will probably never bother to show his daughter such a photograph.

The destruction of physical buildings is also linked to the deterioration of human values. In Taiwan, the relationship between morality and the construction of the cities is particularly close. Like many cities in Taiwan, Taipei's streets are named for moral virtues. Three major east–west thoroughfares in the northern half of downtown Taipei are named for Sun Yat-sen's Three Principles of the People: from north to south, "nationalism" (*minzu*), "people's rights" (*minquan*), and "people's livelihood" (*minsheng*). The next four major roads, continuing southward, are named for the traditional

Confucian eight virtues, grouped into pairs: "loyalty-filial piety" (*zhongxiao*), "benevolence-love" (*ren'ai*), "trust-righteousness" (*xinyi*), and "harmony-peace" (*heping*). When Mr. Guo asks Peter how he will describe the old demolished market to his soon-to-be-born daughter, he cannot help but list the eight virtues that name those southern east–west streets: "How will you tell her that this piece of land used to have a Zhonghua Market? From the loyalty building by the North Gate, loyalty, filial piety, benevolence, love, trust, righteousness, harmony, peace, straight down to the peace building by the Little South Gate, there was a full row of houses—how will you describe it?" (pp. 33–34). Mr. Guo's curse, "Fucking four safeguards and eight virtues!" underscores the point that Taiwan's values have been demolished along with its buildings—and also elicits tremendous peals of laughter from the audience.[41] Critic Jiang Yan writes, "[this line] is probably the impression of many who live in Taiwan. Old morals are just like the old buildings in the scene when the play begins. They have already turned into ruins."[42] Nevertheless, both demolished buildings and values provoke audience laughter. By laughing in spite of themselves, the audience comes to question the notion of what is comic and what is tragic.

Play Hard further blurs this distinction. On the one hand, the settings are far more hopeful than the demolished buildings of *Oh! Three Diverged Paths*. A construction site for a luxury condominium, a KTV, and even the customs checkpoint at Chiang Kai-shek International Airport are all places people go to live a glamorous life and dream of future plans. On the other hand, these sites of joy can so easily become sites of tragedy. In the course of the play, the KTV becomes the scene of a shoot-out by mobsters, and, as one character notes, people perish in fires in KTVs with alarming regularity. Not long before *Play Hard* opened, some newly built luxury towers collapsed in a mud slide. Soon after it closed, Chiang Kai-shek International Airport witnessed the deadliest airplane crash in its history. In Li Guoxiu's Taiwan, no physical site arouses only one emotion. One journalist remarks, "these places, like the customs point at the airport, the lobby of a KTV, a construction site, and so forth, in the eyes of the people who have lived in Taiwan for a long time, represent joyful hope, and also represent fearful destruction—they are precisely the most symbolic of Taiwan."[43] This dichotomous representation lends itself to a play that engages comedy and tragedy in continuous dialogue with one another.

Like *Oh! Three Diverged Paths*, *Play Hard* also sees destruction in the less physical realms of history and morality. Older Brother is the guardian of historical memory, repeating stories over and over until his relatives no longer wish to hear them. When Mr. Guo complains of his brother's repetitions of his story of the war, Older Brother says, "I'm afraid I'll forget, so I want to say it over and over!"[44] The scene "Searching" ends when Older Brother begins his story of the February 28 Incident, and everyone else walks away. Older Brother continues on anyway. Though an earnest chronicler, he is an unreliable one. Throughout his story of the war, the others must correct the details, which apparently change each time the story is told. Despite Older

Brother's efforts, historical memory is being demolished. If the older Guo brother is lost in past events, the younger one is obsessed with moral decay. In Part III, he decries the loss of Confucian virtues in general. In Part IV, he specifically opposes his brother's decision to marry A-man on the grounds that such an act would disrespect his brother's late wife. Mr. Guo's wife scolds him for clinging to outdated values: "A-lin! Look at present reality. Don't be too conservative!" (p. 40). As these two brothers cling to the past in different ways, Li shows how historical and moral destruction are unavoidable.

Destruction can also be quite funny, though. Older Brother's tale of suffering during the war is among the funniest moments in the play. He gets lost in the memory of saving his brother's life, while, in the present, A-man busily changes his diaper. As he reaches the climax of the story, told in that character's usual Taiwanese language, his brother seems more interested in the content of the diaper:

> OLDER BROTHER: It was I who saved A-lin's [Mr. Guo's] life! In 1943 during the Japanese era, the American army bombed Taiwan. A bomb broke off a corner of the Presidential Palace. All of Taipei was a big mess. At that time, I was gathering vegetables at the side of the Dragon Mountain Temple market, when a bomb exploded at my side. In my arms, I was holding A-lin, at that time three years old. He wasn't hurt, but my whole body was covered with . . .
> MR. GUO: Shit!
> OLDER BROTHER: My whole body was covered with shit—What?! Covered with blood, not shit! (p. 40)

The laugh line, which itself arises from an interruption, serves to interrupt the serious story and ensure a lighter tone. So, too, do the numerous corrections of Older Brother's story, particularly those that Mr. Guo, Mrs. Guo, and A-man all provide simultaneously—it seems that everyone knows the story better than its raconteur. An elderly man's growing dementia may not exactly be a laughing matter, but Li Guoxiu enables his audience to find humor in a potentially upsetting situation.

One scene in *Play Hard*, however, truly pushes the envelope as to what might reasonably be considered comedy. The Guo family's ancestral temple, the setting for two earlier scenes including "Searching," makes a ghostly appearance a third time in "Smoke and Fire," the final scene before the epilogue. This three-part scene, set on "no day, no month, no year," represents Little Deng's vision for his yet-to-be-made film (p. 42). The first part is set in the Vancouver airport after Taipei has been destroyed and all who can flee have fled. Mr. Guo, his two daughters, Peter, and his parents are waiting to see if Mrs. Guo has made it out, but the last flight arrives and she is not on it. A distraught Mr. Guo runs back through the gate, shouting that he must return home to Taiwan. At that point, a gauzy scrim descends amidst sounds of guns and fire. The ancestral temple appears, but the tall buildings, which surround it in the earlier two scenes, are gone. After a momentary reminder that it is actually a scene in Little Deng's movie, the lights dim, with sounds of bombs in the background. Following slides of destroyed buildings, the lights slowly rise to reveal the temple in ruins, with Mrs. Guo and Older Brother standing in front of it. Mr. Guo arrives to find his wife unable to understand why he has returned; his brother, who has completely lost his mind from fright over the bombing, is unable to understand anything at all. Older Brother, the declining guardian of past memories, now remembers nothing. History is literally and symbolically destroyed. Mr. and Mrs. Guo support each other in tears; the lights dim; the film-within-a-play, and the play proper, comes to an end. The play never names the aggressor, but no one in the audience can possibly not know: the PRC. It was, in fact, the panic of two years earlier, when the PRC shelled the Taiwan Straits prior to the 1996 presidential elections, that inspired Li Guoxiu to turn the focus of *Can Three Make It?* from the three Chinas back to Taiwan itself and give the question of "Stay or go?" a greater urgency.[45]

The scene chillingly clarifies why people in Taiwan, in Li's view, "play hard." At any moment, everything the Taiwanese people have built could all be destroyed. Li Xingwen explains the central topic of *Play Hard*: "In Taiwan, where society is in never-ending chaos, the people's lives each and every day are just like 'playing hard,' for they do not know when a crisis will stealthily, suddenly appear."[46] The reaction that Li Guoxiu sees, and encourages, in his plays is to turn this and any potential negative into a positive. In a scene in *City Panic* where the three actors debate Taipei's virtues, or lack thereof, all three participants agree that Taipei succeeds precisely because of its less-than-ideal characteristics: "If / not tense / not busy / not crowded / this city fundamentally could not be flourishing."[47] Such seeming contradictions are the essence of life in Taiwan in the post–Martial Law decade. Crime, an issue in all parts of Li's series, is on the rise, but rising crime is symptomatic of a new democracy.[48] At the end of *Play Hard*, Li Guoxiu shows a giant-sized puppet of Li Denghui (Lee Teng-hui) arriving in Canada after fleeing Taiwan; such political caricatures, unthinkable a decade earlier, illustrate Taiwan's dramatically increased freedoms of speech and expression.[49] Whatever concerns Li Guoxiu's scene of destruction in *Play Hard* indicates for the future, it pointedly demonstrates a positive feature of the present. Under Martial Law, could such a scene ever appear? Wang Yaling ends her article with: "In the end, is this kind of philosophy of life pessimistic or optimistic? I'm afraid this is an unsolvable question."[50] No one, not even Li Guoxiu himself, knows the answers to the questions posed by his plays.

There are certainly audience members who come to Li Guoxiu's plays primarily for the comedy. One 1997 year-end review of the arts attributes the success of theater companies, particularly larger ones, to the large number of comedies, believing that in a year of social chaos, people flocked to these funny plays to escape from society's troubles.[51] The review gives no specific evidence, but it certainly seems a reasonable hypothesis. Even Jiang Yan's analytical review begins by conceding that "Many in audiences viewing

Ping-Fong Acting Troupe's performances probably feel that Li Guoxiu is very good at 'making laughter.'[52] In his own performance, Li adds stage business that contributes far more to eliciting laughter than to developing themes. However, *Play Hard*, like the rest of the *Can Three Make It?* series, cannot be wholly characterized as an escape. It undermines the very notion of escape, for even a comedy theater, like a KTV, an airport, or a construction site, can become a scene of tragedy. In *Can Three Make It?*, audiences find tears in a place where they expected to find laughter. Fang Guoyan ends a review of *Oh! Three Diverged Paths* with: "This is a performance abundant with amusement. The roles are a microcosm of the multitude of living things; in addition, the form also reflects this era's fast-paced changes, confused direction, and lack of time to stop and think."[53] In a city where people never have time to stop and think, Li Guoxiu forces them to. They cannot escape from society's troubles, for Li bombards them precisely with images of those troubles, incorporating the most relevant, timely issues drawn from daily life around him. Sitting still in a dark theater, his audiences must confront a vision of their greatest fear and think about the most unthinkable tragedy—and still leave the theater laughing.

NOTES

1. Chou Yang-sun (Zhou Yangshan), quoted in "Restore faith in government," *Free China Review* 47.7 (1997), 25.
2. For consistency, I use *pinyin* to romanize personal names, even though *pinyin* is not yet standard in Taiwan. Lee Kuo-shiu is the spelling used on most of Ping-Fong's English-language documents; Hugh K.S. Lee is also used occasionally.
3. Li Guoxiu, *Sanren xingbuxing I* (Taibei: Zhoukai juchang jijinhui, 1993). Part I ran for 29 performances in Taipei and Kaohsiung, between September 25 and October 25, 1987, with 3 additional performance in Taichung and Chiayi in 1988. See Li Guoxiu, *Sanren xingbuxing IV—Changqi wanming*, program (Taipei: Pingfeng biaoyanban, 1997), p. 69.
4. Li Guoxiu, *Sanren xingbuxing II—Chengshi zhi huang*, photocopy of manuscript, 1988. Part II was performed 40 times between December 17, 1988 and January 27, 1989 in Taipei, Kaohsiung, Tainan, Taichung, and Chungli. See Cai Zhuer, "Li Guoxiu xinong wuye de chengshi," *Zhongguo shibao*, December 26, 1988. Li Guoxiu, *Changqi wanming*, program, p. 67.
5. Li Guoxiu, *Sanren xingbuxing III—OH! Sanchakou* (Taibei: Wenjianhui, 1995). Part III ran for 31 performances in 1993 in Taipei, Kaohsiung, Tainan, Taichung, and Chungli. See "Biaoyan," *Xiuxian shenghuo zazhi* (May 1993), 148; Li Guoxiu, *Changqi wanming*, program, p. 65.
6. Li Guoxiu, *Sanren xingbuxing IV—Changqi wanming*, production script, 1997. Part IV ran from May 14 to June 30, 1997 in Taipei, Taichung, Kaohsiung, and Tainan. See Li Guoxiu, *Changqi wanming*, program, p. 3.
7. Li Guoxiu, interview by author, tape recording, (Taipei, Taiwan, July 2, 1998).
8. For a thorough history of the Little Theater Movement, see Mingder Chung, "The Little Theater Movement of Taiwan (1980–89): in search of alternative aesthetics and politics," (dissertation, New York University, 1992).
9. Li Guoxiu, interview by author.

10. Gu Mengren, "Zhiyou sange ren ye xing?," *Minshengbao* (October 1, 1987).

11. Wang Yaling, "Taiwan daduju huo beijing shihui baixing zhen wanming," *Zhongguo shibao* (November 1, 1997), 47.

12. Shi Meihui, "Changqi wanming xingla fengci Taiwan," *Lianhebao* (October 5, 1997), 18.

13. Li Guoxiu, quoted in Lu Jianying, "Changqi wanming fanying huangmiu Taiwan," *Zhongshi wanbao* (September 28, 1997), 7. The same line headlines are seen in Xu Xiangxin, "Li Guoxiu dasuan Changqi wanming," *Taiwan ribao* (August 21, 1997), 15.

14. Li Guoxiu, *Changqi wanming*, p. 21.

15. Chen Youjun, *Minshengbao* (April 1, 1988), 8.

16. Chen Sufeng, "Pingfeng biaoyanban dailai chengshi fengci baoxiao xiju Changqi wanming you xinxin xiaofan gangdou wenhua zhongxin," *Taiwan xinwenbao* (October 23, 1997).

17. Wu Wenzhi, "Sanren xingbuxing—Changqi wanming," *Jin zhoukan*, 46 (1997), 132.

18. Zhang Jinghan, "Xiao, ye hui liu yanlei! Ping Li Guoxiu de Oh! Sanchakou," *Gongsheng shibao* (June 19, 1993), 28.

19. Yang Liyin, interview by author, tape recording (Taipei, Taiwan, April 17, 1998).

20. Li Guoxiu, *Sanren xingbuxing I*, pp. 70–71.

21. Li Peiyun, "Pingfeng jijiang tuichu xin chengshi xiju," *Taiwan* xinshengbao (May 12, 1993), 8.

22. Li Lianzhu, "Li Guoxiu Changqi wanming zuo deng chang," *Dachengbao* (October 5, 1997), 8; Xu Meihui, "Pingfeng Changqi wanming you laile," *Qingnian ribao* (October 2, 1997), 9.

23. Li Guoxiu, *Changqi wanming*, p. 32.

24. Quoted in Chung, 71.

25. Chung 20.

26. Pingfeng biaoyanban, "Pingfeng biaoyanban guanzhong qun tongji fenxi," photocopy, 1997.

27. Li Guoxiu, *Sanren xingbuxing I*, p. 25.

28. Chen Zhengxi, "Xiaokan aile jiayuan: ping Sanren xingbuxing IV—Changqi wanming," *Biaoyan yishu* 60 (1997), 80.

29. Li Guoxiu, *Sanren xingbuxing IV—Changqi wanming*, performance by Pingfeng biaoyanban, Taibei shejiaoguan (Taipei, Taiwan, October 13, 1997).

30. Li Guoxiu, *Oh! Sanchakou*, p. 67.

31. Yang Liling, "Wenle sici, sanren daodi xingbuxing?," *Biaoyan yishu* (1997), 13–15.

32. Gu Mengren, "Zhiyou sange ren ye xing?"

33. Chen Youjun, "Yinshang Taiwan wutaiju Ying Ruocheng genzhe hahaxiao," *Minshengbao* (May 20, 1993), wenhua xinwen 14.

34. "Xiao nao bei xi zhong, mengchuo xiandairen tongchu!," *Gongsheng shibao* (May 1, 1993), 28.

35. Zhang Jinghan, "Xiao, ye hui liu yanlei!," 28.

36. Pingfeng biaoyanban, "A Short Introduction to Pin-Fong Acting Troupe" (Taibei: Pingfeng biaoyanban, 1997).

37. Zhang Jinghan, "Xiao, ye hui liu yanlei!," 28.

38. Li Guoxiu, *Sanren xingbuxing I*, p. 8.

39. Li Guoxiu, *Chengshi zhi huang*, p. 5-1.

40. Li Guoxiu, *Oh! Sanchakou*, p. 34.

41. Li Guoxiu, *Oh! Sanchakou*, 35; Li Guoxiu, *Sanren xingbuxing III—OH! Sanchakou*, videotape, vol. 1 (Taipei: Pingfeng biaoyanban, 1993).

42. Jiang Yan, "Wo lei siwei bade—tan Sanren xingbuxing—Oh! Sanchakou," *Minzhong ribao* (May 31, 1993), 25.

43. Jiang Shifang, "Changqi wanming xieshi you mohuan," *Zhongguo shibao* (September 28, 1997), 23.

44. Li Guoxiu, *Changqi wanming*, p. 40.

45. Wang Yaling, "Taiwan daduju huo beijing shehui baixing zhen wanming," *Zhongguo shibao* (November 1, 1997), 47.

46. Li Xingwen, "Xizhaoyan, mingzhaowan! Chengshi xiju diyi zhaopai—Pingfeng biaoyanban de Changqi wanming shengya," *Jiaoliu* 36 (1997), 56.

47. Li Guoxiu, *Chengshi zhi huang*, 4-1-2.

48. Hung-mao Tien (Tian Hongmao), quoted in "Change with stability," *Free China Review*, 47.7 (1997), 8.

49. "Constructive discontent," *Free China Review*, 47.7 (1997), 6.

50. Wang Yaling, "Taiwan daduju huo beijing shihui baixing zhen wanming," p. 47.

51. Wang Yaling, "Jiuliu piaofang dimi, Yijiujiuqi shengmingli zhaxian, Yinyue piaofang xiahua, Daxiaojuchang yipian rongjing," *Zhongguo shibao* (January 30, 1998), 47.

52. Jiang Yan, 25.

53. Fang Guoyan, "Sandi sanren sanchakou," *Mingshengbao* (May 22, 1993).

9

Tales of a Porous City: Public Residences and Private Streets in Taipei Films

Yomi Braester

In Taipei, walls crumble, ceilings cave in, and spaces portend their impending destruction—or so the city is portrayed by some of its most prominent film-makers. The directors Edward Yang (Yang Dechang) and Tsai Ming-liang (Cai Mingliang) present two mirroring aspects of urban ruin. Tsai has focused on sites of doom and vanishing cityscapes. In *Dong* (*The Hole*, 1998), two residents cope with the growing porosity of their damaged and leaking apartments, while Taipei is under quarantine because of an epidemic outbreak. The short *Tianqiao bu jian le* (*The Skywalk is Gone*) focuses on the skywalk in front of the New Railway Station, which was torn down since filming Tsai's *Ni neibian jidian* (*What Time is it There?*, 2001). *Bu san* (English title *Goodbye, Dragon Inn*, 2003) takes place in Fuhe Grand Theater in Yong-ho, designated for demolition and razed soon after the shoot. Edward Yang's Taipei, on the other hand, is mostly affluent and chic. Yet glittering images of the prosperous city provide an ironic commentary on the breakdown of interpersonal relations. The deep unrest is foregrounded against the fashionably designed hangouts of the jet set.

In an earlier essay, I traced Taipei's "poetics of demolition" to specific social issues. In this chapter, I stress the images of apocalypse.[1] I revisit my readings of Stan Lai's *Feixia Ada* (English title *The Red Lotus Society*, 1994) and Tsai Ming-liang's *Aiqing wansui* (*Vive l'amour*, 1994) and proceed to contrast these films with Edward Yang's *Majiang* (*Mahjong*, 1996). All three present Taipei as a city on the verge of mental and physical breakdown. With the radical change in Taipei's spatial semiotics, collective memory is destroyed. Rather than simply lamenting the death of an imaginary metro-politan utopia, the films trace the urban ruin to the collapse of the distinc-tion between the private and public realms and, at the same time, show the creative potential in embracing semipermeable borderlines. Insofar as the "public–private distinction has been a key organizing principle, shaping the physical space of the cities and the social life of their citizens," the distinction defines the normative and legal use of space, delimits the self, and regulates the public sphere.[2] This binary opposition is, however, artificial, as public and private spatial functions bleed into each other. The films in question acknowledge the anxieties triggered by spatial ambiguity but also recognize the potential in liminal spaces that defy demarcation.

THE POETICS OF DEMOLITION

These films present a poetics of demolition as they capture the liminal moment at which demolition sites can be taken at face value rather than as markers of what has been destroyed or what will be constructed. The poetics of demolition is a strategy for pointing at the existential negotiation between spatial belonging and urban alienation. Equally important, the poetics of demolition allows cinema to take part in the public debates on urban planning and channel civic resistance to more a complex politics of memory.

The poetics of demolition feeds off the sense of doom associated with late twentieth-century cities. *The Hole*'s description of a millenarian catastrophe should be viewed in light of cultural events such as Superman's death. On November 18, 1992, in a last valiant defense of Metropolis, the man of steel faced the monstrous character Doomsday, saying, "Nobody tears apart *my* city and gets away with it!" The death of Superman, as Marc Kipniss argues, denotes the death of the dream of the modern city.[3] Metropolis is a city with which Superman—who made his appearance in 1938, a time of faith in urban growth—can identify (*"my* city," original emphasis) and for which he is willing to die. His death accompanies the destruction of glorified urban spaces and their heroes. The new urban subjects are antiheroes, living in alienating and torn-up spaces, who must find an existence that transcends the unstable structures they inhabit. The metropolis is no longer "their" city; they are left only with longing for a city that might have set clear borders to accommodate their bodies and contain their memories. Taipei films show how the architectural environment is reappropriated and urban space is reconfigured to suggest both ruin and redemption.

The failure of material barriers to separate personal spaces from those of public activity allows a cinematic representation of issues, some of which are symptomatic of contemporary crowded cities, others specific to Taipei's urban growth. Beginning with the expansion west of the city walls in the nineteenth century, continuing with the walls' destruction and the development of the new districts to the east in the early twentieth century, and through the demolition of many pre-1945 Japanese-style residences in favor of multistoried, functional housing of modernist design, the transformation of the city's physical boundaries reflected political and social changes. Since the 1970s, when the government developed the infrastructure for the service sector, a two-fold pattern emerged, namely the formation of a large and densely populated metropolitan area and precipitated suburbanization. The major change in the perception of private and public space resulted from the government policy to gentrify the city center, the concomitant regulation of land use for residential building, and design of open urban spaces.

Tsai's, Lai's, and Yang's films refer directly to the ambiguous spaces that proliferated in the aftermath of the economic growth and remained in the gray zone in the tug-of-war between developers, municipal policy makers, residents, and social activists. Those spaces include parks planted on grounds formerly occupied by quasi-legal housing, night-time makeshift stalls, restaurants built hastily and without attention to fire regulation, bubble economy startups, and fashionable bars for expats and other nouveau riches working for multinational corporations. These locales act as reminders of the erasure of older Taipei landmarks. The poetics of demolition provides a critique of Taipei's architectural spaces and Taiwan's politics of memory.

McDonald's as a Metonymy for the City

The connection between the demolition of the cityscape and the erasure of memory is one of the central themes in *The Red Lotus Society* (1994), the second film by Stan Lai (Lai Shengchuan), playwright, stage director, and founder of the drama troupe named Performance Workshop. As the Chinese title—literally, "Ah Da the flying knight"—suggests, the plot revolves around a young man, about 20 years old, who becomes interested in the martial art of *qinggong*, which purportedly allows the practitioner to "vault," or hover and fly. The young man's search for the secret bearers of the vaulting tradition leads him through a series of formative experiences, which modify his ideal of the ancient martial art and adapt it for modern city life. As Ah Da wanders through Taipei, the city is revealed to be a monument for forgetting, a space not only of decadent consumerism and speculation but also a metropolis in the process of being demolished and reconstructed, a city that burns down and leaves no spaces for personal memory or collective identity.

Ah Da's formation leads him through a gamut of practices that show the permeability of the private and the public. His journey begins at a McDonald's, where he tries to promote a program for quick English learning. More than merely fast food restaurants, the McDonald's franchises have come to define Taipei's cityscape in the 1990s. Unlike the symbol of life-on-the-run that they have become in the United States, McDonald's franchises in Taiwan encourage customers to stay longer and provide a uniquely quiet, sterile, and smoke-free environment. McDonald's restaurants present themselves as teenagers' dream palaces, providing an illusion of leisure and affluence. They are saccharine places of refuge from the crammed study spaces of the *K-shu* (study halls) and make-up schools. As Li Qingzhi notes, a few McDonald's franchises in Taiwan have been decorated to evoke children's tales.[4] This reflects the rising power of underage consumers, but also the desire to create a new myth out of familiar urban spots and present customers with a fantasy of private space in the midst of the crowd. Ah Da's odyssey for a city he can call his own starts, forebodingly, in such a place of consumerist phantasmagoria.

After McDonald's customers ignore his slick sales pitch and his intrusion into their space, the young Ah Da finds temporary refuge in a public park, where an old man has gathered an intimate group to tell his stories on brave vaulting adepts. Taipei parks, as I discuss later, provide specific ways of reappropriating time and space. Lin Wenqi notes the irony of the fact that the old man's narration takes place in the park next to the History Museum.[5] The park serves as the location of storytelling, which negotiates between the myths introduced by the mainlanders, who came to Taiwan in the 1940s, and the recently created myths of the "new Taiwanese" (*xin Taiwanren*), the generation that is in the process of construing an identity that would replace both the definitions based on the memories of the mainlanders and the indigenous Taiwanese. The story of the secret Red Lotus Society is told first by a mainlander, then by a Taiwanese. At the same time that the custody of the narrative is handed over to the Taiwanese, the locus of the new myth shifts from a pan-Chinese view to the city spaces of Taipei. Lin Wenqi further claims that *The Red Lotus Society* and other urban films of the 1990s parody the national identity promoted in earlier films; the city replaces the State. Yet the new urban allegory is as fallible as national allegory—the apprentice who takes the old storyteller's place indulges in fancy no less than his predecessor. The garden is not simply an antithesis to the museum; it is rather an ambiguous space that, although appropriated by the small group of eccentrics, nevertheless, retains a public dimension.

Ah Da's inventory of Taipei liminal spaces continues when his vaulting teacher dismisses him. The young man follows a lead and helps blind masseurs, among whom he hopes to find a secret master. Most of his clients are underworld mobsters, accompanied by prostitutes in hotel rooms rented by the hour. Ah Da enters these dens by the service doors and becomes familiar with the back alleys behind Taipei's affluent shop fronts. Next, the young man becomes an entrepreneur: "I'll teach you real martial art," says the lady boss, "the martial art of earning money." Yet when Ah Da opens a private door and witnesses the boss's own vaulting practices, he gets fired. The business consists of a teleprinter communications center, which turns all commerce virtual and spaceless. When the virtual speculation turns sour, all that is left behind is a few empty rooms, and Ah Da is seen roaming through the vacated offices that convey no sense of belonging. As an apprentice in realty speculation, Ah Da learns how, in Taipei's bubble economy, busy spaces can be reappropriated or even vanish in no time.

A SKY OF ONE'S OWN

After his training in the Dao of fast food and the Zen of real estate, Ah Da finally masters vaulting and learns how to fly. Becoming a flying knight (*feixia*) is the ultimate modern fantasy of appropriating urban space. Although the knight errant appears in premodern literature, the flying knight did not become a popular theme until the turn of the nineteenth century, and especially after Hong Kong cinema depicted flying knights in the 1950s.[6] The marketing blurb on the videocassette jacket for *The Red Lotus Society* describes the film as "a filmic legend of the modern city" (*xiandai duhui chuanqi dianying*). Inasmuch as the knight errant is associated with the "rivers and lakes" (*jianghu*), the uninhabited periphery, the urbanized knight errant in *The Red Lotus Society* continues to reside in the social margins. Flying is Ah Da's only way of finding a space of his own in the city.

Ah Da follows in the steps of many urbanites who have aspired to observe cities from above. The cinematic imagination, from *Metropolis* to *Blade Runner* and *The Fifth Element*, followed and envisioned the city as an aerial maze navigable by flying vehicles. The flight of fancy that sent the modern urbanite in search of an existence above the city structures would culminate in imagining fictional characters capable of flying, from *Superman* to *The Matrix*. Umberto Eco draws attention to the uniquely twentieth-century characteristics of Superman. The man of steel responds to the particular frustrations of the modern city dweller, living in "an industrial society . . . that has usurped [one's] decision-making role."[7] Superman defies the limitations of city spaces—his speed and X-ray vision break through the limits of space and even time, because he can exceed the speed of light. His double identity, as the privacy-seeking Clark Kent and the limelight-prone Superman, evidences the ambiguity inherent in the dream of flying.

Ah Da shares Superman's lonely double life, practicing vaulting in secret while continuing his drab existence. He lives in the city but takes incognito flights, not divulging, even to his best friend, his identity as the mysterious flying man. Yet Ah Da operates in the days after Superman's death and signals a post-Superman urban disillusion. Unlike the American comic book hero and the native cartoon character Xiao feixia ("Little Flying Knight"), Ah Da is no lifesaving hero; rather, he must submit to the city. He becomes more and more lonely, set apart from those around him, who die one by one. Ah Da's mastery of vaulting complements his tutelage in the dream palaces and back alleys by making him fully aware of the illusion that Taipei spaces foster. Private abodes provide little shelter, nor is public space accompanied by any sense of community.

TAIPEI BY AIR

Taipei's airspace has created a unique urban experience. As several shots in *The Red Lotus Society* remind the viewer, airplanes constantly invade the city. Planes approaching Songshan Airport fly low over Taipei. Urban planner Li Qingzhi, in his *Bird Country Madness: Spatial Culture in Fin-de-siècle Taipei*, observes how people visit Alley 180 of Binjiang Street, at the end of the airport runway, to watch the planes take off. Li writes:

> The sky-scrapers and overpasses bring charm to life in a crowded city . . . but in the heart of every urban person remains the impetus of "wanting to fly," a desire to take off the heavy shackles of the city. . . . A good city . . . must also

provide some spaces with a sensation of flight, so that urban residents should be able to imagine flight in the city, give freedom to their minds and relieve urban stress.[8]

Ah Da's rooftop has a view of the newly built Shin Kong Mitsukoshi Building, 244 meters high with its terrace offering a bird's-eye view of the city (opened in January 1994, as the film was being shot), and his exercises of climbing up stairs are photographed from an angle that takes Ah Da over the high-rise. The low-flying airplanes and observation balcony promise a new, liberated relationship to the city. The novel visual experience is stressed in scenes that take viewers over Taipei's streets at dizzying proximity to the tall buildings. These point-of-view shots from Ah Da's perspective were taken by a remote-controlled minuscule helicopter. The high-tech "Redheaded Fly" was equipped with a camera in its head and could easily maneuver through city spaces.[9] The resulting shots show Ah Da's escapades as a cinematic fantasy—an out-of-body experience tantamount to a human-sized airplane's foray into the city.

The need to escape the city by flying is foregrounded when, toward the end of the film, Ah Da is trapped in a fire and is pushed out of the window. He flies to a nearby rooftop and collapses there. When he regains consciousness, he looks back to see the charred building. The scene resonates with Taipei of the late 1980s and early 1990s, where restaurant and karaoke bar fires were frequent. Such fires resulted from shoddy and illegal construction, entrepreneurial greed that led to the opening of restaurants and KTV bars in unfit quarters, and neglect by city regulators. The catastrophes, involving dozens of casualties at a time, were reported on front pages and widely televised. Despite reprimands issued to administrators and offers of resignation, the fires became a symbol of Taiwan's unmonitored economic growth, governmental mismanagement, and unchecked social change. Ah Da's flight from the burning restaurant presents a fantastic escape from such an urban catastrophe and stands for an alternative individual agency. Stalking the city rooftops and finally flying above the buildings, Ah Da literally finds an existence above and beyond Taipei's apocalyptic cityscape.

The Flight of Memory

Although Ah Da reappropriates Taipei's spaces, his exploits reflect the city's spatial disintegration. Lin Wenqi notes that Ah Da's vaulting signals the loss of collective identity and the advent of Taiwan's "cultural schizophrenia."[10] Ah Da's bird's-eye view, concludes Lin, becomes the last and only way to comprehend the city and its inhabitants as integral entities. Insofar as Ah Da yearns for such an ideal Metropolis, even his mastery of flying cannot reconstitute the city or preserve its mnemonic landscape. Although he internalizes the teaching of previous generations and masters the vaulting art of the Red Lotus Society, nevertheless, the collective memory of his community is receding. His father dies in a violent incident; the storyteller, who remains the only witness to the Red Lotus Society, suffers a stroke and loses his speech; Ah Da's urban odyssey ends in the fire that kills his lover, his childhood friend, and his boss. Ah Da copes with these losses by making his body into a repository of memories. A blind masseur tells him, "Our bodies are like our minds. They retain all sorts of memories. Especially traumatic memories will crystallize into lumps like this one. If you can work slowly and dissolve it, the horrible memory will disappear from the brain."[11] Ah Da searches Taipei's streets for lost memories and residual pain, and harnesses their energy for his art of vaulting. Stan Lai notes that the human body was weighed by traumas: "If we could remember [everything], we would fly."[12] Ah Da is the only one who preserves this ability. As a series of incidents destroy his intimate spaces and close friends, he is left an incognito vaulting master in a city that does not remember him and in which he has nothing to remember.

The dissolution of memory in *The Red Lotus Society* is reflected in Taipei's changing skyline and vanishing cityscape. The film takes the viewer through many sites of construction and demolition. One is reminded that through the 1980s and 1990s, Taipei landmarks gave way to new ones—the old railway station was razed to make room for the project that included the Shin Kong Mitsukoshi building; Zhonghua Market was demolished in 1992 to make way for a new raised freeway; architectural relics from the period of Japanese occupation, such as the Sanyezhuang Building (1907–1990), were torn down, and projects such as the new City Hall on Jilong Road provided new foci of urban activity. Li Qingzhi even finds a potent symbol in the giant plastic dinosaur skeleton that has been hanging over the M Restaurant on Bade Road since 1989: Li sees the dinosaur as an atavistic resistance to civilization, a monument to humanity's nearing extinction, for "fin-de-siècle Taipei is a city of extinct life."[13] Such modernist nostalgia aside, Ah Da's aerial gaze shows a city that has left no traces of Taipei's previous cultural landscape.

The Red Lotus Society foreshadows other films that document the transformation of Taipei and its spatial ambiguity as a city that cannot be pieced together, presenting dissonant architectural and temporal registers. Urban landmarks become metaphors for experience fetishized, consumed, discarded, and forgotten. Ah Da tries to find in Taipei a map of his mental geography. Instead, he finds out that the cityscape is not a memory palace but a maze of forgetting. Insofar as spaces reify experience in material form, the continuous demolition of Taipei tears down its memories.

Ah Da's attempt to store the city's past in his body brings to mind Steven Shaviro's contention that the cinematic experience circumvents the linguistic system of signification and privileges bodily perception over visual semiotics.[14] The poetics of demolition in *The Red Lotus Society* points to an alternative, tactile rather than visual, awareness of urban spaces. Paradoxically, this sensibility reduces consciousness to a memory of the now and erases past experience. The body becomes the last refuge of memory because of the failure to establish architectural spaces of individual autonomy and communal identity.

AT HOME IN PUBLIC SPACE

Whereas *The Red Lotus Society* focuses on the ambiguous space of the body, Tsai Ming-liang and Edward Yang present a more comprehensive criticism of Taipei's changing topography. Of special interest is Tsai's *Vive l'amour*, shot at the same time as *The Red Lotus Society* and released a couple of months after Lai's film. It is the second in Tsai's Taipei trilogy, after *Qingshaonian nezha* (English title *Rebels of the Neon God*, 1992) and before *Heliu* (*The River*, 1997), and paves the way for the exploration of demolition, urban cataclysm, memory, and identity in the director's later films. The story line of *Vive l'amour* follows a female real estate agent, Ms. Lin, and two men: Xiaokang, selling space for cremation jars in an interior burial complex, and Ah Rong, offering smuggled goods at a makeshift sidewalk stall. Their emotionless love triangle takes place in these temporary, borrowed, and impersonal spaces. The two men have each stolen a key to the same apartment for sale. They reside in a twice-reappropriated place—they live clandestinely in an apartment that is in the real estate agent's temporary custody. The woman also conducts her intimate life in public spaces, including the use of the apartment for a one-night stand with the sidewalk vendor. As critics have noticed, the apartment in *Vive l'amour* does not signal home, which is replaced by empty spaces and empty desire.[15]

The film camera stalks the protagonists and stresses the penetrability of Taipei spaces. In Taipei's congested urban environment, "going fishing" entails going to the neighborhood artificial fishing pond, or (as I happened to observe in September 1994, around the time *Vive l'amour* was released) a man can practice golf in a parking lot during office break, using an invisible club and ball. Under these circumstances, city dwellers have come to expect a form of privacy in public places by ignoring others' appropriation of the same spaces. The resulting invisibility of the urban subject gives inexhaustible opportunities for voyeurism but also allows for the devaluation of the gaze as a tool of social interaction. Since private and public are blurred, space is not possessed and vision need not be transgressive.

In one of the opening shots of *Vive l'amour*, one of the male protagonists, Xiaokang, looks at himself in a 7-Eleven security mirror. Although he is subjected to store security surveillance, his self-absorbed observation of his own image ignores others' gazes and neutralizes their potential intrusiveness. The awkwardness of the situation is emphasized for the film's spectators by the fact that Xiaokang's gaze is trained directly at the camera. Chris Berry notes how this scene is emblematic of performativity in the social margins and symptomatic of the "failure or refusal to participate in existing kinship systems."[16] It is an extreme case of the invisibility of the urban subject in public space. In later scenes, the camera follows the protagonists to the apartment for sale and shows them in the most private situations— masturbating, wiping off in the bathroom, trying to commit suicide. Intimacy becomes, at best, banal, or—as in the sex scenes—even impersonal and disaffected. In a daring shot, the immobile camera focuses for seven minutes on Ms. Lin's face as she cries in the open-air theater of the Ta-an Forest Park. The relentless shot stresses the woman's exposure, as she makes a spectacle of herself in the middle of an 800-seat arena. This is the film's last shot; yet it offers no catharsis or resolution. The reappropriation of public spaces for intimate behavior only stresses the debasement of emotion in the urban setting.

THE RETURN OF SUPPRESSED SPACES

The symbolism in *Vive l'amour* should be understood in light of the specific urban locations and of the Ta-an Forest Park in particular. The film originated in the director's experimental theater piece *Gongyu chunguang waixie* (*Let the Spring Light Out of the Dorm*, 1992) and the abstract relations developed in the stage play.[17] In this sense, the cityscape is "an extension of the mindscape."[18] Yet the film clearly relies on concrete references to Taipei landmarks and, as Peggy Chiao remarks, presents a "Taipei flesh and blood."[19] *Vive l'amour* continues a trope present already in *Zaoan Taibei* (*Good Morning, Taipei*, 1980; dir. Li Xing) and *Niezi* (English title *The Outsiders*, 1986), which portray Taipei's parks as "the locale of deviant activities carried on outside the official orbit of the city life."[20] The location of the crying scene in the Ta-an Forest Park stresses the failure of urban spaces to provide the city dweller with any sense of identity, stability, or communal integrity.

The Ta-an Forest Park was at the center of debates in the late 1980s and the early 1990s. The project, known as Park No. seven in earlier blueprints, restructured a 26-hectare block in Taipei's east side to provide the city with much-needed green lungs.[21] Although already designated for public use in the Japanese city plan, it served as a residential area since the early 1950s and contained a veterans' village (*juancun*), a quasi-legal settlement for the dispossessed remnants of Chiang Kai-shek's military. In 1985, the municipal government decided to retake possession of the area. Starting in April 1992, 1348 houses, of which 1257 were declared illegal, were demolished.[22] The large-scale project aroused public controversy.[23] In view of the publicity of the park project, when the protagonist of *Vive l'amour* sets foot in the park, she enters spaces already pregnant with the connotations of strong-handed government intervention in urban planning, disregard of city dwellers, and political dispute over Taiwan's national myths. Tsai's camera catches the park at a point of transition, just as it opened to the public—soon after the evacuation, during the initial stages of landscaping, and before it became fully functional. The woman protagonist walks through a lunar landscape that still carries the scars of demolition. The park under construction presents upturned earth and bare cement, resembling bombarded ruins. The city portrayed in Tsai's film acquires undertones of a millenarian cataclysm, but also more concrete allusions to the city's urban dysfunction and civil unrest.

The destruction of urban spaces is accompanied by the deterioration of memory. The dead are no longer buried on hilly slopes overlooking the city but rather discarded into a private condo refitted for this purpose—a commodified and sterile space. Arguably, the space most emblematic of the characters' inability to create a meaningful memory is the apartment for sale. Although they all inhabit the same place, each protagonist reappropriates it for different purposes and enacts his or her own fantasies in it. They practically never share the apartment and express no interest in making it into a permanent love nest. The apartment remains as if uninhabited, and through the entire movie, the bed is never even covered with a sheet. Although each of the characters returns to the bed as the locus of desire, they just as readily leave it to return to their lonely existence. The condo is neither a private nor a public space. Although the three protagonists come back to the same place time and again, it is as if they always go there for the first time. Their actions acquire no meaning and create no memories. Like the woman's repeated crossing of the road next to the sign "No Jaywalking"—indifferent to any potential transgression—the spatial practices in Tsai's film resist all regulation, ritual symbolism, and meaning formation.

POROUS SPACE

A complementary image to the city in ruins can be found in the works of Edward Yang, who, like Tsai, has dedicated his films to exploring Taipei. Yang's were among the earlier films to document Taipei's neglected areas, such as the slums in *Qingmei zhuma* (English title *Taipei Story*, 1985). Yang's *Kongbu fenzi* (*Terrorizer*, 1986) anticipates Tsai's *Vive l'amour* in focusing on a single apartment, visited and appropriated by various characters, neither of who claims ownership over the place or finds shelter in it. The beginning sequence, in which the condo's windows are shattered in a police shoot-out, sets the tone for the entire film in which private spaces are constantly transgressed and intruded into. The ambiguities of space are at the focus of Yang's later films. *Mahjong* criticizes private apartments, public cafés, and urban projects for failing to protect and serve Taipei's citizens.

In one telling scene, a young hairdresser known as Hong Kong brings home a woman, Alison, whom he had picked up at a bar. In the morning after, he demands that Alison sleep with his roommates. Throughout the scene, Alison and the four men shuttle between two bedrooms, at times dragging each other along, in a maneuver that disorients the woman and leaves her vulnerable. The intimacy of the apartment and the sense of privacy provided by the dividing walls are undermined by the residents' scheme of claiming all spaces and their contents as shared property. At one point, a roommate consults the woman in private, carefully closing the door behind him. The gesture is a charade, as all the men are in cahoots, and the sense of intimacy is illusory. The camera keeps shooting through half-open doorways into the private bedrooms, panning from one to the other, thereby emphasizing the spatial continuity over the divisions. As the roommates exploit the space to destroy any sense of privacy, the apartment ends up as a fluid space where no boundary is taboo.

It is illuminating to juxtapose the scene with Tsai Ming-liang's *The Hole*. In both cases, a passage opens between clearly demarcated residential spaces. In Tsai's film, the hole in the floor of one apartment and the ceiling of the other is an unwanted gap, and any passage through it constitutes a transgression (or, in a final gesture, transcendence). In *Mahjong*, the apartment walls stay solidly in place, yet they become socially fluid. The characters constantly move across boundaries and realign space-bound relations.

Hong Kong's apartment is one of many spaces in *Mahjong* that have been emptied out of any privacy. Angela's condo, for example, mirrors the young men's apartment to the point of becoming Hong Kong's retribution. Angela, a woman in her forties, brings over her women friends to share Hong Kong in a manner similar to the way he had treated Allison. The scene ends with a shot of Taipei's skyline, with the humiliated Hong Kong's crying heard in the background. The walls of Angela's condo are, in fact, alleged to be literally permeable. Hong Kong's friend, pretending to be a fengshui master, analyzes the location and states that Angela was an empress in a past life and that the condo is inhabited by the spirits of all those wronged by Angela's previous incarnations. Angela is purportedly dislocated from her palace, and the condo is ostensibly "out of alignment." The situation may stand for Taipei—it is as if the city has no claim to its geographical location. Citizens are subjected to forces beyond their control and are left unprotected by the city's architecture. Like Angela, they are no more than guests in their own abodes.

The apartments in *Mahjong*, constantly intruded into, resonate also with the dysfunctional public spaces. The plot is motivated by a scene of accidental meetings at the Hard Rock Café, which exemplifies the blurry line between private and public. Hard Rock Café is a liminal space—like T.G.I. Friday's (a central location in *A Confucian Confusion*), the Café has become a mainstay of Taipei transnational culture, a place to demonstrate one's trendiness. It is the meeting place of expats, who cash in on their racial status and cultural capital of familiarity with Euro-American ways of life, and locals whose over-eager affectation of American accent and attitude betrays their unease.[24] It is apt that the Café is the geographical and social epicenter of the film, as it is both typical of Taipei and antithetical to the native geography, illusively intimate, porous enough to enable social transactions but also to expose the dealers for what they are.

A WOMAN CALLED MATRA

Mahjong refers most directly to Taipei's particular spatial constructions in the character of Marthe, a young French woman who flies over and goes to Hard Rock Café to find her lover, Marcus. When Marthe is disappointed with the womanizing Marcus, she is offered help by Hong Kong's roommates. The Taiwanese men call her Ma Tela, as the French company Matra Transport, the contractor for Taipei's Rapid Transit System (RTS). Marthe is, in fact, the antithesis to Matra and transnational business—a romantic who comes to Taiwan not to take advantage of local economy but rather to find personal happiness. Her adaptation to Taipei includes a new understanding of the city's public spaces.

In the mid-1990s, Matra became a symbol for the mismanagement of Taipei's urban development, akin to the evacuated veterans' villages and the burning restaurants alluded to in Lai and Tsai's films. The Mucha line of RTS, built by Matra, finally opened in February 1996, at the cost of $885 million, five years behind plans, and after a two-year test period that witnessed burst tires, a derailment, and a fire incident. Marcus comments: "That's really funny. Those blokes call you Matra? Do you know why Matra is so well known here? It's not because it knows how to build an underground for these people, it's because it knows how to tell these people what they want. These people shelled out four times the going rate for a metro that still doesn't work!" Marcus's description, drawing on his simultaneous fascination with and scorn for Taipei's residents ("these people"), is, nevertheless, informed by the citizens' perception of lack of agency brought about by the failed urban management. The train fire, on the Mucha Line's first trial run in October 1994, became a symbol of Taiwan's social and political shortcomings. Marthe, on the other hand, gives the lie to the apocalyptic vision inspired by Matra. She and Hong Kong's roommate Luen Luen escape the dysfunctional spaces of the shared apartment and Hard Rock Café. Unlike Lai's and Tsai's protagonists, Marthe manages to carve room for herself in Taipei's public spaces.

Marthe's success is made clear in the last sequence, which begins with Marcus's harangue on Matra, spoken as the two drive through the Taipei night. The city lights are reflected on the windshield through which we see Marthe and Marcus. As in the later *Yi Yi*, which makes prominent use of semitransparent glass shots, the image alludes to the illusory nature of Taipei's glitzy surface, where visual stimuli distract from the social and architectural barriers to an unmediated experience of the city. Marthe realizes the illusion fostered by watching the city glide by from the protected space of the car and walks out on Marcus. She meanders through the streets until she rejoins Luen Luen. The film ends with their prolonged kiss, accompanied not by a sweeping cinematic score but rather by the sounds of a Taipei night market. Whereas Tsai's *Vive l'amour* concludes with the woman crying in the open air theater, in line with the collapse of private and public spaces, *Mahjong* points to the possibility of appropriating Taipei's public spaces. Defying the lack of privacy, the couple kisses, oblivious to their surroundings and find their home in Taipei's streets.

Although critical cinematic treatment of Taipei's growth dates back to the early 1980s, prominently in Yu Kan-p'ing's and Wan Jen's films, Stan Lai's, Tsai Ming-liang's and Edward Yang's works provide especially powerful urban parables.[25] They capture Taipei's particular economy of space and focus on specific locations to reveal them as sites of erasure of memory and destruction of identity. An apocalyptic vision emerges, in which Taipei buries its past under its own structures. At the same time, the ambiguity of purportedly private or public spaces also points at redemptive options. Chang and Wang argue against the prevalent view of *Vive l'amour* as simply a sign of doom and desolation. Instead, the Ta-an Forest Park becomes "Paradise Regained," a borderland that both deterritorializes and reterritorializes desire.[26] The other films too draw out the full implications of a post-Superman Metropolis, one that lives on beyond its doom, and demonstrate the double function of urban spaces as scars—on the one hand, indicating the sites of earlier constructions and serving as markers for collective memory and, on the other hand, defining and reconstructing the city through the history of its ruination. Like the camera-yielding characters in Edward Yang's films (especially in *Terrorizer* and *Yi Yi*), citizens and filmmakers can reconstitute an alternative, hopeful image of Taipei.

NOTES

1. Yomi Braester, " 'If we could remember everything, we would be able to fly': Taipei's cinematic poetics of demolition," *Modern Chinese Literature and Culture* 15: 1 (spring 2003), 29–61.

2. Ali Madanipour, "Introduction," *Public and Private Spaces of the City* (London: Routledge, 2003), p. 1.

3. Marc Kipniss, "The death (and rebirth) of Superman," *Discourse* 16.3 (spring 1994), 144–167.

4. Li Qingzhi "Kuaican chengbao" (Fast-food castles), *Niaoguo kuang—Shijimo Taibei kongjian wenhua xianxiang* (Bird Country Madness: Spatial Culture in Fin-de-Siècle Taipei) (Taipei: Chuangxing chubanshe, 1994), pp. 32–33.

5. Lin Wenqi, "Jiuling niandai Taiwan dushi dianying zhong de lishi, kongjian yu jia/guo" (History, space and home/state in Taiwan urban film of the 1990s), *Chung-wai Literary Monthly* 27:5 (October 1998), 108.

6. Liu Damu, "Cong wuxia xiaoshuo dao dianying" (From chivalric fiction to martial arts), in *Xianggang wuxia dianying yanjiu (1945–1980)* (*A Study of Hong Kong Swordplay Film, 1945–1980*) (Hong Kong: Urban Council, 1996), pp. 33–46.

7. Umberto Eco, "The myth of Superman," *Diacritics* (spring 1972), 14–22.

8. Li Qingzhi "Feixinggan de dushi kongjian" (City spaces imbued with a sense of flying), *Niaoguo kuang*, pp. 160–161.

9. Lü Yuezhu, "Hongtou cangying zhen lafeng" (The red-headed fly truly draws wind), *Zhongguo shibao* (January 12, 1994); Lan Zuwei, "Yaokong feiji + 35mm sheyingji: guopian feiqilai luo!" (Remote-controlled plane + 35-mm camera: Chinese film has taken off!), *Lianhebao* (January 12, 1994).

10. Lin Wenqi, "Jiuling niandai Taiwan dushi dianying," pp. 115–116.

11. The relation between memory and modern Taiwan's identity is consistently examined in Stan Lai's work. Stephen Chan observes that Episode Four ("Memory and Amnesia") of Lai's *Na yi ye, women shuo xiangsheng* (*That Evening, We had a Cross-Talk Show*, 1985) implies that all experience recedes into forgetting unless it becomes part of a collective historical narrative Stephen Ching-kiu Chan, "Temporality and the Modern Subject: Memory in Lai sheng-Ch'uan's The Evening, We Put Up a Show of 'Hsiang-Sheng,' " *Tamkang Review* 18,

1-4: 1-37. The plot of *The Red Lotus Society* also resonates, in many ways, with Lai's previous film, *Anlian/Taohuayuan* (English title *Peach Blossom Land*, 1992, adapted from the 1986 stage play), which is also preoccupied with the relation between contemporary Taiwan and the experience of aging mainlanders.

12. Stan Lai (Lai Shengchuan), personal interview, September 2, 1999.

13. Li Qingzhi, "Xiaomo shengming de chengshi" (A city where life idles away) and "Konglong zhenghouqun" (The dinosaur syndrome), *Niaoguo kuang*, pp. 35, 132–133.

14. Steven Shaviro, "Film theory and visual fascination," *The Cinematic Body* (Minneapolis: University of Minnesota Press, 2000), p. 36.

15. Wen Tianxiang, *Guangying dingge—Cai Mingliang de xinling changyu* (*Freeze-Frame in Chiaroscuro: The Spiritual Site of Tsai Ming-liang*) (Taipei: Hengxing 2002), 102; Zhang Dachun, "Chule quqiao hai you shenme—Cai Mingliang Aiqing wansui li de jia/yuwang" (What is there other than the body's husk?: Home/desire in Tsai Ming-liang's *Vive l'amour*), in *Aiqing wansui*, ed. Cai Mingliang et al. (*Vive l'amour*) (Taipei: Wanxiang, 1994), pp. 184–186.

16. Chris Berry, "Where is the love?: The paradox of performing loneliness in Ts'ai Ming-Liang's *Vive L'Amour*," in *Falling for You: Essays on Cinema and Performance*, ed. Lesley Stern and George Kouvaros (Sydney: Power Publications, 1999), pp. 153, 171.

17. Wen, *Guangying dingge*, pp. 98–101; see also Olivier Joyard and Danièle Rivière, *Tsaï Ming-Liang* (Paris: Dis Voir, 2001).

18. Zhang Aizhu, "Piaobo de zaiti: Cai Mingliang dianying de shenti juchang yu yuwang changyu" (Imagining queer bodies: the erotic site/sight of Tsai Ming-liang's films), *Chung-wai Literary Monthly* 30:10 (March 2002), 80.

19. Jiao Xiongping, "Guji de taibeiren—Aiqing wansui: Cai Mingliang de dushi beige" (Lonely Taipei people: *Vive l'amour*—Tsai Ming-liang's urban threnody) in *Aiqing wansui* ed. Cai Mingliang et al. (*Vive l'amour*) (Taipei: Wanxiang, 1994), p. 153.

20. Hsiao-hung Chang and Chih-hung Wang, "Mapping Taipei's landscape of desire: deterritorialization and reterritorialization of the family/park," in *Xunzhao dianying zhong de Taibei*, ed. Chen Ruxiu and Miao Jinfeng (English title: *Focus on Taipei through Cinema, 1950–1990*) (Taipei: Wanxiang, 1995), p. 115.

21. Even with the completion of the park, Taipei's parks comprised only 2.41% of the city's area (compared to Tokyo's 6.2%, New York City's 12.75% and Paris's 26.06%). Lin Chongjie, "Jingying chengshi de xinling" (Administrating the city's soul), in *Shimin de chengshi* (*City of the Urban Citizens*), ed. Lin Chongjie et al. (Taipei: Chuangxing chubanshe, 1996), p. 119.

22. Taibeishi zhengfu gongwuju gongyuan ludeng gongcheng guanlichu (Public Parks—Road and Lamp section of the Public Works Department of Taipei Municipal government), "Taibeishi da'an Qihao gongyuan jianjie" (Brief introduction to Taipei's Ta-an Park No. Seven), February 1992 (publicity pamphlet).

23. A more detailed account of the debate is presented in my previous essay and in my book, *Witness against History: Literature, Film, and Public Discourse in Twentieth-Century China.* (Stanford, CA: Stanford University Press, 2003).

24. I thank Tzu-i Chuang for her insights on the social significance of American chain diners in Taipei life and in Yang's films.

25. See Braester, "If we could remember everything, we would be able to fly" and Hong Yueqing *Chengshi guiling—dianying zhong de Taibei chengxian* (City Degree Zero: Cinematic Representation of Taipei) (Taipei: Tianyuan chengshi, 2002).

26. Hsiao-hung Chang and Chih-hung Wang, "Mapping Taipei's landscape of desire," pp. 122–125.

PART III

THE MORAL SUBJECT UNDER GLOBAL CAPITALISM

10

Reproducing the Self: Consumption, Imaginary, and Identity in Chinese Women's Autobiographical Practice in the 1990s

Lingzhen Wang

"Living as a woman in silence," Yu Luojin lamented in 1982, "is not as tough as telling the truth in public." Yu Luojin published three autobiographical works before she finally sought political asylum during a trip to West Germany in 1986. At least 10,000 characters were removed from her first autobiographical novel when it was published in 1980, due to the "jarring" (*ci er*) personal voices, including her depiction of her wedding night and her different views on love, marriage, and sex. Her second autobiographical novel, which was based upon her love relationship with an associate chief editor of *Guangming ribao*, was banned shortly after it was published in *Hua cheng* in 1982. It was criticized as exposing private matters in public and advocating improper relationships. As a twice-divorced woman in the early 1980s, her fame was raised through public gossip as well. She was attacked as a nonserious (*bu jiandian*) woman in the most important newspaper and journal in Beijing and was negatively stamped as a writer on private affairs (*yinsi zuojia*).

In the 1990s, however, in the autobiographical works by Chen Ran and Lin Bai, for example, gendered perspectives predominate, sex becomes a major topic, and privacy is the trademark of their popularity. Personal voices triumph as the most conscious and valuable presence, whereas public morality regarding love, marriage, and sex is mocked, transgressed, and rendered nearly irrelevant. Chen Ran titled her autobiographical novel *Siren shenghuo* (*A Private Life*),[1] intending to "dissolve the public, grand and collective model of literary representation endorsed in previous periods";[2] and the publication of the novel won her the popular title of "privatized/personalized writer" (*sirenhua/gerenhua zuojia*). Lin Bai also adheres to personalized writing. In her "Memory and personalized writing," Lin Bai states that the public-oriented and collectively framed memory destroys personal memories and thus makes personal selves disappear.[3] The title of her autobiographical novel, *Yigeren de zhanzheng* (*A Self at War*),[4] well indicates the personal and self-referential criteria and characteristics of her writing. In 1998, *Juedui yinsi: dangdai Zhongguoren qinggan koushu shilu* (*Absolute Privacy: Extempore Recordings of Contemporary Chinese Emotions*),[5] a collection of interviews with contemporary young people conducted by a woman newspaper reporter, An Dun, became an instant hit and the success of the book led to further publication of several other books on privacy and private affairs. For a while, the term *yinsi* (privacy, private affairs) became a hot and seductive trademark, which not only sells but also consumes people's emotional lives.

Obviously, society has changed. In the 1990s economic structures, political policies, moral standards, social relationships, and concepts of literature and self have gradually replaced as well as mixed with those in the past. Women's autobiographical writing is no exception. It has been dramatically reinvested, reproduced, and redefined in the 1990s by women writers and the demands of the cultural marketplace. In this chapter, I will focus on three topics concerning women's autobiographically oriented writing in the 1990s: the relationship between women's autobiographical writing of the 1990s with that of the 1980s; the emerging writing structure as a creative means of consumption; and the representation of the affective mode of identity formation.

RESIGNIFICATION OF THE PERSONAL: HISTORICAL CONNECTION AND DIFFERENCE

The connection between Chinese women's autobiographical writing in the 1990s and that in the early 1980s has been largely understated or overlooked as more critical attention has been paid to their thematic and historical differences resulting from the market economy and cultural commodification since the early 1990s. A close examination of the positions and perspectives of the women writers in the two decades, however, will reveal an intertwined relationship between them.

In my previous studies of Chinese women's autobiographical practice in the twentieth century, especially in the early post-Mao era, I retheorized the feminist concept of the personal.[6] The personal in my writing takes the human subject and its experiences as the site of negotiations of different public and private forces. No longer holding the status of objective truth and the origin of knowledge as claimed by Western feminists in the 1970s, experiences are the material location where different forces come into play with each other. A subjective perception is also required for any experience to be meaningful. In other words, experiences are taken not as external events or purely linguistic production, but subjective—mediated stories. The personal, therefore, refers to a state of individual embodiment of the interactions among different historical forces including public dominant discourses, social institutions, conventions, inter-subjective relationships, as well as physical and affective activities and subjective imagination and fantasies. The formation or trajectory of an identity is always a particular/singular negotiation among diverse historical forces. With a particular history or state of being, the personal sometimes conforms to, sometimes conflicts with, and sometimes subverts the current dominant ideologies. In the early 1980s, Chinese women writers succeeded in carving out a literary space for different personal voices; in studies of women writers in the 1990s, I found that the personal is still one of the most important and pertinent concepts, even though the meaning of the personal has been differently signified.

In the early post-Mao era, the state started relaxing its control over gender and class relationships and, as a result, conventional prejudice against women regained its popularity.[7] At the same time, Chinese women's personal lives were still largely defined in relation to social obligations and public moral standards, and literature remained highly centralized and focused on political and social subjects.[8] In order to transmit their gendered and personal voices, Chinese women writers like Zhang Jie, Yu Luojin, and Dai Houying had to seek cover behind various legitimate and socially sanctioned principles, such as Marxist theory on love and marriage, truth telling, and equality between men and women. Their gendered and personal messages had to be conveyed along with these publicly trumpeted social themes; the result was a new literary space where diverse personal voices could speak and be heard by sensitive readers of the time. Wang Anyi, a writer from a younger generation in the early 1980s, enthusiastically responded to the message on the personal in her "Nüzuojia de ziwo" (The self of women writers):

> It is still vividly before my eyes, the exciting reception of "Love Must Not Be Forgotten." [by Zhang Jie] . . . It is already very extraordinary that a trivial private matter (*xiaoshi*) could become a public short story, but it goes further. What is more important is that this private matter (*sishi*) does not establish a connection with social and political requirements, but just relates to personal (*geren*) emotions and feelings. For many years our literature has been confined to the extreme of collectivism, with nobody having a self, . . . People had no preparation to receive a purely private expression. This ("Love Should . . .") may be regarded as the first appearance of the personal and private expression/mind in literature after so many years. . . . [A]nother short work "Shi maisui" (Gleaning) [also by Zhang Jie], more thoroughly belongs to the personal. To be honest, it was not until I read "Picking Up Wheat Heads" that I first realized the possibility for myself to become a writer. Before that, I had had a fear of literature as a great difficulty. I had been full of emotions and I had made a great effort to connect these emotions with the collective/dominant consciousness of a social mission. But everything had been abortive. I have claimed several times that, "in the past I wrote my diary as fiction, but now I am writing my fiction as a diary." [Yu Luojin's] *A Chinese Winter's Tale* (*Yige dongtian de tonghua*) has furthered the personal trend. . . . [It] is a real story of the author, a private fiction (*si xiaoshuo*), and it developed the personal features of literature to its extreme.[9]

Terms like *sishi, geren,* and *si xiaoshuo* already appeared in Wang's highly reflexive writing in the 1980s, illustrating the initial formation of a gendered literary tradition in the early post-Mao era and, at the same time, foreshadowing a further personalized mode of writing by women writers in the 1990s. If women writers in the early 1980s broke the silence and carved out a particular space for expressing gendered, subjective, and personal voices, in the 1990s, this space has been further expanded and diversified with different social, cultural, and individual features.

In the 1990s, as a result of the fully developed market economy and irresistible commodification of daily lives and cultural production, women's personal writing has proliferated, generating great profit and visibility. With subjective, fragmented, mirror/memory-oriented, and monologue-like characteristics, women's autobiographical writing since the early 1990s has repeatedly centered on such subjects as female bodies, sexual desire, mother–daughter relationships, homo/self-erotic relationships, pleasure/pain, and fantasies. How should we relate all these new features of Chinese women's autobiographical practice to the logic of commodity and consumption in a market economy, and what are the new significations of the personal in a new historical circumstance? In the rest of this chapter, I would like to address these questions by focusing on three women writers and their autobiographical writing in the 1990s: Chen Ran's *A Private Life*, Lin Bai's *A Self at War*, and Wang Anyi's *Youshang de niandai* (*Years of Sadness*).[10]

WRITING AS CONSUMPTION: MIRROR, IMAGINATION, AND PLEASURE

In recent scholarship, the concepts of consumption and commodity have been reformulated to suit diverse and different contexts—physical, social, and cultural. In his study of shopping in North London of the eighteenth century, Daniel Miller argues against a tendency to use consumption/shopping as merely a motif in generalizing about the capitalist spirit or to symbolize social distinctions.[11] Instead, he states that consumption/shopping might be involved in the creation of value and relationships that might manifest elements of cosmology. "Commodities do not have meaning . . . Rather they are meaningful—they come to matter as means for constituting people that matter" (p. 152). He concludes saying, "shopping may be many things within diverse contexts" (p. 155). In other words, consumption is not merely a part of capitalism, the logic of which is expansion and for which it matters little how goods are consumed within this or that context just as long as they sell. Similarly, the consumer is not merely expressing some spirit of capitalism. The study of consumption demands contextualization because consumption manifests different ethics in different circumstances. It is neither purely active, rational, and based on free choice nor totally passive, irrational, and destructive.

The insight of Miller's argument that consumption can produce different cultural and historical meanings within different contexts is very useful in the study of Chinese women's autobiographical fiction in the 1990s, when books had become cultural commodities and the logic of consumption was manifested in cultural activities like reading and writing. It is undeniable that, in the 1990s, even autobiographical works were packaged as seductive commodities to sell. The provocative titles of Chen Ran and Lin Bai's books, *A Private Life* and *A Self at War*, grant immediate pleasure to readers as they invite them to consume through peeping at the intimate lives and private emotions of other people. The beginning several pages of Chen and Lin's autobiographical novels are also written in a way to both meet and direct the consuming desire of readers/consumers. In addition to fragmented thoughts on time, death, mental illness, and love, Chen Ran, in the beginning part of her *A Private Life*, includes a striking visual ink image that looks like a female genital organ; Lin Bai starts her *A Self at War* with a young girl's self-gazing and self-touching (masturbation), followed by kids' sex play, death, and peeping at the genital organ of a women who is giving birth to her child. Readers are led immediately to the most intimate details of the narrators' lives. No longer strictly subject to political, moral, and social controls, sex and sexuality in the literary discourse of the 1990s functioned to advertise, to seduce, and to sell. The seductive tension between looking or peeping and being looked at is consciously staged in the beginning part of both Chen and Lin's novels, and readers are encouraged to consume the stories through reading/peeping into the most private areas of other people's lives.

At a different level, however, as Miller has forcefully pointed out, shopping, selling, and other commercial activities cannot be isolated from a contextual frame and specific historical consequence where meaning is located and reproduced. The commodification and consumability of women's autobiographical work in the 1990s have also helped change ideas and concepts regarding literature, morality, identity, self, as well as the relationship between public and private. The criteria of individual identity and self have been transformed from previously external, social, and political categories to subjective interior, intimate relationship, emotion, sexuality, and fantasy.[12] Sex and sexuality are no longer a public taboo but linked to market, consumption, individual expression, fantasy, and pleasure.[13] This shift has produced different cultural and historical meanings, which, in turn, signify different identity formation, human relationships, and self-writing. Women's autobiographical writing in the 1990s functions not only to satisfy the desire of public consumption (buying and reading) but also to change some social standards and cultural values and to resignify the personal in a new historical context.

In *The Romantic Ethic and the Spirit of Modern Consumerism*, Colin Campbell argues that modern consumerist hedonism is not about the satisfaction of need (physical or sensory) but about the pursuit of the experience of pleasure for its own sake.[14] The key to the development of modern hedonism lies in the shift of primary concern from sensations to emotions (p. 69); and the images that fulfill this emotional desire are either imaginatively created or modified by the individual for self-consumption (p. 77). That is to say, modern individual hedonists tend to employ their imaginative and creative powers to construct mental images, which they consume for the intrinsic pleasure they provide, a practice best described as daydreaming or fantasizing. According to Campbell, the illusion of depth provided by a mirror, or by perspective in a painting, is not the product of wish fulfillment, but a phenomenon in which one accepts as natural the discrepancy between our knowledge and our experience of objects. In other words, the modern consumerist hedonist treats the illusion from a mirror as real whilst knowing that it is indeed "false." In terms of ego or identity formation, if Lacanian imaginary denotes an image stage where the infant, existing without a self in the undifferentiated world, sees the unified image in a mirror and is pleased to identify with it; the modern hedonist, existing as an autonomous self and fully aware of the illusory character of the image in the mirror, desires as well to make him/herself return to that imaginary stage and longs for something pleasurable and unknown. This imaginary and conscious pleasure-seeking logic of modern consumption provides great insight into Chinese women's autobiographical practice in the 1990s as it well illustrates the writing structure underlying Chen, Lin, and Wang's autobiographical works—the structure that repeatedly crystallizes a self in the past in order to consume, to reimagine, and to fantasize for pleasures/pains.

The most important object that has functioned to structure Chen's and Lin's autobiographical novels is the mirror. The mirror, in their writing, introduces a logic that focuses on both self and other; it both reflects and creates; and, similar to Campbell's view, it does not rid people of the awareness of illusions it creates and yet it produces immense pleasures/pains for protagonists/narrators. The mirror in both Chen's and Lin's writing is used primarily for self-looking, self-reading, self-objectification/alienation, self-consumption, and self-identification. The relationship between the female protagonists and the images in the mirror is mostly a narcissistic, masochistic, erotic, and consuming one. At the same time, however, their strong consciousness of the illusion/otherness that the mirror brings and of the acts of both looking at oneself and being looked at complicates the simple self-love/torture economy, and introduces a third party (other) whose invisible, but unwavering, eyes are constantly watching and, thus, framing the gazing subject in front of the mirror. In the context of the consumer culture of the 1990s, one of the most activated frames of the mirror was that of consumption, including self-consumption.

In the beginning part of *A Private Life*, Chen writes about how the first-person narrator feels alienated from the so-called normal consciousness and from herself, and how she, while watching/consuming an American movie titled *Jing zi* (*The Looking Glass*), identifies with the vague image appearing in the mirror on the big screen:

> I often feel that I am divorced from common senses, that all around me there are enemies; that I am no longer myself, but have become someone else—even sexless. This is exactly like the person in the American film *The Looking Glass*, who stands alone in front of the bathroom mirror, whose bright surface the steam has covered over with a layer of mist. Though the window is tightly

closed, a soft breeze still finds its way into the room, swaying the shower curtain, so that it covers the private parts of the person before the mirror. The person shut her/himself off in the bathroom out of self-love, because s/he has exposed her/his mind and body to the filthy world outside for too long a time.

There are invisible eyes lurking everywhere in the air, malevolently watching this person.

You don't know this person's sex because the person doesn't want you to know.

I often think that I am that person in the mirror. Clearly, it is from the vague image in the mirror that I recognize myself, a combination of analytical observer and one who is analytically observed, a person whose sexuality has, as the result of a variety of outside factors, been obscured or neglected, a sexless person. Because this person shines with great splendor, it can assume any number of forms. (pp. 6–7)

The mirror, here, provides a form of identification through illusion and the vague image in the mirror questions any solid identity in reality. To identify with the vague image of another person in the mirror is to look for a self-form that blurs the line between self and other and which promises many possibilities and fantasies. Narcissism, here, connotes more than just self-love because it simultaneously dissolves self-identity in reality: an ambiguous and sexless person. The constant awareness of looking and being looked at splits within any unified identification and renders the otherness as part of self and self as part of the other. The uncertainty about oneself and the desire to experience pleasure through imagination and fantasy repeat throughout Chen's novel. Toward the end of the novel, the narrator shuts herself in her own bathroom, staring at herself in the mirror, just as the person in the movie does.

Across from the bathtub there was a big mirror. In it I could see a young woman lying on her side in a tiny swaying white boat. I watched her. The lines of her face were beautifully soft and gentle, her skin was fair and delicate. Tumbled loosely around her neck, her fragrant hair was like a dark glistening flower floating on a pool of water. . . .

I stared at myself in the bathroom mirror, as if I were judging some other girl altogether. . . .

. . .

Then I did something to myself.

. . .

The experience of appreciating beauty and the fulfillment of desire brought perfectly together.

. . .

That evening in the bathtub, I sank quickly into dreams. (pp. 261–263)

The self-othering or self-objectification caused by the logic of the mirror constructs a distanced mental image (the appreciation of the beauty) that grants a self-erotic relationship—an image the narrator consumes to fulfill the desire for the intrinsic pleasure it provides. The mirror also fulfills the narrator/protagonist's desire by introducing another female figure, who is imagined simultaneously as ideal mother, erotic other, and ideal self-model. I will focus on these significant female figures in the three women's writings later. Throughout Chen's novel, there are many mirror scenes and, at a more general level, her writing itself functions as a mirror, which reflects, distorts, creates, and strives for a state of daydreaming which produces pleasure as well as pain.

This writing structure is also reiterated and foregrounded in Lin Bai's *A Self at War*. For Lin Bai, the mirror is the very form in which the war with the self begins.[15] On the very first page, Lin quotes two paragraphs from one of her previously published stories and they read:

> The warring self refers to a palm clapping itself, a wall blocking itself, a flower destroying itself. The warring self refers to a woman marrying herself.
>
> Looking at herself in a mirror, this woman both brims with self-love and harbors a faintly masochistic heart. Any woman who marries herself unquestionably possesses two, irreconcilable natures, and looks like a two-headed monster. (p. 3)

The statement of self-war or one person's war immediately inaugurates the state of self-split/conflict (two-headed) and self-uncertainty, and, thus, the space for reimagination and recreation. The narrator/protagonist's constant nostalgia for, and struggle with, past experiences in Lin Bai's novel indicate an undiminished desire to search for pleasures/pains, which are simultaneously narcissistic, masochistic, erotic, and imaginative. Self-war indicates self-obsession, self-destruction, and self-recreation.

Like the surface of a mirror, memory also serves as a source of subjective imaginations and fantasies. "Personal memory is also one kind of personal imagination." To write about one's past experience is to look into the mirror of time to construct images of the past and then consume them through objectification and imagination. Lin Bai, in her "Memory and personalized writing," states that "the personal memory does not refer to the authentic, accessible reality of past, but to a gesture/attitude and an ability to use the material of memory to imagine" (p. 249). In *A Private Life*, Chen claims, "The creative imagination is the mother of all memories" (p. 90). After depicting a steaming sexual encounter between the narrator's friend Yi Qiu and Yi Qiu's boyfriend, the narrator writes:

> It has been said that it is only before and after the occurrence of the real and fleeting phenomena of life that we experience them. The actual events that we think we perceive are only dreamlike fabrications invented by our own bodies. Only now, after fifteen years, when I recall from among those already faded and dim past events, that disturbing scene I had covertly witnessed (or perhaps I have desired to witness) from outside the door to Yi Qiu's inner room, do I finally understand that the scene as I perceived it is of my own making now, an experience produced by my imagination at this moment.
>
> The creative imagination is the mother of all memories. (p. 90)

Fully aware of the false status of memory as fabrication, both the narrator and writer continue to daydream in the direction that grants subjective, emotional, and bodily pleasures. In Lin Bai's fiction, the first-person narrator often has the illusion that she herself is a pure fabrication. She tells a story about how she was followed by a young woman on a Beijing street. After she stopped and talked to that woman, she found that the woman's story and dreams were completely identical to her own:

> Her words made me constantly feel cold. I murmured: Who are you? Are you my shadow, or my fabricated character? . . . Please tell me, please tell me, who are you? Are you my fabrication?
> That woman looked at my eyes and said word by word: Just the opposite, you are in fact my fabrication. (p. 15)

The dialogue between the two figures also illustrates the relationship between the narrator and the image in the mirror or between the writer and the protagonist in the text. Furthering Campbell's view that a daydreamer knows what is an illusion and what is real, Lin Bai suggests that the greater pleasure or pain can only be experienced at the moment when the discrepancy of the imaginary and the real has been consciously blurred and reality itself becomes illusion.

> Imagination and reality are just like water and mirror. Standing in between, Duomi sees two selves.
> The self in the water,
> The self in the mirror.
> The two reflect each other, changing unpredictably like a kaleidoscope. (p. 20)

Lin Bai also inserts plots of her previously published short stories in her autobiographical novel and weaves together pure imagination and historical facts. In fact, Wang Anyi, in her autobiographical novel *Jishi yu xugou* (*Actual Reports and Fictional Construction: One Method of Creating the World*), already plays with the two concepts of historical fact and subjective imagination by combining the depiction of her life stories with her own fabrication of the maternal genealogy. However, Lin Bai's novel is less conceptually constructed or divided and, thus, foregrounds the desire to consume and destroy as well as to fabricate and re-create.

The metaphor of the mirror presented in Chen and Lin's writing manifests the logic of modern consumerist hedonism that is self-de/centered, emotional, pleasure-seeking, daydreaming, and desire-laden. This writing structure, as an effective way of consumption, has transformed the function of women's autobiographical writing in contemporary China. In the early and middle 1980s, women writers played a significant role in diversifying literary production through personal modes of writing. Writing autobiographically, at that time, meant to tell one's own stories, which were different from the dominant social discourses, to address questions like "who am I," and "what is truth," and to reveal ignored or suppressed subjective emotions and experiences. Writers such as Zhang Jie and Yu Luojin wrote about problems and questions they were encountering as women in Chinese society, and, consequently, their works were read by the public as autobiographical and factual. In the 1990s, however, writing autobiographically was less about self-expression, truth-seeking, or transgression of public morality. Whether it was factual or fictional, autobiographical writing in the 1990s conveyed a desire to consume one's own experiences and fantasies for individual pleasure or pain (aesthetic, psychological, or even physical), a personal need to reflect, re-create, and daydream, and an obsession with the nostalgic and narcissistic gesture of looking back at the self in the past, not to solidify the self, but to question and to continuously re-imagine. Depiction of private life no longer denoted any absolute facts linked to the authors in society, but functioned more to sell the product (book). It also granted the power to face oneself in public and the power to re-imagine and to re-create a self through writing. Therefore, the personal has been re-signified by the dynamic modern consumerism in a new historical context.

THE AFFECTIVE MODE OF BEING: SHAME, IDENTITY, AND WRITING

The different historical contexts in the 1990s have re-constructed the meaning of cultural products and provided different forms of expression. Chinese women's autobiographical writing, as cultural commodity and product of modern consumption, in turn, has also reshaped concepts such as privacy, self, body, sex, writing, and imagination. What accounts for the specific historical significance of women's autobiographical practice in China of the 1990s, however, is not limited to the general modern consumerist pleasure-seeking spirit. The desire to consume one's past, the need to re-imagine and re-create, and the narcissistic drive for looking at oneself through writing, as I have argued, have been made visible in the frame of modern hedonistic consumerism. At the same time, the desire, need, and drive also point to something else, a residue or an invisible space that resists being totally consumed or erased in the process of consumption, informing readers of particular ways of negotiating a past and a self in a consumerist society. It delineates a mode of existence but has no content of itself; it is the force that moves the narrative forward and simultaneously attempts to return it to its origin. It functions like a formless and invisible core driving women writers in the 1990s to write and rewrite their self-stories. This something, as I shall discuss in the rest of the chapter, can be termed shame, one particular affective mode of being. If, in the 1980s, women writers foregrounded their subjective views of history, society, and self, in the 1990s, the affects such as shame, distress, and guilt underpin autobiographical practice by women writers like Chen Ran, Lin Bai, and Wang Anyi.

Since the beginning of her writing career, Wang Anyi has continuously produced autobiographical stories: the series about Wenwen (1978–1982),

Liushijiu jie chuzhongsheng (*The '69 Middle-School Graduates*, 1984), "*Wo de laili*" (*My Origin*, 1985), *Wutuobang shipian* (*Utopian Poems*, 1993), *Jishi yu xugou* (*Actual Reports and Fictional Construction*, 1992), *Shangxin Taipingyang* (*Sadness for the Pacific*, 1993), and *Youshang de niandai* (*Years of Sadness*, 1998). Writing, for Wang, started with self-writing, and, to a large extent, is self-writing. From socially accepted personal idealism to a search for roots of the nation and the self to an internal monologue about her past and fantasies, the personal has produced different meanings in her 20-year autobiographical practice. Her *Youshang de niandai* (*Years of Sadness*) furthers her inward exploration of her childhood experience and touches upon the invisible core of personal identity. Like Wang Anyi, Chen Ran and Lin Bai also probe deeply into their childhood and adolescent experiences to address the problem of a particular mode of personal identity, in spite of the highly consumable characteristics of their stories.

The writing of *Years of Sadness* is inseparable from the consumerist mode of nostalgia popular in China of the 1990s, but it also rests on an undissolvable personal and affective underpinning. The book's first-person narrator tells about several seemingly trivial, yet embarrassing, humiliating, and agonizing episodes of her childhood experiences, which have been unconsciously suppressed by society and the narrator herself, until one day they are triggered by a sobbing woman in a dark movie theater. Those past episodes include losing movie tickets on two occasions before entering movie theaters and the consequent embarrassment, nervousness, and distress; the strong emotions that grew out of her feeling that her mother did not treat her as well as she did her elder sister; the clash between her desire to befriend other children and her shyness; her secret admiration for and overdone imitation of a girl in the neighborhood; her disappointment in her own appearance; a miscommunication with her math teacher and the humiliation she felt from his interrogation; her sister's betrayal of her in front of the math teacher; her fear of loneliness and of darkness; and, finally, the most unspeakable and shameful experience of being sent to the hospital for examination and treatment of genital infection caused by the sting of an insect. From these private and emotional episodes, we see a young, shy, and sensitive girl who, in her early years, is confused, ignored, unprotected, and deeply hurt. She is lonely and insecure among people; she lacks means to express herself and to communicate even with her mother; she feels rejected by people and excluded from the external world, and constantly feels awkward and inadequate.

Andrew P. Morrison in his "Shame, ideal self, and narcissism," points out that shame reflects feelings about a defect of the self, a lowering of self-esteem, falling short of the values of the self-ideal.[16] The external danger from the experience of shame is abandonment or rejection (p. 352). Freud also linked shame to fears of bodily exposure and nakedness: shame originates in being naked in front of the gaze of the onlooker.[17] Helen Lewis has distinguished two general states of shame, one of which she terms "overt, undifferentiated," and the other which she calls "bypassed" shame.[18] Overt shame refers to feelings experienced by a child when he/she is in some way humiliated by another person. Bypassed shame comes from unconsciously experienced anxieties about inadequacies of self. It links directly to feelings of ontological insecurity; it consists of repressed fears that the narrative of self-identity cannot withstand engulfing pressures on its coherence or social acceptability.[19]

Although different forms of shame exist in Wang Anyi's story, it is bypassed shame that stands out as the constantly evoked mode of being in *Years of Sadness*. This bypassed shame, as I will discuss later, has its particular historical origin in the structure of society and family during the Mao era.

Chen Ran's and Lin Bai's novels, despite their daydreaming features and consumerist structure, are also permeated with a deep sense of shame, which results from feelings of inadequacy and insecurity of oneself in society. Chen Ran's narrator refers to her own problem as *canque*—that is, being crippled and defective: "Sex is never my problem. My problem lies somewhere else— a crippled and defective person in a crippled and defective time" (p. 8). The stigmatized term *canque* was, in fact, given to her by her teacher T in primary school. Teacher T once asked the narrator's mother to take her to a hospital to check for some defective problems (*canque*) in her brain because she didn't speak much in school. The stigma had affected the girl since then. In chapter six, "I am a stranger to myself," the narrator concludes that during those years of primary and middle schools, she was totally an outsider: "The happiness to be able to fuse with other people harmoniously is what I lack forever (*canque*)" (p. 63). In *A Private Life*, Chen Ran tells stories about a girl's attempt to secure or to re-imagine a coherent identity while repeatedly thwarted by the external uncontrollable world. As a child, she lived a lonely life and only enjoyed talking to herself. In school, she was humiliated by her teacher, the most abusive and humiliating case being when he touched her breast and genital area while arrogantly telling her where the "private areas" (*sichu*) were. At home, her domineering father forced her old loving nanny to leave and made her mother an unhappy woman and her a much-ignored child. Although the narrator felt relieved when her parents finally got divorced, her life had become defective in another sense. After years of struggling to reemerge as a confident woman, she was unexpectedly left totally alone by all the people she had loved: her beloved neighbor Widow He (He guafu) died in a fire, her lover, Yin Nan, left her for a foreign country, and her mother died of cancer. Refusing to accept the cruel reality, she shut herself off from the outside world. She was then sent to a mental hospital. The spell of *canque*, that is, the mental problem, the crippled and distorted life, the fragmentary sense of self, and/or the feeling of being abandoned seems not to be easily broken.

Lin Bai's *A Self at War* centers on an orphan-like girl, Duomi, and her coming of age experiences in a small town in the south. When she was only three, her father left her mother and her; when she was about eight years old, her mother had to leave her in order to work in the countryside as a medical worker, and, consequently, Duomi had to live, day and night, all by herself in an empty hospital dormitory. She had no neighbors in the four-floor building except for an old woman living further down on the first floor. The emotions she experienced during those nights constituted her sense of being: abandoned, alone, and in fear. Duomi's childhood was full of scary and adventurous events, as well as nightmare and loneliness. She repeatedly dreamed about the death of her relatives and her mother and feared she would become an orphan abandoned by her mother. At the age of nineteen, she published eight poems and two of them were found to be copied from other people's collection. The plagiarism brought her so much shame that it took her more than ten years to be able to finally face it and talk about it. Duomi's story is one of rejection. Toward the end of the novel, in spite of her many heart-wrenching experiences elaborated in the novel, Duomi concluded that, in her life, she had been totally rejected by society twice: one referred to the plagiarism at age nineteen, the other to her marriage at the age of thirty. She married an old man in order to stay in Beijing. The primary fear and experience of being rejected by her mother had obviously foreshadowed her later experiences.

How is childhood or adolescent experience related to the affective sense of shame? What role does the mother figure play in the child's early years? Why does the sense of shame repeatedly appear in these three women's autobiographical writing and what is its relation to Chinese history and society at large? What is the function of writing, then, in dealing with the sense of shame and how should we re-view these women writers' continuous effort to write and rewrite the self?

In fact, in the early and middle 1980s, women writers like Yu Luojin and Xu Ran[20] had already begun exploring their childhood experiences. The fear and anger caused by being abandoned by their parents permeate many women writers' self-writing, especially in the 1990s. The Chinese Communist Party has always trumpeted its role in women's liberation, especially in reconstructing women as socialist producers. The mother figures in women's autobiographical writing of the 1990s almost all belong to the category of active socialist career women. They devote themselves to their public careers; they depreciate the value of personal life and are incapable of establishing strong emotional relationships with their children. Normally they don't have satisfying family lives, and pay little attention to their children's physical and emotional needs. Because of high political demands and their strong sense of responsibility for their jobs, they are often absent from home. In several pieces of Wang Anyi's autobiographical writing, the revolutionary mother is both a central and powerful figure of the family and a distanced and insensitive person who is always busy with her work and dogmatic in her views of history and reality. There is no emotional and intimate relationship between mother and daughter. In *Years of Sadness*, the mother repeatedly overlooks the daughter's needs and demands, and, for the most part, has little clue about her daughter's distress and suffering. At one point in *Actual Reports and Fictional Construction*, the narrator/daughter suddenly realized that the mother herself had been an orphan and felt deeply disappointed and sad about the fact.

In Chen's *A Private Life*, the narrator comments:

> My father and mother were both perpetually wrapped up in their own work, with no interest at all in the little events of everyday life. . . . I know she [my mother] loved me very much, loved me intensely, but it was an abstract, general kind of love, not the conventionally more common maternal kind of love of a hen for the egg she has laid herself. My mother did house work when she had to, but with no passion or willingness. It was just because she loved me, she sometimes was willing to make some sacrifice. But her serious sense of sacrifice pressured me and made me feel so uncomfortable that I never wanted her to get more involved in the trivial and insignificant house work. I have always felt that having ambitious, work-driven parents is not by any means a fortunate thing for a child. (pp. 147–148)

Furthermore, the mother in Chen's novel is a weak and naive woman who needs care and help herself. The narrator often feels guilty and ashamed because of her mother's inability to stand up for herself and her daughter.

For the orphan-like Duomi in Lin Bai's *A Self at War*, her mother is a stranger from an early age and she refuses to accept the belated care her mother eventually offers.

> Because she [Duomi] had been used to a home with the absence of the mother, when her mother was around, she felt uncomfortable. . . . If [her mother] was in the room, she would find an excuse to leave. I had not been conscious of the hunger of my skin until years later when I was carrying my baby and touching her face and body. I realized how a living child in need of caress from their intimate ones. If she/he did not have it, she/he would feel hungry. Is it true that a living and hungry child has the inclination for masochism? (p. 19)

No longer confined by any socially sanctioned values and collectively demanded experiences, women writers in the 1990s were able to articulate their personal affective/defective mode of being, but the affective mode they expressed, especially shame, drew them even closer to each other for an inescapable, shared experience of the past. The dominant socialist ideology, revolutionary ethic, and gender and family relationships promoted in the Maoist era are revealed to have contributed to the historical and psychic patterns of life shared by these women. Although all the daughters within the texts attain, as adults, a certain understanding of the historical situations their mothers faced, they nevertheless cannot stop feeling anxious about their own existences, a mode of being caused by the lack or loss of the love-object at an early stage.

Lack or loss of love-object and self-model, according to psychoanalytic theory, causes narcissistic injury. In his "Some narcissistic consequences of object loss: a developmental view," Robert L. Tyson tries to separate the narcissistic constituents in reaction to object loss from the major theories on mourning and melancholy, and to identify narcissistic sources as well as to make a developmental assessment of the patient's narcissistic status at the time of object loss or subsequently.[21] In his three metaphorical strands or components of narcissism—feelings of omnipotence, feelings of self-constancy, and feelings of self-esteem—the second is most relevant to our discussion. Self-constancy concerns the continuity of the sense of identity over time (p. 258). The emerging sense of self is reflected in the gradual attainment of self-constancy, which is an open-ended process just as the attainment of object constancy is. The real object is important to "refuel" the constant self. If the real object was absent for some period, the integrated self-image will no longer be the source of comfort, and the sense of self-constancy (p. 259) will be threatened. According to Anthony Giddens, lack of coherence in object ideals, or the difficulty of finding worthwhile ideals to pursue, will result in shame anxiety.[22] Shame is directly related to self-identity and narcissism because it is essentially anxiety about the adequacy of the narrative by means of which the individual sustains a coherent biography.

The withdrawal or absence of maternal care and self-ideal causes the fearful feeling of being rejected and abandoned in the child (the narcissistic injury), and that further leads to the experience of disturbed self-acceptance and self-adequacy. The affect of shame that is contingent upon specific stimuli can sometimes produce a long-term or repeating effect on people. According to Donald L. Nathanson, proto-affect shame is a major force in shaping the infantile self, and remains so throughout life.[23] For the narrators/protagonists in these three women's autobiographical writing, lack of love and attention from the mothers and subsequent lack of self-models lead to the pattern of repeatedly experiencing a defective sense of self, the proto- or historical affect of shame. "We are alone," the narrator in Wang Anyi's *Years of Sadness* reflects, "Naked, without armor or covering, we might be ambushed at any time" (p. 344).

Although the lack of maternal figures early in life defines the self, it does not determine the self; this lack may lead to a negative affective mode of being, but it also produces the creative drive for reimagining one's life and identity. The anxiety and shame generated by the absence of the mother do not end in themselves. Instead, they engender the desire and need to reflect, reimagine, and to re-create. In an important attempt to cope with the past experience, memory, and current emotional state of being, women writers like Wang, Chen, and Lin have actively and repeatedly engaged themselves in self-writing. The role of the imaginary was, therefore, double-edged in China of the 1990s: it produced pleasures for both the public and the self to consume,[24] but, at the same time, it provided a major means for these writers to negotiate their past, to articulate a particular mode of existence, and to construct an alternative mirror image for self-re-creation and female identification.

One of the most recurring themes in these women writers' renegotiation of life and self is the (re)creation/imagination of desired or ideal mother in the life of the daughter. The mirror, which reflects the logic of the (public and self) consumerism of the 1990s, also functions in these women's writings as an empowering frame through which a new and alternative way of forming mother–daughter relationships and self-identity can be seen. Indeed, the mirror in Wang's, Lin's, and Chen's works is often closely connected with the ideal maternal figures the narrators have imagined; in these figures, they can not only perceive an ideal to emulate but also build a female emotional and even erotic bond, absent in their relationships with their biological mothers. The heroines' strong feelings of disappointment with, and sometimes anger at, their own mothers are interwoven with an undiminished desire to search for, and create, an ideal (m)other and self through imaginary and literary practice. Only in front of these desired maternal figures/mirrors are the heroines/narrators able to feel a self reborn and re-created.

At the very beginning of *Years of Sadness*, Wang Anyi writes:

> Standing at the entrance to a pitch-dark movie theater, wrapped in the purplish red velvet curtain, I heard the stifled sobs of that woman. . . . She sat in the seat nearest the entrance in the last row, holding a flashlight; the crying woman was an usher. This scene didn't frighten or startle me and I didn't even wonder why she was crying. It was just that I couldn't help myself. I started crying, too. It was like popping a cork. In that instant, my sorrow burst out, gushing into my heart. (p. 322)

This crying woman, a total stranger, released the narrator's unconsciously suppressed memories of the past and the sorrow that had delineated her identity. At that moment, the narrator could not help identifying herself with the sobbing woman. That woman was the narrator herself in the mirror. Her ears had searched for the external echo of her own sob for a long time. "It was not until that moment when I was wrapped in the purplish red velvet curtain and heard the stifled sobs of that woman usher in the movie theater did all my own feeling of sorrow and depression obtain a name" (p. 330). Unlike the busy, insensitive, and disciplined mother, whose presence often frustrated the narrator, the crying woman made the narrator feel that she was, in a sense, reborn. Wang Anyi starts her narration with this significant moment and keeps returning to it many times in this short autobiographical novel. Later in the novel, Wang Anyi writes, "We don't see our situation clearly. Sometimes, the situation only becomes recognizable through the help of other people. Like a mirror, the specificity of their circumstances reflects ours. It is just like the moment when I was standing in the entrance to the movie theater, wrapped in a purplish red velvet curtain, and saw that woman crying" (p. 344). If the moment plays a defining role in the narrator's recollection of herself in the past, the repeated references to this very moment also indicate that the narrator constantly needs an other that mirrors the self in a coexisting and sharing way.

In *A Private Life*, Chen Ran creates a female ideal (m)other/self, Widow He, with whom the narrator/protagonist is not only emotionally tied but also erotically involved. In a way, Widow He is also the imagined mirror of the narrator/protagonist. Comparing her own mother and Widow He, the narrator writes:

> (Widow) He and my mother possessed a similar graceful beauty, but they were very different in personality. . . . Quite unlike my parents, she was never

pressed for time. Her passion for living came from the core of her being. All through my growing years, every woolen sweater and every pair of woolen drawers that I wore, she had knitted. . . . In addition to having the same refined female intellectual characteristics as my mother, she also had the charming "house wife" appeal. (p. 148)

In contrast to her own biological mother, Widow He is an ideal maternal figure for the narrator. However, she is not merely an ideal mother, but also an intimate, erotic other who fulfills both the emotional and the physical needs of the narrator:

I wanted to tell her that over the years she had always been the one that I truly loved, that I cherished my memories of the way she loved me and looked after me when I was little, that I thought always of her intimacy and tenderness, and that as the months and years fell away, these unexpressed feelings grew stronger day by day. I didn't need anyone else to enter my life or my body. (p. 151)

When she started undoing my blouse, the sound of my wildly beating heart so unsettled her that her fingers began to fumble with the buttons. I said nothing, letting her do with me as she wished. When she had undone my blouse, she didn't take it off; she simply spread it open, . . . Then she stepped back several paces so that we were not too close together, yet not too far apart; . . .

Then she began undoing her own blouse and stood facing me in the same attitude in which I faced her, so that we could enjoy one another. A vague anxiety was unsettling me. I longed feverishly for her to reveal her beauty to me totally. Her every movement and gesture overcame me with its perfect beauty, and filled me totally with desire.

She was my mirror. (p. 157)

Lack of maternal love ignites the desire to search for an ideal mother, who then not only provides unconditional love but also bodily pleasure for the self. "The way she treats me lets all the words disappear on my lips. I would try to say something, but I could never find the right words. Only my body itself could tell her" (p. 152). The emotional and erotic relationship between the protagonist and Widow He transcends the limits of conventional space and produces powerful re-imaginations of mother–daughter bonding, self–other interaction, and the formation of self-identity.

[Widow] He was a house made of mirrors that belonged to my innermost being. In it, no matter where I was, I could always see myself. All its blank spaces were my silences, all her joys were smiles reflected on my face. . . . She . . . made me feel like she was my mother, but she was definitely not my mother. From when I was very small, she had stood there helpless and alone waiting for me, waiting for me to become a woman. The air around her filled with anxious concern and longing. (p. 152)

In Lin Bai's *A Self at War*, similar older female figures appear at different moments of Duomi's life. Among them are the pretty ballet dancer Yao Qiong, the nameless, noble old lady in a costume of the 1930s or 1940s, the single and beautiful teacher, Mei Ju, and the fictional character Zhu Liang. These stand out as mysterious and extraordinary women who, as the splendid surface of a mirror, repeatedly lead Duomi to strange places where different concepts of time, space, and relationship apply.

> Mei Ju was the woman whom Duomi called teacher. Mei Ju was in her 40s, looked beautiful and cold. She never got married and kept a slender body. To Duomi's surprise, Mei Ju's breasts were still firm and up.
> . . .
>   Mei Ju lived alone in two rooms, . . . Whether at night or during the day, the curtains always hung low; the shaded rooms were cool and dark.
>   There are many mirrors.
> . . .
>   Where ever you were in the room, you felt someone at your back, staring. In any corner, you saw yourself standing directly in front.
> . . .
>   Every time she returned to Mei Ju's home, Duomi felt that she had entered an extraordinary time-zone, a labyrinth, a place also where many phantasms gathered.
>   After a while, Duomi realized that every time she returned here, memories and past events emanated from the reflecting surfaces and reverse sides of the walls, corners and mirrors in this strange room. (p. 93)

It is in such spaces as Mei Ju's room—full of mirrors and occupied by an older and mysterious woman—that Duomi is able to be connected with her own past and sense of being. Past events "lined up in front of her, she reached out to stroke them, and, sometimes, they yielded enticingly; like lightning, a passageway flashed from their center" (p. 94). Indeed, it is in Mei Ju's room that the narrator/Duomi suddenly feels the urge to write an autobiographical novel (p. 92).

Like the female usher in Wang's writing, who provides such an illuminating moment that the isolated and fragmented girl/narrator is suddenly able to relate to an other emotional being and to her lost self in the past, Mei Ju and other women in Lin's novel also offer Duomi unexpected moments of returning to the suppressed or repressed—the most shameful experiences as well as the wildest fantasies.

As with the relationship between the narrator and Widow He in *A Private Life*, Lin's novel also implies an erotic love relationship between Duomi and other women. Duomi's irresistible desire for Yao Qiong's body and her obsession with Zhu Liang's beauty well indicate that these other women are not only the ones the narrator wants to be (self-model), but also the ones she desires to love (love-object).

Autobiography, according to Janette Rainwater, is a corrective intervention into the past, not merely a chronicle of elapsed events.[25] Thinking back to a difficult or traumatic phase of childhood, the individual talks to the child-that-was, comforting and supporting it while offering advice. ". . . The basic purpose of writing autobiographical material is to help you to be done with the past . . ." (p. 56). This self-therapeutic function explains one important and new aspect of Chinese women's autobiographical practice in the 1990s. However, self-therapy is not the only function or effect. On the contrary, Chinese women's autobiographical writings in the 1990s, as I have mentioned, have signified diverse meanings. To write autobiographically in the context of 1990s is, first of all, to realize the potential value of writing as a commodity for public consumption, to consume the self in an imaginative and creative way, and to address the lack or loss in the past, not merely for the possibility of getting over it, but, more importantly, for recognizing the very defining mode of being that it has initiated for the self. To write autobiographically in the 1990s is also to continue the gendered personal mode of writing that was initiated by women writers in the early post-Mao era to probe into the historical and social causes that directly or indirectly constitute intimate experiences. Finally, to write autobiographically in the 1990s is to refuse to let go of one's past without reflection, and to resist a kind of total consumption that tends to destroy all boundaries in its process: for Chen Ran, "Time elapses while I am still here"; for Lin Bai, writing is constantly at war with the self; and for Wang Anyi, the last sentence of her writing offers, "The sun is bright and beautiful, the time of the past suddenly falls into the instinctive dark shadow" (p. 362). But we know that the process of self-negotiation continues; with the arrival of another scene like the sobbing woman in the dark theater (the mother mirror), a past emotion (sorrow, perhaps, or shame) will burst out again, gushing into hearts as well as words.

NOTES

An earlier version of this chapter appeared in Lingzhen Wang's book, *Personal Matters: Women's Autobiographical Practice in Twentieth-Century China* (Stanford University Press, 2003), and is included here with the permission of Stanford University Press.

1. Chen Ran, "Siren shenghuo," *Hua cheng* 2 (1996); A Private Life trans. John Howard-Gibbon (New York: Columbia University Press, 2004).
2. Chen Ran, "Zuojia de gerenhua" (The personalization of writers), in *Ah-er de xiaowu* (*The Small Room of Ah-er*), ed. Chen Ran (Beijing: Huayi chubanshe, 1998).
3. Lin Bai, "Zhishen yu yuyan zhong" (Situated in language), in *Xiang gui yiyang miren* (*Seductive Like Ghosts*), ed. Lin Bai (Taiyuan: Shanxi shifan daxue chubanshe, 1998).
4. Lin Bai, "Yige ren de zhanzheng" (A self at war), *Hua cheng* 2 (1994).
5. An Dun, ed., *Juedui yinsi: Dangdai Zhongguoren qinggan koushu shilu* (Beijing: New World Press, 1998).
6. Lingzhen Wang, "Retheorizing the personal: identity, writing, and gender in Yu Luojin's autobiographical act," *positions: east asia cultures critique* 6:2 (1998).
7. Ibid., 413–415.
8. See Link's and Kinkley's introductions in Perry Link, ed., *Stubborn Weeds: Popular and Controversial Chinese Literature after the Cultural Revolution* (Bloomington: Indiana University Press, 1984); and Jeffrey C. Kinkley, ed., *After Mao: Chinese Literature and Society, 1978–1981* (Cambridge, MA: Harvard University Press, 1985).
9. Wang Anyi, "Nüzuojia de ziwo" (The self of women writers), in *Gushi he jiang gushi* (*Stories and Telling Stories*), ed. Wang Anyi (Hangzhou: Zhejiang wenyi chubanshe, 1991), pp. 155–156.

10. The page references of the three novels belong to the following editions: Chen Ran, *Siren shenghuo* (*A Private Life*) (Nanjing: Jiangsu wenyi chubanshe, 1996); Lin Bai, *Yigeren de zhanzheng* (*A Self at War*) (Hohhot: Neimenggu renmin chubanshe, 1996); and Wang Anyi, *Youshang de niandai* (*Years of Sadness*) (Taipei: Maitian chubanshe, 1999). Translation of *A Private Life* is from John Howard-Gibbon's text with my modifications; translations of other novels and essays by these three writers are done by Mary Ann O'Donnell and myself.

11. Daniel Miller, *A Theory of Shopping* (Ithaca: Cornell University Press, 1998).

12. Lingzhen Wang, *Personal Matters: Women's Autobiographical Practice in Twentieth Century China* (Stanford: Stanford University Press, 2004), pp. 172–175.

13. Qi Shuyu, "Shengcun jingyu, xing he ren de miankong" (The conditions of existence, sex, and people's faces), *Shichang jingji xia de Zhongguo wenxue yishu* (*Chinese Literature and Art in the Market Economy*) (Beijing: Beijing University Press, 1998), pp. 127–156.

14. Colin Campbell, *The Romantic Ethic and the Spirit of Modern Consumerism* (New York: Basil Blackwell, 1987).

15. In 1997, in the version published by Jiangsu wenyi chubanshe, Lin Bai changed the title of her first chapter from "A Self at War" to "Jing zhong de guang" (The Light in the Mirror).

16. Andrew P. Morrison, "Shame, ideal self, and narcissism," in *Essential Papers on Narcissism*, ed. Andrew P. Morrison (New York: New York University Press, 1986), pp. 348–372.

17. Anthony Giddens, "The self: ontological security and existential anxiety," in *Modernity and Self-Identity: Self and Society in the Late Modern Age*, ed. Anthony Giddens (Stanford: Stanford University Press, 1991), p. 66.

18. Helen B. Lewis, *Shame and Guilt in Neurosis* (New York: International University Press, 1971).

19. Giddens, "The self: ontological security and existential anxiety," pp. 65–66.

20. Yu Luojin, in her second autobiographical novel, *Chuntian de tonghua* (Springtime Tale) starts exploring parent–child relationships; Xu Ran, daughter of the well-known woman writer, Yang Mo, focuses on mother–daughter relationships in *Qing-lan yuan* (Blue Indigo Garden), which was coauthored by her mother and her.

21. Robert L. Tyson, "Some narcissistic consequences of object loss: a developmental view," in *Essential Papers on Object Loss*, ed. Rita V. Frankiel (New York: New York University Press, 1994), pp. 252–253.

22. Giddens, "The self: ontological security and existential anxiety," p. 69.

23. Eve Kosofsky Sedgwick, "Queer performativity: Henry James' *The Art of the Novel*," *GLQ: A Journal of Lesbian and Gay Studies* 1:1 (1993), 12.

24. When I interviewed Wang Anyi in May 2000 and asked her about the intimate details depicted in her *Years of Sadness*, she said that writing about those past experiences had brought her aesthetic pleasure.

25. Janette Rainwater, *Self-Therapy: A Guide to becoming Your Own Therapist* (London: Crucible, 1989).

11

Urban Ethics: Modernity and the Morality of Everyday Life

Robin Visser

Post-Mao Urban Fiction and the Ethics of Authenticity

The moral philosopher Ross Poole introduces his book *Morality and Modernity* by categorizing the modern dilemma of ethical positioning: "The modern world calls into existence certain conceptions of morality, but also destroys the grounds for taking them seriously."[1] In contemporary China, ethical categories have particular salience, as the post-Mao era has seen China's strong tradition of literature as moral discourse threatened by a market-driven popular culture often unmindful of moral mission. By exploring intersections of the narrative and the normative in literature, one can interrogate the shifting relations among text, ethics, and everyday life in late twentieth-century China, uncovering correlatives between fiction and the ethical issues that arise in conjunction with modern commercial life.

In this chapter, I will explore these intersections between the narrative and the normative in fiction set in urban China of the 1990s, where characters negotiate new ethical terrain within the broader context of modernity. While I do not subscribe to a univalent understanding of modernity, I use the term in two distinct senses here. First, I refer to a mode of life in which one's own rational faculties reign in lieu of arbitrary, external authorities. The subtle demise of the *danwei*, or socialist "work unit," is a key contributor to the new cultural logic of China's urban space, as individuals are increasingly free to make their own decisions about livelihood and lifestyle. In addition to the historical argument of rationality, where the rise of a semi-civil society in China is affording increased autonomy from the state, I also refer to a more concrete notion of modernity. Among many contemporary urban Chinese, there is a self-consciousness about being modern, a taken-for-granted feature of life embedded in everyday thinking and behavior. The increased possibilities for autonomy in China's contemporary urban culture have caused the average citizen to reexamine his/her values in conjunction with lifestyle choices, an especially difficult task given the new stratification of society due to market forces.

Before addressing the various ethical strategies engaged in contemporary urban fiction, I will briefly discuss the sociological and cultural context for these works. The *danwei* system, first initiated with the advent of industrialization in the early twentieth century, provided its occupants with a place to work, sleep, eat, and receive all life essentials without leaving the walled enclave that marked the boundaries of their "unit." The *danwei* defined urban culture to such a degree that some analysts have gone so far as to equate the two cultures during the Maoist era. During the Maoist era, life in the city was not so much an experience of "the crowd," "night life," "material desire," "alienation," "risk," "stimulation," and the like, as it was a constant negotiation of the confines of an administrative community situated within the larger urban environment. However, as Chinese citizens divorce themselves from government institutions in increasing numbers, becoming employed by foreign-owned companies or establishing themselves as entrepreneurs, founding research institutes and consulting firms, or operating as independent writers, filmmakers, and artists, a new cultural logic is becoming operative. The hybrid space of contemporary Chinese urban culture is a post-revolutionary society permeated by market values.

While the urban wealthy in previous Chinese dynasties remained in close cahoots with government bureaucrats who maintained the upper echelons of power, in the 1990s, money itself became synonymous with power. Thus by the late twentieth century, both the traditional Confucian mores demeaning merchants, and modern socialist values condemning capitalists, had been largely undermined. According to cultural critic Li Jiefei, in the late 1980s, Chinese urbanites begin to openly flaunt their wealth without concern for appearing unethical, and "[by the early 1990s] nearly everyone became willing to openly state that the reason they worked so hard was for financial gain, no longer considering it immoral to do so."[2] Further, new technologies of transportation, communication, and socialization have intensified domestic and global flows of population, commodities, and information. Hence the urgency with which ethical questions are explored in urban fiction of the 1990s derives, in part, from the fact that a broader sector of society is impacted by the logic of the marketplace than in previous periods of urbanization in China. Nonetheless, Chinese cultural theorists such as Dai Jinhua and Luo Gang have pointed out the fallacy of prematurely assigning the western implications of citizenry to contemporary Chinese society. Dai Jinhua argues that cultural *discourse* of the 1990s, rather than material conditions themselves, actively works to construct and validate the values of a Chinese middle class, thereby negating decades of socialist striving for a class-less society by unambiguously endorsing class-based status. Luo Gang also decries the fact that theorists are far too eager to make ready connections between a *shichang shehui* (market society) and the independence from the state resulting in an active *gonggong changhe* (public sphere). He agrees with Dai that the "middle class" has become a misleading code word in cultural discourse for China's imminent emergence as a new modern state girded by a "civil society." Luo argues, instead, that the public sphere in

China will follow a unique trajectory that differs from the progression theorized by Habermas in relation to the former Eastern Soviet bloc.[3]

It is in this context that new ethical dilemmas arise for urban Chinese citizens. Under the logic of the market, altruism, or the aspiration to an ideal "higher" than pure self-interest, is considered irrational behavior. Yet while the persistent rhetoric of loyalty to the state above self rings hollow to the average Chinese citizen, shadows of both socialist and Confucian ethics remain. How, then, does one live in a society in which the kind of identity presupposed by the market is that of an individual whose well-being may best be achieved in ways that detract from the overall social well-being? Morality in the modern world, including in contemporary urban China, is often asserted nostalgically as a bygone, inaccessible entity. Of course there are modern ethicists who dispute the notion that modernity is unable to sustain a moral grounding. Charles Taylor, for example, has provided an elaborate framework for reclaiming what he terms the "ideal of authenticity," which underlies, but has been misconstrued by, the culture of individualism and moral relativism operative in contemporary Western societies.[4] Jürgen Habermas, in his comprehensive theorizing of modernity, amends Max Weber's exclusive emphasis on instrumental rationality by introducing the notion of communicative interaction and its salutary ramifications for the public sphere.[5] Although their projects differ in approach, both Taylor and Habermas attempt to negotiate the gap between self and other, subject and society. In other words, they try to bring together the two questions that dominate ethical inquiry yet suggest sharply incommensurable points of view: the ethical question addressing the public sphere, "How ought one live?" and that determining individual morality and the constitution of the self, "What ought I to do?" Rejecting a Nietzschean genealogy of morals, and subsequent deconstructionist discourse, which concludes that acts and motives are contingent, overdetermined, invariably self-interested products of prevailing ideologies, these critics argue that ethical principle is still relevant to public life.

In China, many of the cultural debates of the 1990s were, likewise, centered on morality and the relationship between individual action and social good, particularly in the absence of restraints on human behavior, which prevailed under socialist modes of production. For the most part, these debates divide along lines reminiscent of Hume's ethical legacy from the Enlightenment, in that they fail to provide a determinate relation between the proposition of *ought* and *is*. In other words, one group generally adheres to a sense that individual choices *ought* to be other than they currently are, whereas another believes that we should embrace what *is* and stop trying to prescribe an *ought* other than what exists. The former tendency is evident in the nationwide debate over the "loss of the humanistic spirit (*renwen jingshen*)" launched by liberal cultural intellectuals in Shanghai who criticize the effects of market reforms resulting in the increasing irrelevance of the humanities under the monopolization of the public sphere by the commodity. They lament the vulgarization of society, maintaining that Chinese society has "lost" its moral sensibilities and no longer adheres to any sort of *zhongji guanhuai* (ultimate concerns).[6] Not unlike Robert Bellah, who decried the threat that utilitarianism and expressive individualism pose for public life, these scholars seek to recover a language of commitment to a greater purpose.[7] On the other hand, those critics who disagree with such a dour assessment of contemporary culture instead celebrate the "postmodern sensibilities" exhibited by the very works criticized by *renwen jingshen* advocates. Notably, two of the most prominent targets of the *renwen jingshen* debates, Wang Shuo's fiction and Jia Pingwa's *Feidu* (*City in Ruins*, 1993), also represent breakthroughs in urban fiction. Postmodern critics predisposed to praising these innovative urban narratives extend their approbation to subsequent urban fiction of the 1990s, celebrating its absence of "interiority" in an "unreflective" writing that directly represents the raw, vulgar reality of contemporary urban culture.[8] For example, Chen Xiaoming sees in these city narratives a desire to "capture the external shape of contemporary life, to plunge into this life on its own terms, so as to be freed, in the process, from the Enlightenment nightmare long bedeviling literature." He goes on to claim that:

> Life in this age already has no interiority. People are obsessed with elevating themselves from poverty, and are continually incited by the prospect of instant riches. Writers of the "belated generation" have a firm grasp on such tendencies of our time. Without any polishing or ornamentation, they put in front of us the chaotic and vibrant conditions of such a life, presenting a swift, indiscriminate flux of phenomena. Their method of directly representing the appearances of life serves to highlight the rawness of a coarse and vulgar reality.[9]

Chen and other "post" critics, such as Zhang Yiwu, have devoted many writings to the cause of rejecting what they believe to be the elitist and moralistic tradition of modern Chinese literary discourse.

The debates of the 1990s between those advocating a return to Enlightenment values and those promoting postmodernism seem to confuse moralizing with morality. Perhaps because urban novels of the 1990s are written neither as national or cultural allegories, as were the avant-garde works of the 1980s,[10] nor as the thinly veiled didacticism that has dominated so much Chinese literature, these tales of everyday life are assessed either as decadent deviations from literature's true purpose, or refreshing departures from the plague of authorial judgment. Yet Chen Xiaoming's laudatory claim that urban writers of the 1990s lack "interiority" is not supported in close readings of the fiction that he commends. There is no mistaking this fiction's blunt verisimilitude; yet one cannot consider it "unreflective." China's late-twentieth-century urban tales, far from being raw, unreflective narratives, are permeated with questions of individual morality and "ultimate concerns." In this chapter, I will examine the ethical questions confronted by modern Chinese urbanites in works of the 1990s by three authors representative of contemporary urban fiction. Qiu Huadong (b. 1969), Zhu Wen (b. 1967), and He Dun (b. 1958) write novels dominated precisely by one of the key questions debated by ethical philosophers—that of individual action and its relationship to the greater good.

In addition to content, the style of post-Mao urban literature is often criticized for lack of imagination and experimentation due to its forthright depictions of contemporary everyday life.[11] What is fascinating about this stylistic turn is precisely its emphasis on the everyday and the relationship of such a move to historical shifts in modernity. Looking at it from the perspective of urban modernity in art, it is quite remarkable the way in which Dutch, British, and Americans pioneered new art forms that, despite the separation of centuries, exhibit a common thread celebrating ordinariness. Each of these innovations corresponded to what Peter Taylor terms the three "hegemonic cycles": Dutch-led mercantile modernity, British-led industrial modernity, and American-led consumer modernity.[12] Whereas the "High Tradition" dominated seventeenth-century Europe and its culture of absolutism, the Dutch developed a counter-baroque style of "realism" based on scenes from the world in which they lived. Dutch genre painters drew directly on their own experiences to mirror life as they saw it. These artists painted to sell their works, rather than relying on commissions, thereby creating the first art market. During the Song dynasty, a similar phenomenon occurred in the transition from *gongting huajia* (court painters) to professional artists who sold their works to urban citizens, often depicting scenes from everyday life, such as that in *Qingming shanghe tu* (*Spring Festival on the River*, early twelfth century). Here, we see a direct relationship between depictions of everyday life and a market economy. Again, the English novel of the eighteenth century relied on depictions of comfortable middle-class life to appeal to a mass market. And by the mid-twentieth century, Hollywood films turned from portrayals of glamor to showing more secure, cozy, and domestic scenes of everyday American life. The same bourgeois domesticity is evident in all of these genres—ordinary people living comfortable lives. Likewise, new urban fiction portrays the comforts of the Chinese middle class; yet this mode of existence is immediately put into question. While appreciative of comfort, the characters rarely revel in their bourgeois status without deliberation, often resulting in radical lifestyle changes.

QIU HUADONG'S *FLY EYES* AND THE DILEMMA OF THE QUOTIDIAN

In the 1998 novel *Yingyan*, or *Fly Eyes*, the Beijing writer Qiu Huadong (b. 1969) recounts five stories on the lives of professional youth in Beijing and, consciously modeling himself on Dos Passos, he provides a pastiche of individual lives that inform the complexity of the city. Each of the characters in his novel acknowledge that they are *pingmian ren* ("two-dimensional" people) who resist delving into existential questions. Yet while they indulge in hedonistic urban pleasures, they also admit they are "bored" and "disgusted" with such a lifestyle. What distinguishes Qiu's depiction of this generation is his characters' uneasy self-consciousness about their own superficiality. As in most contemporary urban novels, each of Qiu's characters make abrupt lifestyle changes in the early 1990s, often from idealist artists, poets, or scholars, to business-persons in every conceivable line of work. In recollecting the idealism of their pasts, those satiated with the get-rich materialistic lifestyle of the 1990s even attempt to return to a slower, simpler way of living. However it soon becomes obvious that the "thinkers" and "closet idealists" in his stories are unable to survive in the metropolis. Those characters that attempt to find deeper sense of meaning and value in the city perish in the attempt, whereas the "survivors" live prosaic, middle-class lives.

The first of the five stories features Yuan Jingsong, a 20-something fashion magazine photographer whose daily routines are particularly poignant demonstrations of urban decadence. Jingsong's habits include spying on his newlywed neighbors through the zoom lens of his Nikon camera from his high-rise apartment on the Third Ring Road, obsessively watching Sharon Stone films, and stalking women along Beijing's thoroughfares. There are multiple textual indications that his obsessions arise from his sense of modern isolation in the crowd, as demonstrated during a ride on the Beijing subway.

> He entered the subway car and sat down. Looking all around him he suddenly realized how strange it was. Everyone sitting there was thinking their own thoughts, some even using the newspaper to hide their faces as they read, and others still wearing their sunglasses. In a word, not one person was willing to make eye contact with anyone else.[13]

As Georg Simmel theorized about turn-of-the-century Berlin, the modern metropolis is governed by a need to distance oneself from other individuals in the crowd. Simmel spoke of the "fear of contact, a pathological symptom which spread endemically, a spatial fear stemming from the too rapid oscillation between closeness and distance in modern life."[14] Fifty years later the novelist Zhang Ailing described the same tendency in cosmopolitan Shanghai in her 1943 short story "Fengsuo" (Blockade), where the passengers in a stopped tram furiously read everything at their disposal to avoid making eye contact with others.[15] Such mental distancing becomes essential to maintaining one's identity in the crowd, but inevitably creates a sense of isolation.

In the story, Jingsong's desire to reverse the isolationist aspects of the modern metropolis and create meaningful connections with others motivates him to enact extreme measures. He quits his job and attempts to live as a "nature man" within the city. Camping out by the foul moat that had surrounded the former city wall, Jingsong's organic form of contact with the crowd dispels his loneliness, and he regains a sense of social connection and intimacy by sending hand-written letters to his friends instead of using computers or fax machines.

When he happens to photograph a robbery and murder, his life becomes infused with social meaning as he becomes obsessed with a new goal for his life: to single-handedly crack the case. When he finally apprehends the murderers, however, he is helpless to defend himself and they easily dispose him. Since Jingsong had already tipped off the cops, they arrive in time to arrest the murderers, but find Jingsong, whom they label an "anonymous bystander," shot to death at the scene. The story concludes bluntly with the evening paper's account of Jingsong's death: ". . . At the scene there was also an anonymous man who got caught in crossfire while crossing the road. The police are investigating his identity" (p. 69). The irony is obvious—the attempts of this would-be hero to counter the alienating effects of the city and infuse his modern life with meaning are quixotic. Yuan Jingsong dies in the city as an inconsequential, unknown entity, the very fear that grips Liu Heng's alienated Beijing protagonist in *Heide xue* (*Black Snow*, 1988), one of the first post-Mao urban novels. Such narratives castigate the operative logic in the market economy of the 1990s: to quote Allan Bloom, a well-known critic of the moral mediocrity bred by modernity, "there is nothing particularly noble about [modern life]. Survivalism has taken the place of heroism as the admired quality."[16]

Qiu follows this first story with another tale of quixotic attempts to find meaning outside the strictures of the urban marketplace. "Wild Nights," part two of *Fly Eyes*, recounts how four of Yuan Jingsong's former classmates try to dispel the boredom of their daily routines in the city by playing madly at "night games." The opening scene, in which they lie alongside the tracks of an oncoming train in a game of "Who dies?" exemplifies the extremes to which they go to seek their thrills. Each of the four manifest troubling signs of maladaptation to city life. Zuo Yan isolates himself from the others and is obsessed with video games, VCDs, and even ventures out to the tracks to "play" the game by himself; Qin Jie, an ex-poet who owns a sports car dealership, gets high on the "speed" of fast cars and fast women; Yu Lei is ousted from his house by his "wife," a woman he had pragmatically married in order to register for an apartment; and He Xiao throws away his money in the stock market ignoring his home life altogether.

Bored by "night games," He Xiao persuades the others to get a pilot's license and so they can do "air art" for kicks. One day the friends enter forbidden airspace above Beijing's commercial district, where the police threaten to shoot them down if they don't halt. The others turn back but He Xiao keeps flying into the commercial district above the Third Ring Road.

> "He's crazy." Qin Jie said, "He's truly insane." But He Xiao was very sober. His flying skill was very good, but he realized he was running out of fuel. He didn't have any other choice. Blinded by the sunshine glaring off the glass walls of a shopping center he closed his eyes and crashed into it. From a distance the remains of He Xiao's helicopter looked like a tree branch sticking out from that seventy-floor building. (p. 111)

Qiu Huadong repeatedly utilizes such disjunctive "nature metaphors" to describe gruesome urban scenes. Here the impassivity of the shiny modern symbol of progress mocks any attempts by these urban novelty seekers to alter the capitalist forces shaping the modern metropolis.

Two of the friends, shaken by He Xiao's death, decide to leave their ranks in the "newly emergent middle class" by being airlifted to the wilderness, where they attempt to live as *yeren* (savages), completely cut off from civilization. Only Zuo Yan remains in the city. The story ends with Zuo Yan in a cozy apartment making love to his new bride whom he'd met over the internet, dreaming of one "savage" cannibalizing another in the barren northeastern forest where Qin Jie and Yu Lei had been airlifted (p. 152).

Again, this urban fable foregrounds the modern ethical dilemma. Those characters that attempt to find deeper sense of meaning and value in the city perish in the attempt, whereas the survivors live prosaic, middle-class lives. Zuo Yan, the "survivor" of the story, does so by reinvesting himself in the very scripts which dominate modern urban life. With the advent of modernity, ordinary life itself becomes a central moral value. Work and family are affirmed, typically, in opposition to allegedly more transcendent values, say, of philosophic contemplation, religious devotion, or revolutionary zeal. Here, as in many of Qiu's stories, the "idealists" are unable to survive in the metropolis.

Nonetheless, Qiu's narratives consistently problematize urban middle-class life. This story ends with Zuo Yan's post-coital dreams of his friends:

> That wild man in the forest didn't have a partner, only himself, or perhaps he relied on his partner's flesh to survive. The sun peeked through the depths of the forest and seeing it he was suddenly aroused. Knife in hand he let out a sharp whistle as he ran wildly toward the sun. The tone resonated in all four directions, a lonely yet glorious sound. Zuo Yan rolled over and this dream disappeared. Now in his dreams he was fleeing through the city in his car, with another black Nissan in hot pursuit. He couldn't relax at all as he drove madly through the streets of the city. (pp. 152–153)

In the end, Qiu Huadong's tales of bourgeois life, like Dorothy Lessing's *A Proper Marriage*, emphasize the terror inherent in the claustrophobic predictability of middle-class life.

Zeng Hao (b. 1963) is a Beijing-based *xin xingxiang* (new imagist) painter, who, like Qiu Huadong, subverts middle class representation by introducing anxiety into his images of interiority and domesticity. In paintings such as "*5:00 P.M. in the Afternoon*" (1996) (figure 11.1), a miniaturization of a couple in their modern apartment, a sense of angst arises from a skewed spatial relationship within an overwhelmingly empty environment. The insecurity within the interior space derives from its "collectivity," since everything in it represents knowledge shared by society at large. The space has no set boundaries, only stereotypical images. Zeng's paintings of these miniaturized lives, like Qiu Huadong's urban tales, disembody middle-class representations by foregrounding their reproducibility (figure 11.2). Further, "the miniature," as Susan Stewart explains, is something that does not attach itself to lived historical time.

> Unlike the metonymic world of realism which attempts to erase the break between the time of everyday life and the time of narrative by mapping one

Figure 11.1 Zeng Hao, *5:00 P.M. in the Afternoon* (1996), oil on canvas, $78\frac{1}{2} \times 68\frac{1}{2}$ in (200 ×175 cm), collection of the artist.

perfectly upon the other, the metaphoric world of the miniature makes everyday life absolutely anterior and exterior to itself. The reduction in scale that the miniature presents skews the time and space relations of everyday life, and as an object consumed, the miniature finds its "use value" transformed into the infinite time of reverie.[17]

The illusion of modernity, like the "miniature," derives from its narrow focus on the infinite present. Many of Zeng's paintings have titles indicating a moment rather than an identifiable date, in history: *December 31st, Thursday Afternoon* (figure 11.3), *Yesterday, Friday 5:00 P.M., 17:05, July 11th*, resulting in a sense of perpetual present. This "flattening," or

Figure 11.2   Zeng Hao, *September 12th* (1997), oil on canvas, 71 × 59 in (180 × 150 cm), collection of the artist.

self-conscious "forgetting" of the past is also one of the hallmarks of urban fiction of the 1990s, which results in a sense of distorted reality by only concerning itself with the present.

The first two stories from *Fly Eyes* are followed by one in which the death of the heroic figure appears more tragic than quixotic. In "Two-dimensional people," Qiu juxtaposes the lifestyle choices of two brothers. As the story

Figure 11.3 Zeng Hao, *Thursday Afternoon* (1995), oil on canvas, 71 × 59 in (180 × 150 cm), collection of the artist.

opens, the younger brother has changed his career from philosophy student to night club disc jockey, much to his elder brother's dismay. At large in the wee hours of the night, often frequenting other clubs after getting off work, the DJ's new job places him in a context of heightened danger, as organized crime in the city operates on much the same hours. Unaware of the perils, he declares himself a "two-dimensional man" who "belongs to the night," and soon hooks up with He Ling, an alluring "woman in red" who shares his values. The elder brother's job is hazardous by choice—he is a beat cop responsible for busting organized crime rings in Beijing. Predictably, He Ling, herself helplessly caught in a tangled web of crime and unable to "escape the city" where "bullets fly and people die," implicates Tian Chang, whose elder brother must defend him from a notorious mobster and dies in the process (p. 268).

Once again, the "hero" figure perishes whereas the "petty man" (or self-styled "two-dimensional man") survives and "gets the girl." However, the story doesn't end here. Whereas characters in a previous story leave Beijing and tour China's major cities before returning to the capital, the survivors in this story narrow their world even further. They now consider Beijing to be their roots and any attempt to "escape" by exploring other cities, let alone the countryside, is considered futile. Thus when the DJ and his girlfriend feel disgusted with the city, instead of leaving it they decide to "tour" the city by chartering a gondola through the Hucheng River, the ancient moat that surrounded the Beijing city wall. Here Qiu creates an absurd metaphor indicating that Beijing already contains all the "sites" one could need in life. He Ling declares, "we can't escape the city. As soon as we leave [Beijing] we'll want to return, because this is our stage, it is the place which nourishes dreams, and we depend on it for our very breath" (p. 250).

On their tour, they disembark at shopping centers, amusement parks, and other urban gathering places. At an amusement park, the bemused couple observes idiosyncratic individuals who try to escape their problems by engaging in obsessive repetition. They marvel at fanatic pinball players. They are preached to by a young man positively evangelistic about the joys of "flying" on a trampoline, which he bounces on each day after work. They query a middle-aged man obsessively tossing basketballs into a hoop, who barks back that he is trying to forget a painful divorce. And when a blind girl wins a gambling prize, she is unable to bask in her good fortune; instead, she alienates the well-wishers by launching into her bad-luck story of being blinded due to a chemical plant explosion in the city. After observing all of these desperate souls, the couple is more depressed than ever:

> They wanted to quickly forget the faces of those "losers" they saw at the amusement park, because those faces left them with something deeply painful. Those people seem to live in the dark, like a group that has been abandoned by something, immersed in an extremely simple kind of happiness. They are all "two-dimensional people." (p. 280)

The couple is particularly repulsed by the superficiality of contemporary urban practices because they see their own reflection in those faces in the crowd, as individuals who are lacking in substance or character.

In order to reverse the hollowing experience wrought by modern urban life, Qiu's characters adopt the prevalent discourse of the middle class. One of the most prominent characteristics of the middle class is the belief that one must organize one's activities and identities around certain "goals"—that without these goals life would be "pointless" or "meaningless." After completing their one-night tour of the city, the couple decides to renounce the "two-dimensionality" of their night life, vowing, instead, to embrace a mainstream lifestyle of "substance":

> We had lived for such a long time as "night fanatics" . . . so we were shocked to once again see the city as day was dawning. It was full of life, because newly awakened people were moving about it with purpose, dashing about to start a new day, all "addition-type" people . . . Suddenly He Ling and I had a feeling that we would bid our night life adieu, say goodbye to our two-dimensional lifestyle, and directly engage in the daytime. Precisely! From this day on we will directly engage in the daytime and go about "adding," vigorously pursuing that reliable, substantive part of life. We'll work hard, earn money, buy a house, buy a car, buy a television, have a kid, respect our parents, take on the most tiring and banal responsibilities of life. Charge forward! Yes, this is what we concluded after our "tour." Charge forward! Charge into life and be a person of substance. We smelled the fresh morning air, that kind of air which would sustain our breathing for the next half of our life. Charge forward! (p. 293)

The revolutionary zeal with which the couple affirms middle-class values brims with tongue-in-cheek cynicism, especially given their awareness of the superficiality of consumer culture. The couple had once castigated those who devote themselves to "adding" material possessions until they become surfeited with the complexity and emptiness of such a life, whereupon they simplify their life by "subtracting"—ridding themselves of these burdens.

Such sarcasm about the predictability of everyday life, rather than leading to a radical redesign of society, actually bolsters the status quo. The individual's self-conscious distancing from the social arrangements to which he is party gives him a sense of satisfaction with his own lot, which is incompatible with a desire for change. Ben Xu argues that the new social conservatism among Chinese middle-class intellectuals is due to a "rejection" of the radical "academic myth of antitraditionalism" of the 1980s and capitulation to the state agenda of renewed nationalism of the 1990s.[18] Yet it is also a manifestation of modernity under the logic of the urban marketplace: the bourgeois reinforcement of the status quo. Meng Fanhua accurately characterizes the "new cultural conservatism" that prevails among China's urban elite:

> First, it rejects radical criticism and opts for moderate and steady discursive practice. Second, it gives up anxious concern about and questioning of the collective, focusing on the personal; third, it declines quests for ultimate values, goals, or faith, and is instead concerned with solutions to local problems.[19]

In Qiu Huadong's city narratives, the characters who successfully negotiate the city space exhibit precisely these characteristics, whereas those who engage in seeking for ultimate values, radical lifestyle choices, and contribution to the collective good, perish.

Qiu Huadong's characters recognize the same dilemma inherent in liberal societies once analyzed by John Stuart Mill, who delineates the contradictions between the principles of free choice and the lived reality of conformity, which is a denial in practice of this very individuality. In Mill's treatise *On Liberty* he states:

> Society has now fairly got the better of individuality, and the danger which threatens human nature is not the excess but the deficiency of personal impulses and preferences. I do not mean that they choose what is customary in preference to what suits their own inclination. It does not occur to them to have any inclination, except what is customary. Thus the mind itself is bowed to the yoke: even in what people do for pleasure, conformity is the first thing thought of; they like in crowds; they exercise choice only among things commonly done; peculiarity of taste, eccentricity of conduct, are shunned equally with crimes; until by dint of not following their own nature they have no nature to follow: their human capacities are withered and starved.[20]

The problem with indulging one's desires in consumer society, it seems, is that it merely replicates the lowest common denominator of the masses rather than expressing personal impulses and preferences.

SEEKING "THE GOOD" IN ZHU WEN'S *WHAT'S TRASH, WHAT'S LOVE?*

Whereas Qiu Huadong's stories in *Fly Eyes* read rather transparently as morality tales, Zhu Wen's novel *Shenme shi laji, shenme shi ai* (*What's Trash, What's Love?* 1998) explores ethical questions far more subtly.[21] Zhu Wen's comic novella *Wo ai meiyuan* (*I Love Dollars*, 1995) shook the literary establishment with the carefree manner in which the young male protagonist, a Nanjing author in his early twenties, has casual sex with prostitutes and even arranges for his father to join him in his escapades. This attempt to turn sexual conservatism of the 1980s on its head (while adding a twist to the notion of filial piety) is one of the hallmarks of urban literature of the 1990s—a celebration of individuality and social freedom often expressed in sexual licentiousness.[22]

What's Trash, What's Love? is a more in-depth reworking of themes raised in *I Love Dollars*. Zhu Wen depicts the angst and confusion plaguing Xiao Ding, a floundering Nanjing writer in his late twenties, and his circle of friends, which is not easily remedied by lucrative jobs, free love, drugs, or even sacrificial volunteer work. Rather than writing about such aimlessness in a didactic, moralizing manner, Zhu Wen meticulously recounts his protagonist's thoughts and actions, leaving the reader to draw his or her own conclusions. Xiao Ding is a conflicted character who obstinately refuses to assist a friend's search for his daughter (who had been kidnapped and gang-raped, an increasingly common occurrence in the Chinese metropolis), but offers to work as a volunteer in a futile attempt to find purpose. The novel ends as it opens, with the protagonist alone in a crowded bar, his mouth gaping wide in a ludicrous silent scream, an appropriate coda for a work that depicts modern urban life as cyclical and meaningless.

The contingency of modern urban life is foregrounded in *What's Trash, What's Love?* As one of a growing number of freelance artists, there is no work unit to monitor Xiao Ding's comings and goings. His days are not governed by any organizing principle—they blend together just as his frequent naps fuse his waking and sleeping hours. Like most characters in urban fiction of the 1990s, Xiao Ding appears to be strictly controlled by desires for sex, nourishment, sleep, and autonomy. Although he initially maintains a modicum of social interaction, he becomes increasingly cranky and withdrawn, especially after contracting venereal disease. Toward the end of the novel, he rarely makes contacts with others, preferring to isolate himself within his apartment. On the one hand, he ostensibly values his privacy and prevents others from encroaching it, apparently so that they will respect his autonomy. He is only willing to help others on his own terms, and views any attempt to force his hand as a violation of his agency. Yet, as the novel progresses, it dawns on him that something is amiss in such an autonomous lifestyle, and he begins a fruitless search to make what he refers to as "real contact" with others.

One of the most humorous incidents occurs when Xiao Ding, bored by his bohemian lifestyle, seeks out a charitable agency to do volunteer work. When the director of the Love and Virtue Foundation interviews him, however, she utterly fails to comprehend that he would be willing to do "something for nothing," and becomes obsessed in discovering his ulterior motive for volunteering. Xiao Ding's altruistic aspirations are thwarted, as "Love and Virtue" remains firmly wedded to the logic of the marketplace. This ludicrous illustration of the utilitarian ethic dominating consumer society demonstrates that it becomes "common sense" to assume that self-interest is the only real motivation for behavior.

After his "voluntarism" fiasco, Xiao Ding's laissez-faire approach to life suffers a severe setback. Whereas he once felt free to indulge in sex at whim, he has painfully experienced the consequences in his diseased body, and where he had once felt no qualms about living his life strictly based on his own desires, a low-grade anxiety now plagues him. In a final scene, Xiao Ding tries to explain to an ex-girlfriend his quest for "real contact" with life. She naively concludes that "sexual contact" is what he is really after, but much to Xiao Ding's chagrin even *this* idea now repulses him! He realizes, for the first time, that he is, in fact, in search of something more substantial than the superficial life he had been living. Ultimately, the protagonist attempts to answer the question implied by the novel's title—is there, in fact, a "greater good" such as "love" to be achieved in this life? Or is it all, in the final analysis, simply trash? This question is pursued in the novel by exploring the relation of self to others. In the absence of the regulation provided by the state-owned work unit, the individual is afforded so much autonomy that he is almost at a loss. Not only must he regulate his daily routines and coordinate his social activity, with the deterioration of ethical norms inherent in socialism, it becomes incumbent upon him to develop an entirely new value system.

The final image of the novel, Xiao Ding's mouth gaping open as he sits alone in a bar, calls to mind classic motifs of urban alienation such as that encapsulated in Edvard Munch's *The Scream* (1893), where the subject's angst is inextricably tied to the presence of nameless "others" who highlight his sense of aloneness. Zhu Wen's portrayal of Xiao Ding's foiled attempt to do good, and his new self-awareness in the wake of sexual disease, seems to corroborate Nietzsche's claims that the alleged good of altruism is parasitic on egoism, and that sickness is necessary for self-knowledge. Xiao Ding exhibits what Nietzsche termed passive nihilism; one who takes a last desperate stand on behalf of morality in the belief that morality and meaning are lost but *ought* to exist, rather than being an active nihilist who not only accepts the loss of morality but celebrates it. Indeed, in a group interview with Zhu Wen and other Nanjing writers in 1997, they agreed that their writing demands a degree of courage, which, few in society can muster, for their work impels them to "gaze directly upon the purposelessness of modern life."[23]

HE DUN'S FATALISTIC CITY NARRATIVES

He Dun differs from Zhu Wen and Qiu Huadong in that his morality tales lack the sardonic edge of the former writers. Instead He Dun delineates the moral fallout accompanying urban business success stories in a matter-of-fact way. He Dun graduated from art school in the 1980s and taught art in a Changsha middle school for a number of years before quitting his job to do business in interior design. His lifestyle change from idealistic academic to practical businessman followed the pattern of many in the early 1990s who chose to "*xia hai*" ("take the plunge" into business). With his changed lifestyle came an evolution of values and worldview, so he began to write to describe attitudinal changes accompanying the "new state of affairs" (*xin zhuangtai*) of the 1990s, where individual choices abound and personal ethics become redefined and reexamined. He writes realistic accounts of Changsha closely based on personal experience, and first gained critical acclaim for his 1993 novellas *Didi ni hao* (*Hello, Younger Brother*), *Shenghuo wuzui* (*Life is Not a Crime*), and *Wo buxiangshi* (*I Don't Care*).[24]

He Dun's novella *Hello, Younger Brother* features a young man, Deng Heping, disillusioned after failing to get into Beijing University and unmotivated by his subsequent job as an elementary school teacher in the late 1980s. After impregnating his girlfriend, he is kicked out of his parents' house, quits his job, and joins a classmate selling cigarettes on the open market. Through this pursuit, he falls in love with the man's wife, Dandan, whose contacts lead him to a job managing a nightclub. After his classmate is executed for dealing heroin, and Heping's own marriage to a singer-turned-movie-star sours, he marries Dandan and the couple start an extremely successful business supplying decorating materials. However the story ends on a shocking note. Just as Heping has established himself in a profitable job with a lovely wife, his wife and unborn child are killed in a motorcycle accident. In *Hello Younger Brother*, the value of material success in the 1990s is shown to be as ephemeral as political or academic success proved to be in the 1980s.

He Dun provides detailed descriptions of conspicuous consumption in the 1990s. Xiaobing Tang points out that

> Heping first signals his rise in status by smoking an American brand of cigarette, and his footwear progresses from generic "pointy and shiny black shoes" to "Italian-made crocodile skin shoes," which he is quick to put up on a table as a means of convincing his friends of his ambition. When the business of his Hongtai Decoration Materials store flourishes, bringing in a net profit of 700,000 yuan (equivalent to US$85,900), he rewards himself by upgrading his Chinese-made Nanfang motorcycle to a Royal Honda.[25]

The sign value of objects reinforces a logic of differentiation and establishes a distinctive hierarchy of taste, status, and identity through participation in what Baudrillard terms a "social discourse of objects" contributing to a "general mechanism of discrimination and prestige."[26]

According to Dai Jinhua in her perceptive article on the politics of Chinese pop culture in the 1990s, the Chinese media in the mid-1990s contributed to this logic of differentiation by defining their targets in terms of middle-class taste and consumption levels. She provides an example from a 1995 issue of *Best Buys* (*Jingpin gouwu zhinan*), where an article gives detailed instruction about what merchandise to buy to live up to a given income level. She also mentions a commercial for housing that simply states, "for those who have high status" (*wei mingliu bianxie shenfen de jianzhu*), concluding that commercial culture has entered Chinese public discourse as unambiguously class biased.[27] He Dun's city narratives consistently portray the truth of this statement. Heping has already "read" the "political economy of the sign," to borrow Baudrillard's terminology, and is well-aware of the utilitarian function served by his consumption. By flaunting his material success Heping is able to attract more business, simultaneously enticing friends and lovers.

He Dun destabilizes such capitalist power dynamics in his fiction by recalling their radical divergence from the ethics of an earlier age governed by ideals of social equality and socialist mottos of "to each according to his or her need." The opening and closing scenes of *Hello Younger Brother* provide an ethical framing to an otherwise fairly straightforward narrative. The novella opens with a description of Heping's revolutionary father, who was appointed assistant county head at age 26 after leading a brigade of communist guerrillas in ousting his own landlord father from his estate. Yet while Heping's father had a seemingly bright future, due to subsequent political upheavals and his own father's landlord background, he never advanced much beyond his initial position. Heping's success, on the other hand, starts at age 26, and by the time he is 30, he truly seems, in the words of Confucius, to have "established himself."

It is ironic that Heping's tragedy is related to the transgressive transformation of the political *guangchang*, or "square," and all it represented to his father's generation, into the commercial *guangchang*, or "shopping plaza," of his own generation in the 1990s. Yet consumer culture, like revolutionary politics, fails to ensure stability. Recognizing the contingent nature of success in the market economy, most characters in He Dun's fiction adopt a fatalistic worldview. In the closing scene, the narrator recounts his "younger brother's" agony over his wife and unborn child's tragic fate via a series of "what ifs": "If" Dandan hadn't insisted on going to the department store on Shaoshan Road to buy an artificial flower arrangement for the living room of their newly decorated apartment, "if" his Honda motorcycle had been repaired on time, then his wife's last, primal scream would not eternally haunt Heping.

Earlier in the novella, Heping's initial reunion with Dandan is also credited to fate:

> That morning as Didi (Younger Brother) rode his motorcycle to Double Swallow Wonton Shop he bumped into Dandan who was just leaving the shop. How lucky! If he was still at home talking with his wife, if he had given the "Mainland Girl" film script a serious read, he wouldn't have run into Dandan today, and probably wouldn't have run into her in a lifetime. Dandan's uncle had just arranged a job for her in an office on Hainan Island. If that morning Didi had, as usual, spent five mao at that dumpling stand to buy two *baozi* (steamed buns), he wouldn't have run into Dandan. It just so happened that in the past few days that man from Hubei only put a tiny amount of filling in his *baozi*, infuriating Didi each time. Yesterday he bitterly censured the peddler, "Your *baozi* are getting worse and worse! They're not even worth biting into!" Today he didn't even glance at him as he rode past. Of course Didi could have gone to another stand or to a noodle shop to eat breakfast, but it was probably providence that he passed the Double Swallow Wonton Shop, not thinking about wontons, but fifty or so meters past the shop he suddenly realized he wanted them. (p. 333)

A similar litany of coincidences conclude the novella, framing Heping's greatest "success" in life by circumstance. While the notion of *yuanfen*, or "destiny," is the bedrock of traditional Chinese popular belief, He Dun's recurrent references to fate strike the reader with renewed force in the wake of twentieth-century campaigns to eradicate "superstitious ideas" in mainland China.

The rise of superstitious practices in the 1990s is often directly related to the market economy. He Dun elaborates upon this fact in one of his more ideologically explicit novels, *Ximalaya shan* (*The Himalayas*, 1998). As his teacher-turned-businessman protagonist puts it,

> the majority of Chinese businessman in the 1990s aren't controlled by faith or ideology, they don't talk about beliefs or politics or ideas, and they certainly don't talk about movies or art, what they talk about is superstition. That's their belief system![28]

He proceeds to enumerate the ways in which superstition rules Chinese business practices, where diviners are called on to determine auspicious dates on which to break ground for a new building, or to buy a car, or to choose lucky names for the business. Although such reliance on luck might seem to detract from entrepreneurial initiative in a burgeoning commercial society, often the notion of fate functions as a form of consolation, such as in "Life is not a Crime" where an economically struggling teacher attempts to diffuse his wife's jealousy over a classmate's business success by declaring, "his fate is just better than mine, that's all" (p. 69). In the final analysis, a fatalistic mindset can comfort an underdog or loser, while simultaneously allowing for self-congratulation when one becomes successful, as the teacher does eventually.

The question of personal worth and individual ethics is raised in more detail, if less subtly, in He Dun's novels such as *Women xiang kuihua* (*We are Like Sunflowers*, 1995) and *The Himalayas*, which introduce protagonists in search of spiritual ideals in the midst of a decadent urban environment filled with sex, violence, and corruption, only to find that reality fails to provide a grounding for previously held ideals. His protagonists eagerly engage in the commercial activities of the 1990s while remaining spiritually at a loss. In *The Himalayas*, the lifestyle of the metropolis is contrasted both with that of a parochial town and of the pristine Tibetan mountain range.

Luo Ding and his wife, Huang Jiangli, are Changsha middle-school teachers in their early thirties. The novel describes Huang Jiangli's struggles with Principal Peng who refuses to promote her, Luo Ding's gradual rise to prominence in the "Grand Cultural Development Company" where he has relocated, and the tension that builds between the couple as their values come into conflict. The couple married after meeting at their middle-school job in the 1980s; attractive and artistic, they seemed an ideal match. Ten years later, disillusioned with her dead-end job in Changsha, Huang Jiangli makes up excuses to spend more and more time with her parents in Whitewater, the small county seat of her youth. She reunites with high-school classmates who still reside there, and spends her time socializing, gossiping, and dancing with them. She soaks in the fresh air and regains her small-town "heroine" status, admired by the townspeople for her beauty and musical abilities. Luo Ding, however, finds life in this town to be suffocating; as disgusted as he is with Changsha's pollution, he finds himself longing to return to his home there: "no matter how good a county seat may be, it's always twenty years behind the provincial capital" (p. 86) he declares to his wife, whom he denigrates for being so "countrified" (p. 362).

Luo Ding also seeks to escape the pressures of the urban grind, but for him this takes the form of dreaming of travel to the Himalayas. He has never been to the range, and it functions symbolically in his subconscious as the ultimate utopia. Even before he begins to make money, Luo Ding senses that capital will not satisfy his deepest longings; however he feels pressured by his in-laws to raise his menial social status as a teacher. Consequently, when Luo Ding is promoted to company manager and supplied with a pager, cell phone, motorcycle, and expense account, he immediately shows off his new belongings and revels in his new status when he visits Principal Peng, who has terrorized their lives in the school *danwei* with his petty autocracy. He blows smoke from his expensive American-brand cigarettes in Principal Peng's face as he tells him off, the experience considerably enhanced when his pager and cell phone sound simultaneously, "fucking ringing off the hook!" (p. 364). As in He Dun's earlier novellas, commodities conspicuously serve as power brokers, immediately raising an individual's social status.

The perks of Luo Ding's new job not only boost his social standing, they also alter his perception of the world. Whereas he had previously spurned the come-ons by a divorced female colleague, Chou Yuanyuan, it is precisely at this juncture of the novel that he first finds her attractive. Prior to this, Luo Ding considered himself attracted to "gentle, virginal" women like Jiangli, not women with a "strong sex drive" like Yuanyuan (p. 95). He had been disgusted by Yuanyuan's brash reversal of gender roles by inviting him out, paying for dinner, opening doors for him, getting into cabs after him, etc. (p. 169). Taking her up on a "business invitation" to tour Shenzhen, he allows "thoroughly modern Yuanyuan" to "remake" him, teaching him to dance disco, directing his purchase of a new set of clothes to "make the man," and exposing him to a "real city" where he dazedly counts the stories on the shiny skyscrapers.

In the end, however, Luo Ding is inconsolable when Huang Jiangli finally leaves him to take a new job in Whitewater, and he never fully adapts to his new lifestyle in the daily company of business persons. The novel is rife with a sense of pathos and nostalgia for a sense of goodness that seems irretrievably lost in the modern world. As Luo Ding mutters to himself, "even the good girls like Xiao Liu (his secretary, who has recently started drinking and swearing with the boys) change in such a society" (p. 377). He senses that the only possibility of regaining a sense of moral integrity is to retreat into a backward town as his wife did, or to leave civilization altogether. Luo Ding opts for the latter. He convinces Chou Yuanyuan to travel with him to the Himalayas, but she returns alone, reporting that he died there in an avalanche. In the final chapter, Xiao Liu recounts Luo Ding's departure:

> Director Chen didn't agree to the trip, saying there was too much work to be done. I remember how Luo Ding looked as he was leaving. He threw down his motorcycle key, his cell phone, and his pager on Manager Yang's desk and said, "Manager Yang, I'm returning this stuff, I'm leaving." He also turned around to look at me and gently said, "I'm leaving, Xiao Liu." I clearly remember he said "leaving" and was stunned, because he should have said "see you later" instead of "leaving." Was this some kind of sign? (p. 408)

In *The Himalayas, What's Trash, What's Love?*, and *Fly Eyes*, the protagonists seem incapable of establishing a moral basis for modern urban life. Once they become self-conscious, they resort to extreme measures to extricate themselves from the ethical dilemma of engaging in the mundane everyday life of modernity with its apparent lack of idealism and purpose.

NARRATIVE ETHICS AND CONTEMPORARY CHINESE URBAN FICTION

City narratives in China of the 1990s highlight the ethical issues that emerged as the crumbling ideologies of the 1980s became supplanted by the logic of the market, leaving individuals with the burden of creating new belief systems. In the novels I have examined here, fictional characters respond to the ethical dilemmas posed by consumer modernity in a variety of ways. In *Fly Eyes*, Qiu Huadong's characters attempt exaggerated heroics, hermit-like retreat, and mock allegiance to prosaic middle-class values as a means of instilling their lives with purpose. Zhu Wen's protagonist is a passive nihilist, self-aware but unable to enact a meaningful modern existence. He Dun's characters take solace in traditional values, countering the ills of consumer modernity by resigning themselves to fate or by rejecting the city for a pristine, rural existence.

Qiu Huadong acknowledges the challenge of narrative ethics in his brief rejoinder to the many critics who have accused urban writers of the 1990s of moral decadence. In his essay "Who is the enforcer of morality?" he criticizes those who indiscriminately confuse an author's moral code with that conveyed in his fiction:

> During a period in which the economy is rapidly developing without the control of a cultural and ethical system, it is necessary to be vigilant about spiritual values. Who, however, acts as the enforcer of that morality? Who is authorized to be the judge? Unfortunately it seems to me the time when we can establish a space where multiple value systems can co-exist remains in the very distant future.[29]

The critic Li Jiefei concurs that the proliferation in the 1990s of "narratives of desire" (*yuwanghua xushu*) is not merely a response to market demands by lowering literary standards to create best-sellers, but rather a sensitive reflection of recurrent real-life dilemmas.[30]

Yet while "post" critics such as Chen Xiaoming initially praised these urban narratives, his more recent assessments are more critical, perhaps due to a renewed emphasis on leftist narrative ethics in the latter half of the 1990s. He states,

> the majority of "belated generation" authors over-emphasize the superficial aspects of contemporary life, especially the emotional state of urban life (*chengshi shenghuo de qinggan zhuangtai*), rarely expressing the tremendous conflicts arising from rapid accumulation of capital. The "belated generation" is full of vitality but lacks profundity.[31]

Although leftist scholars criticize the lack of class analysis in these works, neoliberal scholars largely criticize post-Mao urban fiction for failing to enlighten.

There is, however, an ethical dimension to these narratives, which, as I have argued, is their most defining feature. In Geoffrey Harpham's *Shadows of Ethics*, he describes ethics as that point where literature intersects with philosophy by addressing ethical questions through plot. Harpham suggests that:

> We can conceive of narrative form as a representational structure that negotiates the relation . . . of *is* and *ought*. The most general and adequate conception of a narrative plot is that it moves from an unstable inaugural condition, a condition that *is* but *ought not*—through a process of sifting and exploration in search of

an unknown but retrospectively inevitable condition that *is* and truly *ought-to-be*. Narrative plot thus provides what philosophy cannot, a principle of formal necessity immanent in recognizable worldly and contingent events that governs a movement toward the eventual identity of *is* and *ought*.[32]

In this sense, Harpham echoes the Aristotelian ideal put forth in *Poetics* that poetry is more philosophical and more morally serious than history, since poetry speaks of universals, history of particulars.[33] Narrative literature shares structures and assumptions with other forms of social understanding; as such, narrative can serve as the "example" to illustrate the moral choice that is, of necessity, the ultimate end of ethical inquiry. In the Chinese urban fiction discussed in this chapter, the characters not only act, they eventually reflect on their actions with the recognition that something is amiss in their modern urban lifestyles. In most cases, these authors conclude their narratives in an open-ended fashion, resulting in moral ambiguity. They may not achieve satisfactory answers to their attempts to transform what *is* into what *ought* to be; yet these authors unquestionably probe ethical issues arising in relation to their urban reality. Post-Mao urban narratives suggest an ongoing inquiry into the relationship between authenticity and the public sphere by grappling with universal ethical questions arising in conjunction with modern commercial life. The real paradox of ethics is that a discourse that seems to promise answers is so obsessed with questions.

NOTES

1. Ross Poole, "Introduction," *Morality and Modernity* (Routledge: London and New York, 1991), p. ix.
2. Li Jiefei, "Xulun er: Zhongguo chengshi wenxue jiushi pingshu" (Introduction II: A critical overview of previous histories of Chinese urban literature), *Chengshi xiangkuang* (*City Frame*) (Taiyuan: Shanxi jiaoyu chubanshe, 1999), pp. 39–40.
3. See Dai Jinhua, "Invisible writing: the politics of Chinese mass culture in the 1990s," *Modern Chinese Literature and Culture* 1:1 (spring 1999), 43–44; and Luo Gang, "Shei zhi gonggong xing?" (Whose public characteristics?), *Shanghai wenxue* (*Shanghai literature*) 5 (1999), 76–78.
4. See Charles Taylor, *The Ethics of Authenticity* (Cambridge, MA: Harvard University Press, 1992).
5. Habermas's arguments in *Theorie des kommunikativen Handelns* 2 vols. (Frankfurt: Suhrkamp, 1981) are summarized in Poole, "Liberalism and nihilism: the project of liberalism," *Morality and Modernity*, pp. 78–85, and in Charles Taylor, "Conclusion: the conflicts of modernity," *Sources of the Self: The Making of the Modern Identity* (Cambridge, MA: Harvard University Press, 1989), pp. 509–510.
6. The *renwen jingshen* debates were sparked by responses to a series of roundtable discussions sponsored by the journal *Dushu* (*Reading*). The minutes of these discussions are published in *Dushu* 3, 4, 5, 6, 7 (1993). Follow-up articles are collected in Wang Xiaoming, ed., *Renwen jingshen xunsi lu* (*Thoughts on the Humanist Spirit*) (Shanghai: Wenhui chubanshe, 1996). Wen Liping summarizes the discussions in "Guanyu renwen jingshen taolun zongshu" (A summary

of the humanist spirit discussions), *Wenyi lilun yu piping* (*Literary theory and criticism*), 3 (1995), 119–134; 4 (1995), 123–138. Ben Xu, in turn, summarizes Wen's article in " 'From modernity to Chineseness': the rise of nativist cultural theory in post-1989 China," *positions east asia cultures critique* 6:1 (1998), 203–223. See also "The making of the post-Tiananmen intellectual field: a critical overview," in *Whither China? Intellectual Politics in Contemporary China* ed. Xudong Zhang (Durham, NC: Duke University Press, 2001), pp. 1–75.

7. Robert Bellah, "Private life: individualism," *Habits of the Heart* (Berkeley: University of California Press, 1985), pp. 131–133.

8. Urban fiction of the 1990s is often referred to by the epithet "xin zhuangtai" (new condition; new state of affairs), resulting from intense discussion in the early 1990s by the Nanjing-based journal *Zhongshan* and Beijing-based *Wenyi zhengming* on how to describe urban fiction of the 1990s by Liu Xinwu, Wang Meng, He Dun, Han Dong, Zhang Min, Zhu Wen, Lin Bai, Chen Ran, Qiu Huadong, Wang Anyi, and others. Other labels for these writers include "new urbanite fiction" (*xin shimin xiaoshuo*), "new generation" (*xinsheng dai*), and "belated generation" (*wansheng dai*). See *Liu Xinwu Zhang Yiwu duihua lu: "Hou shiji" de wenhua liaowang* (*Record of Conversations between Liu Xinwu and Zhang Yiwu: Gazing at "Post-Era" Culture*) (Guilin: Lijiang chubanshe, 1996), p. 222.

9. Chen Xiaoming, "Jianyao pingjie" (Brief commentary on He Dun's "Life is not a crime") in *Zhongguo chengshi xiaoshuo jingxuan* (*Anthology of Chinese Urban Fiction*), ed. Chen Xiaoming (Lanzhou: Gansu renmin chubanshe, 1994), p. 304; and "Wanshengdai yu jiushi niandai wenxue liuxiang" (The belated generation and the literary trends in the nineties), preface to He Dun, *Shenghuo wuzui* (*Life is not a Crime*) (Beijing: Huayi chubanshe, 1995), p. 6.

10. Some scholars consider the rejection of metaphors of the nation-state, the main literary strategy from the May Fourth period until the 1980s, to be one of the key distinctions of urban fiction of the 1990s. See Zhang Yiwu, "Hou xin shiqi wenxue: Xin de wenhua kongjian" (Post-new era literature: a new cultural space), *Wenyi lilun* (*Literary theory*) 1 (1993), 184.

11. Li Tuo, a critic responsible for popularizing the works of avant-garde writers of the late 1980s both in China and abroad, was the most virulent among several who decried the style of new urban literature at a conference sponsored by *Beijing wenxue* (*Beijing literature*) in Beijing in June of 1997, attended by both "avant-garde" and "new urbanite" writers.

12. Peter Taylor, *Modernities: A Geohistorical Interpretation* (Cambridge: Polity Press, 1999), p. 30.

13. Qiu Huadong, *Yingyan* (*Fly Eyes*) (Changchun: Changchun chubanshe, 1998), p. 2. Subsequent page references noted in the text.

14. Georg Simmel, *The Philosophy of Money*, trans. T. Bottomore and D. Frisby (London: Routledge, 1978), p. 474.

15. Zhang Ailing, "Fengsuo," *Zhang Ailing wenji* (Hefei: Anhui wenyi chubanshe, 1992), vol. I, pp. 99–111.

16. Allan Bloom, "Relationships: Self-centeredness," *The Closing of the American Mind* (New York: Simon and Schuster, 1987), p. 84.

17. Susan Stewart, "The miniature: miniature time," *On Longing: Narratives of the Miniature, the Gigantic, the Souvenir, the Collection* (Durham: Duke University Press, 1993), p. 65.

18. Ben Xu, "Contesting memory for intellectual self-positioning: the 1990s new cultural conservatism in China," *Modern Chinese Literature and Culture* 11:1 (spring 1999), 159.

19. Meng Fanhua, "Wenhua bengkui shidai de taowang yu guiyi—jiushi niandai wenhua de xinbaoshouzhuyi jingshen" (Escape and support in an age of cultural collapse: the neoconservative spirit of 1990s culture), *Zhongguo wenhua* (*Chinese culture*) 4 (1994), 53.

20. John Stuart Mill, "Applications," *On Liberty* (London: Dent, 1964), p. 190.

21. Textual references are to Zhu Wen, *Shenme shi laji, shenme shi ai* (*What's Trash, What's Love?*) (Nanjing: Jiangsu wenyi chubanshe, 1998).

22. Zhu Wen's decadent writing of sexuality is perhaps one of the major reasons critics have not been fully appreciative of his fiction. Li Jiefei is an exception, and makes the astute point that narration of corporal desire is one of the defining features of urban fiction of the 1990s, unlike the idealization of romantic love, which defined most writing in the 1980s. He agrees that using sex as an easy means of "approaching another," debases its meaning; however he points out that it is a fundamental characteristic of a commercialized urban society. See chapter two, "Quti de yuwang" (Corporal desire) in *Chengshi xiangkuang*.

23. Author's interview with Zhu Wen, Han Dong, Lu Yang, Wu Chenjun, and other Nanjing writers and artists, August 1, 1997, Nanjing.

24. Subsequent references in the text to all three novellas are from He Dun, *Shenghuo wuzui* (*Life is Not a Crime*) (Beijing: Huayi chubanshe, 1995).

25. Xiaobing Tang, "Decorating culture: notes on interior design, interiority, and interiorization," *Public Culture* 10 (1998), 534.

26. Jean Baudrillard, *For a Critique of the Political Economy of the Sign*, trans. Charles Levin (St. Louis: Telos Press, 1981), p. 30, quoted in Xiaobing Tang, "Decorating culture," p. 535.

27. Dai Jinhua, "Invisible writing: the politics of Chinese mass culture in the 1990s," *Modern Chinese Literature and Culture* 11:1 (spring 1999), 44.

28. He Dun, *Ximalaya Shan* (*The Himalayas*) (Bianyuan wenzong. Nanjing: Jiangsu wenyi chubanshe, 1998), p. 358. Subsequent page references included in the text.

29. Qiu Huadong, "Shei shi daode zhifaren?" (Who is the enforcer of morality?), *Nanfang zhoumo* (*Southern weekend*) (April 25, 1997), 5.

30. Li Jiefei, *Chengshi xiangkuang*, p. 79.

31. Chen Xiaoming, "Zhijiexing: huidao shishi benshen" (Immediacy: returning to the facts themselves), *Fangzhen de niandai: Chao xianshi wenxue liubian yu wenhua xiangxiang* (*Age of Imitation: Surrealist Literary Developments and Cultural Imaginations*) (Taiyuan: Shanxi jiaoyu chubanshe, 1999), p. 187.

32. Geoffrey Galt Harpham, "Ethics and literary study," *Shadows of Ethics: Criticism and the Just Society* (Durham, NC: Duke University Press, 1999), p. 36.

33. Aristotle, *Poetics IX*, in *Critical Theory Since Plato*, ed. Hazard Adams (New York: Harcourt Brace Jovanovich, 1971).

12

CAPITALIST AND ENLIGHTENMENT
VALUES IN CHINESE FICTION
OF THE 1990S: THE CASE OF YU HUA'S
BLOOD MERCHANT

Deirdre Sabina Knight

Recent reports of the HIV infection spreading through blood collection centers in China signal particularly troubling uncertainties about the effects of market transition on the bodies of Chinese citizens. Although health officials estimate that 840,000 Chinese citizens are HIV positive,[1] some doctors working in Henan Province worry that more than a million people there may have contracted the AIDS virus through selling blood.[2] In light of these prognoses, a harrowing set of questions arises concerning what might have been taken as ironic metaphor in Yu Hua's (1960–) prescient novel, *Xu Sanguan mai xue ji* (Xu Sanguan the blood merchant, *literally* Record of Xu Sanguan selling [his] blood) (1995).[3] If the prospect of economically desperate peasants contracting HIV provokes a sense of outrage, the unease derives from convictions that the state should regulate such practices to protect its citizens. Yet, transition from Communist Party dominance over economic planning and industry to a still undefined mix of socialism and capitalist markets demands new negotiations of norms and values that can either enhance or jeopardize precisely such protections.

In a very different, and admittedly academic context, Western analytic philosophers committed to critiquing capitalism are increasingly seeking to argue questions of moral and political philosophy in order to continue to make a case for values, principles, and programs capable of promoting equality, community, and human self-realization. Whereas many Marxists once held development toward these values to be inevitable, the absence of an organized working class and ecological limitations preventing the material abundance Marx predicted have made normative moral and political advocacy necessary to advance considerations of alternatives to capitalism. In a soul-searching examination of the relationship between self-ownership, freedom, and equality, British philosopher G.A. Cohen (1941–) confronts the central place of self-ownership to both Marxist and libertarian thought in order to bolster the Marxist challenge to libertarianism.[4] In light of the relevance of libertarianism to current debates in China about the appropriate scope of government, this chapter draws on Cohen's discussion of self-ownership to explore one representation of China's market transition in recent Chinese fiction. For although neoliberals often view state intervention as a major obstacle to market development, constituencies concerned with redressing poverty and inequality generally support government social spending and the regulation of entrepreneurs' pursuit of profits. Through interpreting Yu Hua's *Blood Merchant*, I argue with Cohen that analysis of the uses of self-ownership diminishes its attractiveness as a primary value in favor of values less complicit with capitalist principles.

I came to this topic when I first considered the title "Contested Modernities," and I asked myself what might be the most important conflict inherent in the uses of the term "modernity."[5] In particular, what are the conflicts that appear in twentieth-century Chinese literature, and to what end does Chinese fiction explore the age we name modernity? One crucial dilemma in pursuing definitions of the project of modernity lies in the intimate relationship between Enlightenment values and capitalism. How does one reconcile (i) a commitment to Enlightenment values that many of us, following German philosopher Jürgen Habermas (1929–), wish to redeem and pursue, with (ii) the complicity of these noble values with social formations and practices of exploitation that we wish to protest or at least question?[6]

Contemporary Chinese fiction offers one avenue for considering recent controversies over what defines modernity and what its legacy is to become. Do these works continue to stage struggles identifiable as part of the project of modernity, including modernist aesthetic reactions to projects of development and modernization?[7] Or has this fiction moved on to another paradigm, such as a postmodern rejection of the meta-narratives of modernity? Moreover, if so, writers might contest two different types of meta-narratives, modernity's meta-narratives of historical events or meta-narratives that give accounts of and thereby often reify the notion of modernity itself.

The stakes behind such questions rise inasmuch as representations of capitalism and capitalist values dominate many recent works. The ascendancy of capitalism is especially evident in the works of the "belated generation" (*wanshengdai*), for the most part writers born in the 1960s, such as Diao Dou, He Dun, Han Dong, Qiu Huadong, Shu Ping, Zhang Min, or Zhu Wen.[8] Critic Chen Xiaoming argues that these writers' works have replaced pursuits of modernist and Enlightenment projects with depictions of the pursuit of profit, commodity fetishism, and consumerism.[9] If these works represent and sometimes even explicitly promote practices that enable capitalist exploitation, to what extent do they also present values that might contest free-market capitalist fundamentalism? In a decade of vast shifts in economic, moral, and gendered power relations, what do these works suggest about the currency of capitalist or socialist ideology? Do they render heroic the pursuit of accumulation and the predatory nature of market society? Or do they bespeak yearnings that oppose the growing hegemony of consumer-capitalism?

Certainly, recent Chinese fiction both reinforces and challenges new regimes of commodification and consumption. Yet some of this fiction also betrays a troubled, but enduring relationship to Enlightenment commitments to social responsibility and progress toward justice and human dignity. In a larger project, I examine several works' treatment of questions of class, gender, ethics, and political disenchantment to posit the perseverance of Enlightenment values. I then compare recent changes in Chinese fiction with the literatures of three other countries (Britain, France, and Russia) during periods of emergent capitalism and market transition. In this chapter, I briefly define the terms of my inquiry, consider the context of Chinese fiction of the 1990s, and then offer an example of the stakes involved in distinguishing between Enlightenment ideals and the more specific capitalist values through an analysis of Yu Hua's *Blood Merchant.*

CAPITALIST AND ENLIGHTENMENT VALUES

To begin this inquiry, it is important to confront two very different problems. The first involves disentangling modernity, capitalism, and Enlightenment from one another conceptually, in terms of life-enhancing and life-negating values. The second problem involves situating these values within the contexts of different histories, West and East. Of course, no one can disentangle these concepts and their histories all at once. Yet one can address particular aspects in specific contexts, and it is for this reason that a contemporary Chinese novel can play a valuable role in redeeming the Enlightenment project's commitment to improving human welfare. Yet before turning to the context of Chinese fiction of the 1990s, here I briefly distinguish capitalist from Enlightenment values in more general terms.

One definition of capitalism identifies an economic system characterized by open competition in a putatively "free" market, in which private or corporate entities own the means of production and distribution and employ wage laborers, and development corresponds to increasing accumulation and reinvestment of profits. Fiction, however, generally examines capitalism not in a strict economic sense, but in terms of its cultural, and specifically moral, ramifications. What values does contemporary Chinese fiction associate with the development of capitalism and the rise of mass industrial or technological society? What does this fiction add to studies of capitalism as a social formation pursued by such thinkers as Herbert Marcuse, Alain Touraine, or Anthony Giddens?[10] Even more urgent, how does Chinese fiction complement the picture of China's economic transformation and its effects on social norms provided by social scientists from China such as Jun Ma and He Qinglian?[11]

Capitalist values and practices include the opportunity for entrepreneurship, the desire for wealth, the sanctioning of acquisition and accumulation, and resultant regimes of consumerism and commodification. An increasingly capitalist system also demands adjustments to rapid change, the ability to update and remold oneself or one's enterprises to profit from a changing environment, and the subordination of other goals to the maximization of economic profit.[12] Greater disparities between rich and poor also lead to the rise of a leisure class and the development of values that regard material labor as unworthy and predatory exploitation as excusable.[13] Risk taking, gambling, outsmarting others, and hardnosed pragmatism all connote hallowed capitalist values.

To simplify, the Enlightenment refers to a philosophical movement of eighteenth-century Europe and America whose advocates sought to use rationalism, empiricism, or a synthesis of the two (Kant's case) to critically examine previously accepted doctrines and institutions. While the diversity and conflicts among thinkers associated with the Enlightenment hardly gave rise to a single coherent movement, certain common themes and values can be identified: first, there is the high estimation of individual reason and secularism. Rather than rely on religious or other traditional belief systems, Enlightenment projects encouraged individuals to investigate the world using reason, analysis, and empirical methods. The quarrel of *les moderns* against *les anciens* did not completely reject tradition, but it subjected traditional beliefs, especially church doctrine, superstitions, and myth, to scrutiny and skepticism that undermined their authority in favor of a this-worldly conception of human responsibility.

Second, Enlightenment projects were based on faith in progress and the idea that human beings can use reason and empiricism to improve their environment and enrich their daily lives. While many thinkers criticize the costs of material progress—especially connected economic, political, and social injustices and the ravages wreaked on the environment, the pursuit of progress has also led to more humane (although not unambiguously so) treatment of criminals and the mentally ill.[14] Along these lines, the Enlightenment's most important legacy is the commitment to freedom and values such as autonomy, equality, justice, and human dignity. The pursuit of such values underlie further commitments to specific political systems, particularly representative democracy, a system that depends on the notion of "one person, one vote" and thus promotes the formation of individual subjects and citizens.

Within the Chinese context, since the late nineteenth century, discussions of Enlightenment notions have largely turned around selected readings and interpretations of Western thinkers.[15] Of course, related notions of enlightenment can be found far back in Chinese traditions, particularly in Buddhist texts and practices and in Neo-Confucian scholarship,[16] but from the late Qing period (1895–1911), and especially in the New Culture Movement (1915–1925) that informed the May Fourth (1919–1927) period, leading thinkers critiqued Confucian traditions in an explicit project to reorient historical and cultural consciousness toward ideas of individualism, dynamism, and teleology. Pressed by urgent concern about China's threatened sovereignty and consequent need for nation building and modernization, these intellectuals turned to Enlightenment ideals in the hope that understanding Western values would enable China to catch up to the West in industrial and military power.

While it is important to keep in mind the heterogeneity of the ideas associated with the New Culture Movement and the limitations of adapting Western terminology in the Chinese context, many of the participants and subsequent scholars have argued convincingly for likening the May Fourth Movement to the European Enlightenment.[17] From the overthrow of the Qing dynasty to the Communist revolution, and from Deng's Four Modernizations to the present market transition, Chinese intellectuals have expressly sought to break with the past and achieve freedoms and amenities promised by the project of modernity and its trope of Enlightenment, or as historian John Fitzgerald more precisely names the Chinese counterpart, "awakening":

> The earliest of China's modern awakenings were awakenings to selfhood and individuality in relation to a rational and material universe. . . . The awakening of this universal self was soon displaced by the awakening of a distinctly Chinese self that preferred to commune with its nation. Defining the particularity of this nation invited reflection, in turn, on the ideal form of a state charged with the responsibility of awakening the people as "self-conscious" citizens. And a determination to "awaken the people" prompted those first awakened (*xian juezhe*) to develop organizations, technologies, and procedures for awakening the people to citizenship and nationhood.[18]

Repressed during the Cultural Revolution, explicit appeals to Enlightenment notions were made again during the 1980s, particularly by social scientists reading both Western Enlightenment philosophy and contemporary Western cultural theory. The Enlightenment promise of national renewal was also central to what Xudong Zhang so rightly names the Deng regime's "political invention" of the "New Era" (1979–1989) by which the regime sought to distance itself from Maoist ideology and gain legitimacy by advancing a rational, progressive, and affluent world.[19] According to Zhang, during the "Great Cultural Discussion" (1985–1989), intellectuals implicitly supported this political invention through their dual commitments to integrating China into the global economy and rebuilding a national culture attentive to local traditions. These commitments led to the pro-science school's interest in futurology and technology and the Chinese Culturalist School's pursuit of what some refer to as a renewed "second Enlightenment" project. This project involved rethinking Marxism and socialist humanism in terms of both traditional Confucian culture and Western theory: "Most important," writes Zhang, "the enlightenment project, the leitmotif of modern Chinese intellectual history, was once again activated in a critical reexamination of the past."[20]

In a careful study of cultural discourses in China of the 1990s, Ben Xu draws attention to the discontinuities in formulations of Chinese appeals to modernity and Enlightenment. Intellectual discussions and official policies of the 1980s, Xu explains, invoked Enlightenment notions to promote programs of gradual modernization and reform that departed significantly from the May Fourth emphasis on modernity as radical revolution and fundamental change.[21] Moreover, even within this gradualist approach, Party officials focused more narrowly on economical and technological development, while intellectuals sought to advance human capabilities and democratic institutions. The Tiananmen massacre, according to Xu, caused another deep rupture in intellectual commitments insofar as it darkened perceptions about the prospects for democracy and bolstered arguments for postmodern rejections of such Enlightenment notions. Xu warns, however, that the "Post-ist" theorists' view that the trauma of 1989 discredited the radicalism of 1980s sociocultural criticism often implicitly endorses neoconservative and neo-authoritarian positions that support the status quo: "Not only is the combined force of a Leninist party-state and a rampant market economy too powerful to allow for effective intellectual opposition or resistance, the reality is too full of incongruities to allow for imagining focused social change and for creating critical initiatives to appeal to the public."[22]

Like earlier scholarship emphasizing the conceptual differences and difficulties of translating these terms and values,[23] Xu's insights remind us of the limitations of theoretical discourses that treat abstractions as if they had concrete material significance. It is also important to remember that in the Western context as well, "the Enlightenment," especially as a noun, is a term more often used in retrospect and was certainly never the name of a unified movement or system of belief. Contested even among their promoters, Enlightenment ideals have been regularly subjected to critique and expressions of pessimism, especially as material experience revealed that quests for power and privilege drove the project of historical modernity as much as worthy Enlightenment principles. From early on, such pessimism was expressed in fictional works such as Voltaire's *Candide* (1759), de Laclos's *Les Liaisons dangereuses* (1782) and de Sade's (1740–1814) project of liberation in which the individual is responsible only to himself and his own pursuit of pleasure. Skepticism regarding the Enlightenment and its ideals broadened further as the industrial revolution, urban centralization, the theories of Marx and Freud, and the World Wars exacerbated anxieties about the direction of human endeavors. In *Dialektik der Aufklärung* (1944), one of the most influential criticisms of the Enlightenment, Max Horkheimer and Theodore Adorno argue that many philosophical concepts originated "in the market-place" to legitimate conditions of domination, and that Enlightenment reason tends to hide modes of abstraction and instrumental rationality that further domination and repression.[24] Specifically, by reducing everything to quantities that could be subject to an omnipotent exchange principle, market rationality disregards qualitative differences that would resist such abstraction if moral criteria were allowed purchase.

Although critics of the Enlightenment hold that capitalist and Enlightenment values are often inseparable, defenders such as Habermas argue against conflating the two. The study of literature can contribute to this debate insofar as much modern fiction, through representing concrete means by which economic power is deployed, stages circumstances of capitalist economic systems that suggest their distance from Enlightenment values. In this way, Yu Hua's novel offers a narrative of historically situated details that can help distinguish between Enlightenment values of freedom, autonomy, and the importance of not treating people as mere means from the more limited and specifically capitalist value of self-ownership.

In selecting and interpreting Yu Hua's *Blood Merchant*, I have to admit that a foreign scholar can hardly hope to be fair and impartial, especially one who feels a similar but forcibly different, that is, Western, ambivalence toward capitalist values. For this reason, I do not presume to unearth or pin down the source of the ambivalence toward capitalist values. Though I explore the novel's internal structures, metaphors, and ambiguities, as well as its relation to the context of sociopolitical and economic changes, I refrain from making claims that the text itself amounts to a particular ideological stance. Such claims would depend on speculations about the author's intentions and the control these intentions might exercise on their product that would disregard the multiple voices, which characterize most fictional works. Instead, I probe the work's ambivalence toward capitalist values, sometimes explicit and sometimes implicit, to demonstrate that such analysis can enhance more abstract philosophical discussions of modernity's precarious contradictions.

CHINESE FICTION OF THE 1990S

If my argument about the ambivalence toward market transition holds, how does recent Chinese fiction show capitalist values as delivering only the material promises of modernity (and perhaps only to the few) and failing to deliver the other promises of modernity, those for social, moral, or legal progress? I explore such questions to make a case for an ongoing commitment to values of justice, dignity, equality, and rationality in a body of fiction that largely spurns this legacy. Presenting this argument to Western readers is especially important in light of the high proportion of works selected for translation that are anti-Enlightenment and antihumanist.[25]

Looking to fiction of the 1990s for some comment on how Chinese citizens have responded to economic restructuring, one might first ask which practices and behaviors writers treat in their works. How does this fiction depict the social consequences of increasing market liberalization? What does it suggest about the types of men and women that Chinese society now selects and shapes?

In addition to a large number of stories about characters becoming small business owners and the social consequences of market liberalization, the 1980s and 1990s brought an increase in literature glorifying deviant behavior. For one, a new gangsta genre named "hooligan fiction" (*liumang xiaoshuo*) showed mafia-like entrepreneurs engaged in prostitution, extortion, and other organized criminal activity. This genre was made famous by Wang Shuo's (1958–) novels and his 1991 television series "Bianjibu de gushi" (Stories from the editorial board).[26] Numerous portrayals of fiscal corruption have also appeared, some specifically targeting joint ventures with foreign capital, as in Liu Heng's *Canghe bairi meng* (*Daydream on the*

Cang river, 1993).[27] Other works treat gluttony, adultery, and legal corruption, as in Mo Yan's *Jiuguo* (*The Republic of Wine*, 1992), sexual excess as in Jia Pingwa's *Feidu* (*The Ruined Capital*, 1992), serial rape as in Su Tong's *Chengbei didai* (*The Zone North of the City*, 1995), or drug addiction and sadomasochism as in Weihui's recently banned *Shanghai baobei* (*Shanghai Babe*, 1999).[28] Some of these works portray not only a tremendous rise in prostitution, but also what appears to be a sexual market generally less tied to the formal institution of marriage. Do such works glorify or problematize the capitalist reconstitution of sexuality in a fetishized mode that can be used to mobilize consumer spending?

A second set of questions asks how writers thematize these practices and behaviors. How do they bring home the impact of destabilizing social and economic changes? To what extent do they reproduce or challenge Western conceptions of capitalist modes of life? Do their works support the views of leftists in China who see contemporary evils as the fruit of capitalism or the views of reformers who blame corrupt systems and dispositions inherited from the Mao Era or earlier?[29] In stories of the brave new capitalist world, do the newly recognizable characters behave as victims, observers, and consumers or perform as agents and entrepreneurs? Does greater availability of consumer goods bring freedom or slavery? One harrowing cultural response to these questions lies in Zhou Xiaowen's 1993 film *Ermo* about a rural woman who sacrifices everything to buy a television set. What standards do such narratives pose for evaluating behavior and social practices? This question is of considerable consequence because simply making standards explicit can sometimes produce comedy, or tragicomedy, as in Yu Hua's novel that is examined below.

Finally, what do these texts suggest has been lost? In addition to subtle but recurrent references to nostalgia for the natural environment, these works prominently record the loss of political idealism about ultimate goals. At the same time, the maturation of political disenchantment seems to lead to a reassertion of specific commitments to family or other individuals that have to be incurred. This renewed emphasis on fulfilling one's commitments brings me to my analysis of Yu Hua's novel.

Yu Hua's novel *The Blood Merchant* offers a strong case of the ambivalence toward capitalist values that I argue marks a significant portion of 1990s Chinese fiction. Beginning with *Huozhe* (*To Live*, 1992), Yu's novels express a strong humanistic tendency that makes them profoundly different from both his own earlier nihilistic stories and the works by Wang Shuo, Wei Hui, or the "belated generation" mentioned above.[30] Turning away from his early phantasmagoric, avant-garde experiments with the boundaries between the real and the unreal, Yu Hua constructs *To Live* and *Blood Merchant* within a realist mode that operates by arousing sympathy for human suffering and reflection about suffering's causes and the responses available to its subjects. Yet, whereas some critics see literature's turning away from avant-garde experimentalism toward humanism as a result of a co-optation by mass culture, I view novels such as Yu Hua's as profoundly critical.

To Live offers the protagonist Fugui's frank account of desperate rural conditions and the arbitrary and murderous political programs that seem to dictate each succeeding eventuality. Thus as Fugui develops from an inveterate gambler and philanderer into a caring husband and father, everyone and everything he holds dear is nonetheless taken away from him. Although a cast of secondary characters serves to expose the brutality of Party officials blindly obedient to commands from the center, Fugui blames himself for reforming too slowly to spare his family the grief he causes them, and it is with a self-deprecating tone that he recounts his moral transformation, including harrowing accounts of how he tried to sell his daughter and how he terrorized his son. The novel ends with the death of Fugui's last remaining relative, his young grandson Kugen. This death seals the family's failure to survive, and Yu Hua leaves us with the prospect of a great socialist future without children. Yet even when a residual life force offers the only justification to go on living, Fugui is not driven to despair but carries on with resignation.

Like *To Live*, *Blood Merchant* underscores the characters' resilience, but it also presents a much greater impression of self-determination. This presentation has to be scrutinized to bring out the novel's critical potential, in part because the later novel employs a very different narrative approach. In *To Live*, the main story is framed by Fugui's encounter with the young, wandering, first-person narrator from the city, an arrangement that results in a more conspicuous presentation of the storytelling. The entire first chapter forms the front-frame, while short back-frames end each of the successive chapters. Structurally, these frames help manage the leaps in time within the fast-paced narrative. By providing convenient stopping points, they also function like the wedge in traditional Chinese *huaben* tales. The uninvolved narrator also mediates the reader's transition in and out of the story. Finally, the humor of these sections increases the affective distance of the narration and offers respite from the intense pathos of Fugui's parsimonious chronological narration of the main story. Finally, the many peripeteia make it difficult to pinpoint a climax in *To Live*, whereas *Blood Merchant* follows a more straightforward climactic progression. A combination of omniscient third-person narration and direct dialogue reinforces the later novel's illusion of objectivity and artlessness, and the characters embody ideas and social processes so seamlessly that nothing theoretical is left exposed. Yet, the novel raises philosophical questions no less urgent for their naturalistic portrayal.

SELF-OWNERSHIP VERSUS AUTONOMY IN *THE BLOOD MERCHANT*

In *The Blood Merchant*, the protagonist's repeated sale of his blood symbolizes the importance of self-ownership, where self-ownership refers to the full sovereignty over oneself and possession of full rights respecting one's body and abilities. British philosopher G.A. Cohen (1941–) attaches great importance to self-ownership because it grounds commitments to liberty, including the Marxist condemnation of exploitation, while at the same time threatening equality insofar as it supports libertarian objections to programs of distributive justice.[31] According to Cohen, libertarians rely on the thesis that self-ownership should guarantee "the right not to (be forced to) supply products or service to anyone" (p. 215) to legitimate a laissez-faire economy that permits differences of talent to produce income disparities, in part by making "not helping" morally distinct from "harming":

> It is useful to remind ourselves, here, why self-ownership excludes a duty to help (save where not helping also counts as harming). If I own myself, I own my parts and powers, which are the wherewithal for helping others. Since it is in general true of ownership that I need not devote what I own to another's benefit, it is true of self-ownership that I need not devote myself to anyone else's benefit, and I therefore have no duty to help others. And harming induced by market competition qualifies as acceptable in light of the concept of self-ownership.[32]

While Cohen respects the logical coherence of the concept of self-ownership, he raises objections to some of the moral and political implications of the libertarian principle of maximal self-ownership and seeks to reduce its appeal by distinguishing it from "not being a slave, possessing autonomy, and not being used merely as a means" (p. 230). Drawing on Cohen's work for my discussion of Yu's novel, I focus first on ways that the notion of self-ownership provides the social, economic, and moral foundations for selfhood and autonomy in the novel. Second, I bring out some of the limits and failures of this notion when it is understood as a universal category. Third, I make explicit how capitalist self-ownership falls short of a meaningful sense of Enlightenment autonomy.

Social, Economic, and Moral Selfhood

The social function of blood selling is established when Xu Sanguan's grand-father conveys to Sanguan that only a man who has sold blood can call his body sturdy (*jieshi*), and when Sanguan's two friends Genlong and Ah Fang first teach him to sell his blood through an initiation process that includes rituals such as drinking excessive quantities of water beforehand and eating pork liver afterward. Selling blood thus functions as a means to male iden-tity formation and for establishing solidarity with others. The invocation of the term "identity formation" here underscores the belief popular among social psychologists and sociologists that the self and its motives are not static, but rather intimately connected to and constructed by social contexts and processes of socialization.[33] Underscoring the function of social interac-tion in interpreting one's place in the world, the social dimension reemerges toward the end of the novel when Sanguan teaches the two Lai brothers the art of selling blood, and again when Sanguan is over 60 and suffers a crisis of identity because a blood taker will no longer buy his blood. These episodes show that Sanguan's blood selling is not only a heart-wrenching struggle for survival, but also a struggle for identity, belonging, status, uniqueness, and coherence. These compelling personal motivations make all the more poignant the paradigmatic way blood selling recruits Sanguan into a capitalist system based on private ownership.

In addition to social benefits, Sanguan's blood selling provides him economic power and moral autonomy insofar as it proves and exploits his self-ownership. Since selling blood constitutes a voluntary exchange within a libertarian system, by engaging in this commerce, Sanguan possesses, as a matter of moral and legal right, the franchise to dispose over himself and his body as a slaveholder could utilize a slave.[34] Self-ownership appears as one plausible foundation for morality due to its broad intuitive appeal: "It's *my* life. It's *my* body. I can do what I please with it, so long as I violate no one else's rights, even if this comes at a significant cost to me, and even if others do not like what I do."[35]

On the economic level, self-ownership appears to allow Sanguan a considerable degree of self-determination. He sells his blood first to found a family, specifically by buying material goods so that Xu Yulan will marry him. On their first date, Xu even counts on his fingers how much money he has spent before asking Yulan when she will marry him. The humor of this passage is undercut, however, when Yulan protests about the unfair nature of Sanguan's assumption that she should be indebted to him: "I thought that I was eating for free. You didn't say that once I'd eaten your treats I'd have to marry you" (p. 64).[36] Yet a month later and pressured by her father, Yulan agrees to marry Sanguan provided he is able to meet her material demands. Second, Sanguan sells his blood for property when he uses the proceeds to redeem his family's household possessions after their confiscation by the father of a boy mangled by their son Yile, a son who turns out to have been fathered by another man. The need to compensate the hospitalized boy's family here also recalls the limits of self-ownership, in that people may act on their desires only to the extent that they do not violate the rights of others. Sanguan's third blood sale reinforces this notion when he spends some of the money on gifts for a woman he has just seduced on her sickbed. Though his plan backfires when the gifts alert her husband to the "rape," Sanguan is able to assuage his wife's anger over the adultery by surrendering the remaining cash for her to purchase new clothes.

After his family has eaten nothing but gruel for 57 days during the Great Leap Forward (1958–1960), Sanguan sells his blood a fourth time to buy them a proper meal. During the Cultural Revolution (1966–1976), he sells his blood a fifth time to give money to his two sent-down sons so they can eat better and buy their team leaders gifts that might facilitate earlier transfers back to the city. Less than one month later, he sells his blood a sixth time for connections, exchanging economic for social capital, when he uses the money to entertain Erle's team leader. Finally and within just a couple more weeks, Sanguan sells his blood a series of at least five more times to raise money to pay Yile's medical bills once Yile has been sent to a Shanghai hospital for aggravated hepatitis.

Advantages and Liabilities of Self-Ownership

Insofar as Xu Sanguan's sale of his blood heralds the appeal of the free exchange of goods, Yu Hua's novel can be interpreted as reinforcing the positive possibilities of a market system. Through highlighting the ability to sell oneself and one's labor power at the most optimum times, the novel demonstrates the ability of the protagonist to make and act on his own choices and to control his own life. This presentation of individual agency supports a libertarian theory of self-ownership that underlies much of the logic of present market reforms toward a capitalist economic system that treats labor power as a commodity and depends on the production of commodities for market exchange (rather than for direct consumption). "The libertarian principle of self-ownership," writes Cohen, "says that each person enjoys, over herself and her powers, full and exclusive rights of control and use, and therefore owes no service or product to anyone else that she has not contracted to supply."[37] Such a principle may appeal since it appears to defend autonomous decision making, but it assumes an ideal of autonomy that fails to take into account structural and social factors such as the costs of healthcare in the event of self-harm.

At the same time, the novel also exposes contingent factors influencing self-ownership, and this attention to differences indicates ways in which the category is not a universal one. For one, in several instances, connections and bribes are necessary before the blood taker will accept Sanguan's blood. For another, with or without consent, self-ownership rights may be alienated or transferred, as in marriage. For example, in describing Xu Yulan's lack of freedom in deciding her betrothal, the novel shows the way gender often works as a roadblock to idealized notions about self-ownership that might purport to make it a foundation for equality. The gender imbalance is made clear first when Yulan's other suitor, He Xiaoyong, forces her to have sex with him, and again years later when Sanguan learns of the rape and focuses only on how the act violates his legal ownership of his wife: "But Xu Yulan was a woman Sanguan had spent money to marry and bring home" (p. 97). His illiberal, self-centered reaction to Yulan's assault recalls an insightful point made by Wang Dewei (David Wang) in his introduction to the novel: To Sanguan, the foundation of his marriage is based on the sacrifice of virgin blood.[38] Yet since under his interrogation, Yulan tells Sanguan that it was he with whom she slept first (p. 79), the novel leaves ambiguous whether the grievousness of the sexual betrayal here derives from the loss of the hymen blood that determines Yulan's value in this sexual economy or from an act of adultery that led to the birth of Yile.

Despite these qualifications regarding the serious liabilities of an overly idealist notion of self-ownership, the numerous ways Sanguan uses blood selling to found and care for his family recall the importance of this Enlightenment notion for personal accountability in the fulfillment of one's commitments. At the same time, since Sanguan repeatedly subordinates and exploits his self-ownership to meet his obligations to his family, a question arises as to whether the novel makes self-ownership a normative value of independent importance, or whether its importance derives from its connection to other moral values. Even as Sanguan acts within an unpredictable social framework marked by conflicts over sexual access to women, children's violence and state political domination, his moral orientation derives from an emphasis—perhaps a Confucian emphasis—on fulfilling one's roles in the family.

In addition to loyalty to family, the novel introduces other distinct standards of moral and social responsibility. For one, in a characteristic Enlightenment move, the novel satirizes superstition at the same moment that it presents a case for forgiveness and the value of human life. Specifically, when He Xiaoyong is hit by a truck from Shanghai and lies in a coma in the hospital, a fortune-teller advises He's wife that the only way to save him is to have his son climb atop He's roof and scream for his father to return. Since He has only the illegitimate son fathered when he raped Xu Yulan, Yulan convinces Sanguan that they should help, and Sanguan talks to Yile: "Yile, in the past He Xiaoyong wronged us. That's in the past. We shouldn't still bear a grudge. Now He Xiaoyong's very life is at risk, what's important is to save his life. Whatever you say, He Xiaoyong is also a person. When a human life is at stake, then one should save it. Besides he's your blood father" (p. 191).

Self-Ownership as Short of Autonomy

In showing the characters' ethical transformations as they embrace moral standards, in this case humanist ones, such passages suggest the priority of the values of survival and self-sacrifice for the good of others over the ideal of self-ownership. In describing at length Yile's suffering as he sits on the roof, the novel makes clear that the adults' concern to save He's life leads them to disregard Yile's reluctance and to force him to participate in their superstitious attempt. Yet even as they violate Yile's self-ownership by stranding him on the roof, he exercises autonomy by refusing to do their bidding until Sanguan is brought in to coax him. As if understanding that he needs to appeal to Yile's own interests, Sanguan promises to be Yile's blood father (*qindie*) if the later calls out to He's spirit. Sanguan performs his vow by cutting his own face and threatening, with blood running down his cheek, to take a knife to anyone who again dares to say that Yile is not his own son.

In another example of personal transformation, Sanguan goes from bearing his wife great hostility for her affair with He Xiaoyong to risking social ridicule in order to provide for her: during the Cultural Revolution, when Red Guards force Yulan to stand on a street holding a sign saying "Prostitute Xu Yulan" (*Jinü Xu Yulan*), Sanguan brings her food and water. Moreover, when compelled to conduct a home struggle session against Yulan in which Yile says he hates his mother and loves Sanguan, Sanguan confesses his own infidelity so that their sons will judge her less harshly: "I'm just like your mom; we've both committed mortal errors. You shouldn't hate her" (p. 217).

As Sanguan owns his transgression to convey to their sons that people are both fallible and capable of forgiveness and moral development, his integrity reinforces the positive aspect of self-ownership. Yet the personal sphere in which he acts in such instances raises further questions about what grounds the underlying metaphor of self-ownership. In the economic sphere, is it not possible that appeal to this metaphor likens the self to a thing in a way that may undermine precisely those qualities that could distinguish human beings as moral agents, namely the possibility of fulfilling one's projects and commitments to others? Cohen has a phrase that points out the situated nature of any claims of self-ownership: "For market competition harms losers, and market competition is the social soul of self-ownership" (p. 227). Yet it might be worthwhile to redefine the "social soul of self-ownership" as lying in one's relationships and responsibilities to others more generally, a redefinition that could reveal more starkly the antagonism between the pursuit of economic capital in market competition and human self-realization in community. Perhaps it would be better to defend the notion of a self not in terms of ownership, but rather in terms of capacities that can be realized and expanded within given social contexts and communities.[39] In this light, the novel could also be read as a demonstration of the relative richness of Confucian conceptions of the self as constituted through the fulfillment of roles and obligations within a network of relations that allow for the realization of human nature.[40]

In the novel's culminating example of ethical transformation, Sanguan transcends the grudge he bears Yile for having been fathered by another man by acknowledging the mutual affection they have earned through years of fulfilling their roles as father and son. As if to deflate an irrational fixation on blood relations, and to suggest that alliances incurred by choice are at least as powerful, the novel shows Sanguan resolving to sell his own blood at a possibly lethal rate to save the life of his illegitimate son.

Sanguan's risky harvesting of his own blood points out some of the liabilities of an exclusive focus on rights of self-ownership. While the novel posits certain Enlightenment rights and values within a basic normative framework, it challenges the Kantian moral imperative not to treat persons as means only. Although Kant's principle allows for the instrumental use of people on the condition that they are also treated as ends, it seems unambiguous that Sanguan treats himself as a mere means, a fact made painfully clear over the issue of whether the blood takers will allow him to sell his blood at a frequency that endangers his life. Sanguan's insistence on his prerogative to sell his blood is grounded in the notion that self-ownership rights should work against paternalistic intervention. The logic behind Sanguan's assertion of his right to sell his blood is, moreover, mirrored by his protest against having to pay for his own blood transfusion. After he collapses during his third blood donation along his route to Shanghai, the hospital gives him a blood transfusion that costs him the equivalent of selling his blood twice. "Buying and selling has to be just," Sanguan protests. "When I sold my blood to them, they knew, but when they sold blood to me, I didn't know at all" (p. 265). Sanguan's indignation reveals the conflict between individual rights of self-ownership and protective medical benevolence that corresponds to political conflicts between "laissez-faire" strains of liberalism (largely

Anglo-American) dedicated to individual liberty and "étatist," "welfare-state" or "egalitarian" strains of liberalism (largely continental European) that assign the state a strong protective role in promoting social betterment.

The depiction of Sanguan's near self-destruction might also suggest the extent to which the enterprising man of affairs who is assumed sober, hard-headed, and practical turns out to be utopian and monomaniac. When the blood taker at Songlin sends him away because he looks sickly, and Sanguan purposely gets a sunburn that disguises his ill health and convinces the blood taker to buy his blood, does he exercise great ingenuity or great recklessness? As Sanguan gambles with his life, he wins inasmuch as he lives. But he benefits from a kind of moral luck. What if he had died along the way and never reached Shanghai with the money? Since moral standards cannot depend on moral luck, the question arises, does such self-ownership secure autonomy? The answer would have to be no, since most commitments to autonomy aim at a more robust notion. The exercise of autonomy may never escape contingencies, but it would be hoped that its calculus would not depend fundamentally on arbitrary chance.

Furthermore, how much autonomy is possible in the face of the standardizing potential of the market? In his desperate efforts to turn his own body into cash, Sanguan epitomizes one aspect of the Enlightenment mindset. Forced to participate in a modern market economy, a very instrumental rationality sustains his pursuit of his objectives. Yet Sanguan is hardly sovereign. To provide for his family's basic survival, he must subject his body to physical harm, and he cannot set his price. Such self-exploitation is seldom detached from larger economic structures, a fact made clear by Sanguan's dependence on medical institutions, their biotechnologies, and their gate-keepers. By making his own blood an external object for sale, Sanguan suffers objectification, alienation, and self-estrangement of the kind Marx described as constituting the alienation of labor. "First, the fact that labour is external to the worker, i.e., it does not belong to his essential being; that in his work, therefore, he does not affirm himself but denies himself, . . . does not develop freely his physical and mental energy but mortifies his body and ruins his mind."[41] Marx's generalization is given concrete embodiment in Yu Hua's direct, unsentimental way of dispatching the details of Sanguan's ill health during his frantic blood selling: "The Xu Sanguan of this time was pale and thin, his four limbs without strength, his head dizzy and swollen. Blurry eyed, with a persistent ringing in his ears, his bones were aching and sore to the point that taking steps made his legs feel as if they were floating" (p. 262).

Sanguan's repeated sales of his blood may exercise his self-ownership, but the practice is but a pale shadow of autonomy given that the social, economic, and political conditions under which he lives hardly allow him acceptable options.[42] If *To Live* exposed the corruption and brutality of medical institutions under Communism, *Blood Merchant* shows the dark side of medical care in a market economy: "My son's in a Shanghai hospital, . . . I have to raise enough money to deliver to him. If [we] don't have money, the doctors won't give my son injections and medicine" (p. 278). In such a predicament, the right to exploit the possession of one's body seems like a hollow compensation.

Of course, it must be admitted that this objection to a narrow focus on self-ownership reveals a paradox in connected appeals to broader ideals of autonomy. Namely, it may be that individuals could enjoy meaningful moral "autonomy" only under social conditions that would guarantee basic human welfare such that a father would never have to risk destroying his own health to pay for his son's medical treatment. Yet the provision of such public goods would require the state's appropriation of its citizens' labor power and wealth, and herein lies the libertarians' objection, in a way that would violate their economic autonomy. Given this dilemma, the proponents of free-market capitalism legitimate the absence of safety nets by presuming the primacy of self-ownership and consent in the economic realm and by sponsoring cultural products and discourses that bolster the impression of moral autonomy. It is on account of such mystifications that Marxist critics often disapprove of humanistic, "bourgeois" literature, but such works can also offer concrete examples of the contradictions implicit in many capitalist values and the usefulness of complementing individualistic interpretations with social ones.

As described above, the main ways that Sanguan does exercise autonomy lie in his personal ethical choices to forgive Yulan and save Yile in their times of need. Yet what happens when Sanguan no longer faces dire opportunities to express altruism? The extent to which Sanguan sees his very identity as depending on his ability to be a subject with economic capacities and provide for his family comes out in the last chapter. Now over 60, Sanguan's life world is much improved. Whereas the Cultural Revolution violated his wife's self-ownership by condemning her to struggle sessions and long days on her feet as an object of public humiliation, and whereas it violated Yile's and Erle's self-ownership by sending them down to the countryside, Sanguan's sons are now back, married with kids, and Sanguan and his wife have enough money. They live amidst new clothing stores and other signs of economic prosperity. Yet Sanguan feels nostalgia about selling blood and craves pork liver, so he decides to sell his blood for the first time in 11 years. "Today he would sell his blood for himself. It would be the first time he sold if for himself . . . Before he ate pork liver and drank millet wine because he'd sold blood. Today it's the opposite. Today he's selling blood only in order to eat pork liver and drink millet wine" (p. 286). Yet to Sanguan's dismay, the young new blood drawer refuses to take his blood because of his advanced age. Upon realizing that no one would want his blood, Sanguan walks around town in circles crying. He worries sadly, what if his family needed money?

Luckily, Yulan can afford to take Sanguan for the meal he wants, and the novel's happy ending might reinforce assumptions that a market society will produce greater production and prosperity. Yet the novel also expresses concerns about changing values and systems for their transmission. For example, what have Sanguan's sons, Yile, Erle, and Sanle, learned about the pursuit of solidarity, health, or dignity from their father? The reader has to wonder when they urge him not to cry in the street primarily out of their concern to preserve appearances: "Dad, don't cry. If you want to cry, go cry at home. Don't make a spectacle of yourself here" (p. 290).

Far from feeling self-congratulatory for his record of self-reliance and risk-taking, at the end of the novel Sanguan appears to be culturally disenfranchised. David Wang has argued that at least when Sanguan sells his blood he exercises a greater degree of self-determination than is allowed the characters of Yu Hua's earlier novel *To Live*. In *To Live*, the communist society that functions in the name of the people increasingly resembles a vampire after the protagonist's son dies in the process of donating blood, and his daughter dies in childbirth due to incompetent medical care.[43] But how much choice do the characters in Sanguan's market world have? What mores or institutions might safeguard against the destruction of moral values and social solidarity in the utilitarian pursuit of economic means?

Furthermore, is it clear that the reader should interpret Sanguan's self-mastery as a sign of the possibilities for the reform of Chinese society at large? To be sure, as China's citizens sustain an unparalleled pace of change, the capitalist market will continue to exercise social influence. An enterprising risk-taker willing to jeopardize his life's blood for his family, Sanguan's farming of his own body also reminds us that the post-Mao de-collectivization of agriculture and the return to peasant family economies are partly to credit for the tremendous rise in China's gross domestic product. Perhaps no system works as peasant family agriculture does to encourage self-exploitation and generate wealth.

China's experience serves to remind us that capitalism is not a monolithic institution, but a set of situated practices. Likewise, in a comparative study of the U.S. commercial and British voluntary systems for collecting human blood, sociologist Richard Titmuss sees human blood as "perhaps the most basic and sensitive indicator of social values and human relationships." Titmuss writes, "If dollars or pounds exchange for blood then it may be morally acceptable for a myriad of other human activities and relationships also to exchange for dollars or pounds."[44] Concern about the appropriateness of commodifying aspects of human personhood is all the more pertinent in light of developments in medical technologies and trade laws that have led to increasing market exchanges in human organs, genetic material, and reproductive services.[45] The issues of self-ownership, autonomy, and selfhood raised in Yu Hua's novel bear on legal and social debates concerning the distribution and commerce in corporeal commodities, from the sales of ova, to the appropriation and patenting of human tissue for the development of cell lines, to a growing illegal trafficking in humans.[46]

Despite making a hero of a self-exploiting peasant, Yu Hua's novel may not promote free-market capitalism over welfare-state capitalism or even market socialism as much as raise questions about whether the supposed laws of markets really harmonize diverse interests. Can human welfare be calculated in terms of economics? Capitalist self-ownership is not the same as autonomy, and values have to be weighed according to moral as well as economic criteria.

NOTES

This chapter was originally published in *Textual Practice* 16 (3), pp. 547-568, and is reprinted here with the generous permission of Deirdre Sabina Knight and *Textual Practice* (http://www.tandf.co.uk/journals).

1. Jonathan Watts, "China offers free Aids test in policy shift," *Guardian Weekly*, April 22–28, 2004.
2. Elisabeth Rosenthal, "Deadly shadow darkens remote Chinese village," *The New York Times*, May 28, 2001, A1 and A6. Infection spread primarily at plasma centers that pooled sellers' blood, extracted the plasma, and then reinjected the red cells back into the sellers.
3. Since the completion of this essay, an excellent translation of Yu Hua's novel has appeared under the title *Chronicle of a Blood Merchant*, trans. Andrew F. Jones (New York: Pantheon, 2003).
4. G.A. Cohen, *Self-Ownership, Freedom, and Equality* (Cambridge: Cambridge University Press, 1995). Cohen's book begins with a critique of Robert Nozick's work, particularly Nozick's *Anarchy, State, and Utopia* (New York: Basic Books, 1974).
5. I am grateful to the conference organizers and participants for their help and questions. For helpful criticism on earlier drafts, I thank David S. Weberman, Edward Friedman, Charles Laughlin and the anonymous readers of the journal *Textual Practice*, in which an earlier version of this article appeared in 2002: Deidre Sabina Knight, "Capitalist and Enlightenment Values in 1990s Chinese Fiction: The Case of Yu Hua's Blood Seller." Textual Practice 16.3 (Winter 2002), 547–568.
6. Habermas, "Modernity versus postmodernity," trans. Seyla Benhabib, in *New German Critique* 22 (winter 1981), 3–15.
7. With this question, I distinguish philosophical projects of modernity, material projects of economic and industrial modernization, and aesthetic, critical reactions named "modernism."
8. For discussion of and examples of works by these writers, see the articles and stories in *Mingbao yuekan* (August 1997).
9. See Chen Xiaoming, "Xianfengpai zhi hou, wanshengdai de jueqi yu weiji" (After the avant-gardists, the belated generation's rise and crisis), *Mingbao yuekan* (August 1997), 33–39.
10. Herbert Marcuse, *One Dimensional Man: Studies in the Ideology of Advanced Industrial Society* (Boston: Beacon Press, 1964); Alain Touraine, *Critique of Modernity*, trans. David Macey (Cambridge, MA: Blackwell, 1995) and *The Post-industrial Society; Tomorrow's Social History: Classes, Conflicts and Culture in the Programmed Society*, trans. Leonard F.X. Mayhew (New York: Random House, 1971); and Anthony Giddens, *The Consequences of Modernity* (Stanford: Stanford University Press, 1990).
11. For a general survey, see Jun Ma, *The Chinese Economy in the 1990s* (London: Macmillan Press, 2000). For a critical account, see He Qinglian, *Xiandaihua de xianjing: dangdai zhongguo de jingji shehui wenti* (Pitfalls of modernization: contemporary China's economic and societal problems) (Beijing: Jinri zhongguo chubanshe, 1998).
12. Geographer David Harvey refers to the restructuring of the global economy since the late 1970s as the regime of "flexible accumulation" to emphasize corporations' greater geographical mobility and flexibility in employment arrangements, markets, products and consumption practices. See David Harvey, *The*

Condition of Postmodernity: An Enquiry into the Origins of Cultural Change (Cambridge, MA: Basil Blackwell, 1990).

13. Thorstein Veblen (1857–1929), *The Theory of the Leisure Class; an Economic Study in the Evolution of Institutions* (New York: The Macmillan Company, 1899).

14. Humane reforms in law and punishments were inspired by the Italian philosopher and jurist Césare Bonesana Beccaria (1738–1794) in *Dei delitti e delle pene* (On crime and punishments) (1764) and by Jeremy Bentham (1748–1832) in *Introduction to the Principles of Morals and Legislation* (1789). Philippe Pinel (1745–1826), a French physician, recommended treating mental illness as a disease rather than as the result of demoniac possession in his *Nosographie philosophique* (Philosophical classification of diseases) (1798). Pinel detailed more humane treatments in his *Traité médico-philosophique sur l'aliénation mentale ou la manie* (Medico-philosophical treatise on mental alienation or mania) (1801).

15. Xiong Yuezhi, *Xixue dongjian yu wan Qing shehui* (The dissemination of Western learning and late Qing society) (Shanghai: Shanghai renmin chubanshe, 1995).

16. See, e.g., Wm. Theodore de Bary, "Neo-Confucian Cultivation and the Seventeenth Century 'Enlightenment'," in *The Unfolding of Neo-Confucianism*, ed. de Bary (New York: Columbia University Press, 1975).

17. See Vera Schwarcz, *The Chinese Enlightenment: Intellectuals and the Legacy of the May Fourth Movement of 1919* (Berkeley: University of California Press, 1986), and John Fitzgerald, *Awakening China. Politics, Culture and Class in the Nationalist Revolution* (Stanford: Stanford University Press, 1996). For a substantive, nuanced discussion of the heterogeneous nature of the May Fourth Movement and literature's subordination to political agendas, see the general introduction in Kirk Denton ed., *Modern Chinese Literary Thought: Writings on Literature, 1893–1945* (Stanford: Stanford University Press, 1996), pp. 1–61, 113.

18. Fitzgerald, *Awakening China*, 6.

19. Xudong Zhang, *Chinese Modernism in the Era of Reforms: Cultural Fever, Avant-Garde Fiction, and the New Chinese Cinema* (Durham and London: Duke University Press, 1997), p. 9.

20. Xudong Zhang, *Chinese Modernism*, p. 46.

21 Ben Xu, *Disenchanted Democracy: Chinese Cultural Criticism after 1989* (Ann Arbor: The University of Michigan Press, 1999), pp. 90–91.

22. Ben Xu, "Contesting Memory for Intellectual Self-Positioning: The 1990s New Cultural Conservatism in China," *Modern Chinese Literature and Culture*, 11.1 (spring 1999), p. 169.

23. Lydia Liu, *Translingual Practice: Literature, National Culture, and Translated Modernity—China, 1900–1937* (Stanford: Stanford University Press, 1995), pp. 10–20.

24. See Max Horkheimer and Theodore W. Adorno, *Dialectic of Enlightenment*, trans. John Cumming (New York: Herder and Herder, 1972).

25. In a recent essay drawing attention to the issue of selection, Howard Goldblatt, the foremost translator of Chinese fiction, self-consciously reflects on his own immense influence on the view of Chinese literature available to readers of English: "Over the past two decades, I have been involved in the production of two dozen or more translations of modern and contemporary Chinese fiction, and while the results of those endeavors can in no way reflect all the literary twists and turns in post-Mao China, they fairly represent my own tastes in literature, some of the strictures in which I work, and, most important, the essence of Chinese novels and short stories to which English-language readers have been exposed." See Goldblatt, "Border Crossings: Chinese Writing, in their World

and Ours," in *China beyond the Headlines*, ed. Timothy Weston and Lionel Jensen (Lanham and Boulder: Rowman and Littlefield, 2000), p. 337.

26. See Geremie Barmé, "Wang Shuo and *Liumang* ('Hooligan') Culture," *Australian Journal of Chinese Affairs*, 28 (July 1992), 23–64. For novels by Wang Shuo available in English, see *Playing for Thrills*, trans. Howard Goldblatt (New York: William Morrow, 1997) and *Please Don't Call Me Human*, trans. Howard Goldblatt (New York: Hyperion East, 2000).

27. For an analysis comparing negative visions of market reforms in Jiang Zilong's "Shoushen ji" (Records from a trial, 1989) and Liu Heng's novel *Daydream on the Cang River* with more optimistic portrayals in Jia Pingwa's stories, see Melinda Pirazzoli, "The Free-Market Economy and Contemporary Chinese Literature," *World Literature Today* 70.2 (spring 1996), 301–310.

28. See my article, "Shanghai Cosmopolitan: Class, Gender and Cultural Citizenship in Wei Hui's *Shanghai Babe*," *Journal of Contemporary China*, 12.37 (November 2003), 639–653.

29. This question was thoughtfully suggested by Edward Friedman, letter, September 6, 2000.

30. Prime examples of Yu Hua's early stories that can be read as nihilistic include "Shiba sui chumen yuan xing" (On the Road at Eighteen, 1986), "Yijiubaliu nian" (1986, 1986), and "Xianshi yizhong" (One Kind of Reality, 1988), collected in *Shiba sui chumen yuan xing* (On the Road at Eighteen, Taipei: Yuanliu, 1990). For English translations of the first two stories and six other good examples, see Yu Hua, *The Past and the Punishments*, trans. Andrew F. Jones (Honolulu: University of Hawaii Press, 1996).

31. Cohen, *Self-Ownership*.

32. Cohen, *Self-Ownership*, 228. On this logic, libertarians can accept taxes to finance police protection of property while rejecting redistributive income taxation on the basis that it violates full self-ownership of one's earnings.

33. See, for example, Tom R. Tyler, Roderick M. Kramer, and Oliver P. John, ed., *The Psychology of the Social Self* (Mahwah, NJ: Lawrence Erlbaum Associates, 1999).

34. This formulation corresponds closely to the definition of self-ownership offered by Cohen, *Self-Ownership*, 68.

35. This line comes from Ernie Alleva's Review Essay of Cohen's work in *Social Justice Research*, 10.3 (1997), 355–372, here 359.

36. All translations from the novel are my own. Page numbers refer to Yu Hua, *Xu Sanguan mai xue ji* (Taipei: Maitian chubanshe, 1997).

37. Cohen, *Self-Ownership*, 12.

38. See Wang Dewei, "Shanghen jijing, baoli qiguan: Yu Hua de xiaoshuo" (Glimpses of scars, wonders of violence: Yu Hua's fiction), in Yu Hua, *Xu Sanguan mai xue ji*, 27.

39. This formulation was inspired by economist Amartya Sen's redefinition of development as a process of expanding the capabilities that people enjoy. See Amartya Sen, *Development as Freedom* (New York: Knopf, 1999).

40. For example, see Tu Wei-ming, *Confucian Thought: Selfhood as Creative Transformation* (Albany: State University of New York Press, 1985).

41. Karl Marx, "Economic and Philosophic Manuscripts of 1844" in *The Marx–Engels Reader*, ed. Robert C. Tucker, 2nd ed. (New York: W.W. Norton, 1978), p. 74.

42. "A person is autonomous only if he has a variety of acceptable options available to him to choose from, and his life became as it is through his choice of some of

these options." Joseph Raz, *The Morality of Freedom* (Oxford: Oxford University Press, 1986), p. 204, quoted in Cohen, *Self-Ownership*, p. 238.

43. Wang Dewei, "Shanghen jijing," p. 26.

44. Richard M. Titmuss, *The Gift Relationship: From Human Blood to Social Policy* (New York: Pantheon, 1971), p. 198.

45. For a thoughtful critique of universal commodification by a legal scholar, see Margaret Jane Radin, *Contested Commodities* (Cambridge: Harvard University Press, 1996).

46. For theoretical discussion of a key legal debate surrounding the appropriation of human tissue from an unknowing patient after a splenectomy, see the passages on Moore v. Regents of the University of California in John Frow, *Time and Commodity Culture: Essays in Cultural Theory and Postmodernity* (Oxford: Clarendon Press, 1997), pp. 154–161, and James Boyle, *Shamans, Software, and Spleens: Law and the Construction of the Information Society* (Cambridge: Harvard University Press, 1996), pp. 97–107.

INDEX